TAKING SIDES

Clashing Views on

Latin American Issues

Selected, Edited, and with Introductions by

Analisa DeGrave
University of Wisconsin–Eau Claire

Eva L. Santos-Phillips
University of Wisconsin–Eau Claire

Jeff DeGrave
University of Wisconsin–Eau Claire

D0001714

Mc Graw Hill **Contemporary Learning Series**

A Division of The McGraw-Hill Companies

*A big thank you goes to our three families
who encouraged and supported us through
all the stages of the book.*

Photo Acknowledgment
Lou Dematteis

Cover Acknowledgment
Maggie Lytle

Printed on Recycled Paper

Preface

Controversy can stimulate debate that results in more complete understanding of an issue. The word *controversy* comes from the Latin *controversia*, meaning "disputable" or something about which there is disagreement. Debates about controversial issues can bring about positive change or solutions to issues many people prefer to ignore or find offensive. By discussing controversial subjects and by presenting reasonable and well-documented arguments, people can persuade others who hold opposing views to understand why they think or believe the way do. This book presents opposing views about Latin America and gives the reader an opportunity to learn about some of the issues that are of concern not only to Latin Americans but also to people worldwide.

Ever since the European "conquest" and early colonial times, controversy has dominated Latin American religious, civil, and political institutions as well as the economic, social, and cultural scene. Today, for example, Latin Americans are divided as to whether women should have more access to legal abortions to prevent the numerous deaths of those who seek illegal abortions or if the existing laws are already too liberal and should be more restrictive. Students will read what two authors have to say about this controversial issue and will be given references for further readings to help them arrive at an informed and reasoned position. Another subject of concern is whether the construction of a dry canal (a railroad connecting the Atlantic and the Pacific) across Nicaragua would be an economic benefit to the country or if it would create substantial ecological problems and provide only monetary gains for the multinational corporations involved and the country's elite. Debating matters such as these will help the student develop skills for conveying thoughts clearly and persuasively both inside and outside the classroom.

This book was created to discuss contemporary issues in Latin America and to nurture debate. *Taking Sides: Clashing Views on Latin American Issues* presents controversial topics for which there are no simple answers; instead, it helps readers develop critical thinking skills so that they may better understand the issues. In reading, discussing, and writing about the topics presented, students will gain a greater understanding of Latin America and the way people think, argue, and ponder controversial issues. Although compelling and well written, the articles provide only a basic framework for issues that often involve multiple and complex perspectives. The readings do not offer a "complete" answer. Therefore, the student will be encouraged to engage in further analysis to help understand the issue more clearly. Students will have the opportunity to voice their opinions based on well thought-out materials and arguments. They will develop their skills in argumentation so that a debate does not degenerate into a thoughtless dispute, but instead remains a reflective deliberation about the issue at hand.

Plan of the book   *Taking Sides: Clashing Views on Latin American Issues* is divided into four parts: Introduction, History, and Politics; Society, Human Rights, and Culture; People, Land, and the Environment; and Economics and Development. Within the four parts, we provide a list of pertinent links to the Internet (URLs) for further reading on the topics covered in each section. Every issue has an introduction that prepares the reader for debating the YES/ NO articles that follow. A postscript accompanies each pair of articles to bring together loose ends and to provide further information, offer additional perspectives, and supplemental readings. Each of the 18 issue questions is driven by two competing articles, creating a total of 36 readings in this volume. Part 4 is followed by brief biographic sketches of the *contributors to this volume* (editors and authors), along with a comprehensive index.

A word to the instructor   *An Instructor's Manual with Test Questions* (multiple choice and essay) is available through the publisher for the classroom. A general guidebook, *Using Taking Sides in the Classroom,* which discusses methods and techniques for using the pro-con approach in any classroom setting, is also available. In addition, an online version of *Using Taking Sides in the Classroom* and a correspondence service for *Taking Sides* adopters can be found at http://www.mhcls.com/usingts/.

    Taking Sides: Clashing Views on Latin American Issues is only one title in the *Taking Sides* series. If you are interested in seeing the table of contents for any of the other titles, please visit the Taking Sides Web site at http://www. mhcls.com/takingsides/.

Acknowledgements   We are grateful to the University of Wisconsin–Eau Claire's Office of Research and Sponsored Programs and the College of Arts and Sciences for funds and allotted time in the preparation of this book. We are also grateful for the assistance of UWEC colleagues Matt Evans, Mimi King, and William H. Phillips; students Anna Baker and Kristin Schuck; UW–Madison colleagues Rubén Medina and Lisa Amor Petrov; colleague Seth Meisel from UW–Whitewater; and photographer Lou Dematteis. To our editor Jill Peter, who carefully evaluated our submitted materials and provided us with excellent direction, goes our deepest gratitude.

Contents In Brief

Contents

Luis Suárez Salazar, professor of history at the University of Havana, believes that Cuban diplomacy and new partnerships have helped create solid relations with its Latin American neighbors. Daniel Erikson, director of Caribbean programs in Washington, D.C., attests that although Cuba is attempting to employ a "good neighbor policy" with many Latin American countries, the majority of these countries are skeptical of Fidel Castroís actions and will continue to ally with the United States.

Issue 4.   Is Plan Colombia Effectively Combating the Drug Industry in Colombia?   51

Robert B. Charles, assistant secretary for international narcotics and law enforcement affairs for the U.S. Department of State, argues that Plan Colombia is succeeding through limiting the flow of drugs to America, defeating terrorists, and protecting democratic rule throughout the Andean regions of Latin America. Linda Panetta, a photojournalist whose work focuses on cultural, environmental, and human rights by focusing on conflict zones around the world—including Latin America—asserts that Plan Colombia has made little progress in the "War on Drugs" and creates more harm than good for both Colombia and the United States.

Issue 5.   Is "Enhanced Commonwealth" the Solution to Puerto Rico's Colonial Status?   72

Previous resident commissioner of Puerto Rico, Aníbal Acevedo Vilá, explains how "enhanced" commonwealth would change the compact established in 1950 between the United States and Puerto Rico and create expanded sovereignty for Puerto Rico, and thereby "eliminate all vestiges of colonialism from the current US–Puerto Rico relation." Dr. Pedro Rosselló, former governor of Puerto Rico, points out the contradictions and ambiguities the status of Puerto Rico has led to in its relationship with the United States and that the only way to resolve this quandary is by rejecting the status quo (commonwealth), and validating "the option under the U.S. sovereignty, namely statehood."

Venezuelan journalist Alejandro Bermúdez discusses the issue of abortion in Colombia and interviews Monsignor Jaime Restrepo, who explains how pro-abortion groups have helped in changing the laws to permit abortions. Peruvian attorney Roxana Vásquez Sotelo argues that Latin American women do not have the freedom or autonomy to terminate unwanted pregnancies, resulting in many illegal abortions. Vásquez Sotelo also indicates that foreign interference helps maintain laws that restrict womenís rights.

Political science professor Mala Htun says that Brazil, which for years upheld itself as an example of a "racial democracy," has come to a realization that racism has and does exist. To counter this finding, affirmative action programs have been created, though not fully implemented. Peruvian anthropology professor Marisol de la Cadena provides an overview of culturalist definitions of race as expressed by Latin American scholars and politicians. de la Cadena explains that common notions of race are challenged by this culturalist definition because race, accordingly, is not defined by phenotype, and instead people are identified in terms of class, decency, morality and education.

Congressman Charlie Norwood argues that the presence of the Minutemen has reduced the flow of illegal immigrants into the United States. Congressman Raúl M. Grijalva contends that volunteer patrol groups on the Mexico-U.S. border are anti-immigrant, racist vigilantes. Instead of further militarizing the border, Grijalva advocates that more attention be paid to the economics, history, culture, and migration patterns of the border region.

Marcela A. Chaván de Matviuk from the Center for Latin American and Latino Leadership in the School of Leadership Studies at Regent University argues that the "relational character" of Latin American culture is a perfect fit for Pentecostal worship and that it directly contributes to the rise in Protestantism in the region. Edward L. Cleary, of the Dominican order, professor of political science and director of the Latin American studies program at Providence College, contends that the growth of Protestantism is not as profound as it might appear and that statistics on religion need to also consider the retention and dropout rates of Pentecostals.

PART 3   PEOPLE, LAND, AND THE ENVIRONMENT   217

Issue 12.   Should DDT Be Given Another Chance?   218

Mr. Driessen, senior fellow with the Committee for a Constructive Tomorrow, believes that the ban prohibiting the usage of the pesticide DDT (dichloro-diphenyl-trichloroethane) has created more problems than solutions since a greater number people have died related to the spread of malaria than would have died from exposure to DDT. Greenpeace researchers Michelle Allsopp and Bea Erry contend that the group of chemicals known as POPs (persistent organic pollutants), which include the pesticide DDT, represent a significant global contamination problem because they are resistant to natural breakdown processes and are highly toxic. They maintain that DDT and other POPs should be phased out of use in Latin American countries.

Issue 13.   Do the Economic Benefits of a "Dry Canal" in Nicaragua Outweigh the Financial, Human, and Environmental Costs?   239

CINN (Canal Interoceanico de Nicaragua), a multinational corporation that is the leading candidate to construct a canal across Nicaragua, argues that the construction of a canal through Nicaragua will provide major long-term economic benefits to Nicaragua by distinguishing it as the nexus of global commerce. Nicaragua Network's Environmental Committee, who seek to strengthen environmental protection in Nicaragua by working with Nicaraguan non-governmental organizations and attracting international support, believe that the construction of a canal through Nicaragua will only benefit a few elites and cause major environmental destruction.

Juan Izquierdo, from the Food and Agriculture Organization of the United Nations, and Gustavo A. de la Riva, from the Centre of Genetic Engineering and Biotechnology, Havana, Cuba, maintain that plant biotechnology, if properly implemented, offers a responsible means to increase agricultural productivity and the possibility to feed future generations in Latin American and Caribbean countries. Silvia Ribeiro, a researcher with the Action Group on Erosion, Technology and Concentration, argues that genetically modified maize has contaminated native crops and is a potential threat to agrobiodiversity, small-scale farming, and cultural identity.

Professors Petras and Veltmeyer maintain that peasant-based social movements are dynamic agents for social change in Latin America. The LulaWatch group points out that although land reform is not new to Brazil, it has always been an economic and social failure. LulaWatch believes that the Brazilian government should halt its "draconian" land reform program.

PART 4 ECONOMICS AND DEVELOPMENT 299

Raúl Zibechi, professor, journalist, and researcher at the Universidad Fransicana de América Latina, details the history behind neoliberal economic policy in Latin America and contends that one of its cornerstones, the privatization of state-owned enterprises, imposes financial and human hardship in the region and is a new form of plundering and conquest. Naomi Adelson, a Mexico City–based freelance reporter, explains that the Mexican government is financially unable to manage its colossal water-related concerns including sanitation, variable population distribution, and high levels of leakage. Privatization ventures, she contends, offer efficiency and the financial resources necessary to improve water services and infrastructure.

Tehsin Faruk and her colleagues at the University of Massachusetts–Dartmouth attest that the FTAA will break down existing trade barriers and promote free trade to the benefit of the 34 participating countries in the Western hemisphere. Oxfam Canada, a non-profit international development organization that supports community programs in food security, health, nutrition, and democratic development, argues that the FTAA is driven by the narrow commercial self-interest of business elites.

Adolfo A. Franco, assistant administrator of the Bureau for Latin America and the Caribbean under the auspices of the U.S. Agency for International Development (USAID), testifies before the Subcommittee on the Western Hemisphere that international aid in Latin America is helping to foment democracy and support development. J. Michael Waller, Annenberg Professor of International Communication at the Institute of World Politics, argues before the same committee that international aid to Latin America has not been beneficial due to corruption, inabilities in effectively managing development efforts, and lack of law enforcement, among other issues.

Introduction

How does one define Latin America? This question is valid in a book dedicated to conflicting views on contemporary Latin America. How is Latin America defined in terms of geography and history? Do historical, political, or geographic definitions of that space coincide with linguistic and sociocultural designations? Are there cultures or nations that do not fit into common notions of what it means to be "Latin American"? Are there one or many "Latin Americas"? How does Latin America fit within all the Americas? Where do "Americans" live?

The region addressed in *Taking Sides: Clashing Views on Latin American Issues* has been identified throughout history by a number of terms. Of course, before the European conquest, the people living in the Americas had their own names for their communities, cities, kingdoms, and empires. For example, the capital city of the Aztec empire, where Mexico City is now situated, was called Tenochtitlán. Tahuantinsuyo is the Quechua word used by the Incas to describe the four regions of their empire in South America. Since the time of the European conquests and colonization of the Americas, a variety of names have been employed to identify the region: the New World, the Indies, New Spain, the Kingdom of Peru, the Americas, Spanish America, Ibero-America, Latin America, and Latin America and the Caribbean. Like any word, these terms have a history and specific particularities. For example, as a consequence of Christopher Columbus' erred assertion that his voyages westward from Europe led him to India in the continent of Asia, the Spanish used the term *las Indias* to describe the lands they encountered in the Americas. However, of the many words listed above, none entirely defines the heterogeneity and history of Latin America. In many cases, they emphasize or exclude particular components of Latin America's history or identity. To offer an example, while the expression *New World* is still used with some frequency, today it is often critiqued as being Eurocentric. In other words, the term originated during the time of European expansion when its inhabitants viewed Europe, the *Old World*, as the center of the world. The expression *New World*, like the verb *discover*, carries a certain weight of colonialism and fails to communicate the vibrant histories of the peoples, tribes, and empires that existed in the Americas before the arrival of the Europeans.

Other terms highlight particular historical and linguistic commonalities in the region. *Spanish America, Luso America, Hispanoamérica*, or *Iberian America*, for example, emphasize a Spanish and/or Portuguese colonial heritage yet exclude the influence of other colonial powers such as the Dutch, French, or English that have possessed or currently hold colonies in the Americas. Another disadvantage in using terms like *Spanish America* is that in highlighting a particular language or legacy, other cultural heritages that have helped to mold the character and composition of the region—indigenous, African, or Asian—are excluded. Like *New World*, words like *Iberian America* or *Hispanoamérica* are also associated with the region's colonial history. And, although this volume utilizes *Latin America* to refer to the subject at hand, it is not without its critics. Both of the words *Latin* and *America* have as their origin a European referent, and the phrase itself is linked to Europe's competing colonial pursuits.

The geographic contours of Latin America are also a subject of debate. According to some people, Latin America includes the entirety of the lands south of the United States including those countries that are not former colonies of Spain or Portugual—Guyana, French Guyana, Suriname, Belize, and the English-, French-, or Dutch-speaking islands of the Caribbean. Many of those who define Latin America in this manner use the term *Latin America and the Caribbean* to define the region to reflect the inclusion of all of the islands of the Greater and Lesser Antilles. Nonetheless, Latin America is perhaps most often identified by historical and linguistic factors to include the former colonies of the Spanish and Portuguese empires. According to this geographic and historical delineation, the core of Latin America consists of twenty countries. In geopolitical terms, Puerto Rico is part of the United States because of its commonwealth status. But, again, when considered according to a historical, cultural, and linguistic perspective, Puerto Rico is viewed as part of Latin America. Discussions of the definition of "Latin America" also point to the significance of the southwestern states of the United States that border Mexico. For centuries, this region of North America was part of the Spanish empire and later became part of Mexico. In other words, many people of Hispanic descent who currently live in that region trace their ancestry to a time when the land was not part of the United States. Recent immigrants from Latin American countries have also contributed to the significant Latino character of the border region. Today the United States is the fifth-largest Spanish speaking country in the world, after Mexico, Spain, Argentina, and Colombia. In fact, after Mexico City and Buenos Aires, Los Angeles, California, is the third largest Spanish-speaking city in the world. Due to these cultural, historical, and linguistic factors, for many, the region forms part of Latin America.

Perspectives and Misconceptions

When studying controversial issues on Latin America one should remember that social, religious, and ethnic beliefs as well as political factors will likely affect your opinion. It is for this reason that one should make a concerted effort to keep prejudices at bay and look at issues from a different and even opposite perspective. For example, if you define yourself as an environmental-ist, you might consider the reality of people who confront the grave danger of malaria yet live in a country where the use of DDT, which controls the spread of the deadly disease, is not allowed. And, to offer another example, if you are from the United States, you should carefully consider the sometimes turbu-lent relationship between Latin America and the United States and its com-plex history before accepting or dismissing the arguments presented on the topic. Moreover, while books, the media, the Internet, and popular culture inform our knowledge of the world, it is always important to consider the source of our information and remember that it may be incomplete or inaccu-rate when applied to all of Latin America. What may be true of Mexico City may not be reflective of the reality of the Bolivian highlands.

There are certain misconceptions or stereotypes that exist about Latin America. One of the most widespread is that Spanish is spoken in all of Latin America. Spanish is the fourth most spoken language in the world; however, it is spoken in many but not all Latin American countries. Portuguese is spoken in Brazil—as well as in Portugal and its former colonies around the globe—and ranks as number six in the world in the total number of native speakers. Like Spanish, Portuguese is a Romance language, and because of its linguistic similarities with the former, certain segments of Brazilian society are fluent in Spanish as well. Nonetheless, Spanish and Portuguese are their second language for millions of people in Latin America. This is often the case for many indigenous language speakers in the region like the Aymara and Quechua speakers of the Andean region of South America, or the Guaraní speakers of Paraguay, Brazil, Argentina, and Bolivia. Millions of people from Mesoamerica—from Southern Mexico to Honduras—speak one of the branches of the Mayan family of languages as their first or second language. Adding to this linguistic variety, French is spoken in Guyana and Haiti; French-Creole is also spoken in Haiti and in many of the smaller islands in the Caribbean (the Lesser Antilles). English is spoken in Belize, Jamaica, and Guyana and is used in many islands of the Lesser Antilles. Dutch is spoken in the Caribbean region in Aruba, Suriname, and the Netherlands Antilles. In different parts of Latin America, other languages such as Japanese, German, Italian and Yiddish continue to be used by immigrants and their descendents. Moreover, depending on their history, Latinos living in the United States may speak any combination of Spanish, English, or Spanglish. In some cases, new immigrants to the United States speak an indigenous language, such as Nahuatl from Mexico or one of the Mayan family of languages from Central America or Mexico.

Related to language, it is common for people outside of Latin America to confuse the dominant language of the region, Spanish, with people of Spanish nationality. In other words, while many people in Latin America speak Spanish, Latin Americans do not have Spanish citizenship unless they have emigrated from Spain. In a similar way, most people in the United States speak English, but are not English unless they have emigrated from England or have dual citizenship.

While it may seem surprising, there are also misconceptions of Latin America's size and location relative to other regions on Earth. For example, many people in the United States believe that Latin America is located more or less directly south of Mexico. However, while this is true for Mexico and the majority of Central America, the overwhelming majority of Latin America lies to the *east* of Florida. So much so, that South America is considerably closer in distance to Africa than is the case for North America. Brazil is 1,770 miles (2,848.54 kilometers) from Liberia, marking the shortest distance between two places across the Atlantic Ocean. This is approximately the same distance from New York City to Denver, Colorado. Brazil is the largest country in the region and is only slightly smaller that the United States (including Alaska); Brazil is 3,284,426 square miles (8,506,663 square kilometers), and the United States is 3,623,420 square miles (9,384,658 square kilometers) (*Hammond Atlas of the World*, 1993). Brazil is also the most populated largest country in Latin America and the fifth largest in the world with 184 million people. Of the former Spanish colonies, Uruguay and Panama have the smallest populations with 3.4 million and 3.2 million people, respectively. With a total of 0.1 million people each, Antigua and Barbuda, Dominica, Grenada, and St. Vicent/Grenadines in the Lesser Antilles have the lowest total populations in the region (*2005 World Population Data Sheet*).

One of the images that people outside of Latin America often have when envisioning the region is that of a rural landscape inhabited by poor indigenous people. It is true that Latin America's indigenous people are the region's most economically disadvantaged group, yet they represent only 10 percent of Latin America's population (World Bank, 2005). Nevertheless, many people are of mixed race and, consequently, defining exactly who is indigenous—and to what extent—is a complex matter. In any case, there are countries whose inhabitants are predominantly of European descent. Government regulations in late nineteenth-century Argentina and Uruguay, for instance, marginalized indigenous peoples and encouraged waves of European immigrants to settle their nations, thus "whitening" their population. In countries such as Bolivia, Peru, Ecuador, Guatemala, and Mexico, however, indigenous populations are significantly higher than in other countries. Nonetheless, the racial constitution of the majority of Latin American countries, including Mexico, could be identified as "mestizo," one of the most common terms used to describe people of mixed indigenous and European ancestry. Significant numbers of Latin Americans of African descent— with a variety of racial combinations—are found in the Caribbean, along the Atlantic coast through parts of Brazil and the northwestern Pacific coast of South America. Beyond the ancestral trio commonly associated with Latin America's racial composition—Iberian (Spanish/Portuguese), indigenous, and African—the region has attracted people from all over the world. In addition to European immigrant groups such as the German and Italian, Latin America is also home to people of Asian, Jewish, and Arab descent. São Paulo, Brazil, for example, has the largest Japanese population outside of Japan. Peru has the second largest population of Japanese descent outside of Asia, and one of its former presidents, Alberto Fujimori, is Peruvian Japanese. In the nineteenth century, Chinese immigrants also came to Latin America, often times as contract workers.

In terms of where people in Latin America live, it is a frequent misconception that Latin America is predominantly rural when, in fact, today almost eight in 10 Latin Americas live in urban environments. During the nineteenth century, the overwhelming majority of Latin Americans lived in rural areas. However, over the course of the second half of the twentieth century, Latin America witnessed a significant increase in urbanization, due in great part to the migration of people from rural areas to urban centers. According to the United Nations Environment Programme, "Latin America and the Caribbean is the most urbanized region in the developing world. Between 1972 and 2000 the urban population rose from 176.4 million to 390.8 million, prompted by better services and job opportunities compared to rural areas" (UNEP Global Environment Outlook).

On the subject of poverty, it is important to note that although people who live in rural environments confront a spectrum of hardships, poverty is not limited to the countryside. In cities like Mexico City, Lima, Caracas, and São Paulo, massive shantytowns reveal the extent of urban poverty. Located predominantly on the outskirts of urban centers, the homes that comprise Latin America's shantytowns are constructed with cheap or discarded materials—cardboard, plastic, wood, and metal. Because these squatter settlements are often illegal, their inhabitants cannot necessarily or regularly depend on access to electricity, water, and sanitation services. Identified by the generic term *barrios populares*, shantytowns or squatter settlements are known by a variety of names, including *favelas* in Brazil, *ciudades perdidas* in Mexico, and *villas miseries* in Argentina. In focusing on shantytowns and urban poverty, it is important to not forget that Latin America is also home to very modern and cosmopolitan city centers where one can readily find high fashion and international and high-tech business.

The coexistence of shantytowns and opulent and ultra-modern buildings in Latin American cities offers just one example of the great economic disparities that persist in the region. According to David de Ferranti, "Latin America and the Caribbean is one of the regions of the world with the greatest inequality." Ferranti and his colleagues of the World Bank add that the "richest one-tenth of the population of Latin America and the Caribbean earn 48 percent of total income, while the poorest tenth earn only 1.6 percent." Ferranti's report also notes that race and ethnicity are significant determinants in economic opportunity. People of African and indigenous descent are "at a considerable disadvantage with respect to whites" ("Inequality in Latin America & the Caribbean: Breaking with History?" 2003). Another World Bank report from 2005 observes that indigenous peoples have the highest rate of poverty in Latin America: "Despite their increased political influence, indigenous peoples in Latin America have made little economic and social progress in the last decade, and continue to suffer from higher poverty, lower education, and a greater incidence of disease and discrimination than other groups" (*Indigenous Peoples, Poverty and Human Development in Latin America: 1994-2004*).

Controversy and Context

Within any field of studies there are unavoidable dangers in focusing on controversy. In the case of Latin America, by emphasizing conflict, one might not capture the beauty and harmony that also exist. Of course, another inevitable consequence of the stressing certain conflicts is that other issues are excluded. For example, this volume addresses the state of democracy and instances of violence in the region, but it does not directly examine the historical legacy of twentieth-century dictatorships or civil wars. On the topic of health, one selection of this book discusses malaria, but one could also examine the quality of health services in general or analyze mental health concerns, physical disabilities, or other diseases like dengue fever or AIDS. *Taking Sides: Clashing Views on Latin American Issues* includes articles on the land and agrarian reform, but it does not look at the access, cost, or quality of education or housing. We have included two environmental issues—DDT and the construction of the "dry canal" through Nicaragua's Atlantic coast rainforest. However, readers interested in furthering their knowledge of environmental issues in Latin America could also examine climate change or the ongoing environmental conflicts in the Amazon rainforest or the Galapagos Islands.

Another danger that at times accompanies discussions of conflict is a tendency to group people together rather than seeing people as individuals. Considering the scope of this volume, it is impossible to avoid this tendency; however, we would like to alert readers to this concern. Moreover, one might also fall into the trap of distilling the identity, hopes, and concerns of such groups and individuals down to one particular issue. For example, while women are directly addressed in the issue questions on abortion and the homicides in Ciudad Juárez, readers should also consider women in relation to the other issues included in this volume. For example, one might consider the relationships between women and land reform or the role of women in Pentecostalism. Directly or indirectly *Taking Sides: Clashing Views on Latin American Issues* discusses a number of human rights issues—indigenous, peasants, and women's rights; land, food, water, and racism, to name just a few—but one could also study the struggle for human rights within gay, lesbian, bisexual, or transgender communities. Readers might also examine the topic of human rights in relation to technology, globalization, or nongovernmental organizations.

With respect to Latinos and Latin Americans in the United States, the editors of this volume highlight the status of Puerto Rico and immigration—the Mexico-U.S. border and clemency for gang members. This focus reflects a decision to limit the scope of this book to the movement of people to places outside of Latin America and, in the case of Puerto Rico, on the geopolitical boundaries of Latin America itself. In doing so, however, we do not examine other issues such as existing differences of opinion between groups or generations of Latino citizens in the United States. Considering this volume's focus on the legal and political status of Latin Americans and Latinos in relation to the United States, it is of utmost importance for readers to recognize that the majority of Hispanics[1] living in the United States are citizens. In fact, seven out of 10 Hispanic individuals in the United States are U.S. citizens, and 60 percent were born in the United States (2000 U.S. Census, "We the People: Hispanics in the United States," 2004).

In a final point about context, when analyzing the issues included in this volume it is important to examine all aspects of the subject by reading the introduction, the Yes and No readings and the postscript. Readers should accept or reject points as they see fit and adopt a view or opinion on the subject. The process of analyzing these issues may reinforce a previously held opinion; however, it may also change the reader's perspective on the issue.

Book Organization and Issue Questions

Latin American Studies is a multidisciplinary field that examines a spectrum of topics related to Latin America, the Caribbean and, frequently, Latinos in the United States. Some of the areas of analysis included in Latin American

---

[1] The most general meaning of the term *Hispanic* refers to people who are from or whose ancestry is linked to a Spanish speaking country or region. However, it is also used to refer to people of Latin American descent who live in the United States and is sometimes used interchangeably with the term *Latino*. The U.S. Census statistic included above includes Spaniards, who are non-Latin American Hispanics.

studies are history, language and literature, geography, economics, art and art history, political science, anthropology, sociology, indigenous peoples, religion, women's studies, the environment, and music. In selecting the 18 issue questions that comprise *Taking Sides: Clashing Views on Latin American Issues*, the editors of this volume have sought to include a variety of controversial issues in the region while at the same time touching on a number of subject areas within Latin American studies.

Taking Sides: Clashing Views on Latin American Issues is organized into four parts. The first part, "Introduction, History, and Politics," provides an overview of a number of issues that appear throughout the book and introduces key historical and political debates on Latin America. In approaching this section, readers might consider the ways in which Latin America defines itself historically and politically in relation to its Latin American neighbors and within the sphere of international affairs. Democracy, the legacy of colonialism, and Latin America's relationship with the United States are also important topics examined in this section. Issue 1 reviews historical and contemporary efforts toward regional unification and introduces readers to a variety of topics that are found throughout the book such as populism, globalization, and free trade. On the topic of integration, Noam Chomsky maintains that for the first time since the Conquest, Latin America is, in fact, moving toward economic, social and political unification and that indigenous and social movements are significant in this process. For his part, Carlos Malamud asserts that previous integration efforts have not yet produced tangible results and that internal issues will continue to hinder integration. Issue 2 offers two conflicting perspectives on the region's democratic future with regard to its political shift to the left and recent developments in Latin American society in general. Carlos Alberto Montaner contends that social unrest—from social movements to kidnappings and gang violence—as well as the political shift to the left with such figures as Venezuela's president Hugo Chávez signal the fragmentation of democracy and a process of "uncivilization" in the region. Offering a diametrically opposing view to that of Montaner, Benjamin Dangl maintains that the rise of the left represents a movement toward more representative democracies, alternatives to unequal trade agreements, and a new focus on human rights and the needs of the people in Latin America.

One cannot study modern Latin American history and politics without considering Cuba's relationship to other countries in the region, particularly with respect to the lingering geopolitical dynamics of the Cold War. It is for this reason that Part 1 includes the subject of Cuban foreign policy (Issue 3). Recently Cuba has worked to establish stronger ties to its Latin American neighbors by providing humanitarian aid. Regarding this facet of Cuba's foreign policy, Cuban Luis Suárez Salazar outlines the diplomatic benefits of these new partnerships through which his country offers educational and medical assistance to other Latin American countries. Daniel Erikson, argues, however, that the majority of these countries are skeptical of Fidel Castro's motives and actions.

To highlight the subject of U.S. foreign policy in Latin America, Issue 4 in this part takes up the U.S.-funded "Plan Colombia." Regarding the program's effectiveness in combating the drug industry in Colombia, Robert B. Charles, of the U.S. Department of State, maintains that in addition to limiting the flow of drugs to the United States, the program is succeeding in defeating terrorists and protecting democracy throughout the Andean region of Latin America. Offering a multifaceted critique of the program, Linda Panetta, asserts that "Plan Colombia" is, in fact, responsible for creating economic, health, and environmental distress.

Latin America's historical, economic, and political ties to the United States are also at play in discussions on the political future of Puerto Rico. For decades, Puerto Ricans have discussed options to resolve what many view as its colonial status as a commonwealth of the United States. In Issue 5, Aníbal Acevedo Vilá argues that enhanced commonwealth would be the most favorable way to expand the island's sovereignty, whereas Pedro Roselló advocates Puerto Rico becoming the fifty-first state of the United States.

While politics and history also inform the debates in Part 2, society, human rights, and culture are its organizing subjects. The deaths and disappearances of hundreds of women in and around the border city of Ciudad Juárez in Mexico is one of the controversies debated in this section. In Issue 6, the Mexican government asserts that it has made considerable steps to stop the killings and bring the criminals to justice. As Kent Paterson explains, however, the family members of the victims and other civil society groups do not think that the Mexican government has done enough and that, in fact, it may be part of the problem. Women, society, and law are also important in the ongoing debate concerning abortion. As is apparent in the two articles selected for Issue 8, competing definitions of human rights and the relationship between the individual, the state, and society are the root of this vigorous discussion. Roxana Vásquez Sotelo's article argues for a loosening of governmental restrictions to permit women to have legal abortions. In accordance to the Catholic Church's definition of life, Alejandro Bermúdez's article makes the case for upholding existing prohibitions on abortion in Colombia.

Religion and racial identity are also addressed in Part 2. While Latin America has long been identified with Roman Catholicism, its religious composition is discussed in Issue 11. Argentinean scholar Marcela Chávan de Matviuk argues that the "relational character" of Latin American culture directly contributes to the rise in Protestantism in the region, whereas Edward Cleary asserts that the growth of Protestantism is not as significant as it might appear. The definition of race and the recognition of racism are examined in Issue 9. In her review of affirmative action programs implemented by the Brazilian government, Mala Htun provides a historical perspective on the Brazilian government's recent rejection of the notion that it is a "racial democracy." Marisol de la Cadena offers an overview of culturalist definitions of race as expressed by Latin American scholars and politicians. She explains that common notions of race are challenged by cultural factors such as class, "decency," morality, and education.

Part 2 also addresses the movement of Latin Americans across the Mexico-U.S. border. The origin and development of the gang la Mara Salvatrucha (MS-13) is worthy of note. While today there is much discussion of the spread of this "Central American" gang northward throughout Central America, Mexico, and the United States, the organization, in fact, originated in the streets of Los Angeles and was then "exported" to Central America. Addressing one facet of the debate on gangs, Issue 7 asks whether illegal Latino gang members, primarily those of Central American origin, should be deported to their country of origin, the position taken by Heather Mac Donald, or if in some cases they should be granted legal clemency from U.S. law. As Greg Campbell notes, for many gang members, deportation to Central America is a death sentence upon their return, as their fellow gang members will kill them. The presence of volunteer border patrol groups along the Mexican-U.S. border is another topic that has garnered attention in Latin America and the United States. In Issue 10, Raúl Grijalva contends that such groups are racist vigilantes, but Charlie Norwood argues that groups like the Minutemen represent a reasonable and just way to address immigration across the border and that their efforts are effective in reducing the number of illegal immigrants entering the United States.

Humankind's relationships to land and the natural world is the subject of Part 3, "People, Land, and the Environment." In approaching the totality of this section readers might consider the dynamics between poverty, economic development and the natural world. At issue here is the precarious balance between human welfare and environmental sustainability as well as competing visions on society's relationship to land and nature. To the question raised in Issue 12 ("Should DDT Be Given Another Chance?"), Paul Driessen answers with the affirmative, contending that environmental groups like Greenpeace are putting people in developing countries at risk by implementing a ban on DDT, which controls the spread of malaria. Greenpeace, however, asserts that the long-term environmental effects to humans and the natural world necessitate phasing out the use of DDT in Latin America. The proposed construction of a "dry canal" (a kind of railway) through Nicaragua is debated in Issue 13. Canal Interoceánico de Nicaragua—a multinational corporation and one of the candidates for building this megaproject—argues that the "canal" would bring great economic benefits to Nicaragua, a country with the notoriety of being the second poorest nation in the Western hemisphere after Haiti. Nicaragua Network's Environmental Committee attests that the construction of a "dry canal" would cause significant environmental devastation and would benefit a limited few. On the subject of genetic engineering, in Issue 14, Juan Izquierdo and Gustavo A. de la Riva argue that plant biotechnology, if properly implemented, could be the solution to hunger and food insecurity in Latin America and the Caribbean. Nonetheless, Silvia Ribeiro contends that genetically modified crops, such as maize, are a potential threat to agrobiodiversity, small-scale farming, and cultural identity, particularly in indigenous cultures. By no means a new controversy in Latin America, land reform is also debated in Part 3 in Issue 15. In their examination of peasant and landless movements in Brazil, Colombia, Ecuador and Mexico, James Petras and Henry Veltmeyer assert that land reform is needed in order to achieve economic justice within today's modern economy. In its analysis of Brazil's Landless Movement, the LulaWatch group argues that land reform has always been an economic and social failure in Brazil.

The object of intense debate in Latin America and in other regions of the world, economics and development are the subjects of Part 4. The World Bank and the International Monetary Fund (IMF), which oversee economic structural readjustment policies in the region, see free trade and privatization as key to economic development. Nonetheless, of late, globalization, free trade, and the privatization of publicly owned entities and utilities, such as water and transportation services, have become particularly explosive issues in Latin America. Like the words *neo-liberal, Free Trade Area of the Americas*, the *World Trade Organization (WTO)* and the *IMF*, privatization is often associated with the fiscal policies of what many define as Washington Consensus. The latter is a phrase originally coined by John Williamson to refer to "policy advice being addressed by the Washington-based institutions to Latin American countries as of 1989." Despite its original definition, many critics of globalization use the phrase *Washington Consensus* as a synonym for *neo-liberalization* ("What Should the Bank Think about the Washington Consensus?" 1999). In Issue 16, Raúl Zibechi details recent examples of public discontent with privatization. He argues that privatization is a new form of plundering conquest, which imposes financial and human hardship. Naomi Adelson presents the case for privatization, noting that, in the face of Mexico's colossal water issues, privatization would improve efficiency, water services, and infrastructure. As was apparent in the public expressions of discontent in the World Social Forums in Venezuela and the massive protests at the Fourth Summit of the Americas at Mar del Plata in 2005, free trade is an incendiary topic in Latin America. In Issue 17, an article in favor of the Free Trade Area of the Americas (FTAA), Tehsin Faruk, E. Bryan Kofton, Dhruv Nag, Cristina Dos Reis, and Kartik Subramanian argue that the FTAA will benefit its member nations in the Americas by breaking down existing trade barriers. Oxfam Canada contends that the FTAA will be detrimental to the environment and efforts to eliminate poverty, and will benefit mainly a small business elite.

Issue 18 offers contrary assessments of the efficacy of international aid in promoting development and stability in Latin America. In his testimony before the U.S. House International Relations Committee's Subcommittee on the Western Hemisphere, Adolfo Franco maintains that international aid to Latin America is helping to promote development and secure democracy. Speaking to the same committee, J. Michael Waller reviews a number of negative trends and details the reasons international aid has not been beneficial to the region.

The topics addressed in *Taking Sides: Clashing Views on Latin American Issues* appear in a variety of contexts and could be distributed under a variety of headings. While examining the specific issue questions in detail, readers should view the book as a whole and consider the potential links between recurring controversial topics. What is the relationship between national sovereignty, free trad,e and the environment? Are there links between poverty, the legacy of colonialism, and populism? How is globalization related to indigenous rights, biotechnology, and the future of democracy? How might the complex and interrelated issues in Latin America be resolved?

On the Internet . . .

Latin American Network Information Center (LANIC)

The University of Texas at Austin's Latin American Network Information Center is an electronic database that contains over 12,000 URLs with electronic resources on Latin America. The content areas listed on LANIC's home page include social sciences, government, economics, education, humanities, internet and computing, science, society and culture, and sustainable development. It also includes country and regional resources as well as links to Latin American media.

http://info.lanic.utexas.edu/

Internet Resources for Latin America (New Mexico State University Library)

Internet Resources for Latin America ("La Guía"), which is compiled and maintained by Molly E. Molloy at the New Mexico State University library, offers an extensive collection of annotated links on Latin America. This useful list includes Latin American and Latin American Studies databases, digital library projects, on-line news, and organizational directories.

http://lib.nmsu.edu/subject/bord/laguia/

Political Data Base of the Americas

Political Data Base of the Americas is "a non-governmental project of the Center for Latin American Studies (CLAS) at Georgetown University in collaboration with the Secretariat for Political Affairs of the Organization of American States and with the support of other institutions in the region." The home page includes information on Latin American constitutions, electoral systems, political parties, democracy, and civil society organizations, among other topics. Information on this site is in English, French, Portuguese, and Spanish.

http://pdba.georgetown.edu/

Perry-Castañeda Library Map Collection: Maps of the Americas

Perry-Castañeda Library Map Collection is part of the University of Texas at Austin electronic resources. Its "Maps of the Americas" page provides links to regional and country maps.

http://www.lib.utexa.edu/maps/americas.html

PART 1

Introduction, History, and Politics

From Tierra del Fuego to the islands of the Caribbean and the Rio Grande northward, history and politics continue to inspire discussion and controversy in Latin America. What are the historical and political factors that define Latin America in the present? In what ways do Latin America's colonial history and international politics inform questions of nationhood and regional identity? What role does history and politics play in Latin America's relationship with other nations in the world?

Understanding the historical and political issues presented in this initial section is helpful for analyzing other related topics that follow in subsequent sections.

- Is Latin America Making Progress Toward Integration?

- Is Democracy Threatened by Social Unrest and the Rise of Latin America's Left?

- Is Latin America Starting to Embrace Cuba's Humanitarian Aid?

- Is Plan Colombia Effectively Combating the Drug Industry in Colombia?

- Is "Enhanced Commonwealth" the Solution to Puerto Rico's Colonial Status?

ISSUE 1

Is Latin America Making Progress Toward Integration?

YES: Bernie Dwyer, from "The Hopeful Signs Across America," http://www.counterpunch.com/dwyer03072006.html (March 7, 2006)

NO: Carlos Malamud, from "The Obstacles to Regional Integration in Latin America," http://www.realinstitutoelcano.org/analisis/852.asp (January 12, 2005)

ISSUE SUMMARY

YES: In an interview with Bernie Dwyer, Noam Chomsky, political activist and professor emeritus of linguistics at the Massachusetts Institute of Technology, contends that for the first time since the Conquest of the Americas, Latin America is becoming more integrated economically, socially, and politically.

NO: Carlos Malamud, senior analyst on Latin America at the Elcano Royal Institute and professor of Latin American history, maintains that efforts toward Latin American integration are doomed to failure and that they have not yet produced any tangible results.

In 1815 Simón Bolívar, the philosophical and military leader of Latin America's wars of independence against Spain, wrote of his dreams for the future of the region. In the now famous "Jamaica Letter" he writes: "It is a grandiose idea to think of consolidating the New World into a single nation, united by pacts into a single bond. It is reasoned that, as these parts have a common origin, language, customs, and religion, they ought to have a single government to permit the newly formed states to unite in a confederation." Yet, Bolívar laments that his dream of an integrated Latin America "is not possible," explaining that while the regions of Latin America have their commonalities with each other, "America is separated by climatic differences, geographic diversity, conflicting interests, and dissimilar characteristics." In the end, however, Bolívar does not entirely negate the possibility that his dream of an integrated Latin America might be realized in the future: "This type of organization may come to pass in some happier period of our regeneration." (Gerald E. Fitzgerald, ed., *The Political Thought of Bolivar: Selected Writings*, The Hague: Martinnus Nijhoff. 1971, p. 41.)

As Bolívar suggests, at the center of the question of Latin American integration is sameness and difference. In other words, do the similarities between the countries of Latin America outweigh its differences? Since the time of the European conquests, Latin America has been predominantly Catholic and shares common linguistic bonds, primarily Spanish and Portuguese. Latin American countries also share similar histories from precolombian times, to European conquest and colonization, to independence, to dictatorships and civil war and, perhaps now, globalization. Despite these similarities, significant differences persist among and even within the nations of Latin America. In 2003 David de Ferranti, the vice president of the World Bank for Latin America explained: "Latin America and the Caribbean is one of the regions of the world with the greatest inequality." In addition to the climatic and geographic diversity that Bolívar noted almost 200 years ago, spectrums of difference in the racial composition, political philosophy, and regional identity of Latin Americans exist.

Attempts at political and economic integration have been made throughout modern Latin American history. Carlos Malamud notes that "[t]he long process of integration has been a veritable alphabet soup with regional and subregional ingredients, spilling across the continent in all directions." For example, in the nineteenth century, we find subregional political entities like Gran Colombia and United Provinces of Central America. In the realm of foreign relations, many nations are members of the Organization of American States (OAS); however, membership in the OAS is not limited to countries historically identified as Latin American (for example, the United States). The Southern Common Market (MERCOSUR) and the Andean Community of Nations (CAN) are current examples of economic integration. Uniting political, economic, and social concerns, the Bolivarian Area of the Americas (ALBA) has gained recent attention throughout Latin America as an alternative to the Free Trade Area of the Americas proposed by the United States.

Inherent to the concept of Latin American integration is the power and control that unity would theoretically provide. Divided, the countries of Latin America, it is thought, are less capable of standing up to external influence. Malamud explains that since the nineteenth century, the British, French, and the United States have used a "divide and rule" or "Balkanization" tactic to realize their imperial ambitions in the region. More than any other nation, however, it is the United States that has stood out and continues to be at the center of discussions about imperial or neocolonial ambitions.

The determining factor in gauging Latin America's efforts toward integration in the following articles relates to the question of external and internal obstacles. While Noam Chomsky does not negate the existence of internal obstacles, he maintains that the region is moving toward integration in great part because it is standing up to the International Monetary Fund and the domination of the United States. In addition to confronting these "external obstacles," Chomsky notes the significance of regional social forums, popular movements, and economic integration. Malamud, for his part, asserts that internal issues, such as a lack of a leadership—that would clearly delineate the goals of a unified Latin America—and an excess of integrationist rhetoric and nationalism, are the main obstacles to Latin American integration.

YES

Bernie Dwyer

The Hopeful Signs Across Latin America

This interview by Bernie Dwyer took place on February 8, 2006 at the Massachusetts Institute of Technology in Cambridge prior to a screening of the Irish/Cuban documentary "Mission Against Terror" about the five Cuban political prisoners incarcerated in the US for taking action in Miami, USA to protect their country, Cuba, against terrorism.

Bernie Dwyer: I am reminded of a great Irish song called "The West's Awake" written by Thomas Davis in remembrance of the Fenian Uprising of 1798. It is about the west of Ireland asleep under British rule for hundreds of years and how it awoke from its slumbers and rose up against the oppressor. Could we now begin to hope that the South is awake?

Noam Chomsky: What's happening is something completely new in the history of the hemisphere. Since the Spanish conquest the countries of Latin America have been pretty much separated from one another and oriented toward the imperial power. There are also very sharp splits between the tiny wealthy elite and the huge suffering population. The elites sent their capital, took their trips, had their second homes, sent their children to study in whatever European country their country was closely connected with. I mean, even their transportation systems were oriented toward the outside for export of resources and so on.

For the first time, they are beginning to integrate and in quite a few different ways. Venezuela and Cuba is one case. MERCOSUR, [the trading association now including many Latin American countries] which is still not functioning very much, is another case. Venezuela, of course, just joined MERCOSUR, which is a big step forward for it and it was greatly welcomed by the presidents of Argentina, Brazil.

For the first time the Indian population is becoming politically quite active. They just won an election in Bolivia which is pretty remarkable. There is a huge Indian population in Ecuador, even in Peru, and some of them are calling for an Indian nation. Now they want to control their own resources. In fact, many don't even want their resources developed. Many don't see any particular point in having their culture and lifestyle destroyed so that people can sit in traffic jams in New York.

Furthermore, they are beginning to throw out the International Monetary Fund (IMF). In the past, the US could prevent unwelcome developments such as independence in Latin America, by violence; supporting military coups, subversion, invasion and so on. That doesn't work so well any more. The last time they tried in 2002 in Venezuela, the US had to back down because of enormous protests from Latin America, and of course the coup was overthrown from within. That's very new.

If the United States loses the economic weapons of control, it is very much weakened. Argentina is just essentially ridding itself of the IMF, as they say. They are paying off the debts to the IMF. The IMF rules that they followed had totally disastrous effects. They are being helped in that by Venezuela, which is buying up part of the Argentine debt.

Bolivia will probably do the same. Bolivia's had 25 years of rigorous adherence to IMF rules. Per capita income now is less than it was 25 years ago. They want to get rid of it. The other countries are doing the same. The IMF is essentially the US Treasury Department. It is the economic weapon that's alongside the military weapon for maintaining control. That's being dismantled.

All of this is happening against the background of very substantial popular movements, which, to the extent that they existed in the past, were crushed by violence, state terror, Operation Condor, one monstrosity after another. That weapon is no longer available.

Furthermore, there is South-South integration going on, so Brazil, and South Africa and India are establishing relations.

And again, the forces below the surface in pressing all of this are international popular organizations of a kind that never existed before; the ones that meet annually in the world social forums. By now several world social forums have spawned lots of regional ones; there's one right here in Boston and many other places. These are very powerful mass movements of a kind without any precedent in history: the first real internationals. Everyone's always talked about internationals on the left but there's never been one. This is the beginning of one.

These developments are extremely significant. For US planners, they are a nightmare. I mean, the Monroe Doctrine is about 180 years old now, and the US wasn't powerful enough to implement it until after the 2nd World War, except for the nearby region.

After the 2nd World War it was able to kick out the British and the French and implement it, but now it is collapsing. These countries are also diversifying their international relations including commercial relations. So there's a lot of export to China, and accepting of investment from China. That's particularly true of Venezuela, but also the other big exporters like Brazil and Chile. And China is eager to gain access to other resources of Latin America.

Unlike Europe, China can't be intimidated. Europe backs down if the United States looks at it the wrong way. But China, they've been there for 3,000 years and are paying no attention to the barbarians and don't see any need to. The United States is afraid of China; it is not a military threat to anyone; and is the least aggressive of all the major military powers. But it's not easy to intimidate it. In fact, you can't intimidate it at all. So China's interactions with Latin America are frightening the United States. Latin America is also improving economic interactions with Europe. China and Europe now are each other largest trading partners, or pretty close to it.

These developments are eroding the means of domination of the US world system. And the US is pretty naturally playing its strong card which is military and in military force the US is supreme. Military expenditures in the US are about half of the total world expenditures, technologically much more advanced. In Latin America, just keeping to that, the number of the US military personnel is probably higher than it ever was during the Cold War. The US is sharply increasing training of Latin American officers.

The training of military officers has been shifted from the State Department to the Pentagon, which is not insignificant. The State Department is under some weak congressional supervision. I mean, there is legislation requiring human rights conditionalities and so on. They are not very much enforced, but they are at least there. But the Pentagon is free to do anything they want. Furthermore, the training is shifting to local control. So one of the main targets is what's called radical populism, we know what that means, and the US is establishing military bases throughout the region.

Bernie Dwyer: It appears, from what you are saying, that the US is losing the ideological war and compensating by upping their military presence in the region. Would you see Cuba as being a key player in encouraging and perhaps influencing what's coming out of Latin America right now?

Noam Chomsky: Fidel Castro, whatever people may think of him, is a hero in Latin America, primarily because he stood up to the United States. It's the first time in the history of the hemisphere that anybody stood up to the United States. Nobody likes to be under the jackboot but they may not be able to do anything about it. So for that reason alone, he's a Latin American hero. Chavez: the same.

The ideological issue that you rightly bring up is the impact of neoliberalism. It's pretty striking over the last twenty-five years, overwhelmingly it's true, that the countries that have adhered to the neo-liberal rules have had an economic catastrophe and the countries that didn't pay any intention to the rules grew and developed. East Asia developed rapidly pretty much by totally ignoring the rules. Chile is claimed as being a market economy but that's highly misleading: its main export is a very efficient state owned copper company nationalized under Allende. You don't get correlations like this in economics very often. Adherence to the neoliberal rules has been associated with economic failure and violation of them with economic success: it's very hard to miss that. Maybe some economists can miss it but people don't: they live it.

Yes, there is an uprising against it. Cuba is a symbol. Venezuela is another, Argentina, where they recovered from the IMF catastrophe by violating the rules and sharply violating them, and then throwing out the IMF. Well, this is the ideological issue. The IMF is just a name for the economic weapon of domination, which is eroding.

Bernie Dwyer: Why do you think that this present movement is different from the struggle that went before, in Chile for instance where they succeeded in overthrowing the military dictatorship? What gives us more hope about this particular stage of liberation for Latin America?

Noam Chomsky: First of all, there was hope in Latin America in the 1960s but it was crushed by violence. Chile was moving on a path towards some form of democratic socialism but we know what happened. That's the first 9/11 in 1973, which was an utter catastrophe. The dictatorship in Chile, which is a horror story also led to an economic disaster in Chile bringing about its worst recession in its history. The military then turned over power to civilians. It's still there so Chile didn't yet completely liberate itself. It has partially liberated itself from the military dictatorship; and in the other countries even more so.

So for example, I remember traveling in Argentina and Chile a couple of years ago and the standard joke in both countries was that people said that they wish the Chilean military had been stupid enough to get into a war with France or some major power so they could have been crushed and discredited and then people would be free the way they were in Argentina, where the military was discredited by its military defeat.

But there has been a slow process in every one of the countries, Argentina, Brazil, Bolivia, all the way through, there's been a process of overthrowing the dominant dictatorships—the military dictatorships which have been almost always supported, and sometimes instituted, by the United States.

Now they are supporting one another and the US cannot resort to the same policies.

Take Brazil; if Lula had been running in 1963, the US would have done just what it did when Goulart was president in 1963. The Kennedy administration just planned a military dictatorship. A military coup took place and that got rid of that. And that was happening right through the hemisphere.

Now, there's much more hope because that cannot be done and there is also cooperation.

There is also a move towards a degree of independence: political, economic and social policies, access to their own resources, instituting social changes of the kind that could overcome the tremendous internal problems of Latin America, which are awful. And a large part of the problems in Latin America are simply internal. In Latin America, the wealthy have never had any responsibilities. They do what they want.

Bernie Dwyer: Do you think that the recent growth and strength of broad based social movements in several Latin America countries have played a significant role in bringing progressive governments into power in the region?

Noam Chomsky: There can be no serious doubt of this. Latin America has, I think, the most important popular movements anywhere: the MST (Landless Workers Movement) in Brazil, the indigenous movements in Bolivia, others. That accounts for the vibrancy and vitality of democracy in much of Latin America today—denounced in the West as "populism," a term that translates as "threat to elite rule with marginalization of the public in systems with democratic forms but with only limited substance," those naturally preferred by concentrated private and state power.

 **NO**

The Obstacles to Regional Integration in Latin America (ARI)

It is often said that regional integration in Latin America is not advancing due to the existence of serious obstacles, generally of an external nature. Euphemisms aside, this generally means US imperialism, which is interpreted as a policy of 'divide and rule' contrary to continental unity. Applying conspiracy theories to the analysis of regional divisions is nothing new. Since the 19th century, imperialism in any of its forms (British, French and American) has been interested in the 'Balkanisation' of Latin America. This argument was present during the entire process of national construction in the first half of the century, with the formation of Uruguay raising conspiracy theories to a high point. In some circles, regional integration is considered a key to fostering development in Latin America. However, no clear explanation is given for this theory, nor is there any explanation of why other regions in the world such as Asia are not integrated but nonetheless are growing faster than Latin America.

The nearly simultaneous occasion of the Ibero-American Summit in Salamanca and the Summit of the Americas in Mar del Plata provides a good opportunity to consider these issues. While not denying the importance of external factors in the internal political life of countries and regions, or the role that Great Britain played in Latin America in the 19th century and that the United States played in the 20th century, I propose to emphasise certain internal issues that generally receive less attention. Though this is not an exhaustive study, I would highlight the existence of two excesses and one deficit as being among the main obstacles to the progress of Latin American integration. The excesses involve the heightened rhetoric and the heavy weight of nationalism embedded in Latin American public opinion; the deficit is essentially the lack of regional leadership.

The Lack of Leadership as an Obstacle to Regional Integration

Let us begin with the lack of leadership. There is no doubt that neither of the two Latin American giants, Brazil and Mexico, have played the role that should correspond to them, given the size, capacity and wealth they would be capable of bringing to the regional integration process. When Argentina's political and economic circumstances allowed it to foment regional integration, it also failed to take the lead in Latin America, being more immersed in its own internal issues than interested in a strategic association with the rest of the region.

This lack of leadership can be explained basically by the lack of any real need for integration, with the various countries being more concerned with their own problems than with what is happening around them. There has also been a significant lack of resources to finance operations of this kind, although this should not disguise the fact that the various governments have lacked the political will to foment integration. However, although the lack of leadership was a key factor in the repeated failures of Latin American integration, most of the common explanations focus on the omnipresence of the United States—and, obviously, we must see in this a clear attempt to avoid accepting responsibility at home.

Academics who study Latin American integration often look to the European Union (EU) for inspiration or appropriate models to foment similar processes in Latin America. Indeed, in the course of European unification, in which the political component was more important than economics, the famous Franco-German axis (now in crisis) played an outstanding role. Without the leadership of Paris and Bonn, European unification would never have reached the point it has, despite the fact that US interests in Europe were, and continue to be, both qualitatively and quantitatively greater than in Latin America. It is true that Europe was a key front in the Cold War, as can be seen in the degree to which NATO was active in the continent, but after the Cuban revolution and the missile crisis, the importance of hemispheric issues began to be felt. Still, it is worth recalling the totally contradictory experiences of NATO and the Rio Treaty (the Inter-American Treaty of Reciprocal Assistance, also known by the Spanish acronym TIAR), both of which arose in the same period in the same Cold War context, but with entirely different results. It is instructive to recall the great boost that NATO gave to European growth, compared with the fiasco of the Rio Treaty, due to a large extent to the deep anti-US feeling in Latin America at the time.

The lack of leadership can also be explained by the costs associated with the exercise of such leadership. It is curious that no one in Latin America has yet wanted to take on the role of regional leader, automatically assuming that the benefits to be obtained would be substantially inferior to the cost involved. This attitude, however, has begun to change now that Venezuela has come on the scene with sufficient resources and a clear idea of what it wants to do with them. As is always the case, when there is a vacuum someone fills it—in this case, due to inaction on the part of Brazil and Mexico. Although Hugo Chávez's Venezuela and Fidel Castro's Cuba have the support of part of Latin American public opinion, the big difference between Chávez and Castro is that the former has the economic resources that the latter has always lacked. This puts the Venezuelan leader in a position to gain political backing in multilateral bodies such as the OAS, through companies such as Petrocaribe, which distributes oil charitably at subsidised prices and finances oil purchases with loans at symbolic interest rates. As a result, it is reasonable to question the permanence of support that is garnered by mechanisms that have little to do with conviction or persuasion.

Nationalism and the Transfer of Sovereignty to Supranational Bodies

Nationalism is the first among the excesses. Despite the continuous stream of declarations (and more on rhetoric later) on—or in favour of—Latin American unity, the fact is that the region has made very little headway towards unification. However, excessive nationalism should not be confused with the autarchy that was dominant from the 1950s to the 1970s and that imposed a near total closure of national borders, preventing any kind of opening to trade or any attempt at integration.

Starting with the initial attempts made by the ALALC (Latin American Free Trade Association), followed by the LAIA (Latin American Integration Association—also known as ALADI, its Spanish acronym) in the early 1960s, and up to the more recent efforts by Central America and the Andean Community of Nations (CAN), there have been very few tangible results. The long process of integration has been a veritable alphabet soup with regional and subregional ingredients, spilling across the continent in all directions. Even Mercosur (the Southern Cone common market), once the most advanced example of subregional integration in Latin America and the model for one and all to follow—in fact the one chosen by the EU as its most favoured interlocutor for negotiations that have turned out be interminable—is now facing serious internal difficulties.

Although the turbulence facing the Brazilian government of President Lula does not favour Mercosur's consolidation, the difficulties of a shared venture by Argentina and Brazil, along with other smaller partners, have been long in the making. To this we must add the possible entry of Venezuela into Mercosur (according to the announcement made by a member of the Uruguayan government), though no one can say for certain how this story will turn out. In all likelihood, if Venezuela joins Mercosur it will mean more problems than benefits for all member countries and it may also have an impact on negotiations with the EU. Brazilian problems also have an impact on the process of creating the South American Community of Nations (one of the most recent attempts at integration, in this case, of South America). This initiative has also been backed by Itamarati—the Brazilian Ministry of Foreign Affairs—but has not been received with universal enthusiasm by the various countries in the region.

In these and other cases, little headway has been made towards the creation of supranational structures capable of developing regional integration. And this is where we come to the question of excessive nationalism: no Latin American country is willing to give up the smallest amount of sovereignty for the construction of supranational institutions, and without such institutions there is no way that regional or subregional integration processes can advance or be consolidated.

The Excess of Integrationist Rhetoric   ⁻

Finally, let us touch on the excess of rhetoric, which is omnipresent in Latin America. We often allude to 'magical realism' in dealing with the issue and this generally gets in the way of a proper diagnosis of what is happening in the region. It seems that Latin American unity is the necessary end of Latin America's historical development—at least we seem to accept this as the gospel truth. We also hear that this is the best way to shake off the heavy yoke of foreign domination: faced with 'divide and rule', the contrary or counter-thesis is the idea that 'in union there is strength'.

From this perspective, Simón Bolívar has lately and repeatedly been presented as the great new apostle of Latin American unity. Even Hugo Chávez's big project to oppose the FTAA (Free Trade Area of the Americas) is ALBA (Bolivarian Area of the Americas). Proof of this was the stage management of the Venezuelan delegation at the Summit of the Americas and at the counter-summit held by the anti-globalisation movements, where Diego Maradona was a star performer.

I do not want go into a detailed analysis of Bolivarian ideas here as they deserve a somewhat longer essay to themselves. Rather, I simply want to suggest that the Liberator's ideas on unification were directly linked to the structure of the Spanish empire in America—an empire already breaking down when Bolívar wrote his famous Jamaica Letter in 1815. Apart from the fact that the figure of Bolívar has nothing to do with Mexican history, we could also ask what Brazil and the non-Spanish Caribbean have to do with his thought and, therefore, what an initiative carrying the Bolivarian label could possibly mean to them.

This is where we come back to the starting point, where excessive rhetoric meets a lack of leadership. Given the lack of clear leadership in the Latin American integration process, and thanks to abundant resources that continue to grow with the rising price of oil, the Venezuelan government has decided to take on the enormous costs of this leadership, which neither Brazil nor Mexico are willing to do. This means that energy is now at the heart of the integration process and, similarly to what occurred in Europe with coal and steel, the idea here is that oil and gas will provide Latin American integration with the required boost. What is overlooked, however, is the political component of the European project. Rhetoric aside, this component has not been clarified in the Latin American context.

This makes it valid to ask—regardless of the impact of this particular case—how long-lasting and sustainable a regional integration process can be if it is spurred on by money, rather than being based on convictions and detailed political agreements. In any case, if the existing deficits and excesses are not corrected, little headway will be made in the regional integration process—a process that appears necessary for the future of the region, but also for Europe and the rest of the world. The excessive rhetoric also tends to minimise the importance of the numerous bilateral disputes in the region and the way in which they may condition the specific results of the integration process (see Carlos Malamud, ARI nr 61/2005, "The Increase in Bilateral Conflicts in Latin

America: Its Consequences In and Outside the Region," available at http://www. realinstitutoelcano.org/analisis/755.asp).

Conclusion

The lack of tangible results in the regional and subregional integration process in Latin America is due more to internal issues than to external considerations. An excess of integrationist rhetoric and nationalism, combined with a lack of leadership considerably hinder any kind of significant headway in this direction. The rhetoric has led to confusion regarding goals and it has been forgotten that without any clear political goals shared by all players, any integration process is doomed to failure. Excessive nationalism has prevented—and continues to prevent—the transfer of the smallest amount of sovereignty for the creation of multinational bodies, which are essential to any integration process. Finally, the lack of clear leadership makes it impossible to give any process the impetus and direction necessary to reach its destination. If these problems are not solved—and insisting on the danger from the north will do nothing to solve them—little headway will be made towards integration, if in fact integration really is the key to removing the obstacles to development in Latin America.

POSTSCRIPT

Is Latin America Making Progress Toward Integration?

$\mathbf{T}$he theme of integration was a key point of discussion in two recent forums in Latin America in 2006—the World Economic Forum (WEF) on Latin America in São Paulo, Brazil, and a regional World Social Forum (WSF) in Caracas, Venezuela. The WEF defines itself as "an independent international organization committed to improving the state of the world by engaging leaders in partnerships to shape global, regional and industry agendas" (www.weforum.org). The goal of the WSF is to create an "open platform to discuss strategies of resistance to the model for globalisation formulated at the annual World Economic Forum." Albeit with distinct areas of interest—economic and social—both forums outlined ways in which Latin America could move toward integration.

The report from the WEF on Latin America summarizes the current state of and central goals for economic integration. From the outset of the report, the WEF concludes that "the immediate outlook for closer relations among Latin American economies is poor. While intra-regional commerce has mushroomed, the Free Trade Area of the Americas (FTAA) and a Mercosur-EU arrangement have stalled." The report also outlined the potential impediments to economic integration. Many participants determined that politics could be one of these obstacles. Eric Farnsworth, vice president, Council of the Americas, cautioned that "The hemisphere has split between countries that want greater participation in the global economy and those that reject the global environment." Some participants expressed concern about the rise of populism. Boris Fausto, historian and professor of political science at the University of São Paulo, Brazil, noted: "We are in a dangerous situation." Despite these potential obstacles, the implementation of several key goals outlined by the report would help to integrate and strengthen the economies of the region. One of these goals is the improvement of infrastructure links such as bridges, railroads, and highways. These developments, it is believed, would "increase intra-regional trade and boost cooperation in strategic sectors such as energy and tourism." On the topic of trade, the report acknowledges that Latin American "countries are discovering each other" and suggested "emphasis should continue to be made on multilateral and regional initiatives. But with those efforts stalled, bilaterals may be the best alternative." The report asserts that the "energy sector may play a leading role in enhancing regional integration."

Turning from economic integration to the WSF, one of the events that took place in the latter was a panel discussion on the "New Paths of Latin American Integration." A common theme of the panel, and the 2006 WSF in general, was the "defeat" of the FTAA at the summit of the Americas in

Mar del Plata in 2005 and the need to unite under a different model of integration in which developing countries would have a stronger collective voice. Mexican academic and human rights activist, Alejandro de Morano, noted that "in the current period of powerful transnational economic forces the only way to achieve this true sovereignty is to unite the continent on a transnational basis." Oswaldo Martinez, the president of the Economics Commission for the Cuban National Assembly, pointed to the Bolivarian Alternative for the Americas as a positive model for integration, maintaining that it offered economic independence and the possibility of reducing poverty in the region. Honduran Rafael Alegría of the international land reform movement *Via Campesina* underscored the importance of changing the internal structure of individual nations to establish a new kind of relationship between people and their government: "National governments must be integrated with the people." In other words, integration, according to Alegría, should not only be between governments but is also a process that should occur at a national level (Alex Holland, Venezuelanalysis.com., January 26, 2006). The need for internal (national) integration is also suggested by Chomsky in his comments on existing economic inequality within the different nations of Latin America. Also central to Chomsky's view of integration is the inclusion of the peoples of Latin America that have traditionally been excluded or underrepresented into positions of political and economic power.

Addressing the thousands of Latin Americans and others who attended the WSF, the president of the host country, Hugo Chávez, began his speech invoking Bolívar's dream of a united Latin America. "Caracas! Here Simón Bolívar was born and here remain the ashes of the Father Liberator, that great man of our America, who one day realized that, like Christ, he would not in his lifetime be able to see or hear, or feel the concretion of the dream, of the utopia. Bolívar said, among so many notable phrases demonstrating his love, his sacrifice and his anguish, he said: 'The grand day of South America still has not arrived. . .'. Bolívar said this shortly before his death in 1830." Has that day arrived as Chávez would seem to proclaim? Are these the words of the leader who will fulfill the dream of a united Latin America? Or, as Malamud suggests, are leaders like Chávez an obstacle to union and an example of an excess of rhetoric? Will populism and nationalism impede the realization of the concept of Latin American integration?

To review a full report from the WEF on Latin America, see http://www.weforum.org/pdf/summitreports/latinamerica2006/default.htm. For information on the WSF, go to http://www.wsf2006.org/index.php. To read the entirety of Chávez speech at the WSF in 2006, see http://www.chavezinenglish.org/2006/WSF2006.html.

ISSUE 2

Is Democracy Threatened by Social Unrest and the Rise of Latin America's Left?

YES: Carlos Alberto Montaner, from "Latin America: Fragmentation and Forecasts," *The Heritage Foundation* (June 2, 2005)

NO: Benjamin Dangl, from "Latin America's Leftist Shift: Hopes and Challenges," Presentation to The Winds of Change in the Americas Conference (March 5, 2006)

ISSUE SUMMARY

YES: Carlos Alberto Montaner, author, political analyst, and university professor, maintains that social unrest and the rise of Latin America's left with such figures as Hugo Chávez and Tabaré Vázquez are a threat to democracy. Montaner argues that a process of "uncivilization" in the region accompanies these developments.

NO: Benjamin Dangl, political analyst and editor of *Upside Down World,* argues that the region's shift to the left offers hope for democracy and that it represents an opening up of economic policy and new focus on the needs of the people in Latin America.

Horrible or hopeful? Anarchy or justice? The fragmentation of democracy or a movement toward it? These are just a few of the polarized viewpoints of the current political and social environment in Latin America. Whether one celebrates or laments its coming, as Carlos Alberto Montaner affirms, "this is the hour of the left," and its recent wave of political victories is one of the most ardently discussed topics in and about Latin America. While significant differences of political ideology distinguish them from each other, to date, some of the recently elected left-leaning leaders include Michelle Bachelet from Chile, Hugo Chávez from Venezuela, Alan García from Perú, Néstor Kirchner from Argentina, Luis Inácio Lula da Silva from Brazil, Evo Morales from Bolivia, Rene Preval from Haiti, and Tabaré Vázquez from Uruguay. And of course, Fidel Castro maintains his position as the prime minister of Cuba as he has since 1959.

There is fervent disagreement on what these political changes will mean for democracy in the region. Nonetheless, many analysts maintain that the rise of the left, in great part, represents a reaction to the economic policies of the past decade and to socioeconomic inequality in general. Senior fellow and director of the Center on Global Prosperity at Independent Institute, Álvaro Vargas Llosa, for example, explains that the rise of what he refers to as the populist left is a response to the "failure or semi-failure of the free market reform in the 1990s" ("Populism in Latin America," Hudson Institute, November 16, 2005). Often identified as the Washington Consensus and neoliberalism, these economic reforms include the privatization of public firms, the deregulation of markets, and austerity. These reforms have met great resistance in Latin America, and, of late, the region has witnessed massive demonstrations and public forums against these economic changes. Those who participate in community forums, protests, and movements often associate these policies with globalization, the International Monetary Fund, the World Bank, the Free Trade Area of the Americas, and the World Trade Organization. Protests and social mobilizations also express concern for indigenous and workers' rights, questions of national sovereignty, a loss of control over natural resources, and the protection of the environment. To this list of concerns, one must also add a critique of the U.S. foreign and economic policy.

As Montaner asserts in the first of the following articles, the shift to the left and recent social upheaval represent a threat to democracy in Latin America. This opinion is shared by other political analyists such as Marifeli Pérez-Stable, vice president for democratic governance at the Inter-American Dialogue in Washington. Pérez-Stable maintains that the "region's bright future, which 15 years ago seemed to beckon, has receded." She highlights Hugo Chávez's "populist delusions" of 21st century social, anti-americanism, "rowdy street protests" and a growing disenchantment of democracy and market reform as evidence of a bleak future ("Populist Delusions Block Latin America's Progress," *The Financial Times,* January 23, 2006). Professor of political science at Cleveland State University, Donald B. Shultz concurs with Pérez-Stable's assertion that the region has gone backward in its movement toward democracy: "The tide of democracy is already ebbing." Similar to Pérez-Stable, Shultz notes that poverty and socioeconomic inequality are impediments to democracy. Shultz outlines a list of other "destabilizing or de-democratizing trends" in the region: a rise in authoritarianism, drug trafficking, narcoviolence, the growth of guerrilla and paramilitary groups, urban violence, impunity for human rights abusers, police corruption, a rise in authoritarianism, and a "generalized breakdown of law and order" ("The Growing Threat to Democracy in Latin America," *Parameters,* Spring 2001).

While he recognizes gradients of difference within the Latin American left, Carlos Alberto Montaner argues that the rise of the left is a threat to democracy and is accompanied by social and economic instability, authoritarianism, and, ultimately, the "uncivilization" of the region. Benjamin Dangl finds hope in Latin America's recent political changes, noting that it introduces a "new space for democracy," economic justice, and a greater concern for human rights.

YES

Carlos Alberto Montaner

Latin America: Fragmentation and Forecasts

The current Latin America outlook is disheartening. The democratic governments of Ecuador and Bolivia are hanging by a thread. In Colombia, as the war goes on without letup, it is not possible to predict whether the Supreme Court will accept the reelection of Álvaro Uribe, despite the clear and popular support he enjoys, in addition to a certain amount of parliamentary support as well.

In Venezuela, it is obvious that Hugo Chávez is accelerating the pace toward "the sea of Cuban happiness." In Argentina, the economy seems to be flowering, but what is really happening is a rebounding, as the foreseeable recovery is taking place after the debacle caused by the devaluation of the peso and the default declared by the government.

In Nicaragua, it is possible that Daniel Ortega will return to power, heading the radical wing of the Sandinistas, supported by a relative majority tired of Liberal Party scandals, and it is easy to predict that if this were to take place, he will make common cause with Castro and Chávez. In México, Manuel López Obrador, a populist, leftist candidate, has a good chance of getting into power, as has already taken place in Uruguay with the victory of Tabaré Vázquez, or when Inacio Lula da Silva won the Brazilian elections.

It seems, therefore, that this is the hour of the left.

All this is accompanied by an evident degradation of political institutions. In many nations—with the clear exception of Chile—the traditional political parties are disintegrating. In all polls, parliaments appear as the most discredited branch of government, and the loss of prestige of the political class is such that the image that best fits the interests of politicians seeking elected office is that of the outsider, somebody that does not come from the system and who will come to clean out the stables of Augias from the indigence that they so shamelessly exhibit.

On the other hand, the judicial branch, in practically all these countries, is also classified as unjust, venal, and corrupt, almost as much as is the police, frequently in cahoots with criminals to commit all manner of abuses against defenseless citizens.

From *American Heritage,* June 2, 2005, Heritage Lecture #883. Copyright © 2005 by Heritage Foundation. Reprinted by permission.

A Journey to the Recent Past in Latin America

This horrible outlook has been aggravated in the last few years. It wasn't exactly this way merely a generation ago.

Let's travel to the past and take a look at the beginning of the 1990s in the Western world. The first thing we notice is the appearance of a powerful center that won the Cold War, made up of the U.S., Canada, Western Europe, and several Asian countries that during the last few decades had successfully integrated into the methods and customs of the West. I am talking about Japan and its four robust followers: South Korea, Singapore, Taiwan, and Hong Kong, the triumphal "Asian Dragons" (also known as the "Asian Tigers"), prosperous and developed.

Within this happy scenario, other hopeful elements can be seen: Two up-to-then-marginal areas of the West, Eastern Europe and Latin America, seem to be taking the road to political stability and economic rationality.

After the fall of the Berlin Wall, the former satellite states of the USSR begin to distance themselves from the tired metropolis, withdraw from COMECON and the Warsaw Pact, and without delay re-institute a market economy, democracy, and pluralism as hallmarks of their new identity. Soon, even the USSR would implode, spawning in its path, among others, nations such as Ukraine, Belarus, Armenia, Georgia, and the remote Central Asian states of the former Turkistan.

In Latin America, these changes come hand in hand with the failure of old populist schemes. The walls that fly off into the wind are protectionism, statism, and the rancorous dependency theory.

Latin Americans—who had seen how the famous Asian Dragons, along with European countries such as Spain and Ireland, had abandoned underdevelopment, taking the path of globalization and good governance—could not go on insisting on old and failed economic ideas, at times coming from populists from the right, such as Juan Perón, and at other times from populists from the left, such as the leaders of the Mexican PRI. Only the Cuban dictatorship maintains its indifference to reality, despite the fact that the sudden disappearance of Soviet subsidies that took place in 1991 meant a crash dive in the consumption capacity of the society to the tune of 50 percent.

This is the moment in time when Salinas de Gortari in Mexico, Luis Alberto Lacalle in Uruguay, Gonzalo Sánchez de Lozada in Bolivia, César Gaviria in Colombia, Carlos Menem in Argentina, Carlos Andrés Pérez in Venezuela, and Alberto Fujimori in Peru—although the latter without much conviction—begin or deepen their commitment to reform. Facing a certain amount of popular resistance, they privatize state-owned enterprises, try to control inflation, and, up to a certain point, open their markets.

In Chile, Patricio Aylwin wisely insists on the economic path blazed by the "Chicago Boys," then working for the recently defeated Pinochet dictatorship, while in Nicaragua, Violeta Chamorro, assisted by the good judgment of her son-in-law and chief of staff, Antonio Lacayo, disassembles with great effort the fateful legacy of the Sandinistas. In some cases, such as Argentina, reforms unfortunately will not be accompanied by the containment of public spending—something that will in the mid term lead to an enormous economic crisis.

The United States—which since the Reagan and "Bush 41" Administrations had been making efforts to create closer trade ties with Latin America—during the first Clinton Administration finally succeeds in incorporating Mexico into the North American Free Trade Agreement (NAFTA), having to defeat in the process a strong alliance of labor unions, protectionist corporations, and a number of nationalists that do not deny their disdain for their Mexican neighbors. At that moment of euphoria, it would seem that the Free Trade Agreement of the Americas (FTAA), a huge hemisphere-wide economic community, would soon become a very beneficial reality for all.

At that moment in time, therefore, in the first half of the 1990s, the forecast called for Latin America to be definitely headed toward modernity, incorporating as the means for development and social and political behavior the same model adopted by the leading nations of the West. At around that time, I recall writing in an article a phrase that later turned out to be sadly inaccurate: "Latin America has come of age." It turned out not to be true. A wide turn toward populism would not be long in coming.

And a Leap to the Future in the Eastern Bloc

In fact, reforms toward a market economy, moderation in public spending, fiscal balance, privatizations, liberalizations, and the control of inflation did not take long in losing their attractiveness in Latin America. Their enemies—neopopulists, coming out of the old Marxist left and at times out of the nationalist right—craftily discredited these measures, creating the label "neoliberalism."

Suddenly, Latin America's poverty was a "consequence of the savage neoliberal tax imposed by the International Monetary Fund, the World Bank, and, in the final analysis, American imperialism." Anyone ticketed with the label "neoliberal" would be politically destroyed, so that adjective was utilized demagogically in any electoral battle. Reforming the state, therefore, lost almost all its attractiveness.

However, this phenomenon seemed to affect only Latin Americans. Eastern Europeans coming out of the Communist bloc had a clear notion that the model to follow was the one used by successful countries, and they understood that, no matter how painful the adjustments would be, it was unavoidable that they needed to follow capitalist rationality.

In the final analysis, the Maastricht Treaties—whereby the euro, the common European monetary unit, was created—looked substantially like the so-called Washington Consensus so greatly derided by Latin American neopopulists. It was unavoidable to privatize state-owned enterprises, to abandon price and salary controls, to stimulate the free functioning of the market, to combat inflation, to limit public spending, and to balance budgets, even though this would lead to a cutback in state services.

What is the result of this divergence between the path followed by the Eastern European countries and those of Latin America? Very stark: Practically all of the 10 former Communist countries that recently joined the European Union have today healthier economies than their Latin American counterparts, and one of them—Slovenia, the most prosperous one—has an annual per capita income of $19,000 in purchasing power parity, practically triple the average PPP of Latin America. In general, these 10 nations, after going through a difficult transition period that included nothing less than the reinvention of capitalism and the reintroduction of private property, report macroeconomic data much better than those achieved by Latin America.

Three Latin Americas

However, it would be unjust to classify all of Latin America as one unitary bloc where only one ideological trend is in vogue. The truth is that there are three large blocs, each with its own characteristics.

There is one Latin America in which Mexico, Central America, the Dominican Republic, Chile, and perhaps Colombia can be included, where it would appear that the majority of society and of the ruling political class agree to some extent in backing the Western capitalist model and in accepting the methods of governance and the public policies instituted by the great nations of the developed West.

There is a second Latin America, undecided and indecisive, in which those favoring reform do not hold any powerful political leverage, made up of three Andean countries—Peru, Bolivia, and Ecuador. In this area, to different degrees, populism, regionalism, Indian nativism, and coca planters coalesce while the frailty and discredit of the political establishment opens the way to any radical adventure of the left, making it impossible to disregard serious secession attempts, such as those happening in Ecuador in the dispute between Guayaquil and Quito, or in Bolivia between Santa Cruz and La Paz.

The third Latin America, made up of governments that take up a broad band on the left, include the Brazil of Lula da Silva, the Argentina of Néstor Kirchner, the Uruguay of Tabaré Vázquez, the Venezuela of Hugo Chávez, and Cuba, for now the only Communist nation remaining in the West, governed for almost half a century by Fidel Castro. Paraguay, in tow of its huge neighbors in the Southern Cone, will probably follow the trend that ends up taking hold in that region of the world. In principle, this third Latin America is a strong populist redoubt, with clear symptoms of anti-Americanism, enemies of the FTAA, and intent on creating an alternative under MERCOSUR, the southern common market.

However, this left is far from monolithic. South American socialism has two very different faces. On the one hand, under modern socialism, we find the Chilean Ricardo Lagos and the Brazilian Lula da Silva, while on the other, radical and authoritarian varieties, Fidel Castro and Hugo Chávez. Evidence points to Néstor Kirchner, the Bolivian Carlos Mesa, and Tabaré Vázquez to inch closer to the ideas espoused by Lagos and Lula than to the revolutionary adventures called for by the Cuban Commander and the Venezuelan Lieutenant Colonel.

In any case, Chávez—who has already announced explicitly the Cuban destination selected for his revolution—and Castro will both persist in their decision to revive the atmosphere of the Cold War in Latin America, with the improbable objective of revitalizing Communism. That is where the support for Daniel Ortega in Nicaragua, Shafik Handal in El Salvador, and Evo Morales in Bolivia is coming from.

Why do they do it? The Messianic aspirations they espouse or the Marxist convictions that they may hold aside, they are engaged in this insane project because of strategic reasons formulated long ago by Leon Trotsky after the Bolshevik Revolution of 1917—because they assume that socialism, if found in only one country, is destined to disappear. For Trotsky, as for Castro and Chávez, the expansion of Communism is a form of self-protection.

The "Uncivilization" of Latin America

Condoleezza Rice is right in paying attention to Latin America. Its problems are grave. In one way or another, they will affect the United States, and they are all interrelated. In a nutshell, all Latin America, although not to the same degree, is confronting a growing onslaught of common criminals, frequently allied to political subversion and driven by two formidable forces—the enormous resources of Colombian narcoguerrillas and the petrodollars of Hugo Chávez, the chief caudillo of the banana left, who is determined to redesign the political map of Latin America.

The best example of this dangerous symbiosis was recently showcased in a devastating event that took place in Paraguay. A few months ago, Cecilia, the young daughter of Raúl Cubas, a former president of that country, was kidnapped and murdered by militants of Patria Libre, an extreme-left political party in Paraguay looking to get millions in ransom. The group belongs to the Sao Paulo Forum, a sort of International that gathers from Chavistas of the Fifth Republic Movement to Nicaraguan Sandinistas, and among which singularly stand out the representatives of the FARC, the Colombian Revolutionary Armed Forces.

In fact, one of the leaders of the FARC, Colombian Rodrigo Granda—to whom the Hugo Chávez government granted Venezuelan citizenship and passport so he could freely move about the world—was the "technical" adviser to these Paraguayan criminals. Soon after these events, Granda was abducted in the streets of Caracas and was "sold" to the Colombian government by a group of Venezuelan military turned into "bounty hunters," which provoked the ire of Chávez and his vice president, José Vicente Rangel, both committed to energetically defending this Colombian criminal.

What is the significance of this deed? Patently, in this case, we can encapsulate the problem and its extraordinary danger. Present is the long arm of the Colombian Communist guerrilla, replete with dollars coming from cocaine traffic and capable of operating in Paraguay, thousands of miles away. Present is the ideological and strategic complicity among Patria Libre, the FARC, and Chavism, a Mafia-type collaboration among groups that have converted kidnappings, murders, and narcotrafficking into a common practice justified as valid elements in "the struggle against Yankee imperialism and cruel capitalism."

Also present, indeed, is the suicidal indifference of the rest of Latin America, a continent that looks at these events as if they were police anecdotes lacking any nexus and not as they are, in fact—coordinated attacks against the heart of democratic stability and social peace in the whole continent.

Add to this outlook the emergence in Central America of the maras, made up of thousands of young gang members, terribly cruel and beginning to establish contacts with Communist narcoguerrillas. It is the perfect marriage—where to find better allies to traffic in weapons and cocaine?

Today, three countries are flooded and almost impotent against this form of massive lawlessness: Honduras, El Salvador, and Guatemala. It is possible that soon the bloodstain will extend into Nicaragua and Panama. Conditions are in place for this to take place: The police is very weak, lacking in resources, and the judicial system is politicized and prone to corruption while jails, overpopulated and violent, are truly schools for turning out criminals.

In large parts of Latin America, something fearsome is taking place: The state is increasingly incapable of maintaining order and guaranteeing the security and property of its citizens. In Argentina, the crisis goes as far as the government being extorted by piqueteros—protestors that demand subsidies in order to regulate their disturbances. In Ecuador, patriotism is beginning to get mixed up with street mutiny. In rural areas of Colombia, Peru, and Bolivia, the situation is even worse, causing great migrations of peasants into cities that are turning hopelessly into Calcuttas, creating ideal conditions for the proliferation of lawlessness.

This situation can be given the moniker uncivilization. Latin America, slowly, is "discivilizing." Governments are losing their ability to exert authority. Societies feel unprotected. Criminals are in charge, at times alone and at others with the complicity of corrupt police. Crimes go unpunished. Judges do not judge in fairness. Parliaments do not legislate with common sense. The rule of law and the delicate institutional fabric of the republics simply become diluted in the face of the generalized impotence of the society.

Therefore, Condoleezza Rice is right in looking south. Not only because it is there—but because it is burning.

Conclusion

In any case, the outlook described is perhaps not as desperate as it seems. It is true that Latin America, in general, is taking up again a good deal of the populist schemes of the second half of the 20th century, but at times it seems that we are in the presence of devices to reach power and not true ideological convictions. Lula da Silva, for example, has not departed much from the fiscal policies of his predecessor, Fernando Henrique Cardoso, and both Kirchner and Vázquez have denied that they are trying to bring back the strong statism adopted in the past by the interventionist left.

There is no doubt, however, that Latin Americans will continue to be the most poor and backward sector of the West until a broad consensus around an economic and political model capable of inducing growth, and substantially decreasing the levels of poverty, takes hold.

Apparently, the only Latin American country where this has taken place is Chile, where almost nobody doubts that success lies in the free market, education, a fundamental economic orthodoxy, and democracy. That is why there is a great possibility that Chile, in the course of one generation, will become the leading Latin American nation to join the first world.

Benjamin Dangl

 **NO**

Latin America's Leftist Shift: Hopes and Challenges

Within the last six years in Latin America numerous social movements have gained momentum in the fight for human rights, better living and working conditions and an end to corporate exploitation and military violence. Recently, left of center leaders have been elected in Bolivia, Uruguay, Chile and Venezuela.

These political leaders, whose victory in office is due largely to these social movements in the streets, have pledged to fight poverty and prioritize the needs of the people over the interests of Washington and international corporations. This resistance is connected to centuries of organizing among indigenous groups and unions in Latin America. I'd like to discuss some reasons why this leftist shift is happening right now and about a few key moments and events in this movement's recent history.

Latin America is currently waking up from a decades-long nightmare brought on by military dictatorships which came to power throughout Latin America in the 1970s and 80s, including Augusto Pinochet in Chile, Jorge Videla in Argentina and General Rios Montt in Guatemala among others.

Under such dictators, hundreds of thousands of innocent people, labeled as "leftist insurgents" by the military, were kidnapped, tortured and murdered. Much of this nightmare was funded by the US government and some of the architects of the repression were trained by US teachers in such places as the School of the Americas in Georgia.

Besides implementing this terror, dictators worked with Washington and multinational corporations to introduce neoliberal economic policies to the region. This economic model, often referred to as the Washington Consensus, opened up markets for investment, put public works in the hands of private corporations, rejected government intervention in the economy, worked to dissolve unions and involved impoverished nations borrowing millions through the International Monetary Fund and World Bank. The debts accrued by military dictators are crippling Latin American countries to this day.

For decades this economic model has ravaged Latin America while IMF officials and free market enthusiasts continue to say, "just wait a little longer, the market will fix everything." Of course, the market hasn't fixed everything. In many ways the current leftist shift in Latin America is a reaction to the failures of these policies.

This article is from a talk given at "The Winds of Change in the Americas Conference" in Burlington, Vermont on March 5, 2006, organized by Toward Freedom. Copyright © 2006 by J. Benjamin Dangl. Reprinted by permission.

Venezuela's Hugo Chavez emerged as a major political leader in 1989, when then President Carlos Perez borrowed billions of dollars from the World Bank, breaking the country with debt and raising income taxes. Riots filled the streets and many were killed. Chavez tried to lead a coup against Perez and failed. It's the momentum from this conflict and discontent which Chavez rode into office in 1998, in a groundswell of support. People were tired of business as usual and the Bolivarian revolution led by Chavez, offered a change.

In 2000, in Cochabamba, Bolivia, a people's revolt against Bechtel's water privatization was successful. The Bechtel Corporation (which has since been contracted to deal with reconstruction efforts in New Orleans and Iraq) pushed this privatization deal with Cochabamba which increased the cost of water by up to 300%. People were billed for using rain water and drinking from wells they had created themselves. Cochabamba residents organized protests, road blockades and city-wide strikes against the privatization. Eventually Bechtel packed up and left town and water was again made a public work.

The house of cards of corporate globalization came crashing down in Argentina in December 2001. The neoliberal policies supported by the IMF and implemented by President Carlos Menem in the 1990s were widely seen as responsible for the collapse. An economic depression which could be likened to the Depression of the 1930s in the US, hit Argentina like a landslide. In one day, Argentina went from being one of the wealthiest countries in the region, to one of the poorest. The government was bankrupt with debt, the banks closed down and factories laid off workers by the thousands. People could no longer get money out of the bank.

As a result, citizens from diverse classes protested, kicking out the president, and demanding the resignation of everyone else in the government and the corporations that were to blame for the mess. "Que se vayan todos," was the cry—"throw them all out" would be the English version of this phrase. At this time, people in Argentina didn't just kick out their corrupt leaders, they organized neighborhood assemblies, barter fairs, urban gardens and alternative currency—all to survive. The country had been broken and in this time of crisis people looked to each other for support, solidarity and created a new world out of the wreckage—without the help of the government. Some workers who were fired took over their places of work—hotels, factories and businesses were occupied and run by worker cooperatives. In fact, this is one of the lasting successes of this 2002 movement; hundreds of factories and businesses are still in the hands of the workers across Argentina.

I have visited a number of these factories and talked with the workers. Many of them weren't anarchists, communists or leftists of any kind when they took over the factories. Some of them were even members of right wing parties. They took over the factories and businesses not for ideological reasons, but because they had no food to eat, because some of them didn't even have enough money to take the bus home when the boss threw them out; so they stayed at the factory. They did this to feed their kids, because there was no other choice.

This kind of crisis is in part what is fueling the revolt in Latin America right now. People are saying, "I can't pay for the water, the food, the gas. I can't afford the hospital fees and want a better future for my children." The neoliberal system doesn't work. People want to try something else. Many hope this "something else" is represented in the political processes led by Hugo Chavez in Venezuela, Evo Morales in Bolivia, Nestor Kirchner in Argentina and others.

Such rebellions in the streets in Argentina to throw the bums out and start another world, in Bolivia to end gas privatization, in Brazil where farmers are taking over unused land—these groups paved the way for the current political leaders in the government, they opened up spaces for people like Chavez and Morales to come to power.

So what does it mean that this leftist movement has come into the political palace?

In the case of Argentina, President Nestor Kirchner has negotiated deals with the IMF to bring his country out of debt and economic depression by not doing everything the IMF says. Since the 2001 crash, Argentina with Kirchner at the helm has set an example by breaking with the IMF and setting the tone at negotiating tables with international lenders. In 2003, Argentina threatened to default on its payments to the IMF, something unheard of for countries of its size. The IMF responded by backing away from some of the policies and interest rates it was demanding. Kirchner's hard line negotiating was an example for other countries and helped Argentina climb out of its crisis.

Tabare Vasquez in Uruguay has made gains in human rights and ending impunity for military officials involved in past dictatorships. Morales in Bolivia has pledged to reverse the negative impact of the war on drugs in Bolivia, nationalize the country's gas (in some form or another), organize an assembly to rewrite the country's constitution and reject US-backed trade agreements. Hugo Chavez in Venezuela has utilized massive oil wealth to fund a social revolution.

However, these leftist governments are far from perfect: Uruguay's Vazquez has gone down a neoliberal path which some argue has gone further to the right than the previous government. Instead of enacting the radical changes his base demands, President Lula in Brazil has strictly followed IMF prescriptions, and instead of using government funds to spur on social projects in education and health care, he has continued making payments on the $230 Billion debt.

Venezuela's political process is largely powered by oil money, meaning the revolution may last only as long as the oil does, and the revolution is not that exportable to countries without such natural resources. Evo Morales in Bolivia has already been accused of working toward gas nationalization deals which are far from what social movements demand. And though the "water war" against Bechtel in Cochabamba in 2000 was successful in kicking the company out, the public water system that was developed in its place has problems with corruption and mismanagement. The momentum and solidarity that exploded in Argentina during their 2001–2002 crisis has all but disappeared. Class divisions, apathy and a lack of civic participation mark the country's social movements.

Other challenges to this leftist shift are posed by the US government and multinational corporations. The US military has set up a base in Paraguay,

200 kilometers from the border with Bolivia. Hundreds of troops are reportedly stationed there. Analysts in Bolivia and Paraguay who I've spoken with believe the troops are there to monitor the Morales administration, leftist groups in the region and to keep an eye on Bolivia's gas reserves (which are the second largest in Latin America) and the Guarani Aquifer which is one of the biggest water reserves in the hemisphere.

As US hegemony is threatened in the region, military and other forms of intervention are not out of the question. As documented by Eva Golinger in her book, "The Chavez Code," the US government supported and helped fund the short lived coup against Hugo Chavez in April, 2002. Washington has worked hard to push free trade deals in Central America, Colombia and continues, along with many corporate media outlets, to demonize the hopeful political processes in Latin America.

Things can't be expected to change overnight. (I heard this phrase a lot while I was in Bolivia recently.) There is reason to be hopeful about what is going on in Latin America. A new space for democracy and a different kind of politics and economics has been opened up; a new era where at best the needs of the people are favored over the interests of Washington and corporate investors.

There also may be safety in numbers. Many left of center presidents are expected to win in Latin American elections in the coming months. On April 9th, Ollanta Humala a leftist social movement leader, is expected to be elected the president of Peru. Left-leaning former Mayor of Mexico City, Andrez Lopez Obrador leads the polls in the Mexican president race. The election there will take place on July 2nd. Elections in Ecuador will take place in October, and socialist Leon Roldos is expected to win.

A progressive trade, political and economic bloc—spurred on by leftist election victories—is also an enormous possibility. This trade bloc would be an alternative to US hegemony and neoliberalism in the region. Chavez is leading the way toward making this a reality. Within such a bloc, instead of bowing to Washington and corporate interests, progressive Latin American nations will unify to create an alternative to exploitative US backed trade agreements. Such regional cooperation and integration offers a long term, sustainable solution to corporate exploitation.

POSTSCRIPT

Is Democracy Threatened by Social Unrest and the Rise of Latin America's Left?

Among the many colorful words used in the current debate on democracy, the "left" and social unrest in Latin America are "civilization" and "barbarism." Employed for centuries to define Latin America and its different peoples, this binary has recently been used to refer to recent political and social developments. Addressing an array of issues that currently confront the region—corruption, a lack of rule of law, gang violence, anti-americanism, kidnappings, narcotrafficking, and chavismo (popular support of Hugo Chávez), Montaner argues that a process of "uncivilization" is occurring in Latin America. He is not alone in the use of this descriptor. In a speech entitled "The Threats to Democracy in Latin America" (2003), author and political commentator, Mario Vargas Llosa, maintained that current indigenous movements were a "threat to democracy because of 'the political and social disorder they generate'." He added that indigenous movements were "incompatible with civilization and development" (quoted in "The Culture of Democracy and Bolivia's Indigenous Movements," Robert Albro, 2005). In an essay on the inauguration of Evo Morales—Bolivia's first full-blooded indigenous president—writer Eduardo Galeano rejects the characterization of Bolivia's recent popular movements: "From the point of view of the civilized media of communication, these explosions of popular dignity were acts of barbarism." However, noting the recent election of Morales and Chile's first female president, Michelle Bachelet, Galeano argues that Latin America is witnessing an expansion of democracy: "Our nations were born false. The independence of the American countries was from the beginning usurped by a very minor minority. All the first constitutions, without exception, left out women, the indigenous, Blacks, and the poor in general" ("The Second Founding of Bolivia," February 19, 2006).

There is even debate over the statistical analysis and the significance of polls conducted on democracy. In 2004 the United Nations Development Program (UNDP) report, "Democracy in Latin America: Towards a Citizens' Democracy," provoked a lively discussion on the state of democracy in the region and the statistical tools used to analyze it. The first round of criticism was leveled at what the UNDP later called a "statistical error." Terry Gibbs of the North American Congress on Latin America explains: "According to Latinobarómetro, the polling firm responsible for collecting the statistics, the UNDP misinterpreted the figures. As a result, the report presented Latin Americans as more pro-authoritarian than they actually are." The initial and incorrect statistic stated that 58 percent of Latin Americans would prefer an authoritarian leader;

however, the correct figure was 43 percent. The significance of this mistake is that the initial error, as both Gibbs and Andrés Oppenheimer of the *Miami Herald* point out, is that the media initially reported that the majority of Latin Americans did not favor democracy, when, in fact, the statistics showed otherwise. Almost 60 percent of Latin Americans support democracy; however, Gibbs notes the "actual figure is still fairly bleak."

Andrés Oppenheimer also critiqued the UNDP, stating that it demonstrated a "double standard in its regional research: It gives generally high marks to Cuba in its annual index of human development [. . .] but it doesn't even mention Cuba in its indexes of democratic development." Oppenheimer questions the report's analysis of democracy as it relates to freedom of the press: "Is it fair to single out Colombia, Guatemala and Mexico as countries with fewer press freedoms than its neighbors without mentioning Cuba, while putting Cuba ahead of some of these countries in a human development index? I don't think so. Either put Cuba in all categories or take it out altogether" ("Revised U.N. data show democracy still prevails," May 13, 2004).

On the basis of the idea that not everyone agrees that market-oriented reforms are an indictor of "democratic development," Gibbs critiques the UNDP report's use of the "Indicator of Economic Reform" as a measurement tool for democracy. Summarizing other findings, however, Gibbs observes that "Latin Americans clearly believe genuine democracy should be directly linked to economic well-being. Despite significant gains in civil and political liberties, many Latin Americans are less and less confident about the ability of electoral regimes to seriously address poverty, provide adequate health and educational systems, and better distribute wealth." ("Democracy's Crisis of Legitimacy in Latin America" *NACLA*, July 2004).

From the "right" and the "left" and everywhere in between, there is a tendency to summarize the policies and character of particular presidents, candidates, and their constituents in groups—"three Latin Americas," "left or right," "(neo)populist or centrist," and "Chávez or Lula." Michael Shifter, vice president for policy at the Inter-American Dialogue and adjunct professor at Georgetown University, contends that "[despite] these labels, viewing Latin America through a strictly "left-right" lens doesn't make sense today. It is too simplistic, and it obscures the region's highly differentiated political landscape. Latin America is undergoing considerable social and political ferment. [. . .] As poll after poll has shown, Latin Americans are disenchanted with politics of all colorations and with the lack of remedies for mediocre economic growth, scant job creation and stubborn poverty." Shifter adds, "[trying] to understand all of Latin America with blanket terms like "left" or "right" makes headlines, but it can lead to misguided, counterproductive policies. It ignores the complicated dilemmas all Latin American leaders must wrestle with, whatever their rhetoric and politics may be" ("Don't Buy Those Latin American Labels," *LA Times*, December 24, 2005).

For regional, national, and international resources related to government and political science, see the University of Texas at Austin's Latin American Network Information Center (LANIC) Web site: http://lanic.utexas.edu/subject/government/.

ISSUE 3

Is Latin America Starting to Embrace Cuba's Humanitarian Aid?

YES: **Luis Suárez Salazar,** from "Cuba's Foreign Policy and the Promise of ALBA," *NACLA Report on the Americas* (January/February 2006)

NO: **Daniel P. Erikson,** from "Castro and Latin America: A Second Wind?" *World Policy Journal* (Spring 2004)

ISSUE SUMMARY

YES: Luis Suárez Salazar, professor of history at the University of Havana, believes that Cuban diplomacy and new partnerships have helped create solid relations with its Latin American neighbors.

NO: Daniel Erikson, director of Caribbean programs in Washington, D.C., attests that although Cuba is attempting to employ a "good neighbor policy" with many Latin American countries, the majority of these countries are skeptical of Fidel Castro's actions and will continue to ally with the United States.

The Cuban Revolution of 1959 marks a watershed moment in modern Latin America history. Since the 26th of July movement overthrew the dictatorship of Fulgencio Batista decades ago, strong divisions persist between those who celebrate and those who condemn the revolution and its long-time leader, Fidel Castro. From economics and women to race and human rights, heated debate continues to surround the successes and failures of the revolution. In the very beginnings of the revolution, many celebrated its promise of social and political change, yet soon others came to fear that Castro would not install a democratic government. For a variety of reasons, Castro would adopt a more centrally controlled Marxist-Leninist model of government, prompting many Cubans to flee the country. Throughout Latin America, people took note of Castro's "Second Declaration of Havana" in 1962 that vowed to take the Cuban revolution to the Andes mountains so that the people of these nations under imperialist governments would be rescued. According to Castro, "The duty of every revolutionary is to make revolution. We know that in America and throughout the world the revolution will be victorious. But revolutionaries cannot sit in the doorways of their homes to watch the corpse of imperialism pass by. The role of [the Biblical] Job does not behoove a revolutionary. Each year by which America's liberation may be hastened will mean millions of children rescued from death, millions of minds freed for learning, infinitudes of sorrow spared the peoples." (James Nelson Goodsell, *Fidel Castro's Personal Revolution in Cuba: 1959–1973*, Knopf, 1975, pp. 264–268.)

As a result of Castro's rise to power, revolutionaries in many countries, as well as progressive democrats, demanded social justice from elites who, for their part, in many cases feared the spread of communism in the region and its potential consequences. Yet, some of these countries were motivated by the outcome of the Cuban revolution and enjoyed degrees of success in mounting a revolution within their country. And, despite the nearly 50 years that have passed since Castro took power, revolutionary groups, such as Colombia's FARC (Revolutionary Armed Forces of Colombia) continue to fight for economic, social, and political reform. However, other efforts, such as the Shining Path in Peru, which is Maoist in inspiration, have been virtually eliminated and no longer pose a significant threat to governmental stability.

In recent years, Cuba has again attempted to reach out to Latin America, but this time with civilian aid programs that offer educational resources to combat illiteracy, provide the expertise of trained Cuban physicians, and make scholarships available to study medicine in Cuba. Nonetheless, this is not the first time that Cuba has offered its resources to its Latin American neighbors. After the Sandinistas came to power in Nicaragua with the overthrow of the Somoza dictatorship in 1979, Cuba sent assistance in the form of medical personnel and literacy campaign workers as well as the technical support to help build up Nicaragua's infrastructure. The Sandinista's relationship with Castro's Cuba strained its relationship with the United States, and the Reagan administration strived to put an end to what it determined to be the spread of communism in the Americas.

Today, due to Castro's thorny position in North-South relations, it seems that the governments of Latin America have some misgivings about Cuba's offers of aid. Daniel P. Erikson, the author of the second of the following articles, contends that "Fidel Castro's relations with Latin America appear to be on the mend," yet explains that Latin America has also taken note of the U.S. disapproval of the newly formed relationship between Venezuelan President Hugo Chávez, Bolivian President Evo Morales, and Castro.

Should Latin America accept this aid and make it clear to Cuba that no strings should be attached? Will Cuba be respectful of such a commitment? Will financially strapped or left-leaning governments be the only ones to accept Cuba's aid? Dr. Suárez recognizes that many Latin Americans are wary of Castro's motivations, but believes that ultimately they will accept the aid and lead to better communication and relations among participating Latin American nations. Daniel Erikson, however, asserts that Castro's historical legacy represents too great a risk for him to be trusted, and that Cuba's latest aid policy will consequently have little impact in Latin America.

YES

Luis Suárez Salazar

Cuba's Foreign Policy and the Promise of ALBA

In his best-known work, Cuban independence hero José Martí called for no less than a "second independence of our America" in the face of American imperialism, or as he termed it, *"la Roma Americana"* (the American Rome). For Cuba's revolutionary government, this required—and still requires—the deployment of an active, multifaceted foreign policy to recalibrate the overwhelming asymmetry of power between Cuba and the United States.

On September 2, 1960, in response to the already recurrent aggressions of the U.S. government against the young Revolution and to a resolution approved at the Organization of American States (OAS) just days before, Cuba's National General Assembly ratified the "First Declaration of Havana." Still a cornerstone of Cuban foreign policy, the Declaration announced Cuba's "friendship with the peoples of the world," and it asserted the country's right to establish official relations with all governments that sought them—including the Soviet Union, China and others in the then-called "socialist camp." In its second article, the Declaration condemned "the open and criminal intervention exercised by North American imperialism for more than a century over all the countries of Latin America."[1]

Since then, I would argue, Cuban foreign policy has retained a clearly consistent trajectory—from its foundational ideas and its choices of regional and international bodies in which to participate, to the strengthening of its diverse international alliances. For example, in opposition to U.S.-dominated "Pan-Americanism," the Revolution has always posited the doctrine of *latinoamericanismo,* adopted in the Cuban Constitution of 1976, which seeks the "integration of Latin American and Caribbean nations that have been liberated of external domination and internal oppression into a community of brotherly nations committed to national and social progress joined by a common history and struggle against colonialism, neocolonialism and imperialism."[2] But as these conditions remain unfulfilled, Cuban authorities have generally maintained a critical stance toward existing regional inter-governmental organizations—be they political coalitions, cooperation agreements or economic integration efforts.

It is no surprise, then, that Cuba has only fully incorporated itself into regional international organizations that do not question its political system, and those in which the United States either does not participate or does not

From *NACLA Report on the America,* vol. 39, no. 4, January/February 2006, pp. 27–32, 44. Copyright © 2006 by North American Congress on Latin America. Reprinted by permission.

wield veto power: the Pan American Health Organization (PAHO), the Latin American Energy Organization (OLADE), the Latin American Economic System (SELA), the Ibero-American conferences, the Association of Caribbean States (ACS-AES) and others. And given the Cuban economy's socialist base, the country does not participate in regional integration schemes that function within the neoliberal capitalist matrix: the Central American Economic Integration System (SIECA), the Caribbean Community (Caricom), the Andean Community (CAN) and the Southern Common Market (Mercosur). These integration efforts surged or regained momentum at the height of the so-called "Washington Consensus," which prescribed a diminished role for the state in social and economic affairs, privatization, deregulation, labor flexibilization and other drastic policies.

Yet amid the formation of these blocs, Cuba has maneuvered its way by signing mutually acceptable, yet limited, cooperation agreements—as with Caricom in 2002, allowing for mutual market access as well as cooperation in trade, tourism and other areas, and the creation of a school to train eastern Caribbean health professionals in treating HIV/AIDS.[3] In the case of the Latin American Association for Integration (ALADI), established in 1980 and which Cuba joined in 1996, the government has reached several "partial scope" (involving fewer than the 12 member countries) economic complementation agreements. And in light of the positive political changes in Argentina, Brazil, Paraguay and Uruguay since 2002, Cuba has sought a "4+1" agreement—allowing trade but short of full membership—with Mercosur, which is slated to induct Venezuela as a full member.

In contrast to such openings, the Cuban state has consistently rejected the prevailing U.S.-dominated Inter-American system, including the OAS, the Inter-American Defense Board and, in the last decade, the Summit of the Americas process—particularly its negotiations over a Free Trade Area of the Americas (FTAA). Cuba has expressed some of its harshest criticisms over recent moves by these institutions to pave the way for "collective democratic interventions" in the internal affairs of nations, as embodied in the OAS's "Inter-American Democratic Charter." In a similar vein, the OAS-ratified "Inter-American Convention Against Terrorism" requires its signatories to ascribe to the insidious notions of "hemispheric security" defined by the current U.S. administration and its allies.

For these reasons, reentry into the OAS (from which Cuba was illegally suspended in 1962) and participation in the Summit of the Americas process (to which Cuba was never invited) do not form part of Cuba's foreign policy objectives. Cuba has categorically opposed a long list of foreign interventions (whether direct or indirect, individual or "collective") in Cuban affairs and those of its neighbors that were led by the U.S. government—with the consent or tacit support of the OAS.

◦◦◦

Besides withstanding relentless attack by ten U.S. presidential administrations, the Revolution has also managed to express its internationalist solidarity with a multitude of struggles for democracy and movements for national and social liberation in the Americas and beyond. It has done so regardless of the social position or political affiliation of their protagonists; of their forms of struggle (armed or unarmed); or of their level of identification with socialist ideals. The varied episodes of internationalist assistance offered by Cuba are well known and need only brief mention: Guyana's People's Progressive Party (PPP) government in the 1960s; Salvador Allende's Popular Unity (UP) in Chile; the military nationalist reformers in Ecuador, Panama and Peru; the positive changes that marked the 1970s in both Jamaica and Guyana; the popular revolutions in Grenada and Nicaragua; and, more recently, the "Bolivarian Revolution" underway in Venezuela. The type of assistance depended on, among other factors, the willingness of the political actors involved, official Cuban opinion on their reliability and the international alignment of forces (including the island's ties with each respective government of the region).

Yet Cuba's solidarity with popular, democratic and anti-imperialist struggles has not prevented it—for the most part—from establishing and maintaining relations of mutual respect with the region's governments that do not interfere in the island's internal and external affairs. Tense relations and even diplomatic crises, of course, do flare up occasionally, as sometimes happens when Latin American governments support the anti-Cuba resolutions hatched by the White House at the UN Commission on Human Rights. But recent diplomatic rows between Cuba and Latin American states—Mexico, Panama and Uruguay—have been overcome and relatively cordial relations have been restored.[4] Cuba now maintains diplomatic relations with 30 of the 32 states of Latin America and the Caribbean, excluding only El Salvador, which does not maintain official relations with the island, and Costa Rica, with which bilateral relations have not gone beyond the consular level since 1959.

As a testament of its goodwill, and independent of its diplomatic or commercial relations on a governmental level, the Cuban state has always offered humanitarian aid to countries afflicted by the social catastrophes that stem from the region's frequent natural phenomena—hurricanes, earthquakes and volcanic eruptions. In some cases, as with Cuba's offer to send doctors and supplies to the victims of Hurricane Katrina in the United States, this aid has been rejected. But the island's medical expertise has helped combat regional pandemics like the mosquito-transmitted dengue hemorrhagic fever. To carry through these projects Cuba lends the services of doctors and healthcare workers through inter-governmental agreements with each nation. For the sustainability of this and similar programs, in 1999 the government inaugurated the Latin American School of Medical Sciences in Havana. The school currently has 8,922 students from 27 countries of the Western Hemisphere, including 71 from the United States. When these students graduate, they will join the 43,000 other students from 120 countries with medium and higher education diplomas provided by scholarships from the Cuban government; more than 20% of these graduates are Latin American and Caribbean.[5]

As part of the Comprehensive Cooperation Agreement signed with Venezuela in October 2000, Cuba agreed to send 20,000 doctors and healthcare workers to assist Venezuela's *Barrio Adentro* (Into the Barrio) healthcare programs, which have provided free medical attention to 17 million poor Venezuelans. At a speech last April at the Karl Marx Theater in Havana, President Hugo Chávez of Venezuela told the audience that so far 90,000 Venezuelans had received medical attention in Cuba, of which some 20,000 had recovered their sight through an effort dubbed "Operation Miracle." And with Cuba's assistance, Chávez expects his government's *Misión Robinson* education programs in the barrios will teach more than 1.4 million Venezuelans how to read and write.[6] As a result of these efforts, Venezuela announced in October that it was an "illiteracy-free territory," a claim certified by UNESCO.

Despite the White House's efforts to portray Cuba as a threat to regional stability and security, the island's economic and commercial relations with the countries of the Western Hemisphere (including Canada) have improved drastically in the last 15 years. This trend will continue in light of Cuba's deepening political and economic relationship with Venezuela.

⋯◉⋯

Today, Cuba's early engagement within Latin America and the Caribbean finds continuity in the nascent Bolivarian Alternative of the Americas (ALBA). Spurred since 2001 by Venezuelan President Hugo Chávez, the ALBA stands in stark contrast to the designs of the new Pan-American order envisioned by the U.S. government. Although the project is still in its infancy, it represents nothing less than a bold new paradigm for the multinational integration of Latin America and the Caribbean.

In December 2004, the two governments signed a joint declaration that defined 12 articles forming "the principles and cardinal bases guiding the ALBA." Taking radical anti-imperialist positions—unlike their counterparts in Argentina, Brazil and Uruguay—Chávez and Castro characterized the U.S.-sponsored FTAA as "the most hollow expression of [U.S.] appetites for domination over the region." They also recognized that integration processes underway in the region, "far from responding to the objectives of independent development and economic complementarity, have served as one more mechanism that deepens external dependency and domination."[7]

The ALBA—which Chávez calls "the dawn of a new era"—contains provisions that seek to address the varied levels of development of each member state by providing for special and differential agreements so that each "nation is guaranteed a share in the benefits of the integration process." The declaration also calls for the ALBA members to privilege "economic cooperation and complementarity over competition between countries and products."

Another important aspect of the ALBA involves attempts to wean Latin America and the Caribbean away from their overdependence on foreign, extra-regional investors. To this end, the two presidents announced the creation of a Latin American Investment Fund, a Development Bank of the South and what resembles an international Latin American credit union. According to the document, such projects are based on the supposition that "commerce and investment are not ends in themselves, but instruments that make possible a just and sustainable development process. True integration cannot be left to the market nor be conceived as a simple strategy to expand foreign markets and stimulate commerce. Integration instead requires the effective involvement of the state as a regulator and coordinator of economic activity."

On the diplomatic front, the ALBA calls for coordinated positions in the multilateral sphere and in negotiations with non-member states and other regional blocs. On this point, the declaration explicitly includes efforts to promote greater democracy and transparency in international organizations, particularly citing the UN and its branches.

The December 14, 2004, accords concretized the goals and application of the ALBA, deepening and broadening Venezuela and Cuba's bilateral Comprehensive Cooperation Agreement of 2000. The agreement is nothing short of a milestone in the outward projection of the Cuban Revolution, because for the first time in its history, it has ratified an agreement leading to the multifaceted integration of Cuba with another Latin American country. The two governments confirmed this by signing a strategic implementation plan in April 2005, and again six months later by ratifying 192 joint projects with an earmarked budget of more than $800 million funded by Cuba and Venezuela.[8]

Among these projects, Cuba's medical support will help Venezuela's construction of 600 comprehensive health clinics, 600 rehabilitation and physical therapy centers and 35 centers fully equipped with top medical technology—all offered to Venezuelans free of charge by trained professionals. As a testament of its solidarity, and notwithstanding the strong strains it causes in Cubans' own medical coverage, Havana has begun sending up to 30,000 of its healthcare workers and doctors to Venezuela to staff these medical centers and to support the *Barrio Adentro* program. A portion of these professionals will also train a new cadre of 40,000 doctors and 5,000 healthcare workers. Meanwhile, back in Cuba, 10,000 aspiring Venezuelan doctors and nurses will receive training, and an estimated 100,000 Venezuelans will receive medical attention for ophthalmologic diseases. Cuba will also maintain its commitment to supporting education through the sixth grade, and strengthening education programs for high school, skilled labor and higher education.

For its part, the Venezuelan government plans to reciprocate with a supply of approximately 90,000 barrels of oil a day as well as other industrial products, technology transfers and scholarships for Cubans to enroll in specialized energy-sector degree programs. Venezuela also agreed to issue credit and will undertake joint investments with the Cuban state in sectors of strategic importance to both countries: nickel, steel, port facility development, shipping, information communications technologies, electricity production, and oil storage and refining.[9]

Venezuelan assistance will spur Cuba's fledgling energy sector—which has recently partnered with foreign firms in exploratory drilling projects—with the added benefit of helping Venezuela's state-run company, PDVSA, cut its costs in supplying oil to Cuba and, from there, to other Caribbean nations. This forms part of Chávez's strategic vision of building a state-run regional energy conglomerate called PetroAmérica.

In September 2005, Venezuela, Cuba, the Dominican Republic and 11 member-states of Caricom ratified the final text of an Energy Cooperation

Accord at the Second Caribbean Energy Summit held in Jamaica.[10] The agreement establishes PetroCaribe as a regional body charged with coordinating the energy policies of its member-states. Venezuela will directly supply the signatories with oil and petroleum-based products under preferential terms. Signatories will receive oil under long-term financing agreements (17 to 25 years) with one percent interest. In cases of deferred payments, "Venezuela shall be able to determine the portion that shall be paid with goods and services for which it shall offer preferential rates," says the agreement.[11] One observer considers the oil deal "an example of the special and differential treatment of less developed nations" that guides the ALBA.[12]

What's more, the agreement establishes the "ALBA-Caribbean Fund." With a startup investment of $50 million from Venezuela, the fund seeks to foment employment, productive activities and services as well as to contribute to cultural, education, sports and public health programs. According to the document, "funds will also be contributed from financial and non-financial instruments. Such contributions may, upon agreement, be drawn from the financed portion of oil invoicing and the savings from direct trade."

❦

These agreements are indeed historic, but they must now confront the practical difficulties posed by the varying political will of each signatory government. They are also dependent on the evolution of Venezuela's political and economic situation, so by implication are subject to the excesses and hostilities of powerful U.S. interests. And as the recent Summit of the Americas in Mar del Plata, Argentina showed, despite the public showing of anti-U.S. sentiment, the leadership of most Latin American and Caribbean countries are still willing to fall in line behind the United States in pursuing FTAA negotiations.

As agreements between Cuba and Venezuela progress, the content of the ALBA will continue to be defined. Already, mechanisms are being designed to facilitate the participation of municipal, provincial or state governments in securing the genuine integration of the region from within and from below.

Despite the differing points of view that exist between Venezuela and Cuba and the majority of Latin American and Caribbean countries, if the energy sector agreements between Venezuela and Argentina, Bolivia, Brazil, Chile and Uruguay as well as PetroCaribe are any indication, it would seem that promising opportunities are emerging for broadening these agreements with existing and future governments of the region.

If such a wave of resistance materializes forcefully, it could tip the scales in cooperation projects, economic integration efforts and political alliances toward new paradigms of self-sustained, long-term development and a genuine integration of Latin America and the Caribbean. In these efforts, countries must not only make a radical break with the "structural adjustment programs" promoted by the Washington Consensus, but they must also specifically reformulate the UN's Economic Commission on Latin America and the Caribbean's (ECLAC) outward-oriented development strategies of "open regional ism" and "productive transformation with equity"—conventional market-based proposals of the past decade's neoliberal reforms.[13] The rise of inequality in what is already the most unequal region of the world should make the failure of this approach readily apparent. Furthermore,, the forecasted productive transformation has not materialized, and any "progress" has come at considerable social and environmental cost.

"Open regionalism" has decidedly failed to deliver the deep multinational integration the region demands. The majority of projects have been oriented toward what Gustavo Magariños, the former Secretary General of ALADI, calls "coercive integration" with the United States and "integration at arm's length" with the European Union.[14] Until recently, the centrifugal forces of U.S.-dependent integration like NAFTA, and the piecemeal liberalization of the hemisphere, have trounced centripetal forces that, in theory, should be driving processes of multinational integration. In fact, it could be said there is always more "opening" and less "regionalism."[15]

The ALBA declaration reasons that the rise of massive economic blocs in the global economy have made the integration of Latin America and Caribbean an indispensable requisite for regional development, but adds that such a process must be driven by concerted efforts for cooperation, solidarity and common will—the only way for "the hopes and necessities of Latin American and Caribbean countries [to] be satisfied and their independence, sovereignty and identity preserved." It is for these reasons, among others, that the departure point for a paradigm shift in regional integration efforts must be a practical and theoretical critique of neoliberal capitalism. As the Cuban Revolution has proclaimed since 1959, only in this way will the dream of those who have fought for Latin America's first independence—and the coming one—be realized.

Notes

1. Primera Declaración de La Habana, en Cinco Documentos (La Habana: Editorial de Ciencias Sociales, 1971).

2. Constitución de la República de Cuba, Departamento Orientación Revolucionaria del CC del PCC, La Habana, 1976.

3. Norman Girvan, "Cuba, CARICOM Cement Ties," Dec. 9, 2002. See ACS Web site: http://www.acs-aec.org/column/index63.htm.

4. In the case of Mexico, bilateral relations have chilled during the government of Vicente Fox (2000–2006). Uruguay under President Jorge Batlle (2001–2005) broke off relations with Cuba. Relations with Panama were severed in 2004 over then-President Mireya Moscoso's pardon of five Cuban terrorists engaged in plots against Cuba and a plan to assassinate President Fidel Castro during his trip to the Tenth Ibero-American conference held in Panama in 2000. Relations were restored in 2005 with the new Panamanian and Uruguayan administrations.

5. Departamento de Cooperación Internacional, *Globalizando la solidaridad* (La Habana: Ministerio de Relaciones Exteriores, 2005), pp. 3 and 12.

6. Hugo Chávez, *ALBA: Amanecer de una nueva era* (La Habana: Oficina de Publicaciones del Consejo de Estado, 2005).

7. "Declaración conjunta del Presidente de los Consejos de Estado y de Ministro de la República de Cuba, Fidel Castro, y del Presidente de la República Bolivariana de Venezuela, Hugo Chávez," *Granma*, December 15, 2004.

8. Ventura De Jesús and Jorge Baños, "Cuba y Venezuela consolidan y amplián la cooperación," *Granma,* October 6, 2005, p. 1.

9. Inter Press Service, "Integración: Un proyecto de largo aliento," *Economic Press Service,* No. 9, May 2005.

10. The only Caricom states that did not sign on to the deal are Barbados, Haiti and Trinidad and Tobago. The last has expressed fears of a dip in its oil profits with competition from PetroCaribe, while Haiti is under military occupation.

11. For text of this agreement, see: http://www.petroleumworld.comstorytt 05071002.htm.

12. Osvaldo Martínez, "ALBA y ALCA: El dilema de la integración o la anexión," *Cubarte: Portal de la cultura cubana,* La Habana, August 29, 2005.

13. CEPAL, "El regionalismo abierto en América Latina y el Caribe: La integración económica al servicio de la transformación productiva con equidad," Santiago de Chile, 1994.

14. Gustavo Magariños, *Integración multinacional: Teoría y sistemas* (Montevideo: ALADI/ORT, 2000).

15. Jaime Estay, "La globalización y sus significados," en José Luis Calva (ed.), *Globalización y bloques económicos: Realidades y mitos* (Mexico, D.F.: Juan Pablo Editor S.A., 1995).

Daniel P. Erikson

 **NO**

Castro and Latin America: A Second Wind?

Is Cuba's influence in Latin America on the rise? Washington seems to think so, and the Bush administration, which sees this as a threat to regional stability, has been sounding the alarm.

During most of the 1990s, Cuba's status as the lone dictatorship in the Western Hemisphere—and one of the few remaining communist countries anywhere—left it isolated and increasingly irrelevant. Under the iron-fisted leadership of Fidel Castro, Cuba struggled to ward off economic collapse as other Latin American countries focused on consolidating democratic rule, expanding trade, and pursuing closer ties with the United States. Most regional governments disapproved of the U.S. embargo of Cuba, which they saw as counterproductive, but few saw any advantage in strengthening their bilateral ties with Havana. In 1999, Mexican president Ernesto Zedillo excoriated Castro for the lack of political freedoms on the island at the Ibero-American Summit in Havana.[1] Excluded from such regional initiatives as the Summit of the Americas and the Free Trade Area of the Americas (FTAA) and denied participation in the Organization of American States (OAS), Cuba appeared to have been permanently relegated to the hemispheric sidelines.

In the five years since Zedillo's speech little appears outwardly to have changed. Cuba remains outside the inter-American system, embargoed by the U.S. government, and criticized for its repressive policies at home. If anything, Castro's rule in Cuba cuts even more deeply against prevailing norms. In a rebuke to democratic opening, the Cuban government cracked down on internal dissent in the spring of 2003, sentencing 75 democracy activists and independent journalists to prison terms averaging more than 20 years. Eschewing diplomatic niceties for Cold War–style confrontation, Castro continues to relish a fight. Recent targets of the Cuban leader's ire have included Mexican president Vicente Fox, Peru's Alejandro Toledo, Uruguay's Jorge Batlle, and even Cuba's crucial economic partner, the European Union. With FTAA negotiations ranking as a top hemispheric priority, and Chile, Colombia, and the Central American nations pursuing separate bilateral trade agreements with the United States, the Cuban government remains unceasingly critical of free trade and regional integration. While most of Latin America favors better relations with the United States, Castro appears to revel in the unrelenting antagonism of the Bush administration.

Yet Fidel Castro's relations with Latin America appear to be on the mend. Last year, the Cuban leader was publicly feted when he attended presidential

From *World Policy Journal,* Spring 2004, pp. 32–40. Copyright © 2004 by World Policy Institute. Reprinted by permission.

inaugurals in Argentina, Brazil, Ecuador, and Paraguay. He has developed a close personal and political relationship with Venezuela's president, Hugo Chávez, the controversial populist who has presided over the leading oil-producing country in the hemisphere since 1999. While Latin American countries continue to support U.N. resolutions condemning the human rights situation in Cuba, an OAS resolution to that effect fell apart in the spring of 2003, spurned by a dozen Caribbean nations and several of the hemisphere's major countries. Cuba's sweeping program of medical diplomacy has earned Havana substantial goodwill in the region, even in Central American countries with conservative governments. . . . In 2002, when Honduras normalized relations with Cuba after 41 years, the head of Cuba's medical brigade became the first ambassador to that country. Today, only Costa Rica, El Salvador, and Uruguay lack full relations with Cuba (and if a leftist candidate wins Uruguay's presidential election this year, that list may be down to two). Meanwhile, Cuba has established closer ties with the new presidents of Brazil and Argentina, and even Mexico appears to be looking for a way to get out of Castro's doghouse. . . . The more U.S. officials have voiced their displeasure at what they see as Castro's guiding hand—for example, in Chávez's political resurrection following a 2002 coup attempt or in the collapse of the conservative government of Bolivian president Gonzalo Sánchez de Lozada in the fall of 2003—the longer Castro's shadow appears to be.

But can it seriously be argued that the democratic countries of Latin America are embracing the hemisphere's lone dictatorship? In 2003, some U.S. analysts worried that Cuba, Venezuela, and the new left-wing governments in Argentina, Brazil, and Ecuador would form an alliance in opposition to U.S. interests and sow regional instability. Apart from Havana's deepening ties with Caracas, that does not appear to have occurred. Efforts by Argentina and Brazil to strengthen ties with Cuba have been notable mainly for their caution, not their ambition. Ecuador's Lucio Gutiérrez has kept Cuba at arm's length. And although the majority of Latin American governments favor maintaining normal diplomatic and trade ties with Cuba, the island simply does not rank as a top foreign policy priority.

Yet Castro's ability to maintain or even improve regional ties is striking because it coincides with a wave of harsh repressive measures against dissidents in Cuba that has led to ruptured relations with the European Union and heightened the island's tense stand-off with the Bush administration. Ironically, Castro has principally Washington to thank for Cuba's rejuvenated ties with Latin America. Since 9/11, the focus on the "war on terror" has led Washington to neglect hemispheric relations. At the same time, the U.S. invasion of Iraq was highly unpopular in the region. Castro, highly attuned to shifts in the political wind, has seized on the widespread disapproval of Washington's approach to the "war on terror" to attempt to renew political and economic partnerships in the region.

Post-9/11 Blues

A week before the September 11 attacks on the World Trade Center and the Pentagon, President Bush hosted a state visit by Mexican president Vicente Fox. There was to be a new focus on hemispheric relations, President Bush promised, and the United States, he said, had no more important bilateral relationship than with Mexico. After September 11, Latin America appeared to slip off Washington's radar screen. The Bush administration continued to pursue Latin American trade initiatives and to offer substantial assistance to Colombia in an effort to control the flow of illegal drugs into the United States, but for the most part its attention was elsewhere. At the same time, the U.S. economy slumped and tourism dropped precipitously, with negative effects on much of the Caribbean, Central America, and Mexico. The worldwide global slowdown that followed was accompanied by specific country crises where the U.S. response was either clumsy or inadequate. Washington's slow response to the collapse of Argentina's economy, its inattention toward the festering political crisis in Haiti, and its ham-handed reaction to the mounting unrest and attempted coup in Venezuela contributed to the perception that Latin America hardly mattered.

Initially, Cuba's relations in the Western Hemisphere also suffered in the aftermath of 9/11. Coincidentally, on that very day, Latin American countries ratified the Inter-American Democratic Charter, which codified protection of democracy in the region and further marginalized Cuba within the inter-American system. Most Latin American governments rallied to the United States, expressing their condolences over the attacks and, in the case of Brazil, invoking the Rio Treaty, under which the attack on the United States was deemed an attack on all the treaty's signatories. Although Cuba had voted for the 12 U.N. treaties against terrorism, Cubans were deeply opposed to the U.S.-led war in Afghanistan; Cuba had been designated a "state-sponsor of terror" by the U.S. State Department, and Cubans worried that Washington might extend its doctrine of preemption to them. This opposition was not widely shared in Latin America, and a public opinion poll conducted in eight countries in November 2001 confirmed that Castro no longer commanded much respect in the region. Castro's negative ratings ranged between 63 and 82 percent. Only in collapsing Argentina did a bare majority—53 percent—express a positive view of the Cuban leader.[2]

At the same time, differences over questions of democracy and human rights were generating new tensions in Cuba's relationship with Mexico, one of the island nation's oldest allies; Mexico is the only country in Latin America to have maintained steady ties with Cuba since Fidel Castro came to power in 1959, and the Cuban Revolution remains a powerful symbol for the Mexican left. Vicente Fox had been elected president of Mexico in 2000, ending 71 years of rule by the Institutional Revolutionary Party (PRI). Although it was the PRI that had traditionally sustained relations with Cuba, Castro's relations with outgoing president Ernesto Zedillo were chilly; Fox's arrival represented an opportunity to turn over a new leaf. Under the Fox administration, Mexico began to seek a more prominent role on the world stage, and its traditional stance of nonintervention in its neighbors' political affairs began to conflict with the desire to promote democratic norms. Foreign Minister Jorge Castañeda, once sympathetic to Cuba, became more openly critical of political repression under Castro. Mexico's position was further complicated by the initially close personal relationship between Fox and George W. Bush, who advocated an uncompromising stance against the Castro regime. This mix of factors soon led Mexico into an unwanted and explosive confrontation with Castro.

In February 2002, as Fox's long-planned visit to Cuba approached, tensions arose between Washington, Mexico City, and Havana. The purpose of the trip was ostensibly to promote cooperation with Cuba, yet the overriding question soon became whether Fox would meet with Cuban dissidents. As U.S. officials pressed for such a meeting, the Mexican government downgraded the trip from a state visit to a "working" visit. Attempting to navigate the diplomatic shoals, Fox met with Castro at length but ended his two-day visit by meeting with dissidents.[3] Instead of smoothing Mexico-Cuba relations, the Fox visit reopened old wounds. Later that same month, Cuban asylum seekers invaded the Mexican embassy in Havana, apparently in response to comments about Cuba made by Castañeda on Radio Martí, the Miami-based anti-Castro radio station. In March, the Fox government awkwardly engineered Castro's exit from a U.N. summit on financing for development in Monterrey in order to ensure that the Cuban leader would not cross paths with President Bush.

The final straw came in April, when Mexico supported a U.N. resolution condemning the human rights situation in Cuba. As a member of few mainstream international organizations, Cuba greatly values its seat in the United Nations, particularly for making its annual case against the U.S. embargo in a resolution overwhelmingly backed by the General Assembly each November. However, in recent years, Cuba has faced the humiliation of a U.N. Human Rights Commission resolution condemning Havana's repression of political and civil liberties. In 2000 and 2001, the Czech Republic proposed the measure, with a split vote among Western Hemisphere countries. But 2002 witnessed the "Latin Americanization" of that effort. Uruguay introduced the measure, which passed with the support of seven Latin American countries, including Mexico, which for the first time departed from its policy of withholding criticism of Cuba in U.N. fora.

Castro, incensed, responded by calling an international press conference to release audio tapes of a private phone conversation with Fox about the Monterrey summit intended to reveal that the Mexican president had ousted Castro as a result of U.S. pressure, and subsequently blasted Mexico's foreign minister, calling him "diabolical" and "sinister." Castro also labeled the Uruguayan president an "abject Judas." Uruguay broke off diplomatic ties to Cuba, and Mexico-Cuba relations sank to a historic low. Fox came away from this contretemps looking like a political neophyte who had been outsmarted by Latin America's sagest politician. The accusations that Fox had ejected Castro from the Monterrey summit at the behest of Washington created a political firestorm in Mexico, with Fox's political opposition having a field day and the media giving the story wide exposure.[4]

But if Cuba's relations with Latin America in 2002 were troubled, Washington's were not much better. The hemispheric trade agenda was beginning to show signs of strain, and anti-Americanism was beginning to seep back into the political discourse. The region broadly accepted the U.S.-led war in Afghanistan, but the subsequent transfer of hundreds of captured Taliban to the U.S. Naval Base at Guantánamo Bay, Cuba, struck many leaders as an effort to flout established international law. And the Bush administration's increasingly hostile posture toward Iraq deeply unsettled the Latin American public. In this atmosphere, Washington could only view with consternation Castro's warm embrace of Venezuela's Hugo Chávez.

The Castro-Chávez Axis

Hugo Chávez, a former army paratrooper and fiery populist, won the presidency of Venezuela in 1998 with the overwhelming support of Venezuela's poor. Chávez first struck up a friendship with Castro in 1995, when he was given a hero's welcome in Havana following his release from prison for a 1992 coup attempt. In campaigning for the presidency, Chávez's promise of a "Bolivarian revolution" was couched in leftist terminology. The newly elected Chávez traveled to Havana in early 1999, in a public embrace of Castro that soon emerged as a political flash point among Venezuela's increasingly polarized electorate.

In October 2000, Castro and Chávez signed the so-called Convenio Integral de Cooperación that has formed the backbone of an "oil for services" arrangement that is economically crucial to Cuba and politically inflammatory in Venezuela. Under this agreement, Cuba receives 53,000 barrels of oil a day at a favorable rate of financing, in exchange for providing technical support and advice on education, health care, sports, and scientific research. The oil shipments represent about a third of Cuba's energy needs, with an estimated value of $400 million—or one-sixth of total imports—making Venezuela Cuba's largest trading partner. Yet for the state-owned oil company, Petreóleos de Venezuela (PDVSA), Cuba's oil imports are barely significant, representing less than 2 percent of annual production. After the coup against Chávez in April 2002, top PDVSA managers immediately suspended the oil shipments to Cuba, acting on the orders of the interim government. But when the new administration, led by businessman Pedro Carmona, made a series of unconstitutional pronouncements, it lost the backing of the Venezuelan generals. Chávez was then quickly swept back into power by the military rank and file amid an outpouring of popular support. Temporarily chastened by his brief removal from office and economic troubles marked by an $8 billion budget deficit, Chávez allowed the suspension to persist until August 2002, when the oil agreement was renewed.

At the time of renewal, Venezuelan officials pointed out that Cuba had held up its end of the bargain, continuing to provide social and technical assistance during the suspension. Nevertheless, as PDVSA struggled to recover from a damaging anti-Chávez strike in 2003, Cuba's missed payments and favorable treatment remained a contentious issue in Venezuelan politics. In early 2004, the *Wall Street Journal* reported that Cuba's debt to Venezuela's state-owned oil company had risen to $752 million—80 percent of the company's debt—and that Caracas had made little effort to collect.[5]

Chávez's open and unapologetic embrace of Fidel Castro has infuriated the right in a deeply polarized country and conjured up the specter of the "Cubanization" of Venezuela. Cuba's deployment of thousands of teachers, doctors, and sports trainers in Venezuela has sparked controversy in both countries. Some Cubans worry that the departure of valued professionals for oil-rich Venezuela will lead to a further fraying of the island's social safety net. Venezuelan educational and medical professionals have expressed skepticism about the need to import foreigners. The political opposition in Venezuela accuses Castro of meddling in the country's internal affairs. The opposition worries that by providing needed services in Venezuela's poorest barrios, the Cubans may in fact be bolstering political support for Chávez among the disenfranchised who have otherwise seen few benefits from his "Bolivarian revolution." The controversy is likely to intensify given recent discussions between Chávez and Castro regarding a medical aid project that would entail sending 10,000 Cuban doctors to treat Venezuela's poor.[6]

U.S. officials have expressed concern that the two countries have entered into a strategic alliance to thwart Washington's objectives in the region. "We certainly see a Venezuela-Cuba axis which is broadening and deepening and which is not conducive to the promotion of democracy and human rights," says Otto Reich, the U.S. special envoy to the Western Hemisphere.[7] Indeed, many U.S. officials have expressed deep concerns that a mix of Castro's smarts and Venezuela's cash could create a hotbed of anti-American sentiment, lead to the rise of new leftist movements, and even pose a security threat to the United States and its allies in the region.

The collapse of the Bolivian government of Gonzalo Sánchez de Lozada last October and the political strength of the Bolivian indigenous leader Evo Morales has only fanned Washington's worries. According to Assistant Secretary of State Roger Noriega, Fidel Castro is "nostalgic for destabilizing elected governments" and has become "increasingly provocative."[8] It is true that many indigenous leaders express admiration for Castro and Chávez at such left-wing gatherings as the Bolivarian Congress of the People, convened in Caracas in November 2003. But it is also true that Bolivia's deep poverty, social tensions, and history of racial exclusion are at the root of country's recent instability.[9] Castro and Chávez are more likely to be ringside cheerleaders than prime instigators of leftist movements in the hemisphere.

The relationship between Cuba and Venezuela merits continued scrutiny. If the two nations were to move toward closer military ties or show signs of actively intervening in neighboring countries, this would lend credence to Washington's fears. Yet what is most striking about this alliance to date is not how much of an impact it has had on regional affairs, but how little. There is no question that Venezuela's oil is crucial to Cuba, and that Chávez derives some political benefit from Castro's support. Yet Chávez owes his rise to domestic political factors that are entirely independent of Cuba, and the loss of Venezuelan oil shipments would be a significant but manageable setback for Castro. Cuba's nearly $2 billion in annual tourist revenues and $1.2 billion in remittances from Cubans living in the United States are both more important economically, and the island has made significant strides in cultivating domestic energy sources and reducing dependency on oil imports. While most hemispheric leaders maintain relations with both countries, they have so far steered clear of allying themselves with the two men and instead focused mainly on regional integration and managing relations with the United States. Castro and Chávez have a penchant for grand rhetoric. But in conjuring a hemisphere united against American hegemony, they remain a distinctly two-man club.

Alliances of (In)convenience

There is little doubt, however, that Castro's star began to rise again in 2003. This was due in no small part to his decades of resistance to Washington in a period of rising anti-American sentiment. It was also due to the emergence of center-left governments in several key countries in the hemisphere, particularly Argentina and Brazil. In Washington, this shift was especially disconcerting because it coincided with a worsening human rights situation in Cuba.

Unease abroad over the Bush administration's steady march toward war with Iraq in the early months of last year was especially prevalent in Latin America. Chile and Mexico, both traditional U.S. allies with seats on the U.N. Security Council, resisted entreaties by Washington to support a second resolution approving military action. On March 19, the day the first U.S. bombs fell on Baghdad, the Cuban government instigated a roundup of dissidents—and subsequently arrested and executed three ferry hijackers trying to flee the island. No doubt the timing of arrests represented an attempt by Castro to crack down on rising domestic dissent when the world's attention was otherwise engaged. But it was the rising tide of anti-American sentiment over the Iraq War that allowed the Cuban government to escape serious negative consequences in Latin America for its mistreatment of dissidents. The war against Iraq was so unpopular in fact that a Zogby International poll of Latin American opinion leaders conducted last November showed that George W. Bush, with an unfavorable rating of 87 percent, had surpassed Castro as the most disliked leader in the hemisphere.[10]

The arrival of new leaders on the Latin American scene in 2003 also gave Castro a number of opportunities to burnish his public image. On January 1, he attended the inauguration of newly elected Brazilian president Luiz Inácio "Lula" da Silva. Later that month in Ecuador, he was given a warm reception at the presidential inauguration of former coup leader Lucio Gutiérrez. This shrewd public diplomacy continued through the spring, when Castro received a hero's welcome at the inauguration of Néstor Kirchner in Argentina, including a standing ovation in the congress and a mobbed speech at the law school at the University of Buenos Aires.[11] Even in Paraguay, a country where Castro had long been considered persona non grata during decades of right-wing military rule, the Cuban leader was smoothly received in August by newly elected president Nicanor Duarte Frutos.[12] Castro drew enormous crowds everywhere he went. Perhaps most markedly, on each occasion the outsized Castro outshone the U.S. representative, who was typically an obscure cabinet official.[13]

If the anti-U.S. sentiment generated by Iraq provided the context for Castro's warm reception in Latin America, it was Brazil's Lula who mapped a path of limited engagement with Havana. As the head of the Workers Party in Brazil and a veteran figure of the Latin American left, Lula had lost three previous presidential elections before his victory in 2002. Castro and Lula have been friends for decades, since the days when Lula was fighting Brazil's right-wing dictatorships. Yet Lula has not pursued a deeper relationship with Cuba to the extent many anticipated, a fact that is consistent with the pragmatism that appears to guide Brazil's new government. It is true that Brazil continues to abstain from criticizing Cuba at the United Nations, and in September, the Brazilian president traveled to Havana to sign trade and investment deals worth $200 million.[14] Anxious to avoid a confrontation with Castro, Lula dodged the issue of political rights and did not meet with dissidents on the island. However, the Brazilian leader kept the trip short, in an effort to assuage U.S. sensibilities.

The newly inaugurated Argentine president Néstor Kirchner traced Lula's footsteps. In 2001, Argentina had recalled its ambassador when Castro accused then president Fernando de la Rúa of "licking Yankee boots" by supporting the U.N. resolution condemning Cuba. Buenos Aires had previously sought to lower tensions with Havana under interim president Eduardo Duhalde by abstaining from the U.N. vote over human rights in Cuba in 2003, and Kirchner had vowed to follow along the same lines. In October 2003, Argentine foreign minister Rafael Bielsa visited Cuba and normalized relations with the Castro government. During the visit, Cuba and Argentina arranged a debt-for-services swap whereby Cuba will provide medical supplies, treatment, and biotech training to Argentina in exchange for cancellation of its $1.9 billion debt to the Argentine government—a move that did little to please Argentina's many creditors.[15]

Lula has largely escaped U.S. criticism for his approach to Cuba, primarily because Washington sees trade as the most important item on the bilateral agenda, and Brazil's outreach to Cuba has been much less substantial than originally feared. The Kirchner administration did not get off so lightly: Assistant Secretary of State Noriega noted the Bush administration's "disappointment" with the "leftward drift" of the Argentine government.[16] Buenos Aires has publicly ridiculed such admonitions, but shows signs of backing away from Cuba. This past January, when President Kirchner met with President Bush at the Summit of the Americas in Monterrey, Mexico, the two leaders avoided the topic of Cuba, but the Argentine president indefinitely postponed a trip to Cuba that had been planned for the following month. The Argentine government also announced that Foreign Minister Bielsa would include the subject of Cuban dissidents on his next trip to Havana. The reality is that Argentina does not consider Cuba to be a foreign policy priority, and the country is preoccupied with successfully renegotiating its debt with the International Monetary Fund (IMF) and dealing with foreign creditors. Nevertheless, much of Kirchner's exceptional popularity in Argentina stems from his assertive attitude toward Washington and the IMF, following the country's economic implosion in late 2001. And Castro remains a figure of respect among the Argentine public. Cordial relations between Buenos Aires and Havana are likely to persist so long as Argentina refrains from criticizing Cuba at the United Nations. Argentina is also pressuring Uruguay to drop its opposition to Cuban membership in MERCOSUR, the Southern Common Market.

Ecuador is the only other Latin American country to abstain consistently from condemning Cuba at the United Nations, but bilateral ties have not strengthened perceptibly since Col. Lucio Gutiérrez, a populist with leftist sympathies, was elected to the presidency in November 2002. Ecuadoran vice president Alfredo Palacio did make a routine visit to Cuba in 2003 and signed several agreements related to medical and sports cooperation, but no presidential visit has been planned.

Colombia's Álvaro Uribe is the latest in a succession of Colombian presidents who say that Cuba has played a constructive role in facilitating the peace process between the government and guerrilla groups, particularly the National Liberation Army (ELN). However, Castro is reported to have tense relations with Manuel Marulanda, the ailing guerrilla leader of the Revolutionary Armed Forces of Colombia (FARC). Castro remains a respected figure among Central America's left-wing parties, like Nicaragua's Sandinista Party and El Salvador's Farabundo Martí National Liberation Front (FMLN), but these parties have failed to win elections, and the conservative governments of Central America remain consistently antagonistic toward Cuba. Perhaps the island's strongest support comes from the small nations of the Caribbean, which have maintained diplomatic relations with Cuba for decades and often side with it in international fora.

Mexico, for its part, has been working to improve its ties to Cuba since the falling out between Castro and Fox. The foreign ministers of the two countries met last September—the first high-level meeting in nearly 18 months. Although both countries have expressed interest in better relations, Havana has indicated that Mexico must abstain from the upcoming U.N. resolution condemning Cuba's human rights record to achieve this. . . .

Don't Call It a Comeback

Despite the renewed appeal of Cuba as a symbol of independence from the United States in a region wary of the Colossus of the North, few countries are anxious to submit themselves to the inevitable diplomatic dustups with Washington that will be provoked by their seeking warmer relations with Castro. So long as Cuba remains the thorn in Washington's side, the path of least resistance will remain by far the most popular course for most Latin American governments. This path consists of siding with the United States on the question of human rights (the common approach in Central America and in South American countries like Chile, Peru, and Uruguay) or maintaining steady, relatively low-profile diplomatic contact with Havana (pursued by Colombia and the Caribbean nations). For those leaders who have tried publicly to straddle the divide between the United States and Cuba, the costs have often outweighed the benefits. . . . Brazil's Lula has managed simultaneously to strengthen relationships with both Cuba and the United States, but his lead has proved hard to follow.

The reality is that Cuba's political and economic model holds little appeal for the democratic governments of Latin America, and relations with Havana tend to rank toward the bottom of their foreign policy agendas. Cuba remains the only country in Latin America and the Caribbean that has not attained full membership in any of the main regional commercial associations, a situation that is unlikely to change in the near future. Worries about the emergence of an alliance of left-wing leaders throughout the hemisphere have proven to be off the mark. The center-left leaders of Argentina, Brazil, and Ecuador have largely pursued moderate policies, guided by pragmatism as much as by ideology. A visit with Castro is useful in establishing left-wing bona fides and asserting independence from the United States, but relations with Cuba's government rarely extend beyond symbolic cooperation agreements and limited trade. Only Venezuela has embarked on a path of deeper engagement. The relationship bears watching, but Hugo Chávez's self-proclaimed revolution, though polarizing and damaging, has fallen far short of its promises. For more than 45 years, Fidel Castro has promoted socialist revolution as the answer to U.S. power in the hemisphere. In the twilight of this performance, Latin America will provide Castro with a respectful audience, but few heirs.

Notes

1. Geri Smith, "Even Fidel's Friends Are Saying Enough," *Business Week,* online edition, November 18, 1999.

2. Nancy San Martin, "Most Latins Disapprove of Castro, Survey Says," *Miami Herald,* November 22, 2001. The countries surveyed were Argentina, Guatemala, Mexico, Nicaragua, Panama, Peru, Venezuela; Latino communities in the United States were also surveyed.

3. Ginger Thompson, "Mexican Leader Visits Castro to Repair Damaged Ties," *New York Times,* February 4, 2002, and "On Cuba Visit, Mexico's Chief Meets Quietly with Dissidents," *New York Times,* February 5, 2002.

4. Tim Weiner, "Fox's Wooing of America Brings Him Woes at Home," *New York Times,* April 26, 2002.

5. Alexei Barrionuevo and Jose de Cordoba, "For Aging Castro, Chávez Emerges as Vital Crutch," *Wall Street Journal,* online edition, February 2, 2004.

6. "Visiting Castro Meets with Chávez," *Miami Herald,* online edition, December 23, 2003.

7. Barrionuevo and de Cordoba, "For Aging Castro."

8. George Gedda, "Castro-Chávez Ties Worry U.S.," *Associated Press,* January 6, 2004.

9. "A Political Awakening," *Economist,* February 21, 2004.

10. Gregg Fields, "Professionals Strong on Lula and Lagos," *Miami Herald,* October 26, 2003.

11. Andres Oppenheimer, "Argentina Gives Royal Welcome to Castro—Or Maybe Not?" *Miami Herald,* May 29, 2003.

12. Pedro Servin, "Castro Draws a Crowd in Paraguay," *Associated Press,* August 16, 2003.

13. Andres Oppenheimer, "Latin American Presidents In Ecuador Ask, Clay Who?" *Miami Herald,* January 16, 2003.

14. Anita Snow, "Brazil and Cuba Cement Ties with Government Accords, Business Deals," *Associated Press,* September 27, 2003.

15. "Cuba/Argentina," *Oxford Analytica Latin America Daily Brief,* October 14, 2003.

16. "Argentina/US: Repairing Relations," *Oxford Analytica Latin America Daily Brief,* January 15, 2004.

POSTSCRIPT

Is Latin America Starting to Embrace Cuba's Humanitarian Aid?

Luis Suárez Salazar gives examples of how Cuba has "incorporated itself into regional international organizations." He explains that the countries that have allowed for this incorporation "do not question [Cuba's] political system, and those in which the United States either does not participate or does not wield veto power." But, despite the fact that changes in policy often require a significant amount of time to take effect, "Cuba now maintains diplomatic relations with thirty of the thirty-two states of Latin America and the Caribbean," with the exceptions being El Salvador and Costa Rica. For countries that face economic hardship and major social issues, it may be difficult to reject the health services and the educational aid that Cuba offers.

However, although Daniel Erikson concedes that Fidel Castro's relations with Latin American governments seem to be improving, "[t]he reality is that Cuba's political and economic model holds little appeal for the democratic governments of Latin America." This may be true, but even though Latin America generally might not espouse Cuba's political and economic ideologies, this is not to say that they will outright reject Cuban assistance. Yet, those countries that do accept aid from Cuba are likely to experience difficulties in maintaining solid relations with both the United States and Cuba.

Currently, Cuba has created a strong relationship with both Venezuela and Bolivia. All three countries have much to gain from partnership, spearheaded by Venezuela's wealth of oil. Chávez's ALBA plan represents, as Suárez Salazar points out, "a bold new paradigm for the multinational integration of Latin America and the Caribbean." It remains to be seen if subsequent agreements similar to or as a part of ALBA may arise in the future between other nations of Latin American and the Caribbean.

However, because of Cuba's anti-American historical legacy of the sixties and seventies, Erikson claims that "few countries are anxious to submit themselves to the inevitable diplomatic dustups with Washington that will be provoked by their seeking warmer relations with Castro." In a speech at the Hudson Institute Center for Latin American Studies, deputy assistant secretary of defense for Western hemisphere affairs, Roger Pardo-Maurer, warned that, "Cuba is back with more experience, but the same vision . . . of a Marxist, socialist, totalitarian state." Pardo-Maurer also elaborates on the latest human rights violations occurring in Cuba supporting the notion that Castro is not to be trusted (July 26, 2005). Yet, Jed Babbin, in his September 2005 article in *The American Spectator,* warns readers that Venezuela's Hugo Chávez is the one who warrants the most concern—not Castro: "Venezuelan strongman Hugo Chavez is Fidel Castro on streroids." Venezuela is the world's fifth largest exporter of oil, and Babbin explains that, different from Castro who does not possess such a resource, Chávez can utilize the economic power of Venezuela's oil reserves to exert political influence on his Latin American neighbors.

Nonetheless, as Daniela Spenser explains in "Cuba: New Partners and Old Limits," Cuba maintains a distinct position in Latin America. She explains: "Cuba continues to play a significant role of resistance in Latin America. This is due principally to the fact that neoliberalism (free trade policies in global markets), far from playing an emancipatory role, has aggravated the conditions of life for vast parts of the population" (*NACLA Report on the Americas, September/October 2005*). Latin America's rejection of neoliberal trade policies is another factor for the recent shift to the left in many countries in Latin America and why Castro's aid package may be embraced.

Will there be more countries accepting of Cuba's humanitarian aid? And what will be the results of all that humanitarian aid? Time, as the old saying goes, will tell.

Consult "Cuba and Cuban Americans on the Internet," a database maintained by the University of Miami Libraries, for information on politics, government, international relations, human rights, and other topics related to Cuba: http://www.library.miami.edu/netguides/cubanet.html. To read speeches, interviews, and press conferences of Fidel Castro in English, see the Latin American Network Research Center's "Castro Speech Database" at the University of Texas at Austin: http://lanic.utexas.edu/la/cb/cuba/castro.html. For a critique of the United States' foreign policy on Cuba, see Lissa Weinmann's "Washington's Irrational Cuba," *World Policy Journal* (Spring 2004, pp. 22–31).

ISSUE 4

Is Plan Colombia Effectively Combating the Drug Industry in Colombia?

YES: Robert B. Charles, from "U.S. Policy and Colombia," Testimony Before Chairman Tom Davis and the House Committee on Government Reform (June 17, 2004)

NO: Linda Panetta, from "Plan Colombia . . . Plan of Death," *School of the America's Watch* (2006)

ISSUE SUMMARY

YES: Robert B. Charles, assistant secretary for international narcotics and law enforcement affairs for the U.S. Department of State, argues that Plan Colombia is succeeding through limiting the flow of drugs to America, defeating terrorists, and protecting democratic rule throughout the Andean regions of Latin America.

NO: Linda Panetta, a photojournalist whose work focuses on cultural, environmental, and human rights by concentrating on conflict zones around the world—including Latin America—asserts that Plan Colombia has made little progress in the "War on Drugs" and creates more harm than good for both Colombia and the United States.

Since the declaration of the Monroe Doctrine by U.S. President James Monroe in 1823, American hegemony in the Western hemisphere has been an incendiary topic. Linking his ideologies with those of Monroe, U.S. President Theodore Roosevelt expanded the powers of the Monroe Doctrine in 1904 via the "Roosevelt Corollary," establishing the policy of U.S. "interventionism" in Latin America. The Roosevelt Corollary stated that the United States would "intervene"—militarily, politically, economically, or via whatever means the United States determined most appropriate—in the affairs of any nation in the Western hemisphere if the United States felt it necessary to do so in order to protect U.S. interests. Since the inception of the Roosevelt Corollary, the United States has engaged in over 70 acts of "intervention," including Plan Colombia, which began in 1999.

Originally known as the "Plan for Colombia's Peace," Colombian President Andrés Pastrana Arango constructed Plan Colombia to bring an end to a long history of bloody battles pitting insurgent groups, such as narco-traffickers, illegal paramilitary factions, and other rebel forces, against the Colombian government. In addition, Plan Colombia was designed to revitalize a failing economy as well as to create a viable anti-narcotic strategy largely based on the manual destruction of drug fields and peaceful negotiations with groups connected to the drug trade such as FARC (Revolutionary Armed Forces of Colombia) aligned with the international support from nations such as the United States.

However, largely due to U.S. influence and American interventionist policy, Plan Colombia migrated from an internally directed peace proposition to a long-term agreement involving U.S. economic aid and military intervention to help support the U.S. "War on Drugs." Although significant portions of the U.S. financial contributions have been earmarked for military support and anti-narcotics operations, Colombian leaders point to other global participants in Plan Colombia and their contributions, which largely focus on social and economic development as well as humanitarian efforts.

Among the many controversial elements of Plan Colombia are human rights issues, drug eradication tactics, U.S.-supported paramilitary operations, and the overall strategies of Plan Colombia itself. Non-governmental organizations such as Amnesty International have issued statements questioning the focus of Plan Colombia, leveling accusations that Plan Colombia is a guise for military intervention as opposed to humanitarian causes and point to a litany of human rights abuses.

Amid the Plan Colombia controversy is the role of the Western Hemisphere Institute for Security Cooperation (WHISC or WHINSEC), formerly known as the School of the Americas (SOA), a training facility located at Fort Benning, Georgia, largely focused on preparing Latin American military personnel for U.S.-endorsed combat missions within Latin America. Some of its graduates include Manuel Noreiga (former dictator of Panama) and Hugo Banzer Suárez (former dictator of Bolivia). Colombia currently has the most graduates of the SOA—over 10,000—accounting for nearly one-sixth of all graduates of the school. Proponents of the school claim these trainees are vital to maintaining peace and security while others blame the school for supporting paramilitary operations that perpetuate insurgency and violence.

With the continued financial support of both U.S. President George W. Bush and the Colombian government, the Plan Colombia controversy is not likely to diminish in the foreseeable future. Robert B. Charles, assistant secretary for international narcotics and law enforcement affairs for the U.S. Department of State, argues the merits of Plan Colombia on behalf of the U.S. government, including the successful eradication of thousands of acres of drug fields, the creation of new opportunities for Colombians, and a reduction in violence and terrorism. However, photojournalist Linda Panetta condemns this policy by pointing out that significant numbers of human rights violations and mass destruction of the environment undermine the intentions of Plan Colombia.

YES

Robert B. Charles

U.S. Policy and Colombia

Testimony Before Chairman Tom Davis and the House Committee on Government Reform

Mr. Chairman, and distinguished members of the committee, thank you for the invitation to discuss Plan Colombia and the State Department's continued efforts during this critical time in Colombia's history. Plan Colombia, complemented by our regional efforts in the Andes, represents a significant investment by the American people and Congress to fight the flow of drugs responsible for ending thousands of young lives each year in America, to fight powerful and entrenched terrorists in this Hemisphere, and to protect democratic rule across the Andean region.

The success in Colombia over the last few years would not have been possible without the strong leadership of President Uribe who took office in August 2002. His administration has taken an aggressive stand against narcoterrorism, which enables our Colombia programs to work. It is my pleasure to be able to testify before you today. . . . [You] have given us the power to make a difference, and this investment in our national security is paying off.

. . . I believe we are seeing real . . . change. . . . First, drug cultivation in Colombia is down for the second straight year. Second, . . . violent crime and terrorist acts are down and falling. Third, respect for the rule of law is expanding and measurably putting down tap roots in new places. Fourth, we are providing meaningful, often innovative, alternatives to poverty-level farmers.

The Andean Counterdrug Initiative (ACI) . . . is a multi-front effort that does not begin and end with counternarcotics. It is our robust effort . . . at creating a sustainable, regional, deep-seated and democratically faithful alternative to the destruction and terror—on personal, national, and hemispheric levels—that comes from drug trafficking and drug-funded terror. In short, what we do in places like Colombia has a direct effect here, in the United States. Our policy and our commitment aim to wipe out narcoterrorists, and help Colombia seize their assets, strengthen Colombia's institutions and increase legitimate economic opportunities for those who wish to live free from drugs and terror. Central to the larger Andean Counterdrug Initiative is restoring, preserving and sustaining the rule of law, in cities, towns, and the countryside. . . .

From Testimony before Chairman Tom Davis and the House Committee on Government Reform, June 17, 2004.

Counternarcotics Achievements in Colombia

The bird's eye view on the Andean Counterdrug Initiative, and Colombia in particular, is encouraging. The commitment of Congress and the effective implementation of our programs are paying off. Drug production is down in Colombia; traffickers are being arrested and extradited and their proceeds are being taken; drug seizures are up; legitimate jobs are being created; Colombian institutions are stronger; and the rule of law expanded.

Eradication

In 2003, INL [Bureau for International Narcotics and Law Enforcement] and the Colombians, working closely together, sprayed 127,000 hectares of the coca crop at 91.5 percent effectiveness, for a net of 116,000 hectares of coca eradicated. At the same time, alternative development programs in Colombia resulted in the manual eradication of an additional 8,441 hectares. Similarly, we sprayed 2,821 hectares of opium poppy while 1,009 hectares were manually eradicated. In 2002, these efforts reduced coca cultivation by 15 percent, and, in 2003, by 21 percent—for a double-digit decline for the second straight year—a first time accomplishment. The 113,850 hectares under cultivation this year represents a 33 percent reduction from the peak-growing year in 2001 when 169,800 hectares of coca were under illicit cultivation. Riding on the success of Colombia reductions, Andean production of coca dropped for the second straight year—this time by 16 percent.

The Colombian government, with USG support, is also making similar progress on opium poppy. In 2003, the Colombian government reduced opium poppy cultivation by more than 10 percent, building on the success in 2002, which had resulted in a 25 percent reduction in cultivation. These efforts have reduced Colombia's opium poppy by 33 percent, or from 6,540 hectares in 2001—to 4,900 in 2002—to 4,400 in 2003. With Colombian heroin victimizing children from Florida to Illinois, New York and Maine to points West, we must make its eradication a priority.

This year our spray goal for coca and opium poppy is ambitious: 130,000 hectares of coca and all opium poppy growing in 2004. To date, we are ahead of schedule on both of these eradication milestones. As of June 16, we have sprayed over 61,000 hectares of coca and 1,600 hectares of poppy. Because opium poppy is an annual flower, all of last year's remaining 4,400 hectares of poppy died last year and have already been replaced by new crops. We have worked out this spray program in full coordination with the Colombian police and armed forces.

. . . Foremost among my concerns is security for our air fleet and pilots—who put their lives on the line every time they undertake a spray mission.

In 2003, INL aircraft took more than 380 hits, and we lost 4 planes. To date this year, we have lost one aircraft in Colombia, but have only taken 79 hits as compared to 142 hits for the same period in 2003. These ground-fire hits are now at the lowest levels in nearly two years.

This reduction is a reflection of our improved planning, changing tactics, increased intelligence coordination, and protective measures that make sure each spray mission is as safe as humanly possible.

In fact, coordination and cooperation between Colombian law enforcement and military elements have also significantly improved. . . . That said, as we are progressively successful on the eradication front, new threats may emerge. . . .

We take environmental concerns very seriously and have sought to be very responsive to members of Congress and non-governmental organizations who have understandably expressed concern about the effects of aerial eradication on human health and the environment. . . . To date, all toxicology tests show that the herbicide mixture used in spraying, in the manner it is being used, does not pose any unreasonable risks of adverse effects for humans or the environment. The accuracy with which the herbicide is applied makes negligible any damage to licit crops grown separately from narcotic crops.

We have increased efforts to track reported health complaints and to investigate any possible connection between spraying of illicit crops and damages alleged in such occasional complaints. We have initiated what amounts to a farmer's "hot line," a channel for any complaints and way to compensate farmers who can demonstrate any harm to health of legal crops caused by spraying. This well-publicized initiative has, as expected, spurred interest. As of May 31, 2004, the Embassy has received a cumulative total of nearly 4,700 complaints. Because the overwhelming majority of the complaints are caused by events unrelated to spraying, NAS Bogotá has only been required so far to compensate 10 persons. Simply put, when investigations verify that a farmer's allegations are true, we compensate them. In most cases, the allegations are false.

Last month, when Colombia's major newspaper *El Tiempo* published an article that quoted farmers alleging that their alternative development crops might have been sprayed, we set up a verification mission with people from the Colombian government. This involved the Complaints Committee and others involved in checking out these claims. Bottom line—the article was grossly inaccurate. Due to prompt response from our Embassy, the Colombian government's manager of the alternative development program immediately sent NAS Bogotá a letter thanking them for the verification and assistance.

Alternative Development
Consolidating gains and sustaining progress requires that those who grow coca or opium poppy be not only discouraged from involvement in the drug trade, but encouraged to enter legitimate markets. Accordingly, done right, alternative development complements interdiction and eradication programs by increasing legal economic opportunities for former producers of coca and poppy. These USAID programs . . . have expanded into other departments with high incidence or threat of coca cultivation. This year, INL-coordinated efforts have already supported more than 7,000 hectares of legal crops, for a cumulative total of 45,000 hectares since 2000. These activities have benefited more than 34,000 families and resulted in the manual eradication of 22,000 hectares of illicit crops. These numbers are not insignificant; they corroborate a sea change or tipping point in the overall effort.

But alternative development is more than alternative crops. Such activities improve Colombia's rural infrastructure so that licit crops can be transported and marketed. The ripple effect means new sharing of technologies, processing, credit, and marketing assistance to legitimate producer associations. Last quarter alone, 188 infrastructure projects were completed for a cumulative total of 835 since 2001. This includes more than 90 schools, 40 water systems, 80 municipal buildings—ranging from homes for the elderly to business centers and community centers. Projects completed also included 195 sewage drains and 35 roads. In addition, as one more indication of democracy and legitimate, accountable businesses are taking root, more than 20 citizen oversight committees were formed last quarter, for a cumulative total of 212. . . .

Interdiction

Interdiction efforts are central to the continuing and measurable success of Plan Colombia. We work closely with Colombia's armed forces and the police. As a result, Colombian forces reported seizures of 145 metric tons of cocaine and coca base in 2003. If sold on U.S. streets, we estimate an additional 1.75 billion dollars would have reached drug traffickers and the narcoterrorism they support. Since President Uribe took office in August 2002, Colombian forces have seized nearly 1,200 kilograms of heroin. INL has worked hand-in-glove with DEA, including support to DEA's Operation Firewall, a maritime interdiction effort off the North coast of Colombia. In addition, we support the DEA Heroin Task Force in Bogotá, made up of over 50 DEA and Colombian National Police officials, that targets heroin trafficking organizations, especially those with regional and international implications. Another good news story seldom written or talked about is Colombia's effective Air Bridge Denial program (ABD). This program was re-started in August 2003 and is proving to be a highly effective deterrent. Since its resumption, the program has sorted thousands of flights, and forced down and/or destroyed over 26 suspected narcotics trafficking aircraft. As of March 1, 2004, the Colombian Air Force and its regional partners had seized roughly a metric ton of illicit drugs through the ABD program. Countless are the flights deterred, deflected or delayed. In 2003, the program resulted in 6.9 metric tons of drugs seized regionally. But the key here is not the number of planes destroyed. To be clear: Our goal is to effectively deter the use of Colombian airspace by traffickers, while protecting civil aviation. . . .

Other Success in Colombia

I would be remiss if I did not point out other equally important achievements. Recently, the Colombian law enforcement authorities, in cooperation with the United States, Canada, and Mexico, completed investigations resulting in charging the leaders and members of two international criminal organizations from Colombia with violations of U.S. laws. The first, Operation White Dollar, targeted the financial service providers working in the black market peso exchange scheme, who facilitate international narcotics trafficking. The second resulted in the charging of the leadership and major players in the Norte Valle cartel with racketeering offenses. The defendants are charged with engaging in a racketeering organization responsible for shipping tonnage quantities of cocaine to the U.S. with furthering the work of the organization by murdering witnesses, and threatening and corrupting members of the

Colombian Congress and more. In both cases, the defendants are being sought for extradition to the U.S. These are two examples of the fact that we are hitting the traffickers and their accomplices hard.

As we are undermining the narcotics industry, we are methodically, unremittingly and decisively extending democracy and strengthening security throughout Colombia's national territory. We are truly witnessing, I believe, the "tip" of a national and perhaps regional tipping point. We have helped fund the establishment of police in 158 municipalities, many of which had not seen any government or security presence in literally decades. As a result of the Colombian government's "police reinsertion program," for the first time in the recorded history of Colombia, there is now a state presence in all 1,098 of Colombia's municipalities. This is an enormous step forward for the people of Colombia and their democratically elected government. As John Locke might say, where there is security and a stable social compact, people will abide the law and mix their labor with the land in a legitimate, lasting way. Due in very large measure to the foresight of this body—the U.S. Congress—in creating, funding and nurturing this pivotal first phase of what was once called Plan Colombia, and now the Andean Counterdrug Initiative, we are seeing real success.

Other developments underscore that we are making unprecedented—but not yet institutionalized—progress: In 2003, Colombia's murder rate dropped by 20 percent, to its lowest figure since 1986. Also in 2003, kidnapping declined by 39 percent from 2002. Finally, forced displacements of persons were cut by 49 percent—a decline for the first time since 1999.

Training of Colombian Nationals

High among our priorities is training Colombians so that they may bear increasing responsibility for programs. This is the natural evolution of programs—a successful seeding and supporting a widening democracy and the rule of law. Accordingly, INL has developed a growing cadre of Colombian professionals to replace USG contractors in flying and maintaining aircraft assets. We have trained 99 pilots and 154 mechanics and crew chiefs since 1999, meeting our own initial training objectives. Due to the increasing size of INL's Air Wing since training targets were first created, we have updated our goals to reduce the number of personnel contracted by the USG involved in operation or maintenance of helicopters. We have recently submitted to Congress a plan entitled *Training of Colombian Nationals for Helicopter Operations and Maintenance Programs,* which will reduce the number of contractor pilots and maintenance personnel in half—from 394 in 2004 to 195 by 2007. We further plan to reduce the contractor presence to 56 by 2009 and 25 by 2010, respectively. In short, as we fight to impose on ourselves real and meaningful management reforms, and move the ball upfield for the American people on both counternarcotics and counterterrorism, we are also cognizant of the need to make the goals more ambitious.

Democratic Institution Building and the Rule of Law

To improve the rule of law, USG projects also have assisted the Government of Colombia in establishing 37 Justice Houses (*casas de justicia*), which increase access to justice for poor Colombians. Make no mistake: this is not a small victory or goal—it is at the very heart, in our view, of sustainable progress and U.S. support. So far, these *casas de justicia* have handled over 2.2 million cases, easing the burden on the over-taxed, inefficient judicial system. Remarkably, the Department of Justice and USAID "Administration of Justice" initiatives have also established 30 new Oral Trial courtrooms and trained over 10,000 lawyers, judges and public defenders in new oral legal procedures designed to reduce impunity and quicken the judicial process. The new accusatorial criminal justice system will be open to public scrutiny and is expected to be more efficient and effective, and thus more worthy of public confidence. Similarly, a so-called "Early Warning System" is up and running. This system monitors potential conditions that might trigger human rights violations in order to provide warning of impending threats. In addition, 11 new mobile satellite units of the national human rights unit have been arrayed around Colombia to provide a more immediate response to allegations of human rights violations in the most remote areas of the country. Together, these projects are creating a civil and human rights protection infrastructure—a climate of respect—so that the Colombian government may be able to prevent or be more responsive to human rights violations.

Also on human rights, the overall Colombian government "protection program" has been expanded to include reliable protection for mayors, local human rights officials, council members, municipal human rights workers, medical missions, journalists, and former mayors. . . . In the second quarter of FY 2004, more than 200 individuals received protection measures for a cumulative total of nearly 3,500. During this quarter, six additional offices are in the process of being armored, for a cumulative total of 83 offices protected as of June 2004. Further, a professional police corps has been trained and equipped to protect judicial personnel, witnesses, and government officials. By providing protection to these individuals and offices, we are playing an increasingly important role in ensuring the ability of Colombia's leaders, including human rights defenders and local officials, to conduct their activities in as secure an environment as possible. . . . [We] are of the view that if conditions for advancement are sustained, the legitimate economy and democracy will grow; build it, and they will come.

Through the office of the Vice President, we are also working with Colombia's local authorities to design and implement Departmental Human Rights Plans. Participatory Planning Workshops have been held already in Cartagena, Bogotá, Cali, Valle del Cauca and Santander de Quilichao. Municipal and departmental planning teams participated in each one of these workshops through a strategic planning exercise.

This is a mosaic—a team effort, both between the United States and Colombia, but also among bureaus and agencies. Besides assisting in placing police around the country, we are funding other initiatives that extend security throughout Colombia's territory. For example, . . . the National Police launched a new country-wide initiative called Departamentos y Municipios Seguros, supported by USAID through Georgetown University's Colombia Program. The program is aimed at strengthening President Uribe's Democratic

Security Policy through a complementary strategy of security plans oriented at the prevention of violence and criminal acts, and implemented by mayors and governors in coordination with the Colombian National Police.

In Colombia, INL also funds a key program, the "Culture of Lawfulness"—a public school-based program that teaches ethics to thousands of children in junior high school. If we can help mold these young people, we can help foster a civic belief that drugs and corruption are wrong. Again, this is a measure of progress. Cultural education and trust in a stable, drug-free future will take time.

Finally, we provide emergency and longer-term assistance to so-called "Vulnerable Groups," particularly Internally Displaced Persons (IDPs). This assistance, administered by the State Department's Bureau for Population, Migration, and Refugees and USAID, includes food, shelter, psychosocial assistance, physical and mental health services, community strengthening, income and employment generation, urban assistance (shelter, water and sanitation) education, and the rehabilitation of ex-child combatants. It also strengthens the Colombian agency responsible for IDP coordination, protection and border monitoring. Working with a municipal focus, the program runs more than 300 projects in 25 departments and 200 municipalities throughout the country.

Last quarter, IDP programs collectively aided more than 190,000 persons for a cumulative total of over 1.6 million persons since 2001. During the same time period, more than 3,800 jobs were created for IDPs and other vulnerable persons, such as youth at risk of displacement or recruitment by illegal armed combatants. To date, IDP programs have provided vocational and skill development training for more than 21,000 IDPs and created over 52,000 jobs. . . . Equally important, access to education was increased during the last quarter for more than 29,000 displaced and other vulnerable children for a cumulative total of 163,900. Finally, more than 700 families who were willing and able to safely return to their original communities, were assisted last quarter, for a cumulative total of 18,090 families, or over 90,000 individuals since 2001. The IDP Program also assisted nearly 350 additional child ex-combatants during the last quarter. By providing viable life and employment options, the program discourages families from taking up cultivation of illicit crops.

Concluding Remarks

We all know the facts, but they bear repeating. . . . Drugs, violence and crime undermine democracy, rule of law, and the stability required for economic development. The drug trade continues to kill our citizens—nearly 21,000 Americans last year, most of whom are unwitting children. The bulk of the drugs arriving in the United States come from Colombia. Let me be bold, unforgivingly clear and unambiguous on another point: The drug trade funds terrorists and violent criminal groups in the Hemisphere and elsewhere. If we want these evils to stop, we must be resolved to halt them now and on foreign soil. For, if we do not, we will most assuredly see them again—on our own doorsteps and street corners. Violence on our television screens against our friends and allies to the south is difficult to bear; but violence in our very midst imposes a burden far heavier on our hearts and lives. INL, and others here today, are determined to hit these threats hard.

Plan Colombia, the centerpiece of our Andean Counterdrug Initiative (ACI) program, is producing results and many success stories. INL's efforts in Colombia have helped reduce drug cultivation in Colombia in 2002 and 2003, after nearly a decade of consecutive increases, increased the effectiveness and coverage of drug interdiction programs, strengthened the presence of the state, the rule of law and the judiciary's ability to prosecute, put traffickers behind bars in the U.S., seized their illegally-gained assets, and expanded economic opportunities for the poor. We continue to build upon our eradication, interdiction, and alternative development results and will stand by the Colombian government in its efforts to topple the drug cartels as it delivers a lasting blow to narco-terrorists.

In short, we need to consolidate our gains and sustain this pace. In FY 2005, our counternarcotics programs in Colombia and the six other countries encompassed by the ACI will continue to pursue vigorous eradication and interdiction efforts to disrupt and destroy the production and transport of drugs destined for U.S. and other markets. . . .

On balance, the USG and the Colombians are on track to dismantle narco-terrorist organizations by seizing their current and future assets in all manners possible. We will face challenges in the coming years that, if not addressed aggressively, have the potential to reverse some of these gains. . . . We must also keep up our support for other allies in the Andes to make sure that the Colombian criminal organizations do not export their processing methods to other countries.

Our basic goals remain: Eliminate the cultivation of drugs, break up narcoterrorist groups by disrupting their routes and seizing their profits, and provide real alternatives to those caught in the illegal trade. . . .

Let me close by offering you this assurance: INL continues to make progress in combating illegal drug production, through partnerships with our foreign allies and with the many federal agencies involved in these efforts. We are committed to fight the scourge of narcotrafficking and narcoterrorism in our hemisphere. Full stop.

Linda Panetta

Plan Colombia . . . Plan of Death

Colombia is a country known for its majestic beauty, abundant biodiversity and extensive rainforests, which lead some people to coin the region the "lungs of the world." Adding to these visual splendors is what lies below the surface. In addition to its acclaimed gold, copper, and silver deposits, Colombia has one of the largest known oil reserves in our hemisphere and is among the top suppliers of oil to the United States. Belying what would appear to be paradise is Colombia's infamous designation as one of the most violent countries in the world.

Overview

My purpose for traveling to Colombia . . . was two-fold. First, to better understand and see first-hand the effects of the US-sponsored fumigation campaign in the Putumayo region. Second, to bear witness to the violence being perpetrated by the Colombian military and paramilitary forces (United Self-Defense Forces of Colombia/Autodefensas Unidas de Colombia, AUC), who act with complete impunity and in conjunction with the Colombian military to instill terror in the populace. The AUC have been designated a "foreign terrorist organization" under Section 219 of the U.S. Immigration and Nationality Act. It is reported that they are responsible for 70 percent of the massacres that have occurred over the last few decades in Colombia, and Amnesty International states that the "paramilitary [have been] responsible for the vast majority of political killings in Colombia in recent years." More than 10,000 Colombian soldiers have been trained at the U.S. Army School of the Americas (SOA), which was renamed the Western Hemisphere Institute for Security Cooperation (WHINSEC), in 2001. . . .

The fumigation program is a US-sponsored "anti-drug" campaign that was attached to a multibillion-dollar aid program developed by the government of Colombia purportedly to deal with the many socio-economic factors afflicting the country. The sequestering of this drug campaign by the US turned what was to be a State-aid program to bring "peace, prosperity, and the strengthening of the state," into a multi-billion dollar US-funded "war on drugs." The bulk of the money—an initial $1.3 billion, now equating to billions—has gone to US weapons and chemical corporations in the form of military training, helicopters, and other fumigation and war related expenses. For Colombia, this campaign has been a war on their ecosystem, crops and forests, and has further eroded their means for subsistence living; it has also created a health and environmental crisis with wide-reaching and staggering consequences. The US aid packages and diversion of weapons have also helped fuel the ongoing civil war which has lasted for over four decades. The end result of billions of US taxpayer dollars being used to bolster the "war on drugs" has been wide-spread destruction and destabilization throughout Colombia while in the US there has been little affect on reducing the availability of cocaine on the streets or its market price. Rather than spend billions of dollars on programs that could potentially save lives by helping individuals end their addiction to cocaine and greatly diminish the demand for the drug, the US—too often addicted to war and flexing its abusive muscles—has opted instead to impose greater punishment on addicts in the US, while its policies continue to displace, kill and maim tens of thousands of victims throughout Colombia.

During our time in Colombia, we met with community leaders, including tribal representatives from various indigenous groups in the Putumayo region (the focal point of Plan Colombia), religious leaders, Colombian officials—including the Vice President, military leaders, the director of the UN High Commission on Human Rights, and the US Ambassador to Colombia. . . .

Health & Environmental Consequences

Throughout our meetings and visits to Putumayo it became vividly evident that, due to the indiscriminate nature of the fumigation campaign, not only were coca crops (the raw material of cocaine) being targeted, but also medicinal plants and food crops were being eradicated and water supplies were being severely contaminated. The primary ingredient used for the fumigations is the herbicide, glyphosate, which is also the main chemical used in the US-sold herbicide: "Round-Up," produced and manufactured by the US chemical corporation, Monsanto. . . .

In Colombia, this herbicide is used in a highly concentrated form (often referred to as "Round-Up Ultra—which is upwards to 25% more concentrated and thus has a greater toxicity than its kin predecessor Round-Up). It is combined with surfactants and other chemicals . . . for greater effectiveness and adherence to coca crops and anything else it comes in contact with—including livestock, birds, food crops, eyes, and skin. . . . To date, the EPA has never tested or approved the combination being used for aerial spraying in Colombia, though it does state that glyphosate-based products such as Round Up could cause "vomiting, swelling of the lungs, pneumonia, mental confusion and tissue damage." Despite this knowledge, and Monsanto's own recommendations that it should not be applied from anywhere above 10 feet, the US has continued to recklessly assert that Round-Up Ultra can be safely applied by crop dusters over vast areas. With no precautionary measures offered to the people, who are unwittingly being exposed to the fumigations, the US continues to reject the reports that show that this program is endangering the welfare of the Colombian people and devastating the ecology.

"Collateral Damage"

Colombian Law 0005 of 2000 which regulated fumigations, states that fumigations will be used only on coca farms larger than 5 acres and that "the application of agricultural chemicals in rural zones cannot be carried out within less than 10 meters by land and less than 100 meters by air as a security border, in relation to bodies of water, roads, nuclei of human or animal populations or any other area that requires special protection." In 2002 US Ambassador Patterson stated that "there is no longer any differentiation between 'small' and the 'industrial' plots. If you grow coca, the Colombian Police will spray it." This change in policy and the indiscriminate nature of the spraying was made evident to us as we visited countless food crops that were fumigated. The stands of rotting bananas on one farm served as evidence to the devastation wrought by a single aerial application. "Now how will I feed my children?" the farmer asked while he despondently tried to comprehend the destruction. Not only was his crop and livelihood destroyed, but he asked us to examine his swollen and glazed over eyes which were severely afflicting him since his exposure to the fumigations. "I had no idea that the cloudy mist trailing from the airplane was going to poison my family and destroy our farm." Another woman, whose brothers were killed by paramilitary forces stated, "They [the narco-traffickers] plant their coca next to our food crops and there's nothing we can do but helplessly watch as our crops are also targeted by the fumigation. And when we raise our voice against the injustice, we are killed." . . .

The negligence associated with the fumigation campaign has not only had disastrous ecological and health consequences for the region, but it has also mostly seen an increase in the expansion of coca cultivation. In 2002, the CIA reported that coca production had increased 25% following the introduction of Plan Colombia in 2000. Although production decreased slightly in 2003 and 2004, there was a huge surge in cultivation in 2005 with over 144,000 hectares being cultivated. Despite any gains that the government may report, the reality is that coca production is still significantly greater today, than it was a decade ago when cultivation in Colombia was at 57,000 hectares. The DEA's 2006 "National Drug Threat Assessment" also reports that "Cocaine supplies appear to be stable at levels necessary to meet current domestic demand, despite record levels of seizures and declines in estimated worldwide production that have been reported over the past few years."

The Colombian Ministry of Foreign Affairs indicates that nearly 30% of Colombia's annual deforestation has resulted from the fumigation campaign. The amount of hectares generally targeted for fumigation, compared with the actual amount of coca being produced in a given area, is roughly a 30:1 ratio. Given the fact that narco-traffickers plow down roughly 2 hectares of rainforests to compensate for every hectare lost by the fumigations, and farmers whose crops are also destroyed in the process often resort to slash and burn techniques to replace their fields, its not difficult to realize the extent of destruction that has ensued. Overall, roughly 2,600 square miles (the combined square mileage of the states of Delaware and Rhode Island is 2,995) have been sprayed with Round-Up Ultra, yet the total land area under coca cultivation has been virtually unchanged throughout the Andean region. Cumulating totals for Peru, Bolivia and Colombia, the US government estimates 198,455 hectares were cultivated in 2000, and 208,500 hectares of coca were cultivated in 2005. . . .

Breaking Down the Cartels

The means by which governments have chosen to counter the production of coca has widely been viewed as indiscriminate, irresponsible and conducted largely without accounting for short or long-term health and environmental consequences. Between 1994 and 1998 it was reported that on average, approximately 45,500 hectares of coca were being cultivated in Colombia. In an attempt to eradicate these crops, more than 140,800 hectares were targeted by fumigations. Due to the indiscriminate nature of the campaign and unpredictable nature associated with aerial "drift," not only were coca crops attacked, but food crops and rainforests throughout the region were also fumigated.

Throughout the 1970's and 1980's, the Medellin Cartel was the predominant coca grower throughout the Andean region. As coca was being targeted and eradicated in Peru and Bolivia the Cartel began to shift some of its production to neighboring Colombia. During this time the US was spending millions of dollars working to take down the Medellin Cartel. When this occurred, there was an abrupt redistribution and decentralization of power that emerged among drug traffickers, as well as a rapid swelling of ranks of paramilitary forces. But repercussions extended well beyond this. In order to build their numbers, influence, and assets the paramilitary groups, taking full advantage of the collapse of the Cartels, grabbed control of the drug trafficking market and spurred coca production at a rate of over 100 percent. By 1999 more than 120,000 hectares of coca were being cultivated in Colombia. By forging ties and collaborating with other drug traffickers, and receiving the support of the Colombian military and the wealthy elite, their numbers quickly grew from 4,000 in 1995 to over 8,000 in 2001. As of 2005, their numbers were estimated to be well over 20,000.

Coca is Big Business for Many Players

. . . Not only is the coca industry big business for in-country profiteers, it also provides US and multinational corporations the opportunity to make millions of dollars by exploiting the "war on drugs." For example, of the $27 million spent on a 1994–'98 eradication campaign, $20 million went directly to Monsanto. Because the campaign was so ineffective—the U.S. blamed the problem on excessive rains in the regions—they decided to increase the amount of applications of glyphosate and put in additives such as "Cosmo-Flux." This agent substantially increases the biological activity of the agrochemicals and is being added at 5 times the recommended dosage. The affect of this and similar agents is catastrophic for the overall ecology of the rainforests, including aquatic life, animals, and the populace who are already being bombarded on a continuous basis by the fumigations. A conservative estimate of the cost of fumigating 1 square mile is roughly $167,000. One can only imagine the cost benefits of investing this money in alternative agricultural projects and drug rehabilitation.

The ultimate result of the failed eradication campaign that began as a $1.3 billion aid package is that a mere 1% has been earmarked for the peace process for which Plan Colombia was originally developed by the Colombian government. More than 80% of the nearly $5 billion in taxpayer dollars allocated since 2000 has gone to the Colombian military and police force (although the vast majority of this aid is recycled back to U.S. corporations for the purchase of weapons, mercenaries, chemicals, and other technologies that support the ongoing initiatives of Plan Colombia). This aid places Colombia 5th in overall world standing as a recipient of US military and other aid—Iraq recently pushed them down a notch from their previous 4th place ranking. . . .

Innocent Victims

As soon as I arrived in the Putumayo I was quickly taken aback by an eerie presence around me. It didn't stem from the numerous bunkers that I saw, or the stares we received from the countless armed soldiers who stood guard. No, probably the most haunting sound I heard from the Putumayo—this majestic Amazon region which borders Peru and Ecuador—was the silence. Occasionally the quiet was broken up by stray dogs chasing one another in the streets and the clatter of horse's hooves pulling carts, but aside from these, the only animals I saw were the victims of the fumigations: a dead ox lying next to a nearby ravine, countless fish floating in the Guamuez River, and two lone and emaciated monkeys poised in a tree that bore little vegetation. In fact, the only place I saw or heard birds flying overhead was at a military airstrip, where we awaited the arrival of our helicopter.

As I tried to zoom in with my camera on a colorful bird perched atop a cable the portending silence was broken by the thunderous roar of several aircrafts approaching from the distance. Distracted, I turned my attention to four planes flying in formation as they shot through a set of clouds; "Those are the fumigation planes!" exclaimed one of the men accompanying us. A few seconds later I glanced back to try and find the bird—but it was gone. At that moment, I pondered how many birds will take flight that day only to be doused in toxic chemicals, how many children will unwittingly be sprayed while playing in schoolyards, how many mothers will unknowingly bathe their infants with noxious water, and how many campesinos will go to harvest their food crops to find them in ruin? . . .

Home Grown Terror

While I was in Putumayo, it was arranged that we would be given an aerial view of the region in a military helicopter. General Montoya, a former instructor and graduate of the SOA, was flown in to accompany us. Montoya, then commander of the 24th Brigade, was responsible for all military activities in the Putumayo region. Many published reports, including by Human Rights Watch, document the 24th Brigade as being responsible for countless human rights atrocities. We also learned that Montoya was cited (in Terrorismo De Estado En Colombia, 1992) as having direct ties to the paramilitary group known as the "AAA." During a meeting with Anne Patterson, then US Ambassador to Colombia, she stated that the 24th Brigade was not entitled to receive funding through Plan Colombia because of the human rights abuses associated with the brigade. She further insisted, and with absolute certainty, that neither US money nor weapons would make their way to this brigade. At this point I shared information with her that Montoya had presented to us in a slide presentation that directly contradicted her assertions; this was bolstered by the fact that Montoya was in charge of all military forces in the Putumayo region and we could see that he was wearing military clothing and carrying weapons that were US-issued. . . .

As stated earlier, the paramilitary depend on the drug trade—they support it and extend its power. This dependence has created an agrarian counter-reform that has had serious consequences on the social character of Colombia, especially for the indigenous populations. As the coca crops overtake the region, the rainforests are being decimated at a staggering rate. The medicinal plants and crops that the indigenous rely on are being displaced and eradicated by the mass introduction of coca crops and the fumigations aimed at destroying them. An additional insidious player is the pharmaceutical companies who have placed patents on medicinal plants and medicines originally discovered and traditionally used by indigenous communities. While the companies make millions on the plants and medicines, the indigenous are warned that they are no longer allowed to manufacture or distribute their traditional medicines now that US pharmaceuticals hold patents on them.

Systemic Exploitation

The indigenous peoples, who were once the majority of the population in regions such as the Putumayo, are now overwhelmingly the minority. Those who have immigrated to the region see coca as a valuable source of cheap and sustainable income. Three to four generations of farmers have now worked the coca fields, and for some, this is the only way of life they know. This is one of the reasons why the paramilitaries have gained so much strength; the farmers don't want to lose the cheap income. Coca is one of the few crops that can be harvested four times annually and guarantees a continual source of income; it generates nearly 3 times as much as coffee and 10 times that of most other crops; overall, it's price has been stable for the last 5 years and since the narcotrafficker picks up the coca from the growers the farmers don't need to haul otherwise potentially perishable goods to the markets.

The paramilitary, whose ranks are bolstered by the Colombian military, use terror against the populace to solicit their allegiance and support. They deem all, whether an active, passive, or presumed supporter of a guerrilla group, as an enemy to be destroyed and they use selective killings as well as indiscriminate massacres to elicit absolute terror in the civilian population. . . .

With millions of dollars being generated annually by the drug trade, drug traffickers have acquired large expanses of territory in the Amazon region that were owned and occupied by indigenous groups. Although many of the indigenous do not have "official" titles for the land, by law, they are protected because of their "perpetual right to ancestral lands." Unfortunately, these laws have been largely disregarded by the Colombian government, which has also granted full impunity to those involved in the violent and forcible exodus of indigenous peoples from these lands. Land-grabs are one of the ways that drug money is laundered; this also provides assurance that land will be available for the ongoing cultivation of coca crops. According to the government comptroller's office nearly 50% of Colombia's arable land is believed to be in the hands of paramilitaries and narco-traffickers. Other means of laundering include diverting resources to the lumber, cattle and the oil industry. This not only secures the flow of money, but it also serves to expand the network and power of the regional armed forces. Ultimately, it empowers them to intensify the violence against the poor, resulting in tens of thousands of people being tortured, killed and otherwise driven from their land each year. Annually, approximately 300,000 people are forced to emigrate from their homes because of the violence and it is estimated that since 2000, over 2 million people have been displaced. This reality puts Colombia second only to Sudan for forced displacements. . . .

Road Less Traveled

Better understanding the reality about Colombia is essential—especially for our members of Congress who may not be fully aware, or have chosen to disregard the grave implications caused by the fumigations and the forged alliances with terrorist groups. Based on their track record, it seems many in Congress have not taken into consideration the socioeconomic effects as well as the degree of ecological and human violence that has resulted from the hundreds of millions of dollars allocated annually to this fragmented country. By overriding the human rights clause in Plan Colombia, side-stepping the Leahy amendment, and showing complete disregard for the well being of the Colombian people . . . our government has been an accomplish not only to murder, but potentially to genocide.

How can the US government justify sending nearly $5 billion dollars of US taxpayer dollars to one of the most corrupt and violent countries in the world? We obviously did not learn our lesson in 2001 after the US handed over $45 million to the Taliban just months before the Sept. 11 attacks in an effort to combat opium production in Afghanistan. It is largely believed that the opium was simply stockpiled and later flooded the US market making the drug even more accessible because of its plummeted price.

The "drug war" has taken the place of "communism" as the new boogieman. No one in Colombia is fooled by the incentives of the US government and soon, with ongoing education, the deception in the US will also be made more transparent. The drug problem is not Colombia's problem; it's a US demand-side problem and should be addressed as such. Congress must re-examine its allocation of funds and place greater emphasis on programs in our inner cities and prisons that help drug addicts get clean. Furthermore, they must immediately stop the annual dispersion of millions of dollars to corrupt and despotic militaries—which inevitably also gets filtered to terrorist cells—and they must admit the failure of Plan Colombia so that it is never repeated.

RAND Corporation, a California-based think-tank, reported that, dollar for dollar, providing drug treatment to cocaine users in the United States is 10 times more effective than drug interdiction programs and 23 times more cost effective than trying to eradicate coca at its source. They also noted that every $1 dollar spent on rehabilitation and treatment gives a return of $7 by decreasing the costs of criminal justice. One can only imagine what $5 billion could have meant for US addicts, their families and communities across the country affected by drug addiction and violence.

Time and time again, from the grassroots level, to senior-level government officials in Colombia, it was made clear to us that the fumigations are being imposed by the United States. No matter how many hectares of coca are destroyed by the fumigations, additional hectares of rainforests (at minimally a 2 fold ratio) will be cut down to keep the supply moving. In the end, once all the forests have been decimated—the medicinal plants eradicated, and all the indigenous peoples have been killed or forced from their land—what will be left? Only the barren soil from which the oil companies and other multinationals will have free range to finalize their annihilation of the Amazon. Before I left our meeting with Ambassador Patterson I posed this scenario to her and asked her what her response were to be if Colombia's ecosystem was destroyed and coca production moved to a neighboring country. Her response was blunt: "Well, at least then it'll no longer be my problem."

Thinking Outside of the Bank

Many farmers, as well as Colombian's then Vice President, Gustavo Bell, support the manual eradication of coca. It is estimated that it takes one worker 10 days to manually pull up one hectare of coca. Even many who are currently growing the coca advocate for this program—as long as they can make a sustainable wage for themselves and their families and they are protected from the threats and assaults of drug traffickers. Unfortunately, the State-sponsored program that was introduced as an alternative pays a farmer a mere $1,000 and allows only one year to not only eradicate the coca, but to produce an alternative crop. Anyone with a basic knowledge of crops and especially those who have an understanding of the soils in the region will affirm that it is absurd to think that this can successfully be achieved in such a short period of time or that it can be sustained for the long term without ongoing assistance. Greater funding, time, technical assistance and an ensuing peace are necessary for this plan to take root. Knowledge of the soils, crop rotation and even basic agrarian techniques will have to be re-taught since the historical memory of many of the coca-growing farmers is based solely on coca cultivation.

Furthermore, despite the fact that the coca plant flourishes in the rainforests, this region is not well suited for most crops. And most of the land that was treated with Round-Up will either remain infertile, or will require several years to regenerate. The rainforests are predominately made up of clays that have a thin organic layer that acts as a soil layer. This layer is dependent on a plush canopy to offer a continuous recycling of organic materials and nutrients. While the organic layer sustains and replenishes the "soil," the covering also provides protection from the heavy rains and heat. However, if the rains are no longer being intercepted by a dense forest canopy, then the nutrient layer not only becomes highly susceptible to erosion and runoff, but the cycle of life is quickly eroded and the land becomes uncultivable. The use of "slash and burn" techniques, frequently used by farmers to clear land for crops, is also a very invasive method and greatly diminishes the sustainability of the land. In order to help maintain the integrity of the region, it is vital to incorporate and support sustainable agricultural systems and to provide the technical assistance to farmers to make sure this happen. Otherwise, as the pillage and uncontrolled annihilation of the ecosystem continues, Colombia, which has the greatest diversity of fauna and flora in the world, will continue to lose both plant and animal species at a calamitous rate. One indigenous tribal leader stated: "We are used to being exploited and attacked [by the US], but now they are killing themselves by taking away the lungs of the world." Another made the appeal: "We beg you, be our voice . . . we are not only being displaced, we are being exterminated." . . .

POSTSCRIPT

Is Plan Colombia Effectively Combating the Drug Industry in Colombia?

With the recent reelection of Colombian President Álvaro Uribe, in one of the most peaceful election processes in recent Colombian history, the Colombian government is likely to continue its support of the U.S. government's actions regarding Plan Colombia. Uribe, considered by the United States to be its greatest ally in support of Plan Colombia, will now serve as president until 2010—the first time a Colombian president has been reelected in over 100 years. Since Uribe took office, Colombia has not experienced the violence of recent decades: Murder has dropped by more than half, and kidnapping rates have been reduced by nearly two-thirds.

Much of Uribe's success is related to his policy of democratic security. This policy states that in order for the rule of law to be effective, the government must achieve a number of objectives, including:

- abolishing sanctuary to terrorists
- creating a transparent and effective government
- establishing effective national security
- eliminating illegal drug trade in Colombia and therefore eliminating the flow of narco-dollars to terrorists and other insurgents who foster corruption, terrorism, and unlawfulness

Uribe has achieved a number of the goals prescribed with the domestic security policy and has returned stability to the office of the president; however, many critics feel that Uribe's counter-narcotics efforts (Plan Colombia), for the most part, have failed. For example, although crime has decreased within Colombia, the amount of drugs that flows into the United States from Colombia has remained largely unaffected since the inception of the domestic security policy. Therefore, the revenues created by drug trafficking have also remained equally unaffected.

Much of the criticism levied against the domestic security policy focuses on the Plan Colombia component of the policy for the reasons indicated above. Uribe has established a strong military presence in Colombia leading to increased security, therefore protecting and ensuring citizens' rights and stability. However, coupled with the increased powers and deployments of the military, justifications of actions undertaken via Plan Colombia in the name of the domestic security policy have reawakened echos of similar policies enacted during the Cold War when Latin America experienced decades of perhaps the most violent and unstable activity in its history. Maintaining

70

"domestic security" was often the rhetoric behind state-sponsored wars against the citizens of many Latin American countries, particularly those who spoke out against governmental policies. Deaths of upwards of 30,000 people in Agentina's "Dirty War," the disappearances of over 3,000 people during Augosto Pinochet's dicatorship in Chile, and the massacre of 20,000 Haitian agricultural workers during the presidency of Rafael Trujillo in the Dominican Republic are just a few examples of prior military and governmental abuses of power. Furthermore, many of these undemocratic policies and actions were endorsed by the government of the United States, much like Plan Colombia.

However, Plan Colombia, despite its weaknessnes, will likely have the support of the United States for at least 4 more years, coinciding with the renewed presidency of Uribe. For more information on the U.S. perspective of Plan Colombia see http://www.fas.org/sgp/crs/row/RL32774.pdf or http://www.state.gov/p/wha/rls/rm/2005/q2/46564.htm. For an anti–Plan Colombia point of view, see Robin Kirk's *More Terrible than Death: Massacres, Drugs, and America's War in Colombia.* For another anti–Plan Colombia perspective, view Dolores Huerta's documentary film *Plan Colombia: Cashing in on the Drug War Failure* (2003). For more information on issues related to Bolivian coca production, see Daniel Kurtz-Phelan's article, "'Coca Is Everything Here:' Hard Truths about Bolivia's Drug War," *World Policy Journal* (September 22, 2005). For a perspective on the coca from an indigenous perspective, see Catherine J. Allen's *The Hold Life Has: Coca and Cultural Identity in an Andean Community* (2002).

ISSUE 5

Is "Enhanced Commonwealth" the Solution to Puerto Rico's Colonial Status?

YES: Aníbal Acevedo-Vilá, from "Rethinking the Future of the US–Puerto Rico Relationship: Towards the 21st Century," Press Release from the House of Representatives (March 4, 2003)

NO: Pedro Rosselló, from "Self-Determination, Civil Rights and the Future of Puerto Rico," Remarks to the Open Forum (October 23, 2001)

ISSUE SUMMARY

YES: Previous resident commissioner of Puerto Rico, Aníbal Acevedo-Vilá, explains how "enhanced" commonwealth would change the compact established in 1950 between the United States and Puerto Rico and create expanded sovereignty for Puerto Rico, and thereby "eliminate all vestiges of colonialism from the current US–Puerto Rico relation."

NO: Dr. Pedro Rosselló, former governor of Puerto Rico, points out the contradictions and ambiguities the status of Puerto Rico has led to in its relationship with the United States and that the only way to resolve this quandary is by rejecting the status quo (commonwealth) and validating "the option under the U.S. sovereignty, namely statehood."

Puerto Rico existed as a colony of Spain for 300 years. But some people, such as the Decolonization Committee in the United Nations, still wonder if it remains a colony, only this time of the United States. In the past, three separate status possibilities dominated discussions of Puerto Rico's future: commonwealth, statehood, and outright independence. Throughout the elections of the last 24 years and at every plebiscite (1967, 1993, 1998), the vote for independence has regularly captured between 3 to 5 percent of the vote, whereas the results for the remaining two alternatives have attracted relatively equal amounts of support. Consequently, the independence movement is not a viable alternative at this time. Therefore, the principal issue concerning the people of Puerto Rico does not revolve around the issue of independence, but how to procure more rights while maintaining a solid relationship with the United States and how to rid itself of the stigma of being a colony.

Spain ceded Puerto Rico to the United States in 1898 after the Spanish American War. Since then, Puerto Rico has remained an unincorporated U.S. territory. In 1917, Puerto Ricans were granted American citizenship and in 1952, the island became a commonwealth, with a local constitution and the right to complete self-government on a local level. However, Puerto Rico remains subject to congressional jurisdiction under the territorial clause of the U.S. Constitution. According to this clause, Puerto Rico does not have voting representation at the federal level, but does possess a "resident commissioner" who has a seat in the House of Representatives, but not a vote. In addition, Puerto Ricans cannot vote in the U.S. presidential election. This lack of voting representation in Congress and non-voting rights for the president of the United States is why many believe that Puerto Rico is currently still a colony of the United States.

According to the Popular Democratic Party (PPD), it is important to recognize that enhanced commonwealth is not the status quo and that the way to eliminate the "colonial" issue is to have the same non-voting representative in Congress and the non-voting rights for the Puerto Rican people. However, the PPD is asking for much more sovereignty than ever before. Under this new status, sovereignty would be shared between Puerto Rico and the United States. And, as part of the agreement, the new status would end Puerto Rico's "territorial" status and provide a permanent union between the two parties, grant Puerto Rico the power to enter into international treaties as if it were an independent country, and authorize Puerto Rico the power to veto some federal laws. However, many believe the U.S. Congress would not approve the proposition of enhanced commonwealth set forth by the PPD because the U.S. government might feel as though they would have nothing to gain by such an agreement.

On the other hand, the party that supports statehood (PNP) says that the only way for Puerto Rico to effectively lose its "colonial" status is to have complete sovereignty and, therefore, independence. The PNP does not believe this will happen because the Puerto Rican people have repeatedly voted against independence, therefore, leaving statehood as the only other realistic alternative. Because the status of Puerto Rico's citizenship is statutory—acquired under 8 U.S.C. § 1402—and not necessarily guaranteed, Congress can revoke statutory citizenship under certain conditions. However, citizenship granted under the fourteenth Amendment—constitutional U.S. citizenship that all 50 states enjoy—cannot be revoked by Congress. Therefore, it would be preferable to become a state, thereby guaranteeing citizenship as well as acquiring voting representatives and the right for Puerto Ricans to vote for the president—eliminating what many Puerto Ricans view as second-class citizenship.

Aníbal Acevedo-Vilá and Roberto Roselló each present what they believe would be the best status for Puerto Rico: enhanced commonwealth and statehood, respectively. Although both authors may have a different opinion as to which status may hold the greatest benefits to Puerto Rico, they both agree that a resolution to the question of Puerto Rico's status be resolved as quickly as possible.

YES

Aníbal Acevedo-Vilá

Rethinking the Future of the US-Puerto Rico Relationship: Towards the 21st Century

I

About a year ago, I addressed a group of students and faculty from the JFK School of Government at Harvard. The title of that conference was: *"In Search of a New Puerto Rican Consensus: 50 Years of Commonwealth"*. On that occasion, I discussed Puerto Rico's struggle to achieve democratic self-government throughout the 20th century and explained why the Commonwealth's Constitution of 1952 was our greatest democratic achievement. Commonwealth status allowed Puerto Ricans to achieve unprecedented economic development, to strengthen our democratic institutions, and to promote our unique cultural identity.

Many people today take those achievements for granted. They seem to forget that before the establishment of Commonwealth, Puerto Rico was a depressed, poor, and undemocratic colony of the United States. Puerto Rico was governed from Washington. Insular governors were appointed by the President, and served at the President's will and many times at the will of Washington bureaucrats who did not understand or care about Puerto Rico, first under the Department of War (from 1900 to 1933) and then under the Department of the Interior (from 1933–1952).

The territorial regime was an economic disaster. Indeed, Puerto Rico came to be known as the "poorhouse of the Caribbean." The per capita income was $121 a year, not much more than at the turn of the century.

Politically, the situation was equally inauspicious. The colonial policy was premised on the racist view that Puerto Ricans were not "mature" enough to govern themselves, nor were they "white" enough to be incorporated as part of the United States. Although Puerto Ricans became United States citizens by virtue of the Jones Act of 1917, their political rights remained very limited and their quality of life was not much better than the one they enjoyed at the turn of the century. Puerto Ricans learned the hard way that neither democracy nor economic progress necessarily followed the U.S. flag in Puerto Rico.

United States House of Representatives, March 4, 2003.

That was the sad reality of Puerto Rico during the first 40 years under the American flag. This began to change in 1940 when the Popular Democratic Party, led by Luis Muñoz Marín, won the legislative elections.

In 1948, Luis Muñoz Marín became the first elected governor in Puerto Rico's history. Two years, later, in 1950, Congress adopted Public Law 600 to allow the people of Puerto Rico to exercise the right to self-determination and draft their own Constitution. The extraordinary nature of this process has been the source of much confusion as to the essence of Commonwealth. On the one hand, unlike an ordinary federal law, or a traditional organic act, this law was a vehicle to establish a compact between the people of Puerto Rico and the United States. Section 2 of the Act provided:

> "This Act shall be submitted to the qualified voters of Puerto Rico for acceptance or rejection through an island-wide referendum to be held in accordance with the laws of Puerto Rico. Upon approval of this Act by a majority of the voters participating in such a referendum, the Legislature of Puerto Rico is authorized to call a constitutional convention to draft a constitution for said island of Puerto Rico."

In other words, the effectiveness of Public Law 600 depended on the people of Puerto Rico's approval in the ballots.

Public Law 600, as approved by Congress, stated "that, fully recognizing the principle of government by consent, this act is now adopted *in the nature of a compact* so that the people of Puerto Rico may organize a government pursuant to a constitution of their own adoption."

Upon approval of the terms of said Act and their own constitution by the people of Puerto Rico, Commonwealth was born. Commonwealth status was the result of a compromise, which permitted Puerto Rico to enjoy a high degree of self-government compatible with the federal system. Contemporary political theorists have recognized the benefits of autonomous arrangements, such as Commonwealth, to accommodate political, cultural and economic goals.

This kind of compact is *sui generis* in the history of the United States and maybe for that reason many have misunderstood it. However, that does not make it less valid or less legitimate. Indeed, in 1953, the United Nations General Assembly approved Resolution 748 (VIII), concluding that the Commonwealth provided an acceptable measure of self-government for Puerto Rico and therefore Puerto Rico was taken out of the list of "non-self governing territory." Resolution 748 recognized that, and I quote, "in the framework of their Constitution and of the compact agreed upon with the United States of America, the people of the Commonwealth of Puerto Rico have been invested with attributes of political sovereignty which clearly identify the status of self-government attained by the Puerto Rican people as that of an autonomous political entity."

From a political perspective, in 1952, Congress devolved the sovereignty to which the people of Puerto Rico were entitled in the first place, therefore ending the colonial regime. In turn, the people of Puerto Rico freely agreed to a compact that entailed a voluntary delegation of powers to be exercised by the U.S. government. Some people question whether such transfer of sovereignty is possible or whether it ever happened. They tend to assess the process from a formalistic and rather narrow perspective. A better reading of the process must include considerations of political theory, constitutional doctrine and international law. Based on this holistic approach it is necessary to conclude that Puerto Rico is a sovereign body politic with the potential of broad autonomy in certain areas and under the federal jurisdiction on others.

The U.S. Congress had then and has now broad discretion under the Constitution and under international law to establish an autonomous Commonwealth, following the federal model of dual sovereignty, out of the reach of its plenary powers. In other words, Congress can expand today Puerto Rico's sovereignty, but cannot diminish it or do away with it.

Beyond the complex legal issues, it is undeniable that Commonwealth has worked. Using its fiscal autonomy and flexibility, Commonwealth combines economic measures and social programs to transform Puerto Rico into a modern and democratic society. Our symbols, our language, our literary tradition, our folklore and high-culture, all resurged with strength and became a healthy basis for a powerful sense of Puerto Rican nationhood. I speak of nationhood in a sociological sense. In that sense, Puerto Rico is a nation.

Moreover, it was Commonwealth that gave true meaning to the U.S. citizenship of the Puerto Ricans. Under Commonwealth, Puerto Ricans have experienced, at last, their U.S. citizenship as a vehicle to achieve democratic rights and to enjoy opportunities for progress. For the majority of Puerto Ricans, their United States citizenship is seen in terms of shared democratic values and aspirations; not in terms of full *vis a vis* partial membership to the Union; they prefer autonomy rather than full integration.

II

Commonwealth has served Puerto Rico well, and it has also been very beneficial for the United States. Puerto Rico contributes to the common defense, and has played an important role in the development of U.S.-Latin-American relationships. Our contribution to the U.S. economy is substantial. Puerto Rico is today the #4 per capita consumer of U.S. goods in the world. In 1999, Puerto Rico alone purchased $16 billion worth of U.S. goods, which translates into over 270,000 jobs in the mainland. The importance of Puerto Rico as a U.S. market must not be underestimated.

Notwithstanding the amazing accomplishments of Commonwealth, it was not meant to be an immutable model. The world has changed since 1952 and the majority of Puerto Ricans would like to see Commonwealth status modified and improved, so it can better adjust to the modern world.

Today, there are roughly 3 competing future alternatives to our current status: Statehood, Enhanced Commonwealth and Independence. Assuming that we can reach a procedural consensus, which we must do before we move forward, the best alternative available to Puerto Rico is the **enhanced autonomic model** or what has been called the enhanced Commonwealth. What I mean is a perfected autonomy with additional tools, particularly economic tools, and enhanced democratic participation for the Puerto Rican people, compatible with the federal system. I believe that this **enhanced autonomic status** is the best route not only for Puerto Rico, but for the United States as well. The idea of enhanced Commonwealth may challenge your assumptions and understandings of traditional concepts of sovereignty, citizenship and federalism. But the world has changed and these concepts are changing as well.

In theory, both statehooders and independentistas alike, have offered compelling arguments to support their status preferences. Statehooders argue that they are second-class and disenfranchised American citizens, and that statehood is the natural course for Puerto Rico. On the other side of the spectrum, the independentistas argue that Puerto Rico is a nation, and as such our destiny is to become an independent republic and a member of the international community of independent countries. Both, as I said, present reasonable, but mutually exclusive discourses.

Let me briefly state the main obstacles to statehood and independence.

Statehood

1. The first reason why statehood is not a truly practicable alternative is that Puerto Ricans do not want it. This is a major obstacle. After over a hundred years of US-Puerto Rico relationship, statehood has never achieved a majority of the popular vote. Commonwealth, as an autonomous model, was chosen by an overwhelming majority of the people in 1952, and it has been favored in every plebiscite since . . . 1967, 1993 and 1998. So, statehood is a problem in terms of self-determination and democracy since the people of Puerto Rico do not want it.

2. The second obstacle to statehood is that Puerto Rico will loose its unique tools for economic development, i.e. fiscal autonomy and economic flexibility because of the reach of the uniformity clause. Statehood is not an economic model in itself. The immediate economic consequences will be: unavailability of special tax incentives to attract industry and investment, imposition of the federal tax structure to our economy, drastic downsizing of local government and, therefore higher unemployment; an increase on welfare dependency; and other side effects. Statehood does not produce new tools; therefore it will perpetuate welfare dependency.

3. The third problem is that statehood is not compatible with the maintenance of a unique and separate nationality. This is a problem for Puerto Rico and the United States, since the overwhelming majority of Puerto Ricans, whether they admit it or not, think that their nationhood and cultural identity is not negotiable. To that extent, statehood is also a self-determination issue for the United States.

4. The fourth obstacle for statehood, at least in the short term, I believe is the legacy of corruption from the last administration. This legacy has hurt us all, and has made being an advocate for Puerto Rico much more challenging. The number of convictions and guilty pleas of persons, who served in leadership positions of the Statehood administration, unfortunately undermines the credibility of those who passionately believe in the statehood cause. I do not believe the leadership of the statehood movement has yet come to grips with how much damage was done to their movement in Washington DC because of individuals in San Juan who, either knowingly participate or turn their backs, while others used public office for political and personal gain.

Independence
1. Independence faces today an even greater challenge since only about 5% of the population favors it.
2. Independence is not compatible with the preservation of U.S citizenship, and the permanence of a stable political bond with the United States, which is so important for Puerto Ricans.
3. From an economic standpoint, independence it is likely to bring unnecessary unrest and lack of economic stability. This will depend on the kind of independence that can be negotiated, but as of today, independence represents economic disaster for Puerto Rico.

You may say about the Commonwealth what Winston Churchill is credited to have said about democracy, this is: "democracy is the worst form of government except all the others that have been tried." I favor Commonwealth not because it is perfect, or sacred, but because it still provides the best model available considering the political and economic realities of the United States and Puerto Rico. From the Puerto Rican perspective, commonwealth is the only status that harmonizes the political, cultural and economic goals of the people.

Any status alternative for the future should be measured from 3 perspectives: economy, democracy, and nationhood/culture. From these perspectives, Commonwealth, as a third way, represents the only alternative that truly can harmonize the seemingly conflicting aspirations of Puerto Ricans and as well as the interests of the United States.

As opposed to statehood, Commonwealth is the flexible model that can evolve and adapt. As a third way for the future, Commonwealth must be enhanced to adapt to the new challenges and realities of the 21st century. Indeed, the "founders" of the Commonwealth thought of it as an important, but preliminary step towards a fully autonomous and democratic status. To truly meet the expectations of its founders, the Commonwealth must be enhanced and strengthened. As Governor Sila Calderón recently said: "Fifty years ago when we entered into the compact with Congress, it fared quite well when compared with the prevailing colonial arrangements then existing in the Caribbean. Half a century later there are areas where that is no longer the case." The enhanced Commonwealth is the route to follow.

III

I will now touch on some of the problematic areas that need to be addressed in any enhanced Commonwealth proposal.

First Problem: *The problem of generic consent.*
This is a problem of democratic asymmetry in as much as many federals laws apply to Puerto Rico, without a formal mechanism of participation by the people. Federal laws that are not essential to the Commonwealth compact should be applicable only if the people of Puerto Rico agree to their application. For example, one may argue that Homeland Security laws are essential to the compact by virtue of the common defense tenet, but that Puerto Rico may be excluded from certain economic laws that do not respond to the Island reality.

Second Problem: *Unwarranted limitations on Puerto Rico's international relations.*

Since Puerto Ricans does not vote for the President and does not elect voting legislators for Congress, there is no legitimate reason to apply the same restrictions that states have in the area of foreign affairs. As a matter of fact, Puerto Rico has an Olympic team, which recognizes the uniqueness of Commonwealth status. Puerto Rico's international presence is a matter of political importance and necessary to promote Puerto Rico's economic and cultural ties with the world.

Third Problem: *Dependency on federal funds.*

The enhanced Commonwealth of the future must dedicate creative energy and explore new effective tools to reduce the levels of dependency of federal funds. This is the only way to be truly autonomous, and to achieve true interdependency, instead of just dependency.

These are just some of the main areas of Commonwealth enhancement. Note that these are not abstract or esoteric proposals. These are reasonable, pragmatic and goal oriented proposals. So, why don't we just go ahead and implement them? Good question.

IV

The problem we have today is that the status issue has been held hostage by local partisan politics. The exacerbated tribalism in Puerto Rican politics has impaired our ability as a people to advance and promote the necessary enhancement of the current status. As I have said before, we need a procedural consensus among Puerto Rican leaders; a new consensus on how to steer a process of true self-determination in which the people of Puerto Rico can freely express their will. Without that consensus, there is no foreseeable way out of the status deadlock.

In 2001, Governor Sila Calderón invited the 3 main parties and the leaders of Puerto Rico's civil society to join the Commission of Puerto Rican Unity and Consensus, a non-partisan commission to agree on the procedural mechanism that will best result in a self-determination process. The purpose of the commission was to work in good faith toward a procedural consensus, instead of having each party and group pushing for their proposal and sabotaging the others. The proposal was truly remarkable because for the first time in Puerto Rico's recent history the party in power set forth an inclusive process; a process that opens the doors of participation to all other parties as well as non-partisan sectors of the civil society.

It is a shame that the leadership of the New Progressive Party, the statehood party, has refused to participate. They rejected this good faith offer to come to the table to talk, to have a dialogue, to express our differences, but to find common ground. Unfortunately, this is not surprising! In 1997, this same party, when they were in power, pushed for a statehood bill in Washington, excluding the Commonwealth party from the negotiations and actually eliminating the enhanced Commonwealth alternative from the proposed ballot.

They invested millions of dollars in lobbyists and political contributions in order to convince Washington that all Puerto Ricans wanted was statehood. The bill, they argued, was about self-determination, but in reality it was an undemocratic process that excluded the choice preferred by the majority of Puerto Ricans: the enhanced Commonwealth. This same day, March 4, five years ago, the U.S. House of Representatives, after a divisive and heated debate, approved the statehood bill by only one vote. That result was a clear defeat for the statehood movement who was expecting an overwhelming favorable vote that night. Their effort, of course failed; the statehood bill never reached the President's desk.

The statehooders have not learned from recent history. They are not willing to respect the democratic process when they cannot manipulate it and control it. They have not learned that no matter how much money or power you have, without consensus among the main parties, nothing will be accomplished in Washington. Today, I call upon the leadership of the statehood party to be brave. I urge them, for once, to respect the democratic process and come to the table in good faith. The Popular Democratic Party and its leader, Governor Sila Calderón, is giving you a last chance: accept it! But, if you shy away from this historic call, rest assured that after 2004, the Popular Democratic Party will steer a process of self-determination.

When the time comes, I will be the first to work with all my heart to complete the unfulfilled autonomous agenda of the generation that created and implemented Commonwealth. There is a lot of work to do, in Puerto Rico and in Washington.

You may ask why would the U.S. be interested in enhancing Commonwealth status? The United States government should favor the enhancement of Commonwealth status, if for nothing else, for 2 reasons: (1) American commitment to democracy; and (2) the possibility of empowering Puerto Rico towards a reduction of economic dependency.

Today, as we face difficult challenges of terrorism, war, nuclear threats, religious hatred, you may ask, why is Puerto Rico important to the U.S.? Why is it relevant? I'll tell you why: Because the root of those problems is the fundamental issue of democracy and liberty. The challenge to the U.S. is that if it cannot do justice and deal with Puerto Rico in an open, fair and creative way, how can they purport to be promoting and bringing freedom and democracy abroad? If we take President Bush at his word, Democracy is God's gift to humanity. The U.S. has a duty to promote a more perfect democratic status in Puerto Rico. And, in my honest view, enhanced Commonwealth is the best way.

Sooner rather than later, the new generation of Puerto Ricans and U.S. leaders will have to face this tremendous responsibility. This responsibility is to equip Puerto Rico with the democratic and economic tools necessary to face the challenges of the new century; to eliminate all vestiges of colonialism from the current U.S.-Puerto Rico relation; and to forge a new consensus on a future relationship. It will not be easy, but we have no choice but to proudly bear this historic burden. I agree with Jose Trías Monge, our preeminent constitutional scholar, that, and I quote: "the United States clearly harbors nothing but good will toward Puerto Rico. It is just a question of taking a hard look at the past about which there are quite a few things to regret, on both sides, and making the decision to forge a brave new beginning."

The message to my generation is this: Let's all start today, full of hope and enthusiasm, to forge that brave new beginning.

Self-Determination, Civil Rights and the Future of Puerto Rico

The State Department is charged with responsibility for foreign affairs. Why then some would ask, are we having here a dialogue on Puerto Rican-U.S. affairs, which to most would seem like a domestic issue?

In short, one may argue that it is because of the ambiguity of Puerto Rico's political status that has caused mixed signals from the federal government and from Puerto Rico. This ambiguity has been validated even by our Supreme Court, which in one of its most infamous decisions established that Puerto Rico was "foreign in a domestic sense."

So it may be appropriate that here, in the U.S. State Department, we discuss the results of this ambiguous, and even oxymoronic policy towards Puerto Rico, which because of its "foreign" component may well be a valid matter of discussion in the seat of U.S. foreign relations. Why is Puerto Rico foreign? Certainly not because it is outside U.S. sovereignty—it is not! Not because it is inhabited by foreigners or aliens—it is not. On the contrary, its residents are U.S. citizens by birth, natural born citizens. Is it because there is a different culture? Not so, as the economic and political culture is strictly American, and the social culture shares its history, heritage and values with the many Hispanic communities in the U.S. that enjoy the full rights of citizens and the full protections of the Constitution.

So why is Puerto Rico "foreign in a domestic sense" and what are the consequences of such a situation? Let us start with a bit of history.

The sinking of the "Maine" in Havana Harbor became the immediate cause of what then-Secretary of State John Hay characterized as "The Splendid Little War." This war, lasting less than a year, set the course that changed the fundamental nature of the young American nation, the United States of America as it entered the 20th century. What had been conceived, and had existed for over a century, as a republic, became a colonial empire, modeled after the same European concept that triggered the rebellion of the original 13 colonies against British colonialism. This chapter of American history began when Congress formally declared war on Spain on April 25, 1898.

Although the acquisition of Puerto Rico was not an original objective in the Spanish-American War, after a brief and successful campaign in Cuba, the U.S. forces led by General Nelson Myles invaded Puerto Rico on July 25, 1898.

From Remarks to the Open Forum, October 23, 2001.

Events followed swiftly. The disembarking military troops quickly established control over the island with almost total absence of resistance. An armistice was announced on the 12th of August. Before the year was over, barely 8 months after the Declaration of War, the Treaty of Paris was signed on Dembeber, 15, 1898. Four centuries of Spanish sovereignty and colonialism in Puerto Rico ended; and a new century under U.S. sovereignty and colonialism was born. Puerto Rico, together with Guam and the Philippines, was ceded to the United States.

The Treaty language left entirely up to Congress the fate of the inhabitants of the newly acquired territories. In its pertinent section it states: "the civil rights and the political status of the native inhabitants of the territories ceded to the U.S. shall be determined by Congress."

What followed the war was the establishment of a new doctrine that permitted, for the first time in the history of the nation, the management of the new territories as permanent colonies. And in the course of these events, changed the very essence, the very soul of the United States.

These events occurred in the context of a national and international scenario at the beginning of a new century that promised to establish the United States as a world power. This resulted in a very spirited debate as to the new role of the nation in world affairs and the presidential campaign of 1900 provided a very public forum for this debate. To quote Judge Juan Torruella: "The presidential campaign that followed between President McKinley and his perennial foe, William Jennings Bryan, became a plebiscite for the controversy regarding territorial expansion, this question being the predominant issue of that contest. McKinley with no other than Theodore Roosevelt as his running mate, thoroughly trounced Bryan. This was considered carte blanche to proceed as to Puerto Rico and the Philippines, and provided the immediate setting against which the Supreme Court decided the "Insular Cases."

The so-called Insular Cases became the foundation of a new doctrine of colonial expansion. The Insular Cases, as commonly referred to collectively, are a series of Supreme Court cases decided from 1901 to 1922, that in conjunction, established and refined the doctrine of incorporated versus unincorporated territories. When referring to this set of court decisions, it is generally acknowledged that the pacesetter case is *Downes v. Bidwell* (1901) and that the final significant decision came with *Balzac v. Puerto Rico* (1922). It was through the application of the decisions on these cases, that in the words of the current Chief Judge of the 1st Circuit of Appeals, "the Supreme Court placed its imprimatur on a colonial relationship in which Congress could exercise virtually unchecked power over the unincorporated territories ad infinitum."

The result of the 1900 presidential elections had settled the political question of imperial expansion, but the validation of derivative issues remained.

The issue was whether the full scope of the Constitution applied to the newly acquired territories or not. The metaphor which surfaced to capture the constitutional question was whether "The Constitution followed the flag"—whether or not, as described by Judge Cabranes, "Certain peoples could be permanently excluded from the American political community and deprived of equal rights." Through the Insular Cases, Judge Cabranes continues "the court effectively answered in the affirmative the question whether it was constitutionally permissible for the United States to possess colonies indefinitely."

A change of major proportions took place through these Court decisions—not only for the territories concerned, but for the essence of the nation. Some consider that a fundamental change in the Constitution, without an outright amendment, was effected. From a constitutionalist's point of view, Professor Sanford Levinson argues that: "the Constitution had in effect been amended as the result of the events of 1898 and the ratifying election that took place two years later."

What so dramatically changed the nature and the self-image of the nation was the novel doctrine of incorporation of territories. In essence, although no mention of this is found in the Constitution, the Court ruled that there were two types of territories: those incorporated, where after a territorial transition, statehood would be granted and the full force of the Constitution was to be in effect; and those non-incorporated, where the privileges and immunities guaranteed by the Constitution need not be extended to their citizens, and where the fate of the territory was to be ruled under the plenary powers of Congress.

Judge Torruella characterized these decisions as the "Doctrine of Separate and Unequal". An interesting historical tidbit is that the same Supreme Court that established the Insular Cases Doctrine, The Fuller Court, has the distinction of creating the infamous "separate and equal" doctrine of *Plessy v. Ferguson,* that gave validation to the practice of racial segregation. It took the Supreme Court 58 years to reverse that discriminatory doctrine with its *Brown v. Board of Education* decision. However, it is now over one century, and counting, that the equally abhorrent doctrine of "separate and unequal" persists. I believe the time is ripe for a similar reversal of this egregious dictum by the federal courts.

What are the consequences of this sad state of affairs? Let us focus on one of the most fundamental rights of a citizen in a democratic society, and in particular in American democracy—the right to vote.

The history of the citizen right to vote in the nation has been a history of progressive enfranchisement. Chief Justice Earl Warren in 1964 put it in perspective: ". . . history has seen a continuing expansion of the scope of the right of suffrage in this country. The right to vote freely for the candidate of one's choice is the essence of a democratic society, and any restrictions on that right strike at the heart of representative government."

But today that history is incomplete. Today we still face an unfinished business of American democracy.

The colonial period was characterized by a markedly limited (from our current perspective) voting franchise extended only to white protestant male property owners. This situation left many totally disenfranchised in the early years of the nation: Women, African-Americans, men without property, those under 21 years old, and non-Protestants. Even the white American male was not totally enfranchised. From this nascent vision of the new democratic experiment that gave birth to the new American republic, a course of progressive inclusion of additional citizen groups has been relentlessly followed. This course has been illustrated by changes in the demographic and immigration patterns, in the social circumstances, and indeed, in the added pressure provided by every expansion of suffrage to citizens. . . .

The Civil War brought an end to the large immigration wave of the mid-nineteenth century, but opened the door to further recognition of citizen voting rights. At the conclusion of the war, the nation ended slavery by adopting the Thirteenth Amendment in 1865. Subsequently, voting rights specifically took a quantum leap as the Fifteenth Amendment clearly prohibited restrictions on voting based on "race, color or previous condition of servitude." In legal terms, this constituted a major expansion of the recognized voting franchise; in pragmatic terms it opened the doors of democratic participation to thousands of previously disenfranchised blacks, through the period of the reconstruction. However, this enhanced participation by black citizens was rapidly curtailed in the post reconstruction era, by state laws and regulations.

In 1896, the Supreme Court justified and validated this retrenchment of the achievements of post Civil War Reconstruction when, in *Plessy v. Ferguson,* it found that state mandated racial segregation was compatible with the Constitutional Doctrine of equality before the law. Thus was born, and lived for decades the abhorrent doctrine of "separate and equal". Of note is the fact that this same Court, the Fuller Court, applying similar racist undertones, went on to establish the doctrine of "separate and unequal" that to this date applies to the U.S. territories acquired after the Spanish-American War of 1898. The same concept that allowed for legal discrimination of African-Americans was utilized to allow the legal disenfranchisement of citizens of the American territories.

The next Constitutional amplification of the voting franchise had to wait until 1920. But then another quantum leap was accomplished by opening the door of democratic participation to fully half of the potential (or rightful) electorate. This achievement became the expanded platform for women to seek full recognition of their civil rights. The enfranchisement of women permitted, indeed stimulated, the claim to all citizen rights for equality under the law. Another pertinent parallel was thus established in history to the current situation of disenfranchised U.S. citizens, who today demand their voting rights as a preamble to their entitlement to all other rights recognized and protected by the Constitution.

Other Amendments followed, expanding and securing the voting franchise. The 23rd Amendment granted the Presidential vote to citizens of the District of Columbia in 1961 (in a "non-state" territory). The 24th Amendment in 1964 established that the rights of citizens of the United States to vote . . . shall not be denied or abridged . . . by reason of failure to pay poll tax or other tax (significant in the uncoupling of voting rights and payment of taxes). The 26th Amendment of 1971 that stated that the right of citizens of the United States who are 18 years or older to vote cannot be denied or abridged on account of age. . . .

And so we arrive at the end of a long story of definition and progressive expansion of suffrage in the U.S. . . . In practical terms, still some obstacles remain as demonstrated by the recent 2000 presidential election, but these are being addressed currently. However, a most obvious deficit of democracy remains. Nearly 4 million United States citizens, residents of Puerto Rico, remain disenfranchised, lawfully and practically—both "de jure" and "de facto." Today Puerto Ricans remain as disenfranchised stepchildren within the great American family. In the progress towards a more perfect union, the achievement of universal suffrage remains a goal unfulfilled.

The same conditions that prevented, at some times in the past for non-Protestants, non-landowners, slaves, blacks, women or overseas citizens to exercise their full voting rights, still persist, after more than a century for the residents of Puerto Rico and the territories.

Two cases have been recently filed to try to secure this most fundamental right for Puerto Rico's residents. Both are based on the premise that voting rights are inherent in citizenship within a democracy, and further that this fundamental right should supercede any voting procedural consideration. Although the Courts have not yet moved to redress a century of discrimination, these cases have served to advance the awareness of the untenable situation of unrecognized rights of U.S. citizens.

Particularly pertinent is the concurrent opinion in one of those cases, of first Circuit Chief Judge Juan Torruella, a Puerto Rican, who reviews the relevant history of disenfranchisement in Puerto Rico concludes: "Although this is not the case, nor perhaps the time, for a federal court to take remedial action to correct what is a patently intolerable situation, it is time to serve notice upon the political branches of government that it is incumbent upon them, in the first instance, to take appropriate steps to correct what amounts to an outrageous disregard for the rights of a substantial segment of its citizenry. A failure to do so countenances corrective judicial action. It may be that the federal courts will be required to take extraordinary measures as necessary to protect discrete groups "completely under the sovereignty and dominion of the United States."

Maybe then, the question to the federal courts is when is the time, and which is the case, "to take remedial action to correct what is a patently intolerable situation?" It took the Supreme Court 58 years to reverse the egregiously outrageous "equal and separate" doctrine of *Plessy v. Ferguson* (1896). It is now over a century since the equally outrageous doctrine of "unequal and separate" of the Insular Cases was established by the same Fuller Court. When is the time? Which is the case? What will be the threshold required for the federal courts" to take extraordinary measures as necessary to protect discrete groups completely under the sovereignty and dominion of the United States? When will, in the words of Judge Torruella, "the conspicuous inattention of the judiciary end?"

But we must ask, why are we hopeful that this longstanding problem can be brought to the forefront and solved with finality? For one, there is a very strong general consensus that the current status must change—although admittedly the direction of change is passionately and violently debated by different observers and engaged groups. What is clear however is that all agree on the need for change. At the same time consensus also exists around the Wilsonian element of self-determination: "For the right of those who submit to authority to have a voice in their own government." Judge Cabranes summarizes the situation thus: "In short it is fair to say that all of Puerto Rico's political movements seek to chart a path towards a post colonial future, whatever form it may take. The central political problem of Puerto Rico remains as ever, de-colonization and how it is to be fully achieved."

Dissatisfaction with the status quo is a powerful element in the eventual resolution of this status conundrum. The fact that the leadership of the Popular Party (Commonwealth), which has represented a position in favor of the status quo over the past half century, now agrees as to the colonial nature of the current relationship, allows for consensus on the urgent need for change. No less an exponent of the Commonwealth status, and one of its founders, former Puerto Rico Chief Justice Jose Trias Monge, now points to the inherent "injustice according to law." He states, "There is no equality or comparability of rights between American citizens residing in Puerto Rico and American citizens residing in the United States."

One conclusion emerges clearly: there is ample consensus for action. As Judge Torruella contends: "on the Puerto Rican side there is almost unanimous agreement on one fact: the present status is unacceptable."

As divisive an issue as the manner and content of de-colonization is, it is fair to say that at least there is another common basis for agreement in the need for change from the status quo. The common element in all diverging visions is for an explicit recognition of the principle of the "consent of the governed," the full participation of the citizen in government. This indeed is the basic foundation of democracy.

Former Governor of Puerto Rico, Rafael Hernandez Colon, a firm advocate of the Commonwealth option, has sensed that, "all factions do agree to end the present undemocratic arrangement, whereby Puerto Rico is subject to the laws of Congress but cannot vote in it."

It is accepted, then, that to unravel the Gordian knot of colonialism in Puerto Rico, both the people of Puerto Rico and the United States Government must engage in defining the valid and effective road to de-colonization. The consequences of continued inaction to both Puerto Rico and the United States would be destructive.

A major responsibility for untangling this century old imbroglio lies unequivocally with the federal government. All three branches of the United States Government must weigh in to eliminate this embarrassing stain on American democracy. But to date that responsibility has not been exercised by any one of the national government branches. Describing the laisse-faire attitude of the federal government, Roberto Aponte Toro writes: "Laid back in their seats, the United States and Congress will constantly reply that they only want to help, but do not know how; that it is the Puerto Ricans' own fault; that they just do not get their act together." In fact, a majority of Puerto Ricans have come together many times, but to no avail. Waiting for clear signs from the political branches, the third branch, the Supreme Court, which originally through the Insular Cases offered legitimating consent to the empire, now carefully avoids the issue.

Unless the federal government finally resolves to implement a process for decolonization and self-determination, the ambivalence, the immobility, the frustrations, and the dysfunction of the present will continue. Unfortunately, the United States Government has never done this. But it must. Despite very clear calls from all sectors of the Puerto Rican society and from the political parties and leaders for a major change in the status quo, the United States Federal Government has so far been unwilling or unable to move the process forward in a definitive manner. . . .

It is clear that a nation that portends to be the beacon of democracy for the world in the 21st century must act affirmatively to confirm its commitment to its fundamental democratic values and sense of justice.

One must understand first which options would offer a solution for change and which would not. It has to be clear that the current status quo, even with superficial modifications, is no answer to final resolution.

As summarized by Trias, "The first step in taking a hard new look at Puerto Rico should therefore be to understand what is wrong with Puerto Rico's present situation—why it has indisputably earned the title of the 'oldest colony in the world'."

What options then are valid and de-colonizing? It is conceivable, though improbable, that one route could be the enactment of a Constitutional amendment that would create a new status within the U.S. federation that is neither a territory (under territorial clause and the plenary powers of Congress), or a state (with all the rights and responsibilities on an equal footing, and the individual immunities and protection of the Constitution for its citizens). As currently contained in the United States Constitution, those two are the only recognized political status jurisdictions under United States sovereignty.

However, the real options that would provide finality to this century old dilemma are the definitive definition of Puerto Rico's status under a separate sovereignty, or under U.S. sovereignty with full citizenship rights, that is, statehood. I agree with a House of Representatives report that states that, "full self-government for Puerto Rico is attainable only through establishment of political status which is based on either separate Puerto Rican sovereignty and nationality, or full and equal United States nationality and citizenship through membership in the union and under which Puerto Rico is no longer an unincorporated territory subject to the plenary authority of Congress arising from the Territorial Clause."

Suffice it to say here that the political branches of the federal government, the executive and legislative, should and must act to recognize fundamental citizen rights by instituting a process of de-colonization toward either of these options. It is redundant, but necessary to add that in choosing the remedy to finally resolve the civil rights and political status conundrum, the rights to self-determination of the people of Puerto Rico have to be central to the process.

We remain hopeful that the federal government will recognize and exert its responsibilities; similarly, that Puerto Rico recognize and exerts its own. It is incumbent on the federal government to validate the option under the U.S. sovereignty, namely statehood, as well as its willingness to enter into any agreements with a new nation with a separate sovereignty. It is then imperative that the informed citizenry of Puerto Rico make a decision as to its final political status. The only status that will not resolve the quandary is the status quo; indeed, the status quo is the problem.

Question and Answer Segment

Alan Lang: Can you tell us more about on-going public education efforts related to self-determination in Puerto Rico and throughout the United States?

Dr. Rossello: Well, there is an on-going process in Puerto Rico that has been changed with some ups and downs. But I think the most significant part, the most significant new element is the one that President Clinton submitted to Congress. Congress approved funding for a process of education concerning the different alternatives, valid alternatives that Puerto Rico would have in a process of self-determination. This funding has already been signed. It has not been utilized. Let me make a plea for those already-appropriated funds to be used at this time so that real valid education concerning options for decolonization can be presented in a very forthright manner to Puerto Rico. . . .

Question: I'm a private citizen. Over the years there have been a number of congressional commissions and committees that I've tried to at least try to understand the Puerto Rico dilemma. Every time including the last one, the Congressman Don Young commission, they failed to capture the boiling of status politics in Puerto Rico. That's where more acid couldn't escape. How would you convince Congress since they are the ones that hold preliminary powers on Puerto Rico to revisit the issue and this time finally reach a decision as to what we are going to do?

Dr. Rossello: think it's a very complicated endeavor and I think that it's not just at one level or at one of the different points of the spectrum of the political and government structure. True, Congress is central to whatever effort has to be made, but let me suggest to you that maybe there's other ways where you can indirectly, in addition to, directly appealing to Congress. Have some influence so that Congress will act and I mentioned one of them, which is through the courts.

I think it's clear in our history that at times the federal government, the political branches of the federal government have been unwilling to act on certain issues. It has taken court decisions to in essence stimulate or force the federal government to act. I think in addition to the efforts that have to continue with the presidency, with the federal agencies on the executive branch, with Congress, we also have to look at opening up an avenue in the judiciary. I make this parallel with the *Plessy vs. Ferguson* case which to me is enlightening because of the similarity of the concepts of time that it was adopted by Supreme Court of the same justices that made those decisions. It seems to me that we should also look at the judiciary as a place where we can recur to a knot, an occurring knot. If the political branches have been unwilling for many years and many decades to do something. Let us think about the possibility of taking what Judge Hoya says, the case and the time. What is the case? We have to look at that. The *Brown vs. Board of Education* case did not just come up. It was really a very studied approach to reversing a very, very sad doctrine that was in place. So I think we should also look at that new avenue. And I'm pleased to say there have been some attempts over the past few years to try to bring this to the floor. We have to look for the adequate case. We have to make sure the Supreme Court looks at this, under strict scrutiny and not necessary whether it's reasonable or not for different treatment to the U.S. citizens of Puerto Rico and the territories. So I submit to you that we have a task before us of maybe opening up a new front that could then in essence direct the federal government in its legislative and executive branches to solve the problem, not necessarily to tell Congress or to tell the Presidency what the solution is, but basically to state that the current situation is untenable.

Question: I'm an attorney. My issue here is really economic. You are looking for political equality for Puerto Ricans. The Congress to some extent sustain a large number of unemployed people in Puerto Rico. What are your thoughts of improving the economic commonwealth of Puerto Rico? What areas you are looking at because I think this would have to be done in order to look at political sustainability of statehood?

Dr. Rossello: Let me say first that maybe you have placed the question the other way around. I contend that the Puerto Rican economic situation would not improve vis a vis the nation unless you do away with the obstacles that being a territory imply. We have seen this. It's been half a century since the so-called commonwealth was established. The difference in economic terms between Puerto Rico and the poor state Mississippi, or any of the states has not budged. It will not. If you have a certain structure you can make improvements on the edges, but if you want to make real changes you have to change the structure. History also tells us that every territory that subsequently became a state improved its economy, without an exception. The latest chapter was Hawaii. Hawaii as a territory was growing in its growth product at approximately 4% per year. In the decade after it became a state it almost doubled that growth and so it makes sense to change the structure so that you can achieve new levels of economic development. I suggest to you that unless you do it you will not get the improvement that you are seeking. The argument then becomes an obstacle for economic development.

Thank you.

POSTSCRIPT

Is "Enhanced Commonwealth" the Solution to Puerto Rico's Colonial Status?

Perhaps Roselló's statement provides the most accurate summary of the point of view that many Puerto Ricans hold regarding their view of the colonial status that their island maintains. Roselló asserts that "a most obvious deficit of democracy remains. Nearly 4 million United States citizens, residents of Puerto Rico, remain disenfranchised stepchildren within the great American family."

Addressing this issue of political isolation and commonwealth limbo that Puerto Rico has been enduring for several decades, Puerto Rican attorney Gregorio Igartua filed an appeal in the spring of 2006 requesting that the residents of Puerto Rico be given the right to vote in U.S. presidential elections. However, in a sign of maintaining the status quo, the U.S. Supreme Court rejected the appeal. Reflective of the Supreme Court's decision, many Americans—particularly those who have little or no connection to Puerto Rico—do not want to see a change in Puerto Rico's status. Citing crime, income, and unemployment levels that do not compare favorably to most U.S. states, many Americans feel that allowing Puerto Rico statehood or enhanced commonwealth status would create additional tax burdens and increased financial obligations in order to support what is perceived to be a relatively less-affluent Puerto Rico.

Alvin Rubinstein, in "The Case against Puerto Rican Statehood," echoes the sentiment against changing Puerto Rico's status by identifying an issue that he feels raises another concern—the question of language. For Rubinstein, language is what unites the United States, and having a state whose main language is not English would form a rift in that unity. However, Christina Burnett in her article, "The Case for Puerto Rican Decolonization," argues that "Puerto Rican statehood does not threaten to create a so-called American Quebec." She also agrees that "unresolved colonial condition has fostered Puerto Rico's damaging brand of ambivalent politics."

Many believe that is up to the U.S. Congress to make the initial moves for Puerto Rico self-determination, and many efforts have recently been made attempting to resolve the issue. In December 2005, a presidential task force recommended that Congress call a referendum on the island's status as a self-governing U.S. commonwealth. In 2000, U.S. President Bill Clinton called for a presidential task force on Puerto Rico's status and in April 2001, President George W. Bush amended this executive order, ultimately leading to the December 2005 report. However, this report did not accept the enhanced commonwealth option that the pro-commonwealth Clinton administration submitted. In fact, the report made it clear that what was needed for a status decision was a two-step approach: (1) whether Puerto Rico wanted to remain a territory of the United States, or (2) they preferred to change their status. And, if a change was in order, then Puerto Ricans would vote for complete sovereignty and independence or for statehood. Those supporting statehood were pleased with this report, whereas those in favor of enhanced commonwealth were left without any options. Yet, many politicians, including members of the House and Senate, were quite critical of the report and thought it was biased toward statehood. These same politicians made statements in support of a constitutional convention on the status of Puerto Rico, as is provided for in the "Puerto Rico Self-Determination Act of 2006" (S.2304/H.R. 4943).

For which alternative will Puerto Ricans ultimately vote? How will the U.S. Congress vote? If history in any way can predict the future, the vote—whether by the Puerto Ricans or by Congress—will remain undecided.

For further reading on these issues and on the third party (PIP—pro independence), the following is suggested: "The United Nations and Decolonization" (http://www.un.org/depts/dpi/decolinization/main.htm). A special press release on June 13, 2005 on the Special Committee on Decolonization: 6th and 7th meetings: Special committee Calls on United States to expedite Puerto Rico self-determination process.

Statehood Issues (http://www.prstatehood.com/issues/index.asp) asks and answers questions that Puerto Ricans and Americans may have about Puerto Rico becoming a state.

For more information on enhanced commonwealth, PR's resident commissioner, Luis G. Fortuño, gave "Opening Remarks before the House Resources Committee" on the President's Task Force on Puerto Rico's Status: http://www.house.gov/list/press/pr00_fortuno/04_25_06.html.

José Trías Monge's *Puerto Rico: The Trials of the Oldest Colony in the World* (Yale University Press, 1997), a classic on the subject at hand, discusses various options for Puerto Rico to end its colonial status.

To know more about the "Presidential Task Force Report on Puerto Rico," see http://www.independencia.net/noticias/hc_editorial_task_ force_report.

On the Internet . . .

Society and Culture in Latin America (Latin American Network Information Center)

Society and Culture in Latin America is one of the resource pages of the Latin American Network Information Center at the University of Texas at Austin. This page of LANIC's database contains an extensive array of topics including the African Diaspora, children and family, disability resources, folklore, human rights, immigration and migration, indigenous peoples, the Jewish Diaspora, labor, the Middle Eastern Diaspora, non-governmental and non-profit organizations, religion and theology, social work, and women and gender studies.

http://info.lanic.utexas.edu/subject/society/

Human Rights Watch—Americas

Human Rights Watch—Americas "is dedicated to protecting the human rights of people around the world" and seeks to "prevent discrimination, to uphold political freedom, to protect people from inhumane conduct in wartime, and to bring offenders to justice." Its home page contains country and regional information and briefing papers on current human rights issues.

http://www.hrw.org/doc/?t=americas

United Nations Women Watch: Latin America

United Nations Women Watch's Web site on Latin America provides links for information on women and economics, human rights, the environment, violence, education, poverty, development, health, food, agriculture, and the media. Most resources are available in English and Spanish.

http://www.un.org/womenwatch/asp/user/list.asp?ParentID=10474

Border and Latin American Information (New Mexico State University Library)

New Mexico State University's Border and Latin American Information site provides links for information on migration, environment, crime and justice, and artistic publications and activities. Its Border Studies section contains a working bibliography of books, videos, databases, and other resources.

http://lib.nmsu.edu/subject/bord/#border

PART 2

Society, Human Rights, and Culture

Latin America is a place of extraordinary heterogeneity; oftentimes, the very definition of what constitutes Latin American society, human rights, and culture is the subject of heated debate. This section addresses the relationships between society and the individual and, in some cases, the balance between government, society and personal freedom, rights, and identity. As the following issues illustrate, underlying these relationships are questions of freedom, security, culture, nationality, religion, gender, race, and ethnicity.

- Has Mexican Governmental Involvement Helped Stop the Killings in Ciudad Juárez?

- Immigration: Should Illegal Immigrant Gang Members Be Granted Legal Clemency from U.S. Law?

- Is Latin America Loosening Its Restrictive Abortion Laws?

- Does Race Matter?

- Do Volunteer Border Patrol Groups Represent a Reasonable and Just Way to Address Immigration Across the Mexican-U.S. Border?

- Is Latin America Becoming Protestant?

ISSUE 6

Has Mexican Governmental Involvement Helped Stop the Killings in Ciudad Juárez?

YES: Undersecretary of Multilateral Affairs and Human Rights, from "Updated Informative Documents Regarding the Mexican Government's Actions in Cuidad Juarez, Chihuahua," http://www.sre.gob .mx/substg/derechoshumanos/juarezingles.htm (August 2004)

NO: Kent Paterson, from "The Juarez Women's Murders: Mothers Step Up Justice Campaign as a Cover-Up Takes Hold," *Americas Program, Interhemispheric Resource Center* (November 24, 2004)

ISSUE SUMMARY

YES: Mexico's Undersecretary of Multilateral Affairs and Human Rights claims that due to recent state and federal governmental intervention, significant gains have been made in the fight against the crimes surrounding Ciudad Juárez and the deaths and disappearances of hundreds of women.

NO: Kent Paterson, a freelance photojournalist and author who frequently writes for the International Relations Center, a policy studies institute that promotes grassroots dialogue and civic action, writes that the Mexican government is not doing enough to stop the "femicide" surrounding Ciudad Juárez and may be part of the problem.

Among the first victims to be noticed in the crime pages of the local press was Alma Chavira Farel, whose death is still used as the marker of the official count. Her corpse was found in January of 1993 . . . she had been raped, beaten, and strangled . . . but there is to this day no explanation of why. . . . The following May, the body of another raped and strangled victim . . . was found. . . . A third corpse appeared in June, stabbed and set on fire. . . . Another . . . had been raped, impaled, and knifed to death; her head had been bashed in.

—Alma Guillermoprieto, *New Yorker Magazine* (1993)

Since the death of Alma Chavira Farel in 1993, approximately 400 bodies of raped, tortured, and murdered women have been discovered in and around the border city of Ciudad Juárez, Mexico. In addition to these 400 instances of "femicide," scores of women from the area have also disappeared during the same time frame. Criminal investigations have led to a number of arrests; however, a large percentage of the crimes remain unsolved. Explanations for the murders include issues related to drug trade, prostitution, family squabbles, the high percentage of female workers employed at border factories.

Aside from the controversy surrounding the motives and circumstances that cause these murders, much of the attention directed toward Ciudad Juárez focuses on the apparent inability of law enforcement authorities to locate and prosecute the people responsible for the murders. Is it estimated that only about 20 percent of all the murders have resulted in a successful prosecution and sentencing. Because of the inexplicably high frequency of impunity, international pressure from non-governmental organizations and human rights advocates such as Amnesty International have attempted to apply international pressure on the various levels of government within Mexico in hopes of inspiring greater efforts and concrete results regarding the hundreds of unsolved murders. However, the Mexican government attests that the estimated number of murders is overstated and that the extent of unresolved cases is not significantly high. Despite this position, governmental involvement has emerged to help the investigatory process—including the U.S. FBI.

Yet, despite intervention at a federal level, the degree of progress concerning the killings has been disputed, and most of the cases still remain unresolved. Accusations of corruption, negligence, incompetence, cronyism, and indifference due to a "machista" culture of male-dominated bureaucracy have created new levels of animosity between human rights advocates and members of law enforcement and government assigned to the various cases. Family members of the victims have organized into several groups, including the Mexico Solidarity Network, designed to attract attention to not only the hundreds of unsolved murders, but also to their claims that the Mexican government is a primary suspect as to why these victims' killers continue to go unpunished.

However, Mexican authorities point to several signs of progress that have appeared since the federal government became involved in the investigations in 2003. Adopting a policy of "full transparency," crime rates dropped by 14 percent after the first year of federal intervention, 153 convictions were issued, and 101 government employees have been identified for negligence and other crimes committed during the handling of various cases. In addition, a number of women's shelters were funded and constructed, and programs were established to protect women.

While recognizing that more work still remains to be done, the Mexican government notes that through the contributions and coordination of both internal and international organizations and led by the Mexican federal government, major steps have been made toward solving and eventually stopping the femicide that has haunted Ciudad Juárez. However, citizen-based policy groups like the America's Program, International Relations Center remain steadfast in identifying continued institutional breakdowns at all levels of government that result in the persistence of these murders even after several years of federal involvement.

Updated Informative Document Regarding the Mexican Government's Actions in Ciudad Juarez, Chihuahua

Introduction

Between 1993 and May of 2004, Mexican authorities have identified 334 homicides of women in Ciudad Juárez, Chihuahua. Of these, 66% are motivated by intra-family or domestic violence, 26% are the result of violent sexual aggression and the remaining 8% have unknown motives. Despite the fact that these homicides were committed for varied reasons, by different perpetrators, under different circumstances and different criminal patterns, their magnitude and context have turned these crimes into a challenge to the Rule of Law and a grave threat to the human rights of women. The government of Mexico is committed to undertake all necessary endeavors to resolve and eradicate the roots that gave way to these crimes. . . .

Actions Undertaken at Different Governmental Levels

The government of Mexico has designed and set in motion a series of actions to resolve the homicides and their causes, based on the diagnostic study prepared by national authorities and the recommendations issued by international authorities interested in the issue which visited Ciudad Juárez, among them the Special Rapporteur for Extrajudicial Executions of the United Nations, Special Rapporteur on the Independence of Judges and Attorneys of the United Nations, the Inter-American Commission on Human Rights' Rapporteur on the Rights of Women, Executive Director of the United Nations Fund for Women (UNIFEM), experts of the United Nations' Committee for the Elimination of All Forms of Discrimination Against Women and experts of the United Nations' Office on Drugs and Crime. These actions are revised periodically to be updated and adapted to arising necessities. Some of the more relevant actions are:

a) State Level Actions

At the state level, the Governor of Chihuahua, Patricio Martínez, created by decree the Chihuahuense Institute for Women (ICHIMU), with a mandate to

From http://www.sre.gob.mx/substg/derechoshumanos/juarezingles.htm, August 2004.

foster the equality of opportunities for women in education, training, health, employment, development, as well as the full exercise of the rights of women and a culture of no violence to eliminate all forms of discrimination. In relation to the homicides of women in Ciudad Juárez, the ICHIMU has taken the following steps:

1. Initiated the Homicide Victims' Family Assistance Program, which includes providing psychological, medical, legal and economic support, as well as help with a wide array of services like access to housing, pension funds, food supply, education and reimbursement for funeral expenses. Currently 39 families in Ciudad Juárez and 2 in Chihuahua have benefited from the program.
2. Communication and coordination between the federal and state governments has improved and has translated into 2 forums for dialogue between governmental institutions and civil society.
3. A national survey about the dynamics of home relationships in 2003, realized under an agreement between INEGI (National Institute for Geography, Computer Information and Statistics) and INMUJER (National institute for Women), in order to obtain statistical information regarding home violence. . . .

The State Attorney General and the Municipal Authorities in Ciudad Juárez have begun training programs for the personnel in charge of the investigations, in order to sensitize them about gender issues and better their investigatory capabilities. An awareness campaign to prevent violence against women aimed at the general public has also been launched. The technological equipment has been substantively improved and special operatives have been implemented in high risk areas.

b) Federal Level Actions

In addition to the strategies of the state government to design and apply an integral program that responds to the diversity of causes that gave way to the homicides, the federal government complements state actions through the Sub-Commission for Coordination and Liaison to Prevent and Eradicate Violence Against Women in Ciudad Juárez, Chihuahua, of the National Inter-Secretarial Commission for Human Rights.

The Commission is made up of federal authorities whose actions may positively impact the situation of women in Ciudad Juárez (Ministry of Health, Ministry of Labor and Social Welfare, Ministry of Economy, Ministry of the Treasury and Public Credit, Ministry of Education, Ministry of Social Development, Ministry of the Interior, Ministry of Public Security, Ministry of Foreign Affairs, National Institute of Women, National Migration Institute and Office of the Attorney General). Similarly, non-governmental organizations participate in the Commission with equal footing to these entities, and as observers the National Commission for Human Rights and a Representative of UNIFEM.

This Commission is presided by Guadalupe Morfín Otero, who in addition is the head of the National Commission to Prevent and Eradicate Violence

Against Women in Ciudad Juárez, Chihuahua, a de-centralized organ of the Ministry of the Interior.

Commissioner Morfín is in charge of designing and executing the Program of Actions to Prevent and Eradicate Violence Against Women in Ciudad Juárez, Chihuahua (40 Point Program), aided by diverse public and private organizations. She is also responsible to promote actions and public policies that include crime prevention, support to crime victims and that foster social reconciliation in Ciudad Juárez, Chihuahua.

Nine months after her appointment, the Commissioner improved the coordination between agencies and has become an effective bridge between authorities and organized civil society. On June 3rd, 2004, she issued her first report (available at www.segob.gob.mx), in which she presents a social diagnostic of the situation in Ciudad Juárez, where she evaluates the 40 Point Program and proposes a new work program.

Since the Commission was established, the Mexican government has sought to provide all necessary resources for its optimal operation. Today, it has an 18 people staff, offices in both Mexico City and Ciudad Juárez, each of the institutions associated with it provide resources for its activities and 14 million pesos have been destined to strengthen its operation (equivalent to 1.4 million US dollars).

According to the 40 Point Program, the federal government entities have realized diverse activities, among them:

a. The installation of 4 shelters for women victims of domestic violence in Ciudad Juárez. Three of these are operated by civil society organizations that work in this arena.

b. Signing 26 cooperation agreements with Non-governmental Organizations (NGOs) in projects for social capital investment, prevention of domestic violence, attention to high risk and vulnerable groups, fostering a culture of legality (rule of law), combating corruption, community education, prevention and attention of addictions and promotion of a gender perspective.

c. The establishment of a Post-grade in Social Capital with international and national experts at the Autonomous University of Ciudad Juárez, the national institute for planning and Research, the Chihuahuense Business Foundation, A.C. and INDESOL.

d. Design of a program for the psychological assistance to the victims of urban violence that will be administered in conjunction with the National Autonomous University of Mexico (UNAM).

e. The design of two national campaigns against domestic violence, one by the National Institute for Women and the other by the Ministry of the Interior, including radio and television media outlets, which began in the month of March.

f. The transfer of a suspect from Chihuahua to the Ciudad Juárez Jail.

g. Plans to establish new community centers in Ciudad Juárez.

h. Opening 29 new day care centers administered by the Mexican Institute of Social Security (IMSS), by civil associations or in conjunction with IMSS and a private enterprise.

i. A data base of at risk children that will allow efficient identification of at risk persons, in order to better asses the social assistance they require.

j. Workshops and classes that seek, among other things, to include gender perspectives in the procurement of justice and the practice of law, as well as to raise awareness among women of their legal rights. Also, the program aims to train human development facilitators.

k. The creation of a Work Group to recuperate public spaces in Ciudad Juárez", which first task is the Project known as "La Acequia del Pueblo" (the Town's Water Gate), which is the basis for the creation of parks expected to indirectly benefit 750,000 people.

l. The establishment of specific programs by the National Council for Mental Health and the National Council Against Addictions in order to provide preventive and rehabilitation services, in terms of psychiatric and addiction problems.

The actions undertaken in the 40 Point Program have represented positive advances, even if modest in nature. An area where there has been substantive change for the better has been public security. Although much remains to be done, the actions in this area have contributed to lowering the criminal incidence rate by 14.5%.

Taking into account these advances, Commissioner Morfín created a new work program in order to more closely follow up on the activities under the 40 Point Program. The new emphasis is placed on the procurement and administration of justice, closer monitoring of the criminal investigations and prosecutions, victim assistance, giving much more attention is given to the families of victims of crime, strengthening of the social fabric and public policies that take gender perspectives into account. This plan has already been discussed with various civil organizations, as well as other governmental entities, and it is currently being revised in order to ensure its prompt implementation.

Investigative and Prosecutorial Actions Undertaken

In terms of investigation, resolution of the crimes and prosecution of the perpetrators, the Mexican government has undertaken several actions, among them:

a. Since 2002, Mexico has received specialized technical and consulting support from the United States' Federal Bureau of Investigations (FBI).

b. On April 16, 2003, the Attorney General of the Republic (PGR) assumed jurisdiction of 14 homicides of women that had been investigated by local authorities up to that point. This number has increased as the years have gone on.

c. Through a Collaborative Agreement, the federal and state governments established the Joint Agency for Investigation for the Homicides of Women in Ciudad Juárez, made up of officers from the PGR and state authorities in charge of the investigations. This agency has evolved over time and its joint efforts have strengthened on a daily basis.

d. On January 30th, 2004, the PGR established the office of the Special Prosecutor for the Attention of the Homicides of Women in the Municipality of Ciudad Juárez, Chihuahua. . . .

María López Urbina was appointed as the Special Prosecutor. She began her mandate on January 30th, 2004, and is a highly regarded jurist and investigator within the PGR.

The Special Prosecutor presented her first report on the 3rd of June, 2004, and informed about the first results of her activities, some of which, according to her work plan, are listed below:

I. Systematizing information regarding the homicides of women and related crimes.   Seeks to establish with clarity the number of victims, motives, patterns in the homicides of women in Ciudad Juárez, through the careful review of open files. This review allows for more reliability and confidence in the numbers and the pursuit of new lines of investigation that may contribute to identify those responsible for the crimes.

On April 7th, 2004, the Special Prosecutor for the homicides of women in Ciudad Juárez of the State Attorney General's Office reported that it had 307 files, corresponding to the 332 homicides registered up until that date. It also informed that of those cases, 218 had been solved (104 with a sentence entered and 114 in the process).

With the help of the National Center for Planning, Analysis and Information for Combating Crime (an institution of the PGR), the Special Prosecutor is inputting 225 files provided by the State government into a data base. This work is 59.61% completed. Taking into account the large volume of work and the necessity to account for her actions, the Special Prosecutor provides information every 4 months about 50 cases that have been examined. The first of these was included in the June 3rd report.

II. Program for addressing the crimes related to the homicides.   Its objective is to identify the federal jurisdiction crimes, as well as collaborate in the determination of possible avenues of investigation and pending endeavors for solving the crimes. As part of this task, possible administrative and penal responsibility of public officials involved in the cases is determined, in order for the pertinent authorities to ensure application of the law.

The resulting analysis of the first 50 files examined is as follows:

> The cause in 29 files is still under investigation. Of these, 20 have victims who have been identified and identification remains pending in 9 cases, which have been referred to the Forensic Genetics Data Bank. Seven of those 29 cases have been determined to be federal jurisdiction cases.

Of the 167 public servants who intervened in the processing of these 29 cases, 81 have been identified as having incurred in administrative or penal violations. Recently, state authorities announced that they had commenced investigation of 21 officers who were referred by the Special Prosecutor as having incurred in probable administrative and penal infractions related to the cases of homicides of women in Ciudad Juárez. Other people identified by the Special Prosecutor no longer work for the State Attorney General or live in the state. However, the authorities are evaluating different means of pursuing these investigations.

The remaining 21 files are being processed: 14 for Murder (intentional killing), 2 for homicide during a fight, 1 for negligent homicide (or manslaughter), 2 for parricide (killing of one's mother), 1 for felony murder (in the commission of a robbery), and 1 motivated by conspiracy to cover another crime. In 19 of these cases a sentence has been entered, against 23 different individuals.

Is Federal Jurisdiction Feasible in All Cases?

. . . [The] fact that the legal framework does not allow for federal jurisdiction to be exercised in all cases has not hindered cooperative efforts between governmental authorities of both levels. The review of case files allows the PGR to evaluate whether federal jurisdiction is viable in more cases than those already transferred. In fact the PGR took over administration of 7 of the last 50 cases reviewed so far.

Lastly, in order to avoid future situations like that of Ciudad Juárez, President Vicente Fox sent a legislative proposal to Congress, as a part of Constitutional reform package aimed at strengthening the Mexican justice system. This initiative intends to increase federal powers to transfer cases from state to federal jurisdiction.

III. Assistance program for reported cases of missing women. This program consists of determining the numbers of cases in which women have been reported missing and, when applicable, take proper action to ascertain their where abouts. The intention is to have precise and reliable information regarding reports of missing women.

In order to accomplish this, the Special Prosecutor created a data base exclusively for the Missing Women in Ciudad Juárez, Chihuahua, and has already combed through data provided by the various organizations involved. The Results evidence that from the year 1993 to March of 2004, there were 4,454 reports of women missing, of which 41 remain outstanding, having found 4,413 women so far.

The data base helped to find 7 women who had recently disappeared.

It is important to point out that there Attorney General of the Republic has specialized units operating in the state, dealing with all the missing women reported. The Attorney General is committed to investigating all reports with seriousness and acting responsibly, taking into account that the disappearances may result in the commission of crimes against the victims physical integrity, including attempts on their life.

IV. Victim assistance program. Its objective is to provide victims and people affected by the crimes under the jurisdiction of the Special Prosecutor, with legal advice and assistance, while at the same time promoting the effective reparations that they may have a right to.

This program provides medical and psychological services for victim's families and scholarships are sought to provide financial aid to those victims' families in need. Also, family members are given periodic information as to the state of investigative efforts.

In addition, the PGR has periodic meetings with NGOs, private charitable foundations and organizations, as well as media outlets.

Additional Efforts

In order to facilitate the work of the PGR, a Forensic Genetics Data Bank was established. The Data Bank stores genetic information obtained from recovered remains and possible family members of the victims, in order to facilitate identification efforts.

In addition, a National Victims of Crime Register Data Base was created, which stores federal crime information. Furthermore, a support fund for families of homicide victims in Ciudad Juárez was recently created. This Fund will receive monies from the federal government (25 million pesos to start) and will be available for donations from the State of Chihuahua. It will also be open to receive donations from public and private organizations, as well as individuals.

The federal and state governments recognize the need and the importance of dialogue and retrospective interaction with society-at-large. Although much work has been done with most of the mothers of the victims and organizations doing follow up on this issue, there are other NGOs that have adopted a more critical stand against the local government and are not willing to engage in a dialogue with these authorities.

Nevertheless, the State government and the Attorney General of Chihuahua have expressed their desire to continue reaching out to the public and remain open to dialogue with any organization interested in doing so. This openness and disposition are evidenced through the Attorney General's participation in the dialogue workshops established by mandate of the Governor of Chihuahua. Although the process has not been exempt from problems, overall the meetings have developed in a positive way.

The Government of Mexico recognizes and is conscious of the fact that changing cultural patterns requires constant effort and the application of public policies that slowly change society's perceptions. It also recognizes that cultural change and advances in the investigations could not be possible without adequate training for its personnel. Therefore the Mexican government has made an unprecedented effort to train personnel involved in these investigations and to ensure their professional permanence in public service. Special emphasis has been placed on the collection and handling of evidence, interviews and interrogations, practical investigation of homicides, kidnapping of minors, gender equality and human rights.

This year new homicides of women have been registered in Ciudad Juárez, motivated by diverse reasons. The treatment and investigation of these unfortunate events has been done with strict adherence to the measures instrumented by the authorities and in some cases several suspects have been detained. The objective is to prevent events of this nature to take place.

Conclusions

Both the state and federal governments have concentrated their efforts in addressing the problems of Ciudad Juárez, Chihuahua. Modest gains have been achieved over time and there is awareness that the actions undertaken have room for improvement. The recommendations of the diverse international organizations complement national diagnostic studies and have been very useful in the design of new strategies.

It is a fact that in the beginning, the dimension of the problem was not clearly evaluated. There were failures that hindered the authorities from intervening in an opportune and effective manner. Nevertheless, one should recognize that these failures have slowly been corrected and that, over the last years, there has been greater follow-up to the investigations, important economic resources have been invested and public policies aimed at building a culture of equity and justice have been adopted. The Government of Mexico reiterates its commitment to continue with these efforts.

Kent Paterson

The Juarez Women's Murders:
Mothers Step Up Justice Campaign
as a Cover-Up Takes Hold

Like other mothers, Patricia Cervantes has heard the promises sung like empty lyrics by a chorus of presidents, governors, and law enforcement authorities. Their reassuring words vow to end impunity and find justice for the murdered daughters.

Cervantes, whose 19-year-old daughter Neyra was raped, tortured, and murdered last year in Chihuahua City, has seen authorities defile her loved one's case to such an extent that someone even put a man's skull on Neyra's skeleton in order to make it appear that a full body had been recovered. She's watched in horror as Chihuahua state police officers picked up her nephew David Meza and then—according to the young man's account—tortured him into falsely admitting to killing Neyra. Speaking to reporters in Ciudad Juarez, Cervantes had a simple message: She wants her daughter's real killers caught. "We don't want words, we want action."

Little has changed in the cases of Neyra Cervantes and the more than 400 women and girls who have been murdered in Ciudad Juarez and Chihuahua state since 1993, according to Amnesty International and press accounts. Dozens more remain missing. About 100 of the victims are thought to have been killed by serial rape murderers. Still, police have arrested no credible suspects in the serial killings, while widely believed scapegoats like Meza remain locked up in jail, and new murders stain an already bloody landscape.

Chihuahua's new governor, PRI member Jose Reyes Baeza, took office on October 3 and was immediately confronted with the femicide issue as a top priority. He appointed a woman, Patricia Gonzalez, as new state attorney general; met with the relatives of murder victims; reshuffled law enforcement and women's services personnel; renamed the organized crime-linked Chihuahua State Judicial Police, and vowed to "lower impunity and clean up the security forces."

But things have not gotten off to a good start for the governor. Within hours of his inauguration, a woman's body was discovered in Chihuahua City. In the next several weeks, 6 other women and girls were killed in Chihuahua City and Juarez. Some of the latest killings follow a previous pattern, when changes in government or public events related to women's rights have been

Kent Paterson, "The Juarez Women's Murders: Mothers Step Up Justice Campaign as a Cover-Up Takes Hold," Americas Program (Silver City, NM: Interhemispheric Resource Center: November 24, 2004).

accompanied by the discovery of new bodies. As if a macabre message were being delivered.

A victim recovered on November 25, the International Day to Eliminate Violence Against Women, has been tentatively identified as Martha Cecilia Vargas, a mother of two who disappeared last August after leaving home to search for work in the maquiladora industry. If the victim's identify is confirmed, the Vargas murder would be the latest example of how authorities have underplayed the true number of missing/murdered women in the borderlands. The young mother's name was not on an official list of 35 disappeared Juarez women released by federal and state officials earlier in November.

A Caravan for Justice

With justice nowhere in sight, Patricia Cervantes and other victims' relatives embarked on a mega-tour of 54 U.S. and Canadian cities in October. Dubbed the International Caravan for Justice in Juarez and Chihuahua and co-sponsored by the Mexico Solidarity Network and numerous local groups, members of the Juarez-based *Nuestras Hijas de Regreso a Casa* (Return Our Daughters Home) and the Chihuahua City-based *Justicia para Nuestras Hijas* (Justice for Our Daughters) spoke to thousands of people, ranging from high school students to seniors, and appeared on local news shows. They testified before the Inter-American Commission on Human Rights (IACHR) in Washington , DC and met with U.S. congressional representatives.

In Las Vegas, New Mexico, the mayor proclaimed a day of solidarity, and new ground was broken when the New York City council passed a resolution promising to disinvest its money from companies that have maquiladora plants in Juarez if they do not do more to protect their workers. For caravan participants like Marilu Garcia, whose 17-year-old sister Lilia Alejandra, was raped and murdered in Juarez in 2001, the tour was bittersweet. "I would have liked to have a caravan for a reason of happiness," said Garcia. "It's shameful that family members have to join a caravan in this way and go to other countries to ask for justice, because they don't get it in their own country." After arriving home on October 31, the traveling mothers had their photos involuntarily snapped by officers with the Federal Investigations Agency (AFI), and some activists reported being followed by the Juarez city police in the days afterward.

The Mexican Government Drops the Ball—Again

Already an international scandal, the unresolved murders of young women in Chihuahua not only call into question the Fox administration's human rights record, but threaten the very premise of governance as well. In Juarez, "the rule of law is broken," flatly states federal PRD deputy Marcela Lagarde, the president of the Mexican Chamber of Deputies' femicide commission.

Fed up with the way the Chihuahua State Attorney General's Office (PGJE) has long mishandled the murder cases, activists last year pressured

President Fox into assuming a greater federal role. He named the former head of the Jalisco State Human Rights Commission, Guadalupe Morfin, as the new Commissioner for the Prevention and Elimination of Violence Against Women in Ciudad Juarez. The President then appointed Maria Lopez Urbina special federal prosecutor. It was widely expected that Lopez Urbina would immediately launch a criminal investigation in search of the murderers.

But one year later, the federal record is beginning to resemble the state one. Although Lopez Urbina's office located some of the missing women alive, it has not detained any serial murder suspects or assigned many new cases to federal investigators. Reviewing old state files, the special prosecutor singled out 129 former and current PGJE officials for negligence and possible prosecution for omission of duties. Lopez Urbina then turned their names over to the PGJE—the same agency whose personnel were accused of committing the violations in the first place—for legal action.

The new PGJE administration has suspended about 20 of its officials, but several have avoided prosecution through legal maneuvers. Notably, Lopez Urbina did not mention two past Chihuahua governors, Francisco Barrio of the National Action Party (PAN) and Patricio Martinez of the PRI, or any of the numerous state attorneys general and Juarez district attorneys as bearing any responsibility in the botched investigations. All the individuals identified by Lopez Urbina were mid- or lower-level officials, and a dozen of them have filed defamation charges against the special prosecutor.

Former Prosecutor for Women's Homicides in Ciudad Juarez, Zulema Bolivar, one of the officials identified by Lopez Urbina for alleged negligence and the current assistant director of the Juarez city jail, created a scandal of her own in November when she declared that her previous superiors, ex-State Attorney General Arturo Gonzalez and former Juarez District Attorney Jose Manuel Ortega, had irregularly yanked her off a notorious 2001 case in which 8 women were found murdered in the middle of Juarez. Two bus drivers are widely suspected of being framed up by the PGJE for the crimes. While Bolivar's declarations signify that her supervisors might have engaged in far more than negligence, neither man was named by Lopez Urbina in her recent reports. Asked by the local press if Bolivar's statements would be investigated, Chihuahua State Attorney General Gonzalez said legal impediments prevented her from doing so. Meanwhile, Ortega continues to work as legal director of the PGJE.

The nonprofit Washington Office on Latin America criticized Lopez Urbina's record so far, noting that the same deficient files she used to identify alleged state law enforcement violations were the basis for statements downplaying femicide. Indeed, Lopez Urbina's murder statistics are far short of the probable number of victims, who are sometimes omitted from the death toll, according to eyewitness and family versions. For instance, on September 23, 2002 , the day ex-Governor Patricio Martinez was in Juarez to inaugurate an ill-fated inter-institutional commission to address the murders, the body of 26-year-old Ericka Perez was tossed onto an empty lot.

The same day Perez's body was found, the skeleton of another suspected murder victim was found behind a maquiladora plant. Also, Juana Sandoval vanished. Four months later, she was found raped and murdered along with two other victims.

Initial police versions in the media reported that Perez had been raped and murdered by strangulation. Then-State Attorney General Jose "Chito" Silva quickly proclaimed that Perez had succumbed to a drug overdose, and her death was not placed in the official femicide roster.

An unemployed maquiladora worker and former employee of the Instituto Mexico private school, Perez disappeared after leaving home to look for work, according to the victim's mother, Elia Escobedo. The distraught Escobedo now must care for Ericka's two children on wages earned from washing and ironing clothes.

Scapegoats Rot Away

Although the Mexican government claims to uphold international human rights agreements disallowing torture, the continued imprisonment of various suspects in the serial murders despite the lack of any hard evidence against them suggests otherwise, because the judges won't admit recantations as evidence. Besides David Meza, other suspects include U.S. citizen Cynthia Kiecker and her Mexican husband Ulises Perzabal. Both claim they were savagely tortured. The couple is currently being tried for the 2003 murder of 16-year-old Viviana Rayas in Chihuahua City, and a decision in their case is expected very soon.

Then there is bus driver Victor "El Cerrillo" Garcia. Detained with fellow driver Gustavo Gonzalez in 2001 for the murders of 8 women, Garcia and Gonzalez accused members of the Chihuahua State Judicial Police (PJE) of torturing them. Gonzalez's lawyer, Mario Escobedo Jr., who complained to colleagues that he was threatened to abandon the case, was later shot to death by PJE officers led by the same commander who had allegedly overseen the detention and torture of the bus drivers. Cleared by a judge, the commander, Alejandro Castro, then went on to work for a while in security at the federal government's anti-corruption ministry in Mexico City. In 2003, Gonzalez himself mysteriously died in a Chihuahua prison before ever receiving a sentence.

Commissioner Morfin gives credence to reports by the United Nations, Inter-American Commission on Human Rights, National Human Rights Commission and Amnesty International that suspects including Garcia have been tortured into confessing to crimes they did not commit. Morfin's office has promoted the application of the Istanbul Protocol, a rigorous method of documenting torture, in confirming suspects' claims. Earlier this year, Morfin secured Garcia's transfer back to a Juarez jail from Chihuahua City and set up interviews with PGR personnel to verify the suspect's torture allegations under the Istanbul standard.

But Morfin's efforts were shot down last month when Chihuahua Judge Gustavo Munoz Gamboa, ignoring both the pending application of the Istanbul Protocol and the lack of any hard physical evidence against Garcia—handed the man a 50-year prison sentence for murder.

The Specter of a Cover-Up Looms Large

With both state and federal efforts mired in chaos, there are several lines of investigation about who is actually responsible for the femicides that merit further investigation. Leads include a network of private computer schools, bars, and businesses operating in both the downtowns of Juarez and Chihuahua City; police officers from different agencies; drug traffickers; wealthy businessmen; politicians; immigrant smugglers; El Paso residents; and elements within the PGJE—the same law enforcement agency supposedly probing the women's murders.

"They're all in this up to their necks, in the murders and kidnappings," charges Evangelina Arce. Frustrated at state inaction, Arce began her own investigation into the 1998 disappearances of her daughter Silvia and a friend, Griselda Mares. She sniffed out a trail that led to two Federal Judicial Police officers as the probable culprits. The men have not been detained, but Arce says she has been under surveillance by Chihuahua state police, beaten up on the street, and hit by a car since speaking out.

Another unpursued lead concerns Hector Lastra, a former PGJE official who was arrested last February on charges of running a prostitution ring of underage teenage girls. Denying the accusations, Lastra was quickly released on bail. Reportedly, Lastra pressured teenage girls working at Juarez fast food restaurants into having sex with prominent businessmen. Clients were allegedly offered catalogues with photos of the girls, whose age and physical appearance resembled those of previous serial killer victims. At a meeting with the Mexican Chamber of Deputies femicide commission in Juarez last month, attorney Lucha Castro, who represents family members of murder victims, said that two of the girls who lodged charges against Lastra denounced that the ring had been taking minors from Ciudad Juarez to the Chihuahua City campaign headquarters of the current Chihuahua governor. Commissioner Morfin, whose office has repeatedly spoken out about the gravity of the Lastra case, earlier requested protection for the family members of the girls involved.

Activists Move Forward

Undaunted, victims' relatives and women's activists are pressing ahead with a multi-pronged struggle. Lawyer Lucha Castro plans to press on with cases filed with the Inter-American Commission on Human Rights that accuse the Mexican government of violating the rights of the victims and their family members. In the United States , activists are supporting resolutions in the House and Senate, sponsored by Rep. Hilda Solis (D-CA) and Sen. Jeff Bingaman (D-NM), respectively, that would offer greater U.S. technical assistance to the investigations and formally put the femicide issue on the agenda of bilateral U.S.-Mexico relations.

In Mexico City, a group of academics and activist have formed Grupo Alternativas, issuing specific recommendations to assign federal jurisdiction to all the murder cases and put one autonomous, unitary law enforcement agency in charge. The plan will be considered by the Mexican Chamber of

Deputies femicide commission, according to commission president Marcela Lagarde. Additionally, the femicide commission intends to review a rash of women's murders in other Mexican states besides Chihuahua, among others, Sonora, Tamaulipas, Coahuila, and Guanajuato.

During the last week of November, dozens of mothers of murder victims traveled to Mexico City to meet with government officials including President Fox and attend anti-femicide demonstrations in the capital city. Among their demands were renewed calls for the federal government to take over the murder investigations; the release of political prisoners, and the installation of 4,000 video security cameras in Juarez. While Fox instructed his cabinet members to work more closely with the mothers, Norma Ledesma, the mother of a 16-year-old computer school student raped and murdered in Chihuahua City in 2002, was quoted as stating that she was "more disappointed than ever" in the government's response to the femicide. A separate, unsuccessful attempt to meet with Fox's wife, Martha Sahagun, likewise prompted denunciations by the mothers. According to Norma Andrade, Lilia Alejandra Garcia's mother, she and her other daughter, Marilu, were detained by police for three hours outside the Mexican White House, Los Pinos, after trying to enter to deliver a petition. Complained Andrade: "the victims are treated worse than the responsible parties and murderers of this femicide."

Some say the Mexican government's time ran out a long time ago. Chihuahua City women's activist Graciela Ramos, who works with *Mujeres por Mexico and Mujeres de Negro,* says her groups advocate bringing international specialists to solve the murders. "In order to get at the truth, let people come who know how to investigate, who don't have any commitments to any party and who don't have to protect any government officials or ex-officials," says Ramos. "For this, a large budget is needed, and a lot of will and determination is required to arrive at a solution."

POSTSCRIPT

Has Mexican Governmental Involvement Helped Stop the Killings in Ciudad Juárez?

Despite both governmental and international intervention, the crimes against women in and around Cuidad Juárez continue. Perhaps the most significant concern related to the femicide is the degree to which the perpetrators of these crimes go unpunished. For a variety of reasons, corruption being the most cited explanation, few criminals have been brought to justice related to these crimes. The controversy will persist until not only the culpable parties are caught and identified, but also punished for their crimes. Between January 1 and April 25, 2006, another 20 women have been beaten, raped, and killed. However, a number of changes have recently been made, and new efforts have been put forth to hopefully lead to more arrests, more prosecutions, and, ultimately, greater justice for victims.

For example, the Mexican government has appointed a new special prosecutor—Alicia Elena Pérez Duarte—who will head the newly formed national special prosecutor's office whose mission will focus on violent crimes against women. However, symptomatic of the problems that have plagued governmental efforts, this new office replaces a similar office that was established in 2004 yet has remained without leadership since October 2005. The original appointee of the office, María López Urbina, resigned from her post due to public pressure related to ineffectiveness after just 16 months of service. Her replacement, Mireille Roccatti, lasted less than a half-year. The greatest distinction within the new office is that it will focus on abuse and murder of women not only in Juárez, but at a national level—a move that many hope will lead to better communication and coordination between states, cities, and all governmental districts within Mexico. Numerous reports of violence against women have also surfaced in Sonora, Veracruz, Chiapas, Oaxaca, and Mexico City, among others. Among her first objectives, Pérez Duarte has pledged to prosecute what are now 177 governmental officials who have been cited for numerous crimes such as alleged participation in the murders, criminal negligence, and a variety of transgressions related to corruption. In addition, Pérez Duarte can employ the powers of the Mexican Supreme Court as well as international tribunals, if necessary. Mexico has also recently appointed a special investigatory commission of a dozen legislators to help create more transparency and infiltrate any internal corruption that may exist.

In addition, through President Fox's willingness to allow international organizations such as Amnesty International, Human Rights Watch, as well as a number of international women's rights groups to monitor governmental activities related to the murders, a new hopefulness for justice has emerged. Fox's policy of "transparency" in government has helped instill confidence that the Mexican government is open to third-party interests by sharing with them information and knowledge related to both the crimes and procedures.

However, the legacy of injustice endures. Inconsistencies and contradictions within the PGR report continue to undermine progress. For example, the PGR dismissed a number of recommendations and issues raised by critics of the government's approach. One of more controversial components of the reports is that the government still remains unwilling to view the crimes from a gender-based perspective, in effect stating that these rapes, beatings, and killings bear no significance to the fact that the victims were female. In addition, the PGR report insists that only 20 percent of the crimes involved "sexual violence"—which is definitionally differentiated from gender violence, domestic violence, and social violence, all of which exclude gender as a factor in their legal definitions. Many argue these legal loopholes that eliminate the recognition of gender as a factor in the femicide are emblematic of machismo in Latin American culture and significantly inhibit the truthful prosecution of these cases. Other issues that remain unresolved are fraudulent arrests coupled with torture-driven confessions, as well as the lack of safety for women working at the maquiladoras.

Since the body of Alma Chavira Farel was found in January 1993, the death toll related to violent crimes against women in Juárez continues to rise. For a copy in English of the PGR's fourth report on the Cuidad Juárez murders, visit http://www.bayefsky.com/html/mexico_cedaw_article8.php. For updated information on the Mexican government's efforts to end the femicide, visit http://www.sre.gob.mx/substg/derechoshumanos/infrjuarez.htm. For the perspective of the Human Rights Watch, visit http://www.hrw.org/reports/2006/mexico0506/6.htm. For the perspective of a Latin-based women's rights organization visit http://www.libertadlatina.org/Crisis_Lat_Mexico_Juarez_Femicide.htm. For more information on the relationship between maquiladoras and women, see Altha J. Cravey's *Women and Work in Mexico's Maquiladoras*. For a visual chronicle of the crimes against women in Cuidad Jáurez, view Lourdes Portillo's 2001 documentary *Señorita Extraviada*.

ISSUE 7

Immigration: Should Illegal Immigrant Gang Members Be Granted Legal Clemency from U.S. Law?

YES: Greg Campbell, from "Death by Deportation," *Boulder Weekly* (May 27, 2004)

NO: Heather Mac Donald, from "The Illegal-Alien Crime Wave," *City Journal* (Winter 2004)

ISSUE SUMMARY

YES: Greg Campbell, an award-winning investigative journalist and current editor of *Fort Collins Weekly*, asserts that granting sanctuary to reformed, yet illegal, Latino gang members who assist law enforcement officials by testifying against gangs is the proper course of action, rather than deporting them back to their dangerous old neighborhoods.

NO: Heather Mac Donald, a lawyer and contributing editor to *City Journal*, claims that sanctuary policies inhibit members of law enforcement from reporting immigration violations to federal authorities, therefore, allowing dangerous illegal aliens to remain at-large and free to commit serious crimes with impunity.

Soon after the assassination of Catholic Archbishop Óscar Romero in 1980, El Salvador became embroiled in a bloody civil war that would last 12 years and cost the lives of tens of thousands. With the financial support of the United States, estimated at approximately $1 billion, the right-wing government supported death squads who engaged in torture and indiscriminate killings. Perhaps the most egregious example of the human rights violations endorsed by the military junta was the El Mozote Massacre, where 900 men, women, and children were systematically tortured and shot in El Mozote's public square due to their alleged harboring of anti-government guerrillas known as the FMLN (Farabundo Martí National Liberation Front). In order to escape death and persecution of this nature, many Salvadorians fled, seeking refuge in Honduras, Nicaragua, and—accounting for nearly one-half of all refugees—the

United States. However, for many refugees, transitioning from the legacy of an arguably U.S.-inspired civil war to American society proved to be extremely difficult, and many found security and opportunity through La Mara Salvatrucha, which has become one of the most violent and powerful gangs worldwide.

MSNBC reports that La Mara Salvatrucha, otherwise known as MS-13, is considered by the U.S. Federal Bureau of Investigation to be the most dangerous gang in the United States. MS-13 is largely comprised of illegal Latino immigrants from a variety of countries including El Salvador, Honduras, Nicaragua, Mexico, and Belize. La Mara was formed in Los Angeles during the El Salvadorian civil war by a group of El Salvadorians who sought to protect themselves against the powerful Mexican gangs of Los Angeles. Since that time, La Mara has spread throughout the United States, maintaining significant membership in New York, Illinois, Michigan, Washington, D.C., and Florida, estimated at nearly 20,000 nationwide. Global membership within the gang is expanding rapidly and is estimated at nearly 70,000 with its highest concentrations in Central America and El Salvador. This growth is largely the result of the U.S. policy of deporting gang members to their home country where they often recruit and eventually bring new members into the United States. The membership of illegal aliens in gangs similar to MS-13 in the United States is unclear, ranging anywhere from 20 to 60 percent or higher.

Deportation is one of a number of methods that U.S. law enforcement officials employ as part of their efforts in treating crimes committed by illegal aliens. However, the issues related to arresting illegal aliens complicate the prosecutory options available to police. Many cities in the United States have clemency laws where it is illegal for police to arrest a person based solely on immigrant status, unless that person is caught in the act of committing a major crime. Therefore, even though a police officer may have firsthand knowledge of the illegal status of a specific gang member, the officer cannot take action until that person has committed a separate criminal act beyond merely his or her immigration status.

However, many gang members who are in the United States illegally want to free themselves from the influence of gangs such as MS-13. Yet, without sanctuary laws, illegal aliens who come forward to police to testify against members of their gang risk deportation and may very likely face serious consequences, frequently torture and death, upon their return to their homeland as a result of their actions against their former gang members.

The issue of granting clemency to illegal aliens who are gang members is a double-edged sword for members of both the judicial and legal branches of government. Heather Mac Donald, a senior fellow at the Manhattan Institute for Policy Research, explains how granting clemency to illegal aliens who may be members of gangs undermines the powers of law enforcement and complicates the U.S.' ability to arrest and prosecute dangerous criminals. Investigative journalist Greg Campbell reveals that by not fully accounting for the political, historical, and social contexts of why many of these illegal aliens seek sanctuary here in the United States, U.S. law enforcement officials may be losing opportunities to disrupt gang activities in the United States and unwittingly sending reformed or non-criminally inclined immigrants back to their homeland where they may be awaiting a sentence of death.

Greg Campbell

Death by Deportation

They say you don't hear the shot that kills you. Bullets always outrun the reports that announce them, and if the aim is good, death comes before the whip-crack of the shot can catch up. There's no telling whether or not this was the case with 16-year-old Edgar Chocoy, who was gunned down March 27 in the streets of Villanueva, a town overrun by street gangs on the outskirts of Guatemala City. The day he was killed, he'd come out of hiding at his aunt's house to buy juice and lingered in the littered intersections of the crime-ridden city to watch a Roman Catholic procession of saints through the streets. He never returned. By the time his family was told of his murder four days later, he'd already been buried in an unmarked grave in a cemetery for the homeless.

Chocoy's death came as a surprise to no one, least of all him. In spite of all of his efforts to avoid this fate, his life ended much as he'd predicted it would—in a flare of violence that's all too familiar in Guatemala's cities. Years earlier, at an age when most children are more concerned with their grades than their imminent murders, Chocoy sought every avenue of escape. Knowing that he'd been "green lighted"—marked for death—by members of a notorious gang he was trying to untangle himself from, he hid out with relatives until that became too dangerous for them, bused alone to Mexico, then illegally entered the United States in search of his mother who'd left him when he was 6 months old. Two years after he left, however, he was deported back to Guatemala by a Denver immigration judge who either didn't believe his testimony that he would be killed there or didn't care. By denying his application for asylum in the United States, Judge James Vandello effectively sentenced him to death.

Two and a half weeks after being returned to Villanueva, street executioners carried out that sentence, just as Chocoy said they would.

He'd heard those bullets coming for years.

Mara Salvatrucha

From the outset, Edgar Chocoy didn't stand a chance. Born to an impoverished Guatemalan family in a city where wild street gangs openly battle overwhelmed security forces, the course of his short life followed those of all too many children in Central America who are abandoned or neglected by their parents. When he was 6 months old, his mother left him in the care of her father so that she could work in the United States. Chocoy lived with his grandfather—who was always either at work or at church—his uncle who sold drugs for a living and his aunt. He'd only met his father once. No one bothered to put him into school until he was 9 or 10.

As solace for his loneliness, Chocoy made friends of the kids he met in the street and at school. Many of the older children came to be like the family he'd never had. The trouble was that they were all members of a street gang that the Central Intelligence Agency calls one of the most notorious of the thousands of gangs that lay siege to Central America: Mara Salvatrucha, or MS. The name is derived from a species of aggressive swarming ants and, according to Al Valdez, an investigator for the Orange County District Attorney's Office in California, formed in the Los Angeles Rampart neighborhood in the 1980s. Its original members were Salvadorian refugees who, during that country's civil war, fought with the paramilitary group Farabundo Marti National Liberation Front and La Mara, a violent street gang.

"Like many other street gangs, MS initially formed for protection, but quickly developed a reputation for being organized and extremely violent," Valdez wrote in a 2000 article for the National Alliance of Gang Investigators. "Mara Salvatrucha is truly an international gang."

In Guatemala, MS is involved in everything from fencing cars stolen from the United States to trafficking military firearms. Members are easily identified by their elaborate tattoos, and their numbers are estimated at 100,000 in Guatemala alone. The extent of their criminal enterprise is massive and involves extortion, bold robberies, random assaults and brutal murders. By the time Chocoy was befriended by the gang, Central American countries began to crack down on the region's estimated quarter-million gang members with bloody results. In response, MS began dismembering victims and leaving notes on body parts warning governments to back off.

It's not known if Edgar Chocoy knew this level of detail about the gang that he suddenly found himself a member of in the summer of 2000. All he knew is that his new "friends" taught him how to rob chains and watches from pedestrians. They gave him a sense of belonging and purpose, however misguided it may have been. As he explained it to the judge during the Jan. 4 hearing on his asylum application, "They were the only friends I had, and I only knew them... I thought they were the only family I had."

It's unlikely that he could have known what he was really getting into; after all, he was only 12 years old at the time.

Deadly Decisions

If his testimony before the Denver immigration court was truthful, Chocoy didn't seem cut out for the violent life of a gangster, even though he soon sported their tattoos, a requirement of Mara Salvatrucha members. According to a transcript of his hearing provided by his attorney Kim Salinas of Fort Collins, he tried to avoid fighting with other gangs or beating people with rocks and bats, as they often did. When a fight seemed imminent, he made up excuses to go home.

If he'd stayed in the gang, he might have eventually toughened up, gotten over his disdain for violence and ended up as one of the thousands of murderers who rule Guatemala's streets. But when he was 14 he visited a different neighborhood and met kids who weren't in a gang. They came from a wealthy family, and Chocoy enjoyed playing soccer with them. He'd visit their homes and play video games, getting a tantalizing taste of the sort of home life he'd longed for but never had for himself. He stopped wearing the tight white T-shirts and baggy pants preferred by the gangsters, and he became more and more scarce at their nightly 6 p.m. "hang-out" sessions, which regularly turned into crime sprees.

By distancing himself from Mara Salvatrucha, Edgar took his life in his hands. One of the rules learned quickly as a member of Mara Salvatrucha is that you do not leave the gang. He was beaten and robbed for dropping out of sight, and finally he was told that he would be killed unless he paid the gang 3,000 quetcales—the equivalent of $375—in a week.

He stopped going to school and went into hiding at his aunt's house. Chocoy probably never saw his new friends again, the ones whose normal lives inspired him to quit Mara Salvatrucha. In fact, he rarely went outdoors at all, doing nothing in his aunt's house except counting the hours. The one time he ventured outside, at night in the hopes of avoiding his MS tormentors, he was chased by them at gunpoint, threatening to shoot if he didn't come to them with the money they demanded.

After that, his aunt's house became a prison. MS members stalked the streets and waited for him across town at his grandfather's house. His aunt finally told him he had to leave because, as he told Judge Vandello, "she didn't want anything to happen to her... She knew that they didn't care about killing somebody."

His mother in L.A., whom he barely knew, sent him money for a bus ticket to Mexico City.

At 14 years old, Chocoy left Guatemala in fear for his life.

Deport Them All

There's nothing unique about Chocoy's flight north in an attempt to escape the violence that is synonymous with Mara Salvatrucha. In the past six months, thousands have done so, a wave of tattooed refugees who see the United States as a safe haven from the persecution they know will befall them for trying to escape Mara Salvatrucha's clutches. Joining them in the exodus north are the gang members themselves who are getting out of the way of governmental crackdowns in El Salvador and Honduras. Guatemala has yet to institute a similarly tough anti-gang dragnet, but it's expected to adopt one soon. All of these refugees and refugees-from-justice crash into one another in Mexican border towns where their wars with one another—as well as with indigenous vigilante groups—simply continue regardless of what country they're in.

Mexico, of course, isn't the last stop—everyone is headed for the border, and MS gangs are present in California, Oregon, Alaska, Texas, Nevada, Utah, Oklahoma, Illinois, Michigan, New York, Maryland, Virginia, North Carolina, Georgia, Florida and Washington, D.C. Most members are in the United States illegally.

The U.S. response to this wave of criminals from the south has been simple: round them up and deport them. In October, local and federal law enforcement conducted "Operation Fed Up" which resulted in more than 60 arrests of Mara Salvatrucha members in Charlotte, N.C., who were immediately processed for deportation.

The main tool used by judges to decide deportations such as these is a 1996 law that banishes illegal immigrants from the United States for life if they break the law, resulting in the biggest dragnet in U.S. history. More than half a million people have been captured and deported and their crimes range from petty theft to murder. According to government figures, in 2003, illegal criminals were being deported to more than 160 countries at a rate of one every seven minutes.

This catch-all approach to the problem has certainly rid the U.S. of some violent criminals, but it's also been disastrous on more than a few occasions. The law doesn't discriminate between volatile MS members and generally law-abiding illegals who may have come to the United States as infants. This is what happened to Eddie and Edgar Garcia of Sanford, Colo. They'd crossed the border at ages 4 and 6 respectively, and their town was filled with stories of how they helped their neighbors, supported their parents, played high school football and made good grades. But when one of them was stopped for driving without a license, they were both deported to Palomas, Mexico, where they hadn't been in 16 years and where they knew no one.

On a more global scale, the "deport them all and let their home governments sort them out" approach is overwhelming these criminals' home governments, according to the results of a six-month investigation by the Associated Press. In Jamaica, one out of every 106 men over the age of 15 is a criminal deportee from the United States.

In Honduras, according to the latest figures from Interpol, murders increased from 1,615 in 1995 to 9,241 in 1998, after the first wave of what is now 7,000 criminal deportees.

"We're sending back sophisticated criminals to unsophisticated, unindustrialized societies," says Valdez, the Orange County gang expert. "They overwhelm local authorities."

But sometimes, those who are sent back are the ones who tried to leave gang life to escape to something better: a home life where instead of robbery, assault and the fear of being murdered, a child looks forward to weekend soccer games and love from his family.

Homeboy Without a Home

Edgar Chocoy found neither of those in his mother's home when he eventually crossed the border and located her in L.A. According to his own testimony, he barely knew her and didn't stay with her for long. He started school in L.A., but couldn't speak English. His MS tattoos made him a target of local gangsters who thought he was a member of a rival gang. Neither school nor life with his mom lasted long: He was kicked out of the school for fighting and kicked out of his mom's house because he no longer went to school.

Scared of the idea of having to live on the street, he fell in with people he'd met on the L.A. streets—all of whom were gang members.

According to Chocoy's Fort Collins attorney, Kim Salinas, he didn't officially join the L.A. gang but he was involved in some of their activities. He transferred drugs from place to place and was given a .25-caliber pistol to protect the gang members. According to his testimony, he did this in exchange for having a place to sleep. In May 2002, he was arrested for possessing a firearm and again on July 28, 2002, for possession of cocaine base. On Jan. 15, 2003, he was arrested again for possession of a firearm.

Because of his young age, his violations were adjudicated, but he was sent to an Alamosa, Colo., detention camp in the custody of the INS because he was in the United States illegally. It was at the detention camp when he first heard of the concept of political asylum, and in October, Salinas began preparing his arguments that if he returned to Guatemala, he would be killed by Mara Salvatrucha gang members.

"I am certain that if I had stayed in Guatemala the members of the gang MS would have killed me," Chocoy wrote in an affidavit. "I have seen them beat people up with baseball bats and rocks and shoot at them. I know they kill people. I know they torture people with rocks and baseball bats. I know that if I am returned to Guatemala I will be tortured by them. I know that they will kill me if I am returned to Guatemala. They will kill me because I left their gang. They will kill me because I fled and did not pay them the money that they demanded."

The gang wasn't the only worry awaiting Chocoy if he were to be sent back—former gang members have everyone to worry about. Not only was he still marked for death by Mara Salvatrucha, but possibly also by the police and vigilante gangs who often take matters into their own hands by leveling street justice upon those they fear will continue their lives of crime once they're returned to Guatemala.

Among his biggest problem were Chocoy's tattoos, which forever branded him as a member of Mara Salvatrucha. When he was in L.A., he'd heard about a group called Homeboy Industries, which specialized in removing gang tattoos, and he'd gone through two of the painful procedures before being moved to Colorado to await his deportation hearing. But having the tattoos removed was just as much of a fateful decision: If an MS member ever found out about it, there would be no way to fake it and profess that he wanted to join the gang again, if only for self-preservation. "They'll know who he is whether he has his tattoos removed or not," Salinas told the judge during Chocoy's hearing. "In fact, arguably that makes him even more of a target because that's more evidence that he did leave the gang . . . and would make him even more subject to their persecution."

At his Jan. 4 hearing, Chocoy pleaded with the judge for his life. His testimony is punctuated by numerous statements that he would be killed if he were returned. As Salinas put it in her closing arguments, Chocoy made a number of bad decisions in his young life, "but he also made a very good decision, that is, to leave the gang," she testified. "But when he made that decision, he was punished by persecution . . . Edgar made a choice to . . . escape from the life he'd known and to escape from the Mara Salvatrucha . . . He was denied that chance because the gang Mara Salvatrucha controls through force and fear because it doesn't serve their interest to have children leave them to play soccer and video games. Edgar made a decision to better his life and for that decision he was beaten, his life was threatened and he was forced out of his home, out of his school and out of his country.

"Edgar's now before you for his final chance to save his life," she continued. "He's asking you not to send him back to a country where he's been identified as one who must be killed. He's asking you not to send him back into the arms of his persecutors. He's asking you for one final chance to escape the gangs and become a child, a child who's safe from fear and danger, a child who's free to attend school, to pursue a career, to live in a home [with] a family . . . He's asking for the opportunity to become a productive adult. He's asking that you not deny him his ultimate chance."

The Death Sentence

In giving his verbal decision about Chocoy's application for asylum, Judge Vandello recapped Chocoy's case and considered a slew of supporting documents, including an affidavit from Bruce Harris, the director of Casa Alianza, a Central American children advocacy group, which said that sending Chocoy back to Guatemala would be a death sentence for him. Vandello read a psychological evaluation which concluded that Chocoy was depressed and suffering from post traumatic stress disorder. He read a letter from Santiago Sanchez, a counselor at Homeboy Industries, who said Chocoy has a lot of support and a suitable home with an aunt in Virginia who offered to raise him, an offer that was initially approved by the Office of Refugee Resettlement. Another letter from a teacher at the San Luis Valley Youth Center said Chocoy was doing well in school and that "he has a positive attitude and . . . has been a valuable asset to their program."

The judge acknowledged several reports on gang violence in Guatemala, including one that said an average of 30 to 40 children are murdered every month in Guatemala in gang-related violence.

Finally, he said he found Chocoy's testimony to be credible.

"He appears to have told his story honestly and directly," Vandello said. "I have no reason to doubt his credibility."

Nevertheless, Vandello denied the asylum application, effectively sentencing Chocoy to death. Vandello declined to comment for this article, but in the transcript from the hearing he based his decision on his belief that Chocoy could safely return to Guatemala and live an anonymous life, in spite of all the testimony to the contrary.

"I also note that Guatemala is a country of 13 million people," Vandello said. "The respondent has to show that his fear of persecution is nationwide, and I find it hard to believe that if he were to go to a part of Guatemala without tattoos and get a job and try to live a normal life, I find it hard to believe that he would be identified as a gang member who defected and then would be harmed. There are many cities and many places he could live I believe without being so identified."

But in his final statements, Vandello seems to imply that Chocoy brought the danger he might experience on himself.

"The United States has many programs to help youths from other countries learn English, get jobs, stay out of gangs," he said. "But he chose to get into another gang, he was arrested by the police twice for carrying a loaded weapon, and another time for delivering drugs, and I find that such a person, even though a juvenile, is not entitled to asylum and should not be granted asylum in the exercise of discretion.

"It appears that he has taken steps recently to try to do something with his life," he concluded. "These steps are very late, and I find that his past speaks . . . more loudly than his present attempt at rehabilitation."

The decision was a blow to Chocoy's advocates.

"I can't believe a judge could say that," says Anna Sampaio, assistant professor of political science at Denver University. "It says there is no purpose in incarceration or rehabilitation. It says you cannot pay for your past. And most importantly, it shows an ignorance, a misreading of what is going on in communities of color, the reasons why kids on the street in Central America wind up in gangs."

Sampaio was originally tapped by Salinas to provide expert testimony on gang life in Guatemala, but was never called to offer her testimony.

"It probably wouldn't have made a difference considering what's happened since 9/11," she says.

According to Sampaio, prior to 9/11, there would have been other processes in place that likely could have stopped the deportation of a minor like Chocoy, but those options have all but disappeared under the new government emphasis on fighting terrorism.

"They now deport first and ask questions later," she says.

The governmental ignorance she refers to stems from a lack of understanding about the economic conditions in Central America and how those conditions impact children.

"You have tens of thousands of kids living on their own on the street by the time they are 3 years old," she says. "They don't make an intelligent decision to join a gang. They decide that the only way to eat and survive is to be associated with a gang. The gang becomes their only family, their protector. There are no government programs to keep them alive. It's a gang or death in most cases. And can a kid under the age of 10 or 12 really understand the decisions they are making without any input from an adult? Edgar's decision to get out of the gang may have been one of his first true decisions after reaching an age where he could decide something on his own."

In the end, the 16-year-old was too tired to fight Vandello's decision. Salinas says he ultimately decided not to appeal because he couldn't stand being locked up until a new hearing could get underway.

Chocoy was returned to Guatemala on March 10.

On March 27, he was shot dead.

Fallout

Chocoy's death has caused an international outcry.

Both Amnesty International and the United Nations High Commissioner for Refugees have issued statements condemning Vandello's decision to deport him. Representatives of U.S. government agencies have been put in the unenviable position of defending the judge's decision, albeit weakly. Associated Press quotes Virginia Kice, a spokeswoman for U.S. Immigration and Customs Enforcement, as saying, "There is a real likelihood that the same fate would have befallen him if he was allowed to stay here."

Wade Horn, the assistant secretary for children and families at Health and Human Services told the *Denver Post,* "Sometimes very bad things happen despite the fact that people do the best they can."

Others put the blame on the home countries.

"I don't think we can control what happens in Guatemala," Jeff Copp, special agent in charge of Homeland Security's Bureau of Immigration and Customs Enforcement in Denver, told the *Post.* Copps's view is, of course, correct, but raises the point that if you can't control what happens in Guatemala's violent streets, perhaps children shouldn't be deported there. It seems that since 9/11 those most familiar with the conditions in the deportee's home country are being given the least input into the deportation process.

"The Chocoy case has made us all more aware of the dangers associated with gang activity in the countries of origin," says Ken Tota of the Health and Human Services Office of Refugee Resettlement. "But it is still not our call. Ultimately it is the Justice and Homeland Security departments that have the final say on deportation. Perhaps we should get more involved during the hearing process."

When questioned about his office's decision to pull its permission for Chocoy to live with his aunt in Virginia, Tota stops short of saying that his office was pressured to do so by Homeland Security. He did however, admit that it was Homeland Security's intervention—the agency sent a record of Chocoy's criminal past to HHS and suggested that he should not be allowed to live with the aunt—that was the deciding factor in rescinding the permission for Chocoy to stay.

"Based on the current laws and the way they are being enforced," says Tota, "it's the criminal background that immediately disqualifies someone for asylum, even if they are minors. We're hopeful that consideration of the conditions in the home country will eventually become more important to the process. We're trying to train our people about the gangs and the consequences of returning children with gang ties. I understand that the Child Protection Act has a clause that would give us more control over the process based on country conditions." . . .

Still, there may be a positive side to the Chocoy tragedy. Tota assures that his office will be more proactive in future cases.

Salinas credits the outrage over Chocoy's murder to the fact that, for a change, news of his fate reached the United States.

"There are a lot of times when we just don't know what happens to people, but in this case his mother was in touch with me and contacted me and said he was killed," she says. "What happens in a lot of cases is that we don't know what happens to people when they go back to their countries . . . [Immigration attorneys] don't know what happens to people who are denied their asylum claims, they never hear from them and they're never in touch with them again, so who knows what happens to them?"

Salinas says the news of Chocoy's death hit her particularly hard; she'd grown close to him during the five months she prepared his case.

"He was a sweet boy who just wanted a chance. He had bad breaks all his life," she says. "I would have been proud to have had him as a son.

"He was a great kid."

The Illegal-Alien Crime Wave

Some of the most violent criminals at large today are illegal aliens. Yet in cities where the crime these aliens commit is highest, the police cannot use the most obvious tool to apprehend them: their immigration status. In Los Angeles, for example, dozens of members of a ruthless Salvadoran prison gang have sneaked back into town after having been deported for such crimes as murder, assault with a deadly weapon, and drug trafficking. Police officers know who they are and know that their mere presence in the country is a felony. Yet should a cop arrest an illegal gangbanger for felonious reentry, it is he who will be treated as a criminal, for violating the LAPD's rule against enforcing immigration law.

The LAPD's ban on immigration enforcement mirrors bans in immigrant-saturated cities around the country, from New York and Chicago to San Diego, Austin, and Houston. These "sanctuary policies" generally prohibit city employees, including the cops, from reporting immigration violations to federal authorities.

Such laws testify to the sheer political power of immigrant lobbies, a power so irresistible that police officials shrink from even mentioning the illegal-alien crime wave. "We can't even talk about it," says a frustrated LAPD captain. "People are afraid of a backlash from Hispanics." Another LAPD commander in a predominantly Hispanic, gang-infested district sighs: "I would get a firestorm of criticism if I talked about [enforcing the immigration law against illegals]." Neither captain would speak for attribution.

But however pernicious in themselves, sanctuary rules are a symptom of a much broader disease: the nation's near-total loss of control over immigration policy. Fifty years ago, immigration policy might have driven immigration numbers, but today the numbers drive policy. The nonstop increase of immigration is reshaping the language and the law to dissolve any distinction between legal and illegal aliens and, ultimately, the very idea of national borders.

It is a measure of how topsy-turvy the immigration environment has become that to ask police officials about the illegal-alien crime problem feels like a gross faux pas, not done in polite company. And a police official asked to violate this powerful taboo will give a strangled response—or, as in the case of a New York deputy commissioner, break off communication altogether. Meanwhile, millions of illegal aliens work, shop, travel, and commit crimes in plain view, utterly secure in their de facto immunity from the immigration law.

I asked the Miami Police Department's spokesman, Detective Delrish Moss, about his employer's policy on lawbreaking illegals. In September, the force arrested a Honduran visa violator for seven vicious rapes. The previous year, Miami cops had had the suspect in custody for lewd and lascivious molestation, without checking his immigration status. Had they done so, they would have discovered his visa overstay, a deportable offense, and so could have forestalled the rapes. "We have shied away from unnecessary involvement dealing with immigration issues," explains Moss, choosing his words carefully, "because of our large immigrant population."

Police commanders may not want to discuss, much less respond to, the illegal-alien crisis, but its magnitude for law enforcement is startling. Some examples:

- In Los Angeles, 95 percent of all outstanding warrants for homicide (which total 1,200 to 1,500) target illegal aliens. Up to two-thirds of all fugitive felony warrants (17,000) are for illegal aliens.
- A confidential California Department of Justice study reported in 1995 that 60 percent of the 20,000-strong 18th Street Gang in southern California is illegal; police officers say the proportion is actually much greater. The bloody gang collaborates with the Mexican Mafia, the dominant force in California prisons, on complex drug-distribution schemes, extortion, and drive-by assassinations, and commits an assault or robbery every day in L.A. County. The gang has grown dramatically over the last two decades by recruiting recently arrived youngsters, most of them illegal, from Central America and Mexico.
- The leadership of the Columbia Lil' Cycos gang, which uses murder and racketeering to control the drug market around L.A.'s MacArthur Park, was about 60 percent illegal in 2002, says former assistant U.S. attorney Luis Li. Francisco Martinez, a Mexican Mafia member and an illegal alien, controlled the gang from prison, while serving time for felonious reentry following deportation.

Good luck finding any reference to such facts in official crime analysis. The LAPD and the L.A. city attorney recently requested an injunction against drug trafficking in Hollywood, targeting the 18th Street Gang and the "non–gang members" who sell drugs in Hollywood for the gang. Those non–gang members are virtually all illegal Mexicans, smuggled into the country by a ring organized by 18th Street bigs. The Mexicans pay off their transportation debts to the gang by selling drugs; many soon realize how lucrative that line of work is and stay in the business.

Cops and prosecutors universally know the immigration status of these non-gang "Hollywood dealers," as the city attorney calls them, but the gang injunction is assiduously silent on the matter. And if a Hollywood officer were to arrest an illegal dealer (known on the street as a "border brother") for his immigration status, or even notify the Immigration and Naturalization Service (since early 2003, absorbed into the new Department of Homeland Security), he would face severe discipline for violating Special Order 40, the city's sanctuary policy.

The ordinarily tough-as-nails former LAPD chief Daryl Gates enacted Special Order 40 in 1979—showing that even the most unapologetic law-and-order cop is no match for immigration advocates. The order prohibits officers from "initiating police action where the objective is to discover the alien status of a person"—in other words, the police may not even ask someone they have arrested about his immigration status until after they have filed criminal charges, nor may they arrest someone for immigration violations. They may not notify immigration authorities about an illegal alien picked up for minor violations. Only if they have already booked an illegal alien for a felony or for multiple misdemeanors may they inquire into his status or report him. The bottom line: a cordon sanitaire between local law enforcement and immigration authorities that creates a safe haven for illegal criminals.

⋘⊙⋙

L.A.'s sanctuary law and all others like it contradict a key 1990s policing discovery: the Great Chain of Being in criminal behavior. Pick up a law-violator for a "minor" crime, and you might well prevent a major crime: enforcing graffiti and turnstile-jumping laws nabs you murderers and robbers. Enforcing known immigration violations, such as reentry following deportation, against known felons, would be even more productive. LAPD officers recognize illegal deported gang members all the time—flashing gang signs at court hearings for rival gangbangers, hanging out on the corner, or casing a target. These illegal returnees are, simply by being in the country after deportation, committing a felony (in contrast to garden-variety illegals on their first trip to the U.S., say, who are only committing a misdemeanor). "But if I see a deportee from the Mara Salvatrucha [Salvadoran prison] gang crossing the street, I know I can't touch him," laments a Los Angeles gang officer. Only if the deported felon has given the officer some other reason to stop him, such as an observed narcotics sale, can the cop accost him—but not for the immigration felony.

Though such a policy puts the community at risk, the department's top brass brush off such concerns. No big deal if you see deported gangbangers back on the streets, they say. Just put them under surveillance for "real" crimes and arrest them for those. But surveillance is very manpower-intensive. Where there is an immediate ground for getting a violent felon off the street and for questioning him further, it is absurd to demand that the woefully understaffed LAPD ignore it.

⋘⊙⋙

The stated reasons for sanctuary policies are that they encourage illegal-alien crime victims and witnesses to cooperate with cops without fear of deportation, and that they encourage illegals to take advantage of city services like health care and education (to whose maintenance few illegals have contributed a single tax dollar, of course). There has never been any empirical verification that sanctuary laws actually accomplish these goals—and no one has ever suggested not enforcing drug laws, say, for fear of intimidating drug-using crime victims. But in any case, this official rationale could be honored by limiting police use of immigration laws to some subset of immigration violators: deported felons, say, or repeat criminal offenders whose immigration status police already know.

The real reason cities prohibit their cops and other employees from immigration reporting and enforcement is, like nearly everything else in immigration policy, the numbers. The immigrant population has grown so large that public officials are terrified of alienating it, even at the expense of ignoring the law and tolerating violence. In 1996, a breathtaking *Los Angeles Times* exposé on the 18th Street Gang, which included descriptions of innocent bystanders being murdered by laughing *cholos* (gang members), revealed the rate of illegal-alien membership in the gang. In response to the public outcry, the Los Angeles City Council ordered the police to reexamine Special Order 40. You would have thought it had suggested reconsidering *Roe* v. *Wade*. A police commander warned the council: "This is going to open a significant, heated debate." City Councilwoman Laura Chick put on a brave front: "We mustn't be afraid," she declared firmly.

But of course immigrant pandering trumped public safety. Law-abiding residents of gang-infested neighborhoods may live in terror of the tattooed gangbangers dealing drugs, spraying graffiti, and shooting up rivals outside their homes, but such anxiety can never equal a politician's fear of offending Hispanics. At the start of the reexamination process, LAPD deputy chief John White had argued that allowing the department to work closely with the INS would give cops another tool for getting gang members off the streets. Trying to build a homicide case, say, against an illegal gang member is often futile, he explained, since witnesses fear deadly retaliation if they cooperate with the police. Enforcing an immigration violation would allow the cops to lock up the murderer right now, without putting a witness's life at risk.

But six months later, Deputy Chief White had changed his tune: "Any broadening of the policy gets us into the immigration business," he asserted. "It's a federal law-enforcement issue, not a local law-enforcement issue." Interim police chief Bayan Lewis told the L.A. Police Commission: "It is not the time. It is not the day to look at Special Order 40."

Nor will it ever be, as long as immigration numbers continue to grow. After their brief moment of truth in 1996, Los Angeles politicians have only grown more adamant in defense of Special Order 40. After learning that cops in the scandal-plagued Rampart Division had cooperated with the INS to try to uproot murderous gang members from the community, local politicians threw a fit, criticizing district commanders for even allowing INS agents into their station houses. In turn, the LAPD strictly disciplined the offending officers. By now, big-city police chiefs are unfortunately just as determined to defend sanctuary policies as the politicians who appoint them; not so the rank and file, however, who see daily the benefit that an immigration tool would bring.

Immigration politics have similarly harmed New York. Former mayor Rudolph Giuliani sued all the way up to the Supreme Court to defend the city's sanctuary policy against a 1996 federal law decreeing that cities could not prohibit their employees from cooperating with the INS. Oh yeah? said Giuliani; just watch me. The INS, he claimed, with what turned out to be grotesque irony, only aims to "terrorize people." Though he lost in court, he remained defiant to the end. On September 5, 2001, his handpicked charter-revision committee ruled that New York could still require that its employees keep immigration information confidential to preserve trust between immigrants and government. Six days later, several visa-overstayers participated in the most devastating attack on the city and the country in history.

New York conveniently forgot the 1996 federal ban on sanctuary laws until a gang of five Mexicans—four of them illegal—abducted and brutally raped a 42-year-old mother of two near some railroad tracks in Queens. The NYPD had already arrested three of the illegal aliens numerous times for such crimes as assault, attempted robbery, criminal trespass, illegal gun possession, and drug offenses. The department had never notified the INS.

Citizen outrage forced Mayor Michael Bloomberg to revisit the city's sanctuary decree yet again. In May 2003, Bloomberg tweaked the policy minimally to allow city staffers to inquire into immigration status only if it is relevant to the awarding of a government benefit. Though Bloomberg's new rule said nothing about reporting immigration violations to federal officials, advocates immediately claimed that it did allow such reporting, and the ethnic lobbies went ballistic. "What we're seeing is the erosion of people's rights," thundered Angelo Falcon of the Puerto Rican Legal Defense and Education Fund. After three months of intense agitation by immigrant groups, Bloomberg replaced this innocuous "don't ask" policy with a "don't tell" rule even broader than Gotham's original sanctuary policy. The new rule prohibits city employees from giving other government officials information not just about immigration status but about tax payments, sexual orientation, welfare status, and other matters.

But even were immigrant-saturated cities to discard their sanctuary policies and start enforcing immigration violations where public safety demands it, the resource-starved immigration authorities couldn't handle the overwhelming additional workload.

The chronic shortage of manpower to oversee, and detention space to house, aliens as they await their deportation hearings (or, following an order of removal from a federal judge, their actual deportation) has forced immigration officials to practice a constant triage. Long ago, the feds stopped trying to find and deport aliens who had "merely" entered the country illegally through stealth or fraudulent documents. Currently, the only types of illegal aliens who run any risk of catching federal attention are those who have been convicted of an "aggravated felony" (a particularly egregious crime) or who have been deported following conviction for an aggravated felony and who have reentered (an offense punishable with 20 years in jail). . . .

Resource starvation is not the only reason for federal inaction. The INS was a creature of immigration politics, and INS district directors came under great pressure from local politicians to divert scarce resources into distribution of such "benefits" as permanent residency, citizenship, and work permits, and away from criminal or other investigations. In the late 1980s, for example, the INS refused to join an FBI task force against Haitian drug trafficking in Miami, fearing criticism for "Haitian-bashing." In 1997, after Hispanic activists protested a much-publicized raid that netted nearly two dozen illegals, the Border Patrol said that it would no longer join Simi Valley, California, probation officers on home searches of illegal-alien-dominated gangs.

The disastrous Citizenship USA project of 1996 was a luminous case of politics driving the INS to sacrifice enforcement to "benefits." When, in the early 1990s, the prospect of welfare reform drove immigrants to apply for citizenship in record numbers to preserve their welfare eligibility, the Clinton administration, seeing a political bonanza in hundreds of thousands of new welfare-dependent citizens, ordered the naturalization process radically expedited. Thanks to relentless administration pressure, processing errors in 1996 were 99 percent in New York and 90 percent in Los Angeles, and tens of thousands of aliens with criminal records, including for murder and armed robbery, were naturalized.

Another powerful political force, the immigration bar association, has won from Congress an elaborate set of due-process rights for criminal aliens that can keep them in the country indefinitely. Federal probation officers in Brooklyn are supervising two illegals—a Jordanian and an Egyptian with Saudi citizenship—who look "ready to blow up the Statue of Liberty," according to a probation official, but the officers can't get rid of them. The Jordanian had been caught fencing stolen Social Security and tax-refund checks; now he sells phone cards, which he uses himself to make untraceable calls. The Saudi's offense: using a fraudulent Social Security number to get employment—a puzzlingly unnecessary scam, since he receives large sums from the Middle East, including from millionaire relatives. But intelligence links him to terrorism, so presumably he worked in order not to draw attention to himself. Currently, he changes his cell phone every month. Ordinarily such a minor offense would not be prosecuted, but the government, fearing that he had terrorist intentions, used whatever it had to put him in prison.

Now, probation officers desperately want to see the duo out of the country, but the two ex-cons have hired lawyers, who are relentlessly fighting their deportation. "Due process allows you to stay for years without an adjudication," says a probation officer in frustration. "A regular immigration attorney can keep you in the country for three years, a high-priced one for ten." In the meantime, Brooklyn probation officials are watching the bridges.

Even where immigration officials successfully nab and deport criminal aliens, the reality, says a former federal gang prosecutor, is that "they all come back. They can't make it in Mexico." The tens of thousands of illegal farmworkers and dishwashers who overpower U.S. border controls every year carry in their wake thousands of brutal assailants and terrorists who use the same smuggling industry and who benefit from the same irresistible odds: there are so many more of them than the Border Patrol.

❧

For, of course, the government's inability to keep out criminal aliens is part and parcel of its inability to patrol the border, period. For decades, the INS had as much effect on the migration of millions of illegals as a can tied to the tail of a tiger. And the immigrants themselves, despite the press cliché of hapless aliens living fearfully in the shadows, seemed to regard immigration authorities with all the concern of an elephant for a flea.

Certainly fear of immigration officers is not in evidence among the hundreds of illegal day laborers who hang out on Roosevelt Avenue in Queens, New York, in front of money wire services, travel agencies, immigration-attorney offices, and phone arcades, all catering to the local Hispanic population (as well as to drug dealers and terrorists). "There is no chance of getting caught," cheerfully explains Rafael, an Ecuadoran. Like the dozen Ecuadorans and Mexicans on his particular corner, Rafael is hoping that an SUV seeking carpenters for $100 a day will show up soon. "We don't worry, because we're not doing anything wrong. I know it's illegal; I need the papers, but here, nobody asks you for papers." . . .

Even where immigration officials devote adequate resources to worksite investigations, not much would change, because their legal weapons are so weak. That's no accident: though it is a crime to hire illegal aliens, a coalition of libertarians, business lobbies, and left-wing advocates has consistently blocked the fraud-proof form of work authorization necessary to enforce that ban. Libertarians have erupted in hysteria at such proposals as a toll-free number to the Social Security Administration for employers to confirm Social Security numbers. Hispanics warn just as stridently that helping employers verify work eligibility would result in discrimination against Hispanics—implicitly conceding that vast numbers of Hispanics work illegally. . . .

For illegal workers and employers, there is no downside to the employment charade. If immigration officials ever do try to conduct an industry-wide investigation—which will at least net the illegal employees, if not the employers—local congressmen will almost certainly head it off. An INS inquiry into the Vidalia-onion industry in Georgia was not only aborted by Georgia's congressional delegation; it actually resulted in a local amnesty for the growers' illegal workforce. The downside to complying with the spirit of the employment law, on the other hand, is considerable. Ethnic advocacy groups are ready to picket employers who dismiss illegal workers, and employers understandably fear being undercut by less scrupulous competitors.

❧

Of the incalculable changes in American politics, demographics, and culture that the continuing surge of migrants is causing, one of the most profound is the breakdown of the distinction between legal and illegal entry. Everywhere, illegal aliens receive free public education and free medical care at taxpayer expense; 13 states offer them driver's licenses. States everywhere have been pushed to grant illegal aliens college scholarships and reduced in-state tuition. One hundred banks, over 800 law-enforcement agencies, and dozens of cities accept an identification card created by Mexico to credentialize illegal Mexican aliens in the U.S. The Bush administration has given its blessing to this *matricula consular* card, over the strong protest of the FBI, which warns that the gaping security loopholes that the card creates make it a boon to money launderers, immigrant smugglers, and terrorists. Border authorities have already caught an Iranian man sneaking across the border this year, Mexican *matricula* card in hand.

Hispanic advocates have helped blur the distinction between a legal and an illegal resident by asserting that differentiating the two is an act of irrational bigotry. Arrests of illegal aliens inside the border now inevitably spark protests, often led by the Mexican government, that feature signs calling for "*no más racismo.*" Immigrant advocates use the language of "human rights" to appeal to an authority higher than such trivia as citizenship laws. They attack the term "amnesty" for implicitly acknowledging the validity of borders. Indeed, grouses Illinois congressman Luis Gutierrez, "There's an implication that somehow you did something wrong and you need to be forgiven."

Illegal aliens and their advocates speak loudly about what they think the U.S. owes them, not vice versa. "I believe they have a right . . . to work, to drive their kids to school," said California assemblywoman Sarah Reyes. An immigration agent says that people he stops "get in your face about their rights, because our failure to enforce the law emboldens them." Taking this idea to its extreme, Joaquín Avila, a UCLA Chicano studies professor and law lecturer, argues that to deny non-citizens the vote, especially in the many California cities where they constitute the majority, is a form of apartheid.

Yet no poll has ever shown that Americans want more open borders. Quite the reverse. By a huge majority—at least 60 percent—they want to rein in immigration, and they endorse an observation that Senator Alan Simpson made 20 years ago: Americans "are fed up with efforts to make them feel that [they] do not have that fundamental right of any people—to decide who will join them and help form the future country in which they and their posterity will live." But if the elites' and the advocates' idea of giving voting rights to non-citizen majorities catches on—and don't be surprised if it does—Americans could be faced with the ultimate absurdity of people outside the social compact making rules for those inside it.

⋅⟨◉⟩⋅

However the nation ultimately decides to rationalize its chaotic and incoherent immigration system, surely all can agree that, at a minimum, authorities should expel illegal-alien criminals swiftly. Even on the grounds of protecting non-criminal illegal immigrants, we should start by junking sanctuary policies. By stripping cops of what may be their only immediate tool to remove felons from the community, these policies leave law-abiding immigrants prey to crime.

But the non-enforcement of immigration laws in general has an even more destructive effect. In many immigrant communities, assimilation into gangs seems to be outstripping assimilation into civic culture. Toddlers are learning to flash gang signals and hate the police, reports the *Los Angeles Times*. In New York City, "every high school has its Mexican gang," and most 12- to 14-year-olds have already joined, claims Ernesto Vega, an illegal 18-year-old Mexican. Such pathologies only worsen when the first lesson that immigrants learn about U.S. law is that Americans don't bother to enforce it. "Institution-alizing illegal immigration creates a mindset in people that anything goes in the U.S.," observes Patrick Ortega, the news and public-affairs director of Radio Nueva Vida in southern California. "It creates a new subculture, with a sequela of social ills." It is broken windows writ large.

For the sake of immigrants and native-born Americans alike, it's time to decide what our immigration policy is—and enforce it.

POSTSCRIPT

Immigration: Should Illegal Immigrant Gang Members Be Granted Legal Clemency from U.S. Law?

Perhaps the most significant underlying issue related to clemency laws and illegal aliens is the subject of immigration reform. Within the first six months of 2006, the United States witnessed demonstrations for immigrants unprecedented in American history, including separate marches estimated at 750,000 participants in Los Angeles in March, up to 500,000 in Dallas in April, and upward of 700,000 in Chicago in May. Although the reasons for participating in the marches were particular to each individual, the overall purpose of the demonstrations was to draw attention to a need for U.S. immigration reform—largely centered on illegal aliens already in the United States.

There have also been at-length debates in the U.S. Congress concerning the most effective method for not only limiting the number of illegals that enter the United States every year, but also addressing what is the best solution regarding the estimated 13 million illegal aliens living in the United States. A number of different proposals were considered—ranging anywhere from the arrest and/or deportation of all illegals to granting citizenship to anyone already in the United States. After much heated debate, one of the most controversial elements of the possible scenarios is the perceived "rewarding" of illegal aliens with citizenship despite having entered into the United States unlawfully.

The issue of granting clemency to illegal aliens has continued to fuel debate by lawmakers, members of law enforcement, Latino communities, scholars, and others. This controversy has provoked groups, such as the Minutemen, to take border patrol issues in the hands of ordinary citizens and led President Bush to call for the eventual deployment of tens of thousands of National Guard troops to the Mexican border to help dampen the immigration issue, which is inextricably linked to national security.

Given the strong correlation between the rapid expansion and proliferation of street gangs like La Mara Salvatrucha as well as their rivals (the 18th Street gang), and due to the increased traffic of illegal aliens crossing into the United States from Mexico, many in the United States feel law enforcement officials are limited in their capabilities to prevent crimes committed by illegal aliens due to clemency laws. However, many feel deportation of these criminals is not always a viable solution and may actually worsen the situation. The deportees may recruit from their home country and help bring more gang members into the United States. In addition, many Americans feel it is only a matter of time before international gangs like La Mara coordinate their effort with terrorist organizations such as Al Qaeda, although no links between La Mara and Al Qaeda have been shown to exist.

One method of dealing with illegal alien criminals that is showing signs of success is to arrest them before they enter into the United States. Through coordinated efforts between a number of Central American countries, Mexico, and the United States, progress is being made. Using a centralized database among several countries and engaging in solid information-sharing practices, prisons in Mexico are beginning to fill with members of MS-13 who had been deported to El Salvador and were making their return journey to the United States. Other internationally coordinated efforts have been discussed with Salvadorian authorities, such as working with the El Salvadorian government to ensure criminal deportees are sent to jail in their home countries with a list of charges as well as bringing members of Salvadorian law enforcement to the United States to better familiarize U.S. authorities with the culture of Salvadorian gangs. El Salvador has passed its own controversial "get tough" policy called the "Mano Dura" or the "Heavy Hand" where law enforcement officials can arrest suspected gang members for reasons related to visible gang-related tattoos, being seen with other gang members, or even simply based on suspicions of gang association, leading to a significant increase in arrests. Gabrielle Banks in "The Tattooed Generation: Salvadoran Children Bring Home American Gang Culture" (*Dissent,* Winter 2000) describes the work of Homies Unidos, a non-profit organization in Los Angeles, and their efforts in El Salvador to create an alternative to the Heavy Hand.

For a comprehensive look at gangs and immigration in America, see Nicolaus Mills, *Arguing Immigration: The Controversy and Crisis Over the Future of Immigration in America.* For the U.S. government's view on illegal aliens and gang activities, see http://judiciary.house.gov/media/pdfs/printers/109th/20528.pdf. For more information on La Mara Salvatrucha, listen to National Public Radio's Mandalit del Barco's perspectives on MS-13 at http://www.npr.org/templates/story/story.php?storyId=4539688. For a critical look at U.S. immigration policy, visit www.newswithviews.com/Wooldridge/frostyA.htm.

ISSUE 8

Is Latin America Loosening Its Restrictive Abortion Laws?

YES: Alejandro Bermúdez, from "Will Colombia Become the First Country in South America to Legalize Abortion?" *Catholic World News* (October 10, 2001)

NO: Roxana Vásquez Sotelo, from "Notes on the Situation of Abortion in the Region," Latin American Center on Sexuality and Human Rights, the State University of Rio de Janeiro's Institute of Social Medicine (May 2005)

ISSUE SUMMARY

YES: Venezuelan journalist Alejandro Bermúdez discusses the issue of abortion in Colombia and interviews Monsignor Jaime Restrepo, who explains how pro-abortion groups have helped in changing the laws to permit abortions.

NO: Peruvian attorney Roxana Vásquez Sotelo argues that Latin American women do not have the freedom or autonomy to terminate unwanted pregnancies, resulting in many illegal abortions. Vásquez Sotelo also indicates that foreign interference helps maintain laws that restrict women's rights.

Although the topic of abortion has clearly been a volatile subject in Western societies, Latin America is recognized as having among the most restrictive laws in the world regarding abortion. The majority of Latin Americans are Catholic, and as a result, most Latin American governments do not allow abortions. To date, only three Latin American nations allow abortions without restrictions: Cuba, Guyana, and Puerto Rico—although it should be noted that most Latin American countries do allow abortions when a mother's life is in danger. Yet, despite this apparent willingness on the part of many governments to take into account women's health, few Latin American countries permit early termination of pregnancy due to rape, incest, or fetal impairment, and even fewer allow abortion for economical or social reasons. Cuba legalized abortion in 1965, resulting from a change in policy linked to the Cuban revolution when religious practices were discouraged by the authorities, therefore virtually removing the Catholic influence on the subject. However, although not prohibiting abortion, Castro has periodically spoken out against abortion. Yet, Puerto Rico, which is 85 percent Catholic, has followed the U.S. federal mandate of 1974 to legalize abortion. And, in Guyana abortion has been completely legal since 1995.

Although the Catholic Church opposes abortion, a virtually incalculable number of illegal abortions still take place in Latin America: it is estimated that more than 4 million women undergo an induced abortion each year. These procedures are performed illegally and usually under hazardous conditions (Alan Guttmacher Institute, 2005). In some countries, such as Mexico, where under certain conditions abortions are allowed, it is difficult for poor women to have the option of an abortion because of "the lack of response within the public health system" (America's Policy.org, March 10, 2005).

Why is this practice so controversial? For some, it is an ethical concern; for others, it is a religious one; for many, it is a women's rights issue or perhaps a combination of reasons. The fundamental question is, of course, how much power should the state or any religious institution have over women's reproductive system? And, an issue that is equally inextricable from the controversy relates to the question of when life begins, therefore identifying a distinction between abortion and murder.

Until recently, abortion in Latin America had been a taboo subject. People may have indirectly referred to its presence in their communities, but abortion was not a topic for outright discussion. Because of the significant number of illegal abortions taking place and the consequent deaths of many women, many studies have been undertaken to understand the relationship between anti-abortion policy and women's health. In Colombia in 1994, the initial results were discussed at what came to be the first pan-Latin American meeting on abortion. These studies illustrated how illegal abortions have had a detrimental effect on women's health and have led to many instances of premature death of women. As a result of this study and others, many women's groups have begun demanding legalization targeted toward women's health, particularly focusing on the safety and legality of early termination of pregnancy. At the same time, other groups are appalled at these demands and do not want their governments to change any law that would allow a greater degree of access to legalized abortions than currently exists. Many blame the interference of foreign governments, religious groups, and outside international groups for not only furthering the legalization of abortion, but also impeding movements that support the decriminalization of abortion.

Of course, many groups—both domestically and internationally—have a certain degree of influence on abortion-related issues in Latin America. Alejandro Bermúdez asserts that Colombia is on its way to legalizing abortion as a result of international organizations and feminist groups pressuring government officials. Roxana Vásquez Sotelo argues that Latin American women do not have the freedom or autonomy to terminate unwanted pregnancies, resulting in many illegal abortions, and also indicates that foreign interference helps maintain laws that restrict women's rights.

YES

Alejandro Bermúdez

Will Colombia Become the First Country in South America to Legalize Abortion?

In early October, members of the executive committee of the Colombian bishops' conference were discussing the conditional support they were planning to give to the "Colombia Plan"—a key US-financed program to bring peace and stability to the country—when the legal advisor of the Episcopate, Andres Arango Martinez, stormed into the room with news that would dramatically change the priorities in the bishops' list of concerns.

Unexpectedly, President Andres Pastrana—a well known Catholic—had signed and approved a new Penal Code in which the Liberal Party managed to insert into the last few lines of an article a text that, in practice, legalized abortion in Colombia.

There was even more bad news: the birth control advocating organization ironically named Profamilia ("pro-family"), a local subsidiary of the International Planned Parenthood Federation (IPPF), announced that the National Institute for Medicines and Food—the Colombian equivalent to the US Food and Drug Administration—had granted permission for the legal distribution of "emergency contraceptives," a euphemism for a pill that causes an early-term abortion. Profamilia will commercially distribute the pill starting next January.

At that moment, the bishops understood that, despite the threat to the life of Colombians posed by rebel groups, paramilitaries, and drug-trafficking organizations, another greater threat was menacing the lives of Colombians, this time in their mothers' wombs. "The first problem was to start a legal battle against an already approved Penal Code which basically said that abortion was not legal . . . but legal," says Arango Martinez.

In fact, article 123 of the new Penal Code clearly states that abortion is a crime, but article 124, according to Arango Martinez, completely contradicts the previous it. Article 124 says: "The punishment applied for the crime of abortion will be reduced by three-fourths when pregnancy is a result of a sexual act, artificial insemination, or zygote transference without consent." It immediately adds: "In the formerly described cases, when abortion takes place in extraordinary motivational conditions, the judiciary official can drop all punishment if necessary."

"Technically, what article 124 is doing is legalize abortion, because the State determines that, in so-called 'extraordinary' circumstances, it can refrain from applying the due legal punishment, a measure not taken in the case of any other crime," explains Arango Martinez. "That is to say, only in the case of abortion, a judge can totally drop the punishment, which is in practice an open door to do so on almost a permanent basis," he adds.

The Problem with "Emergency Contraception"

Regarding the new "emergency contraceptive" promoted by Profamilia, Msgr. Jaime Restrepo, Secretary of the Life and Family Commission of the Colombian Bishops' Conference (CEC), explained that "a simple norm released by a government agency is basically legalizing abortion as opposed to the Constitution and the pro-life sentiment of most Colombians."

In fact, despite Profamilia's claims that the new pill "is in no way a means for abortion, but only to prevent an undesired pregnancy," a council of physicians consulted by CEC revealed that the "emergency contraceptive" contains a drug known as Levonorgestrel, which acts in the woman's body three days after sexual intercourse by preventing the embryo from implanting in the womb. In other words, it kills the new human being.

Msgr. Restrepo said these two separate events—Article 124 of the Penal Code and the new pill—are far from a mere coincidence. On the contrary, he believes that feminist and pro-abortion groups declared a "low-intensity war" immediately after the UN's Beijing+5 Conference held in New York earlier this year. On the occasion of the summit, the bishops' conference and First Lady Nohra Puyana De Pastrana agreed to establish a new way to handle women's issues in dialogue with the Family and Life Commission of CEC. That sudden change in policy irritated feminist nongovernmental organizations (NGOs) accustomed to controlling Colombia's position at international forums and leaving the Church out of the loop.

"Several NGOs harshly complained that the Church was 'interfering' with women's issues, and some of them decided to join forces with other political and social groups to launch the most aggressive campaign ever to legalize abortion," Msgr. Restrepo explains.

One of the most important allies of pro-abortion groups has been the influential newspaper El Tiempo of Colombia's capital city, Bogota, which has been strongly calling for the legalization of abortion. "Our authorities must realize that the liberalization of abortion is a commitment legally and morally acquired by Colombia at several international forums, such as the Beijing and the Cairo summits," said El Tiempo in an editorial note written on October 2.

"Such alleged 'commitments' (to legalize abortion) have never been assumed by Colombia nor even supported in those documents. What exists instead is the government's duty to secure the sanctity of the human life of all Colombians, either born or unborn," rebutted *El Pais,* a newspaper which took the pro-life side in the growing debate.

Carlos Corsi Otarola, a Catholic and pro-life legislator who has been instrumental in the Congress on several occasions opposing previous attempts to legalize abortion or euthanasia, said "pro-life forces represent, without a doubt, the current feeling of most of the Colombian population, as all opinion polls show." He added, "Unfortunately, the pro-abortion forces counter, as usual, with far more means and the support of the big media."

As an example, Corsi Otarola compared the importance of the pro-abortion *El Tiempo,* the newspaper with the largest circulation in the country, with *El Pais,* a respected newspaper that reaches only one third of *El Tiempo's* readership. He also compared the budget of Profamilia, which he claims "has received more foreign money than the Ministry of Health itself," with the brave but poor Provive Colombia, the largest pro-life organization in Colombia, which has to organize several fundraising events to meet its needs.

The Bishops Speak Out

In early October the president of the Colombian episcopate, Archbishop Alberto Giraldo Jaramillo, called members of the episcopate's presidency for an emergency meeting to evaluate the events. After the daylong gathering, a strong document was released. The document, entitled "The Eclipse of Life," not only denounced the campaigns against life, but also called Colombians to protest.

The bishops said in the document that "a massive and aggressive campaign against life has been launched," and claimed that article 124 of the new Penal Code "has been deliberately formulated to subtly legalize abortion in the country."

"We want to express before the whole nation our strongest voice of rejection and protest against this grave attempt against human life," wrote the bishops, who promised to assume "the commitment to fearlessly defend our Constitution, which guarantees the right to life to all Colombians."

Explaining the document, Archbishop Giraldo Jaramillo said, "The state has the duty, according to our Constitution, to defend and protect each human life, especially those of the defenseless." He added, "If the state is not willing to fulfill this commitment, anyone in civil society has the right and the duty to demand respect for the Constitution."

"The bishops of Colombia have said on several occasions that our country is morally sick. And this moral disease is at the root of the wave of murders, kidnappings, drug-trafficking, and political violence which has turned Colombia into one of the most violent countries in the world," the archbishop of Medellin explained. He added that "the decision to bring this violence inside the womb of Colombian women will only foster more violence and deepen our moral disease." In fact, the bishops' document said that "the Eclipse of Life is one of the most dramatic consequences of our morally sick country, and opening the doors to abortion will only aggravate the lack of respect for life."

"Faced with a culture of death, the adequate therapy can only be a spiritual revival and a massive mobilization of people willing to defend the intrinsic value of human life, from its conception in the mother's womb to its natural end by age or disease," the document continued. "The starting point for such a therapy is, of course, the formation of the conscience with strong moral and spiritual values that have to be nurtured first by the family, but also by the school, as well as by public and private institutions."

Explaining the objective of the document, Archbishop Giraldo said that the episcopate was clearly calling for public demonstrations in all possible cities, as well as for a national campaign to pray the rosary during October—the month of the rosary—in families, parishes, and movements, "to request from our Mother of Life the gift of a change of hearts among the heralds of death."

First Public Reactions

Days after the document was released, the first pro-life marches took place in three major Colombian cities: Bogota, Medellin, and Cali. In all three of them, the demand was the same: keep abortion illegal, according to the Colombian Constitution.

The Ministry of Public Health tried to appease the Catholic Church and pro-life forces by stating that the abortion pill RU-486, recently approved by the FDA in the US, would not be accepted in Colombia. "The authorities of sanitary registries will not allow the import or production of the RU-486, because it causes abortion, which is against our Constitution," a statement said.

But neither the bishops nor pro-lifers were fooled by a token that clearly kept things unchanged. The bishops, in fact, quickly responded to the statement by saying that "if health authorities recognize that abortion is against our Constitution, then they should revoke the authorization given to the so-called 'emergency contraceptive.'"

Health authorities did not respond, but a spokesman for Profamilia, Lidia Jaramillo, announced that "there will not be a back step" on the pill, and announced that it will be aggressively promoted under the name of Postinor-Dos.

Congressman Corsi Otarola has said that, despite the well-articulated campaign to legalize abortion, pro-lifers are starting to strike back. The pro-life legislator summarized the key elements of the pro-life campaign:

- Keep the pressure high through public marches called by the bishops.
- Avoid bringing the case of the new Penal Code to the Constitutional Court, which is controlled by anti-life judges, who two years ago made Colombia the first Latin American country to legalize euthanasia.
- Try, instead, to block the application of the Penal Code either by calling it back to Congress or by forcing President Pastrana to object to Article 124.
- Start a legal and medical battle to demonstrate that the "emergency contraception pill" is, in fact, abortifacient, and therefore, unconstitutional.
- Promote a better knowledge of what the Colombian Constitution says regarding the right to life of the unborn.

"We know that the forces of darkness always have more resources than the forces of life," says Corsi Otarola. "That is part of the 'business.' We are used to being the underdogs . . . and we play that role very well."

A Conversation with Msgr. Jaime Restrepo

Catholic World Report spoke to Msgr. Jaime Restrepo, head of the Family and Life Commission of the Colombian Bishops' Conference, about the challenges posed by the pro-abortion campaign and the Church's response.

CWR: Are there grounds to say that there is, in fact, an organized campaign against life in Colombia?

Msgr. Restrepo: There is no doubt. But first you have to keep in mind the context. Colombia is a country that is being torn apart by political and criminal violence. In this environment, when most of the energies of all sectors are concentrated in initiatives to end the violence, out of the blue appear several facts, statements, and acts pushing to legalize abortion. It is evident that there is a campaign, and that such a campaign has tried to catch the whole country off guard.

CWR: But has abortion become an issue that is currently being debated in the public square?

Restrepo: Definitely. Although the "Colombia Plan" agreed upon between the Colombian government, representatives of civil society, and the US government should be drawing the public attention, there are more and more articles, editorials, and opinion columns about the issue of abortion. Recently, for example, most of the media gave great coverage to a so-called "report" issued by a feminist organization, claiming that in Colombia there are currently between 300,000 and 350,000 clandestine abortions being performed each year. The figure is obviously invented and scientifically groundless, but is part of the strategy to create the environment favorable to the legalization of abortion. Of course, neither the bishops' conference nor pro-life groups have remained silent. We have also been taking to the public square, coming out with our own arguments, which despite being far more consistent, don't have as much media coverage as the ones of pro-abortion organizations.

CWR: Which are the most important pro-abortion organizations?

Restrepo: We are suspicious of several NGOs, but most of them throw the stone and hide the hand. The only outspoken pro-abortion organizations are the feminist groups that used to have control over Colombia's stand at international forums, until Beijing+5. These groups put a lot of pressure on the government. Now, we have to admit that the current government at least tries not to allow these pressures.

CWR: And what about Profamilia?

Restrepo: They are definitely the most influential organization promoting birth control in the country. They represent the interests of organizations such as the International Planned Parenthood Federation or Pathfinder. Despite their claim not to be favorable to abortion, they have launched a very aggressive campaign to promote vasectomy and tubal ligation among peasant men and women. Currently they are involved in the promotion of the so-called "emergency contraceptive," which they claim is not an abortion method, even despite medical evidence. Of course, even though Profamilia does not promote abortion openly, they certainly promote the kind of contraceptive, anti-life mentality that favors abortion. In other words, I don't imagine them opposing an eventual legalization of abortion.

CWR: What is the importance of having major newspapers promoting abortion?

Restrepo: It depends. In the case of the daily *El Tiempo,* which is the newspaper with the highest circulation in the country, we are not surprised. It is a militantly liberal, traditionally anti-Catholic newspaper, which has always promoted causes against the Church and religion. It only reflects the philosophy of the Santos family [the publishers], well known in Colombia for their liberal commitment. Therefore, we could not expect otherwise from them. Of course, we are surprised by the passion they are putting into the abortion issue: day in and day out, they bring out an article, a report, an interview with an "expert" to support the myth that there are 300,000 illegal abortions in Colombia and that its legalization is therefore an urgent "lesser evil." Other big media try to be more balanced, but with very few exceptions, most of them make evident, some more, some less, their pro-abortion bias.

CWR: What has been the response of the Colombian bishops' conference in this context?

Restrepo: First of all, we have tried not to be absorbed by the short-term consequences of the debate. This is a long-term battle; of course, with immediate, short-term goals, but basically a long-term one. Our duty and our objective is to make sure that the enduring teaching of the Catholic Church, the Gospel of Life, has an impact in the minds and hearts of Colombian Catholics, and from there to the different levels of the public square. Especially in Colombia, the issue of life and death is a very sensitive one. The Colombian people are sick of violence; they want to end violence; they want the ongoing killings to stop. Colombians are tired of getting a daily dose of murders, kidnappings, massacres, guerrilla attacks, Mafia revenges, and so on. Therefore, the respect for life is not one part of our evangelization, it is our evangelization. We have to bring back the respect for human life, from its very beginning to its natural end. It cannot be otherwise if we want a future for Colombia.

CWR: How is this "pastoral of Life" expressed, for example, in the legal field?

Restrepo: Incredibly, despite the dramatic situation Colombia is going through, several groups attempted, during the draft of the new Penal Code, to clearly support abortion, euthanasia, and genetic manipulation. We had to create a task force to follow closely the draft of the Code, because at each step we would find groups or individuals trying to sneak in something against life. The battle was quite successful until a last minute change modified the original version of the Article 124, which we are now contesting. We have definitely decided not to let the "abortion wave" become a sort of "global fashion" before which we have to kneel down. The truth of yesterday is the same today and always.

CWR: What concrete steps are you planning in the near future to face this current campaign in favor of abortion?

Restrepo: We certainly have several options. We will deliver them at the right moment. At present, we have had an impressive celebration of the Jubilee of the Families, which, in coordination with the Holy See, has also had the motto of "Children, Wellspring of Family and Society."

This has given us the opportunity to reinforce the teachings of the Church in a positive way, in the way that most Colombians love: by demonstrating that babies are never a threat, a "problem," or a "burden," they are a source of joy. We believe, with Mother Teresa of Calcutta, that to say that there are too many children is like saying that there are too many flowers.

At the diocesan level, we are already holding several marches for life, and we are discussing the possibility of holding a national one. What I can assure you is that pro-life forces will not stand still and watch as the lives of the unborn are eliminated before our eyes, either by the law or by chemicals such as the one Profamilia is planning to launch.

Roxana Vásquez Sotelo[1]

 **NO**

Notes on the Situation of Abortion in the Region

Some Starting Points

There is no doubt that one of the issues that generates more controversy in the Latin American region is that of women's freedom or autonomy to decide about unwanted pregnancies. In other words, the debate in question poses the question of whether or not abortion should continue being considered a felony. These debates repeat themselves with more or less similar arguments both in the micro spaces as well as in the macro spaces of social life; eternal discussions at the family dinner table, at the office, among the young and the not-so-young, in parliaments, at the Health and Women's Ministries, in the women's movements and in some other social movements, and of course, in the communications mass media, whether due to some bill, to a close case, to a public policy or to some scandalous or emblematic deed, capable of being capitalized by one of the already known postures.

The first big gap appears in the distances we can observe between what is being discussed and the arguments utilized to defend certain positions, and the concrete practices—behavior that indeed is common to us in many fields, but that turns out to be especially divergent or contradictory when we talk about sexuality or reproduction[2]. A relatively recent study on abortion in Peru[3], performed by the Centro de la Mujer Peruana Flora Tristán (Flora Tristán, Peruvian Women's Center) and Pathfinder International, informs that approximately 410,000 clandestine abortions a year are performed, i.e. more than 1,000 abortions per day, which means that in spite of it being a felony, the need or desire to have it overwhelmingly transcends the limit of penal sanction and is not in line with what is stated in the discourse. On the other hand, the reiterated public proposal of various Ministries of Health of the region related to combating maternal mortality until its eradication, without proposing de-penalization or legalization of abortion, evidences this double-standard with which people intend to confront a problem. If these types of contradictions are maintained, it shall not be easy to advance in the solution of these problems.

The second gap, scandalous and brutally discriminatory, which favors the double-standard thesis, is that for many years all of us, men and women, have known that penal repression only affects poorer women. They are the

From *Latin-American Center on Sexuality and Human Rights,* May 2, 2005. Copyright © 2005 by State University of Rio de Janeiro's Institute of Social Medicine. Reprinted by permission.

ones who die or become infertile, go to jail or have to bribe so as not to be denounced. The circuits for those of us that can afford them are well known; with sufficient money this operation is fast and safe (at least in terms of access to the service).

The third gap is marked by the absence of true laicism in the Latin American States; the separation between State and Church is formal, and has been acknowledged for quite a long time in our Constitutions; however, the basis of legislation or public policy keep on finding support in particular beliefs that pretend to be universally valid. Therefore, they continue imposing on the citizenry a state of affairs that corresponds to the ideas of a group of believers, violating the rights and liberties of the non-believers or of those persons that profess other creeds. They are attempting against the freedom of conscience, but in matters that concern sexuality and/or reproduction, it does not appear as a problem. The political class mostly continues understanding them as private affairs that correspond to morals and not to rights. Therefore, albeit it is necessary to know previously about the male and female candidates' positions regarding certain "important" matters such as, for example, those of an economic nature, the ones referred to sexual rights or to reproductive rights do not need prior positioning and are normally left to the particular conscience of each member of Congress.

Nevertheless, what is there behind so much blindness? What clouds the vision and maintains a drama that affects only certain persons vis-à-vis a situation that for many years now has known of proven solutions and answers in other countries of the planet? A first reason, probably one found at the core, is the ethical, juridical and political tutelage still applied to women; their status as persons capable of discerning and of having autonomy in their decisions does not manage to be totally convincing in these times of our republican life. The argument of life (of the defense of intra-uterine life) turns out to be an excuse, an element that is part of a necessary, although fallacious, argumentative structure. If we examine once and again the value truly granted to life by the defenders of these postures, we shall be able to verify their enormous inconsistency. This struggle of visions and political positions creates a synthesis in the abortion figure; only in this way is it possible to explain the dogmatism and ferocity with which the detractors of women's autonomy and real freedom defend their positions.

The Argumentative Struggle

The general framework of this dispute centers, in the first place, on the scope of the visions that regarding democracy are handled by the various political actors, whether traditional or emergent. Liberty, equality and solidarity for men and women alike? The old motto of the French Revolution (which certainly was not thought having women in mind) is an unfulfilled promise in all our Latin American democracies. However, there are several questions that underlie these emancipating concepts of the 18th Century and turn into challenges to keep on building and therein really lays the core of the dispute: what do we understand by equality? What do we understand by liberty? What are their real scopes? The dimensions of these concepts cannot be analyzed apart from the power asymmetries that are born and reproduced in our societies: asymmetries on account of socioeconomic condition, ethnic/racial origin, age, sexual orientation and gender. These are the ones acknowledged as the ones that stand out the most and give testimony of the outcome of the struggle for visibilization of these structuring forms of discrimination in our societies.

In the identification of the arguments utilized by those opposing the liberalization of abortion we basically find:

a. The idea of a Superior Being—read as God—that grants life and only He (i.e. somebody who is above human beings) can define its ending. This dogma must be understood as the central sign of the transition we are historically living, from the belief in a cosmos organized by a divine entity, to the critical and anxiety-ridden assumption of a notion of liberty and modernity, in which human beings become "owners of our own destiny" individuals.

b. The reinforcement of the maternal role as an idea/argument that has as its objective neutralizing the autonomy and the extension of this condition of women as subjects of rights.

c. The defense of the conceived as holder of rights, more properly as subject, pretending to equal the rights of women with those of the conceived, and as a strategy to put a hold on the liberalizing advances regarding women's autonomy and freedom. In this sense, reproductive autonomy becomes the last symbolic and political bastion in this struggle.

d. The reinforcement of a sexuality and reproduction regulated by the strict canons of marriage and the heterosexual family as the cornerstones of the preservation of a notion of social order and synonymous of well-being and happiness. In this way the bond is tightened between sexuality and reproduction.

This argumentative battery, sustained with more or fewer shades since a long time ago by the conservative sectors of our societies, allied in a particular way to the Catholic Church's hierarchies, has had a strong comeback—as the result of the advancements developed in the fields of sexuality and reproduction, in particular at the international conferences of the United Nations—which is expressed in a visible manner in the alliance of US politics with the Vatican State.

The global gag rule, which is reinstated in 2001 and that precludes organizations from developing actions aimed at working with information, services, legislation and public policies related to abortion, under penalty of loosing the US funds for family planning[4], as well as the set of policies aimed at undermining the health and the rights of women and girls and the exercise of a sexuality different to the heterosexual and reproductive pattern, are good examples of how the current US Administration is acting. "These policies, supported by a Congress controlled by the Republican Party are eroding the health, sexual rights and reproductive rights in four ways:

- Limiting or withdrawing financing for effective programs that are considered incompatible with the conservative values.

- Creating new sources of financing or channeling existing funds through organizations or programs that promote a radically conservative political agenda, without any consideration whatsoever for scientific and public health criteria.
- Censoring information, advocacy and research on integral-health strategies, and
- Trying to go back on prior international covenants and intending to dilute the new agreements that advance health, sexual rights and reproductive rights."[5]

"Due to the strong connections among the Bush Administration, the extreme right and the religious conservative groups, the agenda pursued is an extensive and integral attack on sexual rights and gender equality, and not only a concern on issues circumscribed to abortion or gay marriages."[6] However, in relation to abortion it is presenting a discourse so distorted and dogmatic as the one formulated on the abortion law of partial birth, in which President Bush referred to "children only a few centimeters from birth" when he was speaking about pre-viable fetuses.[7] This fallacious discourse, together with the war policies and the almost total abandonment of progressive positions on the part of the Democratic Congressional representation, has made it difficult for national activists to call attention to Bush's policies until lately. It is even harder for the activists abroad to discern the scope of US policy on sexuality for their own work, their sources of financing and their political situation".[8]

The importance and effects of the US policy, much to our regret, has serious consequences in our region as a result of the political and economic dependency in which we find ourselves in, and as a product of the strong connections of certain US ultraconservative leaderships with the political elites of most of our States. By the same token, the Vatican State utilizes its institutional structure, networks and influences both in the local hierarchies of the Catholic Church as well as within the politician class—which in general takes good care of its close relationships and image before the Church—to achieve its objectives of moral tutelage, particularly in those issues related to sexuality and reproduction, contributing to limit its democratic development from a rights' approach.

Regional Summary

In this section I shall present the main findings in matters of legislation and public policy contributed by a summary performed by CLADEM for the 1995–2000 period, updated later up to 2002 on the situation of sexual rights and reproductive rights in 14 countries of our region.[9] This within the context of the boost to the Campaign for an Inter-American Convention on the sexual rights and reproductive rights.[10] Next, we are adding new updated information[11] in relation to laws, legislative proposals, administrative norms and jurisprudential decisions of certain relevance, which help us understand better the changes and/or movements around the issue, which as we have suggested, must not be analyzed separately from the sexual and reproductive local and international policies.

Abortion is an issue broadly and traditionally addressed by the penal legislation. Its incorporation into public policies is, however, quite more recent. The information collected on this issue in the national diagnoses performed in 2001 and currently updated, allows us to propose the following:

a. Even though in some cases new assumptions of punishment exemption have been incorporated, such as abortion due to rape, and in others penalties have been reduced, we cannot affirm that a flexibilizing trend exists, one that would open the way towards depenalization of abortion.

b. Instead, there is a current of a contrary sign, quite potent, that expresses itself, for example, in a tendency to include the conceived within the right to the protection of life. Argentina, Bolivia, Colombia, Chile, Peru, Ecuador and Honduras (also Guatemala, Costa Rica and Nicaragua) do so in their Constitutions, civil legislation and/or in their minors' or childhood and adolescence codes.

c. The situation of the regulation of abortion in our countries can be summarized as follows:

- Regarding the non-punishable assumptions:
- Therapeutic abortion for reasons of life is permitted in ten countries.
- Therapeutic abortions for health reasons are not punishable in 8 states of Mexico and in six countries.
- Eugenic abortion is not sanctioned in two countries and in seven Mexican states.
- Abortion due to rape is not punishable in six countries.

Puerto Rico is the only country that does not penalize abortion and Panama the one who contemplates all the prior assumptions as punishment exception, whilst El Salvador (since 1977), Colombia, Chile and Honduras have opted for penalization under any assumption.

d. Some countries, such as Mexico, Peru and Bolivia, consider abortion as a public health problem, due to the incidence it has as cause of death among women, especially adolescents. The inefficacy of a declaration such as the preceding one is made evident and lacks consistency in the face of situations in which abortion is penalized, because as long as this persists, women shall continue recurring to clandestine abortions.

There are no figures for all countries and neither is there data disaggregated by age, geographical area or socioeconomic sector. Those that exist stem from non-official estimates, because the ones produced by the Ministries of Health are referred to the entries/exits from public hospitals, which only account for legal abortions and very marginally for clandestine abortions. Nevertheless, these estimates can give us an idea of the monstrous magnitude of the problem.

e. In general, the treatment abortion receives in the public policy of our countries has a double meaning. It is assumed as an event to be avoided and as a health problem that needs to be attended. That is the reason why, most of the times it is mentioned, it appears expressed as an objective of the sex education policy, or related to adolescent pregnancy and, in general, as an issue related to the prevention of pregnancy.

    f. Most of the countries that consider non-punishable assumptions contemplate in their legislations, or as part of their health policy, the rendering of medical attention services for the legal abortions, and in some cases (such as in several states of Brazil), they also propose an integral attention, including psychological care.

    g. The issue of the access conditions to the health services is not only about the legal type barriers, it is also related to the cost of the services. Interruption of pregnancy in cases of rape is attended in at least four states of Brazil totally free and, in general, the police are obliged to inform the victim about the possibility of having an abortion. Only Mexico, Paraguay, Bolivia and Honduras state that attention of abortion –it is understood that only when it is spontaneous or legal– is partially subsidized. Puerto Rico indicates that abortion is only practiced in the private health establishments. The other countries do not inform regarding this issue.

    h. Legislation on injuries to the conceived being has been approved in Colombia, El Salvador, Nicaragua and Peru.

Regarding legislative initiatives it is worthwhile to point out a relative movement, where the most important proposal is undoubtedly that of the Uruguayan feminist movement in a significant alliance effort with other social movements and that proposes, within the framework of the bill to defend reproductive health, the right of every woman to decide over the interruption of pregnancy during the first 12 weeks. On December 10, 2002, the House of Representatives approved said bill with 47 votes in favor, 40 against and 11 absentees. They are waiting the subsequent voting of the Senate.

With a different perspective and with serious restrictions, Provincial Law No. 1044 of the city of Buenos Aires dated July 17, 2003, although it does not permit abortion, it accepts advancing the birth date in cases of pregnancies incompatible with life due to anencephaly, as of the 24th week.

On the other hand, we currently have initiatives of laws on the issue in Argentina, Brazil, Peru, Chile, Paraguay and Nicaragua, the latter being a case of deep concern, since in the context of the penal code reform of that country, even though it still maintains therapeutic abortion and has reduced the penalties from 1 to 3 years for women, it has also introduced the legal protection of the "unborn child", sentencing the male and female doctors to 5 to 8 years in prison, absolute disablement for the exercise of medicine and closing of consultation rooms.

In the rest of the countries mentioned, a set of proposals has been presented, some of which have been stopped several years ago; however, the tendency in most of these shows a sign in favor of de-penalization through the system of indications. In all of the cases these refer to the rape and eugenics assumptions. Also, some few initiatives have been identified that propose de-penalization in all the assumptions for women. On the other hand, there are some proposals that formulate as aggravating circumstance the abortion without the woman's consent. Only two proposals of a contrary sign have been identified, one in Chile and the other one in Peru. The first case deals with the introduction of a new type of felony in the Penal Code related to prenatal diagnoses (presented in January 2004), and in the second one, the initiative is aimed at increasing the penalties in the abortion figures contemplated in the Penal Code (presented in August 2004). It is worth noting the ever-present difficulty of accessing reliable and updated information. Finally, the need arises to underscore the fact that within the eugenics abortion assumption, a constant that appears in the legislative initiatives is the exemption of penalty in the cases of anencephaly fetuses. Seemingly, this could be turning into a new crack from where it would be possible to act in a consistent manner, in a context that in a general way is still perceived with many limitations.

Regarding judicial decisions, an interesting movement related to cases of anencephaly fetuses has been reiterated in Brazil and Argentina. Even though in Brazil they are still awaiting the decision of the Federal Supreme Tribunal, and the Argentinean case was about an authorization for the induction of birth due to the advanced state of pregnancy, we can recognize certain encouraging signs geared towards change.

The largest production, however, is observed in the approval of technical norms for the attention of abortion. It is worth highlighting the two administrative norms designed by Brazil's Ministry of Health; the first one exonerates women whose pregnancy was the result of rape from the registry with the police procedure, and the second one, called *technical norm for the humanized attention of abortion*, which purpose is to offer clinical attention, psychological care and orientation on family planning with the guarantee of confidentiality. On the other hand Colombia, in its sexual and reproductive health national policy, approved in February 2003, establishes as an strategy to strengthen the human resources for the treatment of the birth complications by means of integral strategies that consider biological, psychological and social aspects. Uruguay also approved in August 2004 by means of Ordinance No. 369, norms and clinical guidelines for pre- and post-abortion attention. And Mexico, that within the context of the reform of its General Health Law on January 27, 2004, sets forth that the public health institutions must attend free of charge and under quality conditions the interruption of pregnancy in the assumptions permitted by penal law when the interested woman so requests it. The route of pinpointing through norms of administrative nature, guidelines and procedures tending to guarantee the attention of that which has already been recognized or not sanctioned by law, is an interesting strategy boosted mainly by the feminist movements with actions from within and without the State institutionalism.

In spite of the novelties, abortion continues being a neuralgic point in the issue of women's reproductive rights and a core aspect of the policy of our States, which in most cases tend to continue being bound to ceding vis-à-vis the conservative positions that exert pressure to maintain abortion penalized. Trapped in their own fears and particular interests, the governing classes do not know how to resolve the dilemma: to maintain penalization of abortion and decrease—until it is eliminated—its incidence as a cause of death among women, which is not possible, because it encloses a great contradiction; to develop and/or support proposals that turn into demands from a human rights vision that can strengthen the laicism and plurality of our States, in the face of the risk of losing positions and, more importantly, votes; to assume their obligations to be able to guarantee the strengthening of our democracies and a rights' reasoning in accordance with the political representation and public function they exercise, setting aside their moral particular imperatives.

On the other hand, we cannot forget that the figure of the protection of the conceived being's life can become a real obstacle for de-penalizing abortion and even pushing the trend towards the consolidation of the positions of those that intend to undo the advances achieved so far. There is still a long road ahead of us, with a lot of work in various fronts and on different levels, in which the strengthening of positions and actions to favor a lay culture—not one of faith—of human rights; democratic, not elitist; plural and not mono-chord, becomes a top-priority matter.

Lima, April 2005.

Notes

1. Feminist, Peruvian Attorney-at-Law, currently coordinates the Campaign for a Convention on Sexual Rights and Reproductive Rights.

2. This is a hypothesis picked up from Bonnie Shepard, expressed in her work: The "double discourse" on the sexual rights and reproductive rights in Latin America: the abyss between the public policies and private acts.

3. "Clandestine abortion in Peru: New evidences", Delicia Ferrando, Power Point presentation, Lima 2003.

4. The global implications of the US national and international policies on sexuality, Francoise Girard, p. 2 IWGSSP Working Paper, No. 1, June 2004.

5. Bush's other war: attack on health and the sexual rights and reproductive rights of women, International Women's Health Coalition.

6. The global implications of the US national and international policies on sexuality, Francoise Girard, p. 4 IWGSSP Working Paper, No. 1, June 2004.

7. On November 5, 2003, President Bush signed the law that prohibits partial births. To date the State of Nebraska and judges from New York and San Francisco have questioned the constitutionality of the law, since it does not contain a clause to protect women's health.

8. The global implications of the US national and international policies on sexuality, Francoise Girard, pp. 4 and 5.

9. Regional summary: What remains and what has changed?, Roxana Vásquez and Inés Romero, in *Sexual Rights, Reproductive Rights, Human Rights*, CLADEM, Lima, Peru, 2002. The countries that participated in the study are: Argentina, Bolivia, Brazil, Colombia, Chile, Ecuador, El Salvador, Honduras, Mexico, Panama, Paraguay, Peru, Puerto Rico and Uruguay.

10. This Campaign is being boosted to date by an ever-increasing group of local organizations, regional networks and campaigns from Latin America and the Caribbean.

11. I thank Verónica Aparcana for her collaboration on this part of the work.

POSTSCRIPT

Is Latin America Loosening Its Restrictive Abortion Laws?

Although it is clear that international organizations and foreign governments have a significant impact on the topic of abortion in Latin America, influences outside of Latin America are not solely responsible for the current abortion policies that exist throughout most of Latin America. In Bermúdez's article, Monsignor Restrepo blames organizations such as Profamilia (profamily) because it promotes "the kind of contraceptive, anti-life mentality that favors abortion." Restrepo also accuses a leftist newspaper of spreading misinformation regarding the number of illegal abortions that allegedly occur in Colombia. Vásquez Sotelo, however, maintains that abortion laws should be passed and implemented in Latin America. As part of her argument in support of abortion rights, Vásquez Sotelo argues that while the state avows a secular-based form of government, it violates "the rights and liberties of the non-believers or . . . those persons that profess other creeds." Vásquez Sotelo also blames the U.S.' current administration for limiting or withdrawing "U.S. funds for family planning."

Given that only three countries in Latin America have non-restrictive abortion laws while the overwhelming majority still maintain restrictive laws regarding abortion, it seems unlikely that most Latin American countries will enact more relaxed laws on abortion in the near future. Chile and El Salvador have the most prohibitive laws—abortion is not allowed under any circumstance. Many women in these countries do not have a significant number of contraception options available to them and, as a result, the frequency of unplanned pregnancies, and therefore illegal abortions, is substantially high. Due to similar, yet less restrictive, legislation in many Latin American countries regarding abortion, many women who seek abortions must do so illegally.

But who are these women, and how many of them are having these abortions? And why are they having them? According to IPAS (Protecting Women's Health Advancing Women's Reproductive Rights) in Latin America, there are 900,000 "unsafe" abortions each year in Central America and Mexico along with what is estimated to be another 3 million in South America. IPAS also points out that South America has the highest "incidence ratio" of unsafe abortions worldwide, according to data provided by the World Health Organization. As many as 21 percent of maternal deaths are believed to be associated with abortion in Latin America (The Alan Guttmacher Institute, 2003). Women who seek abortions are from all walks of life, different economic classes, married, or single, and those who have been raped or are victims of incest. However, a few general tendencies exist. Overall, women from lower economic statuses tend to have more illegal abortions than affluent women in Latin

America. However, it is important to note that these results are largely the effect of the opportunities brought by wealth and do not necessarily indicate which women seek abortion, overall. Women with the financial means have the ability to leave Latin America and travel to another country where abortion is legal or where knowledge exists regarding how "to obtain safe medical abortions in doctors' offices" ("An Overview of Clandestine Abortion," The Alan Guttmacher Institute, 2005).

Recently, however, a shift to less restrictive laws in some countries has been visible. According to *Colombia World News* (CWNews.com, May 11, 2006), the Constitutional Court of Colombia lifted the government's ban on abortion by ruling that abortion may be allowed in cases that involve rape, incest, fetal malformation, or danger to the life of the mother. In addition, on December 3, 2005, a *New York Times* article reported that in Brazil, "the world's largest Roman Catholic country, women's groups successfully pushed for new regulations this year that permit a rape victim to get an abortion without providing a police report to doctors, as was required." Yet in other countries such as Uruguay, anti-abortion/pro-life groups won a legislative battle when the Senate failed to ratify the legalization of abortion.

Although many articles on Latin America's stance on abortion have been written, those authored by Latin Americans are few. Most of their abortion-related articles tend to focus on global, as opposed to local, issues such as "The World's Abortion Laws" article by the Center for Reproductive Rights identifying how Latin America and Africa have the most restrictive laws concerning abortion. In another article, "An Overview of Clandestine Abortion in Latin America," the Deirdre Wulf of the Guttmacher Institute notes that although health experts were aware of clandestine abortions in Latin America, it was not until recently that reliable information about these unauthorized procedures existed. Other articles, such as Laura Carlsen's "Women's Rights Eroding in Latin America," discuss issues related to Latin American women's rights and argues that most laws "do not recognize the term 'sexual rights,' and that religious organizations in these countries have been working to eliminate the term 'reproductive rights,' as well." Articles and interviews related to religious leaders, such as "Awaiting Valencia," an interview with Cardinal Alfonso López Trujillo in 2006, criticizes countries that are considering decriminalizing abortion. The Hispanic division of the non-profit Catholic organization Human Life International also has an electronic library with articles on abortion and contraception in Latin America.

What the future holds for Latin America regarding the abortion issue is difficult to predict. Some countries such as Colombia have shown indications of loosening the restrictions on abortion. However, indications from countries like Ecuador reveal that significant change in Latin America's position on abortion is not likely to come anytime soon.

ISSUE 9

Does Race Matter?

YES: Mala Htun, from "Racial Quotas for a 'Racial Democracy,'" *NACLA Report on the Americas* (January/February 2005)

NO: Marisol de la Cadena, from "Reconstructing Race: Racism, Culture and Mestizaje in Latin America," *NACLA Report on the Americas* (May/June 2001)

ISSUE SUMMARY

YES: Political science professor Mala Htun says that Brazil, which for years upheld itself as an example of a "racial democracy," has come to a realization that racism has and does exist. To counter this finding, affirmative action programs have been created, though not fully implemented.

NO: Peruvian anthropology professor Marisol de la Cadena provides an overview of culturalist definitions of race as expressed by Latin American scholars and politicians. de la Cadena explains that common notions of race are challenged by this culturalist definition because race, accordingly, is not defined by phenotype; instead, people are identified in terms of class, decency, morality, and education.

For decades, Latin Americans and people from around the world have wrestled with the issue of race. Although scholars have studied the polemic complexities of the social relationships of various races and ethnic groups, fundamental disagreements still remain regarding what constitutes a person's "race" or even if the term itself contains any validity. Race is often understood as a social construct used by people to categorize large masses of people, usually with the implication that one race is superior and therefore has certain rights and opportunities that are not permissible for the "lower race." But, in Latin America, due the relatively high degree of the intermixing of peoples (known in Spanish as *mestizaje*), many avow that racism in Latin America does not exist. Yet, for most who study race and racism, this belief is unfounded. Social anthropologist Peter Wade ("Race in Latin America," in Philip Swanson, ed., *The Companion to Latin American Studies,* Arnold, 2003: 185–201) believes that race "exists as an idea—often with very potent social consequences."

In "Racial Democracy in the Americas" (J. of Cross-Cultural Psychology, May 2004, pp. 749–50), Yesilernis Peña, Jim Sidanius, and Mark Sawyer outline three major factors contributing to the theory of racial egalitarianism in Latin America. They summarize the elements of this concept, known as the "racial democracy theory" or the theory of "Iberian exceptionalism":

> Iberian conquerors of Latin America had the experience of living under the political and social hegemony of the Moors, a dark-skinned people, for nearly 800 years. . . . [The] Iberian colonists could not then regard the dark-skinned African and Indian slaves as subhuman with the same degree of celerity as the North American colonists found possible. Second, contrary to Calvinists and Puritan doctrines . . . Catholicism regarded Native Americans and even African slaves, as people with souls and equally beloved of God; thus . . . [Catholics were] less averse to mixing with them. Finally, in contrast to the colonists of North America, the early Latin American colonists did not venture into the New World with intact families . . . establish[ing] sexual and emotional relationships with the Indian and African slave women . . . creating a more positive attitude toward those of African descent and resulting in the high rates of miscegenation we see today in Latin America.

Nonetheless, the theory of racial equality is not without its critics. In the first of the following articles, Mala Htun explains that "Brazil has gone from an official 'racial democracy' to a country that acknowledges racism." To effectively combat racism, she asserts, people must acknowledge its existence in order to find ways to eliminate it. In the second article, which focuses on Peru, Marisol de la Cadena, underscores that while racism, in fact, does exist in the region, distinctions among people in Latin America are often understood as cultural rather than racial: "within the Latin American racial field, phenotype (skin, hair, and eye color as well as facial features) could be subordinated to 'culture' as a marker of difference." In her analysis of the concept of "decency," de la Cadena explains how people whose physical features could be identified as one race could view themselves as being a superior race due to their position in society, thereby creating a class-based or education-based distinction as opposed to race-based.

YES

Mala Htun

Racial Quotas for a "Racial Democracy"[1]

When the Brazilian government began considering affirmative action policies based on race, critics claimed they would be impossible to implement because of the ambiguity of the country's racial categories. Given extensive mixing and fluid identities, how can the state determine just who is black? Yet supporters of affirmative action say the question of "who is black?" is disingenuous. Senator Paulo Paim, for example, says that people are happy to acknowledge race when they identify the large number of blacks who live in poverty or prison. But when discussing compensatory policies, they suddenly become ignorant. Their response, he says, is "'how do we know who is black?' That's the first excuse they give. When we talk about the bad side, they identify blacks easily, but when we get to the issue of compensation, they don't know who blacks are!"[2]

For advocates, the answer to "who is black?" is simple: self-identification. Activists joke that if this doesn't work, "in the event of a doubt, call a policeman; they always know."

This controversy incited by affirmative action policies suggests that the state is a major player in racial formation. Its policies, over time, have had the potential to trigger transformations in the significance and understanding of identity in society at large. Unlike the United States and South Africa, Brazil historically avoided state-sponsored segregation and has prided itself on being a multi-hued "racial democracy." The racial democracy thesis insists that the absence of segregation, a history of race mixing and the social recognition of intermediate racial categories have upheld a unique, multi-tiered racial order. In the United States, by contrast, children born of white and black parents are generally classified as black—the "one-drop rule"—creating a bipolar racial system.

It is true that Brazilian culture celebrates racial ambiguity and that racial categories are fluid, but the country is nonetheless profoundly stratified by color. For decades, the state did nothing to alter the situation. On the contrary, it suppressed efforts to challenge the racial democracy myth and sought to whiten the population by encouraging European immigration. Over the past decade, however, that policy has changed radically. Under President Fernando Henrique Cardoso, the government admitted that Brazil is a racist country and endorsed an extreme form of affirmative action—quotas—to address racial inequality. The President created a national affirmative action program; three ministries introduced hiring quotas for blacks, women and handicapped people; the National Human Rights Program endorsed racial quotas; the foreign ministry introduced a program to increase the number of black diplomats; and three states approved laws reserving 40% of university admission slots for Afro-Brazilians. The state expanded these policies under the current government of Luiz Inácio Lula da Silva.

Policymakers were motivated more by conviction than threats or material or electoral interests. Few believed that championing race issues would actually win votes.[3] The changes occurred because greater numbers of people became convinced by an idea advanced for decades by Afro-Brazilian activists and social science researchers: racism is pervasive and will not disappear until something deliberate is done about it. Armed principally with arguments, critics of Brazil's racial order appealed to reason and a sense of justice to advance their cause. In a country struggling to prove its liberal credentials to itself and to the world, claims about the connections among race, equality and democracy found receptive ears.

Beginning in 1995, the Cardoso Administration provided a context that nurtured a transformation of political action on race. Then, preparations for the 2001 World Conference on Racism in Durban, South Africa provoked national soul-searching on racial inequalities. By the time the conference actually occurred, the country was ready for a change in orientation. Pledges made at Durban served as the catalyst for affirmative action policies at home. Social mobilization and presidential initiative were thus framed within unfolding international events.

⋅⦿⋅

While affirmative action was new, Brazil had a long history of anti-discrimination policies. The country's three constitutions in the 1930s and 1940s each proclaimed: "All are equal under the law." In the 1960s, the military government reintroduced the prohibition of racial distinctions and made racism a punishable offense. While these early provisions were mostly symbolic, with the return to democracy in 1985 and the Constitution of 1988, the state began to take more significant action on issues of race.

The 1988 Constitution defined racism as a crime for which bail could not be posted and with no statute of limitations. It also affirmed a commitment to multiculturalism, including the protection of Afro-Brazilian cultural practices, and it granted land titles to surviving occupants of *quilombos,* communities established by runaway slaves prior to emancipation in 1888.

At the state level, there were some policy changes adopted mostly by governors elected in 1982. Opposition parties that emerged in the 1970s and 1980s vied for black support by assuming a role in the fight against racism. In the early 1990s, state governors of Rio de Janeiro and São Paulo created government institutions and advisory groups to address issues of racism and to advocate on behalf of their black constituents. Though these agencies were small and underfunded, their creation implied that some institutions of the

Brazilian state were beginning to reject the thesis that Brazil was a racial democracy.[4]

With the election of Cardoso in 1995, the federal government began to take more initiative with regard to race and for the first time contemplated affirmative action. Meanwhile, Brazil published its tenth report for the United Nations Human Rights Commission. The report, written by the Secretary of State for Human Rights, Paulo Sérgio Pinhiero, proclaimed that affirmative action was compatible with Brazilian legislation and committed the state "to take positive action to promote equality."

The National Human Rights Program, launched in 1996, then proposed specific public policies aimed at black Brazilians, such as support for private businesses that hired them and measures to increase access to universities. The Human Rights Plan represented the first time that racial groups were officially recognized as targets of public policies.[5]

Following the 2001 World Conference on Racism, state agencies at all levels began announcing affirmative action policies. The ministries of Justice, Agrarian Development and Culture adopted 20% to 30% quotas for blacks. The Foreign Ministry also announced an affirmative action program. Historically, there have been almost no blacks in Brazil's diplomatic corps. "We need a diplomatic corps that reflects our multicolored society, that will not present itself to the outside world as if it were a white society, because it isn't," proclaimed Cardoso. The Foreign Ministry's affirmative action program, which began in early 2003, provides yearly scholarships to 20 black candidates to help them study for the public service entrance exam.

On releasing the 2002 Human Rights Program, Cardoso issued a decree that created the National Affirmative Action Program, charged with studying how government agencies could adopt "percentage goals" for blacks, women and the disabled in their own ranks and also in firms that contracted with the government. By the end of 2001, 14 different bills in Congress contemplated some form of racial quotas. On October 9, 2001, the state of Rio de Janeiro adopted a quota of 40% for blacks in its two state universities. The states of Bahia and Minas Gerais followed suit with similar programs.

These policies provoked lively exchanges on the street and in the press. Yet the debate about affirmative action was essentially reduced to a debate about quotas. To favor affirmative action was to endorse quotas; to oppose quotas was to condemn affirmative action in all forms. Quotas, however, are only one among several affirmative action measures both contemplated by official government commissions in the mid-1990s and actually implemented by municipal governments and nongovernmental organizations around Brazil. The full array of policies includes social programs targeted at black neighborhoods, job training programs, preparatory courses for university entrance exams and support for black-owned businesses.[6]

Simplifying the debate in this way served both advocates and opponents. Many activists aimed not only to lobby for new state policies, but also to initiate public discussions about race and to transform a culture that tacitly endorsed racial inequality. It was thus helpful to showcase an issue so provocative that no one could hide from it. Quotas—like abortion or the legalization of drugs—became an "absolutist" issue on which few people lacked a strong opinion. At the same time, aggregating a wider range of policy options into the signature example of quotas helped the cause of opponents. By focusing public attention on a blunt and controversial policy option, opponents could magnify the resistance to *any* type of affirmative action.

One of the most significant aspects of the government's moves towards affirmative action, argues anthropologist Peter Fry, is that they constitute a dramatic break with the past. "For the first time since the abolition of slavery," writes Fry, "the Brazilian government has not only recognized the existence and inequity of racism but has chosen to contemplate the passage of legislation that recognizes the existence and importance of distinct 'racial communities' in Brazil." Even Cardoso publicly declared that Brazilians "lived wrapped in the illusion that this was a perfect racial democracy when it wasn't, when even today it isn't."

❧◈❧

The emergence of a race-based "issue network" marked a shift in social mobilization around race in Brazil. The concept of an "issue network" captures the range of engaged groups and individuals and the specificity of their objectives. Members of issue networks are linked primarily by their shared interest in a particular policy area, not a collective identity, occupational category, place of residence or ideological orientation.[7]

Race-based issue networks had roots in three decades of activism and scholarship around inequalities, particularly during the upsurge in black political mobilization in the 1970s and 1980s. The period saw an increase in identity-based "new social movements" organized around race, ethnicity, gender and sexual orientation. Non-white Third World nationalist movements and the U.S. civil rights movement also influenced Brazilian activists. Yet many of these movements were culturally oriented and community-based. Influencing national policy was not their primary focus.[8]

By the 1990s the group of actors working on race issues had grown and diversified. Journalists, public intellectuals, state officials, economists from prestigious government research institutes, human rights groups, NGOs and members of Congress carried political action from Afro-Brazilian movements and the leftist academy into the social mainstream.

One of the decisive moments in this process came when the federal government's Institute for Applied Economic Research (IPEA) entered the debate. Beginning in 2000, the IPEA released studies, widely publicized in the press, documenting the extent and persistence of racial inequalities in Brazil. The significance of these studies was not necessarily their content, but the fact that prestigious white economists working for the government were participating in such discussions. "It was the first time that the debate left the militancy of the black movement and went to an institution with an undeniable reputation," commented Ricardo Henriques, author of one of the IPEA studies. "The issue had been taboo for academic economists on the one hand and the government on the other. When the IPEA published its studies, the government could no longer remain deaf to the [race] discussion."[9]

A shift in priorities at the Ford Foundation was another important factor. Ford had funded academic centers and research on race in Brazil since the late 1970s. Beginning in the mid 1990s, however, Ford began to focus its support on organizations dedicated to combating racism. Ford initiated a "period of action" in order to "help people who wanted to intervene rather than just gather information," says Nigel Brooke, Ford Foundation representative in Brazil. "We would come out of the closet with regard to our positive view of affirmative action, instead of just supporting research."[10] Edward Telles, a UCLA sociologist and expert on race relations in Brazil served as human rights program officer in Ford's Brazil office between 1997 and 2000. Under his leadership Ford's spending on race issues more than tripled. Ford helped fund Afro-Brazilian movements by endorsing public policy interventions like affirmative action, a network of black attorneys, academic research on race discrimination and policy remedies, and leadership training for black politicians.[11]

Meanwhile, black legislators from the Workers' Party (PT) grew more successful in organizing a black caucus in Congress.[12] The number of self-identified blacks in the Brazilian Congress has historically been low, never exceeding 3% of the total number of federal deputies and senators.[13] But by 2003, nine black deputies from the PT and two other parties, forming a *bancada negra* (black caucus), were meeting on a regular basis with the objective of seeing that race and affirmative action were discussed in Congress and within political parties. There are more "blacks" in the legislature than those nine, but despite their dark skin, they choose not to identify with the caucus.[14]

Black feminists who cut their teeth on global gender politics played key roles in the issue network. Because of their double militancy in the feminist and the Afro-Brazilian movements, they transferred skills and lessons from one struggle to the other. Beginning in the late 1980s and early 1990s, these women began to create autonomous spaces within the feminist movement, organizing national conferences, seminars and formulating their own demands.

Black women's lobbies were active participants in Brazil's preparation for the United Nations Conference on Population and Development, held in Cairo in 1994, and the Fourth World Conference on Women, held in Beijing in 1995. They succeeded in influencing the reports presented by Brazil at both conferences. Through these experiences, black feminists learned how to articulate the local and the global, to speak policy language and to negotiate consensus positions among people of diverse backgrounds. These skills helped the Durban process and the affirmative action movement. As Ivair dos Santos recalled: "We men had barely traveled abroad. But the women had already been to several UN conferences and told us exactly what to do!"

⋯◈⋯

In 1995, a new government sympathetic to an anti-racist agenda assumed power. Fernando Henrique Cardoso embodied cosmopolitan intellectual currents and their penetration into the state. Through personal declarations and appointments of individuals who wanted to take action, and by lending political support to their alliances for change, Cardoso began to change the state's approach to race. The political opening offered by Cardoso created opportunities and incentives for greater civic mobilization, which empowered social actors and lead them to push for greater changes later in his presidency

Cardoso's interest in race can be traced back to the early days of his career as a sociologist.[15] His dissertation explored race relations, as did his first published book and several of his scholarly articles in the late 1950s and early 1960s. In the December 2001 speech in which he declared his support for affirmative action, he noted that for him the issue was very personal "because I spent several years of my life as a sociologist . . . studying blacks and racial discrimination among the poorest sectors of the country."

Presidential initiative was crucial in orchestrating an opening for new policies. As Human Rights Secretary Paulo Sérgio Pinheiro has noted, "In Brazil, an authoritarian, racist and hierarchical country, you need the agreement of the President to advance on controversial causes."[16] Márcio Fortes, secretary general of Cardoso's party, concurs. The quotas, he says, "resulted from the President's determination, the idea being the construction of a more diverse and plural society for the future."[17] But individual presidential effort combined with a lack of partisan and legislative support means recent policies suffer from a fragile institutional architecture. According to Pinheiro, the issue of "fragile architecture" is a problem not just for race discrimination but also for human rights more generally.[18]

The Lula government has built upon the efforts of the previous administration. Lula created a Secretariat for the Promotion of Racial Equality to oversee implementation of the federal government's program, among other responsibilities. He also appointed a record number of blacks to senior posts (though their presence still lags far behind their numbers in society). A new law makes education in Afro-Brazilian history and culture obligatory in public schools. The health ministry now has a special program aimed specifically at black communities and two federal universities adopted admissions quotas. Meanwhile, Congress is currently debating a bill to mandate quotas in all public universities, government service, firms of more than 20 employees and television shows.

The final impetus to state action was the 2001 world Conference on Racism held in Durban. Anticipation of Durban provided an occasion for dialogue on race and a deadline to reach consensus on change. In order to produce an official report, the government convened a committee of state officials, academics and representatives of Afro-Brazilian movements. This committee held seminars and workshops around the country to solicit input, triggering more widespread civic mobilization.[19] NGOs, trade unions and universities sponsored lectures and exchanges. The yearlong preparatory phase culminated in Brazil's first national conference against racism and intolerance, held in Rio in July 2001 with some 1,700 participants from around the country and chaired by then-Vice Governor Benedita da Silva. The report eventually released by the preparatory committee adopted a vanguard position by endorsing quotas and other forms of affirmative action.

These preparations for Durban captured the interest of the Brazilian media. In the months leading up to the conference, newspapers, television and radio stations around the country began to report on racism and inequalities. Reports analyzed academic studies, proposals for quotas and affirmative action, the work of NGOs and debates about gay and indigenous rights. The op-ed pages of major newspapers carried debates over quotas waged by politicians, academics, journalists, Afro-Brazilian activists and government officials. Never before had race been such a big topic in the Brazilian press.

Later, the final document from Durban recommended affirmative action and other policies for victims of racism and called for adequate representation in politics and education, adding force to the positions adopted in Brazil's national report. In much the same way that the Fourth World Conference on Women held in Beijing in 1995 lent international legitimacy to women's demands for gender quotas in politics, the Durban conference backed Afro-Brazilian demands for special rights.[20] As Brazil's UN Ambassador Gelson Fonseca Jr. put it, "Durban was a positive experience for Brazil because it legitimized the debate on racism at the international level and recognized the need for remedial actions to benefit the victims of discrimination." But the most significant change, said Fonseca, "occurred at the domestic level, for it mobilized civil society and public opinion against racism, and strengthened the political will for policies to combat discrimination and led to the first experiences in affirmative action for Afro-descendents."[21]

✦

Despite these gains, a systematic national affirmative action program—one that operates in all government agencies and for which enforcement mechanisms have been created—has yet to be established. Such a program, requiring profound institutional changes and budgetary outlays, would likely encounter greater resistance than the changes made up to this point. Ideas may compel people to change their minds and even certain aspects of their behavior, but alone they seldom build the political coalitions needed to back the allocation of money and changes in the rules. In Brazil's world of pork-barrel politics, old habits die hard. Breaking these habits will likely require threats and incentives in addition to moral conviction.

Even weakly implemented, though, quotas compel people to talk about race. As Senator Paulo Paim noted, "even a law that works only partially is an advance. It generates debate, because then you can ask and force [political] parties to explain, why quotas aren't filled. . . . Laws don't always give the results that we expect, but they offer yet another instrument to do politics."[22] Proposing quotas exposes racism. In short, the appearance of quotas in public discourse prevents anyone from denying that race matters. Given Brazil's myth of racial democracy, this is no small achievement.

The concept of race originated as an attempt by nineteenth-century biologists and anthropologists to rank and evaluate the supposedly inherited differences among human populations. It has long been understood that it has almost no basis in biology.[23] Since it aids social discrimination, it would be desirable to move beyond the concept of "race." But race has validity as a social category. Racial labels define human identities and structure social relations. How can public policy address these concerns while avoiding essentialism? There is a tension between trying to get beyond race on the one hand and forming practical strategies to combat racism on the other. Negotiating this tension—affirming the living practice of race while simultaneously denying its essence—is the challenge Brazil faces.

Notes

1. Mala Htun, "From Racial Democracy to Affirmative Action: Changing State Policy on Race in Brazil," *Latin American Research Review,* Vol. 39, No. 1, 2004.

2. Interview. Brasília, June 19, 2002.

3. Then-Deputy (now Senator) Paulo Paim, for example. is convinced that his disapproval rating in his home state of Rio Grande do Sui increased by 6% because he started to push the issue of race in Congress. Interview, Brasília, June 19, 2002. On the other hand, there is at least one deputy who gets elected by championing race issues. Deputy Gilmar Machado calls himself the "candidate of the race" and "100% black" in his campaign material. and dedicates at least half of his budgetary amendments to the black community in his state of Minas Gerais. Interview, Brasília, November 13, 2002.

4. George Reid Andrews, *Blacks and Whites in São Paulo, Brazil, 1888–1988* (Madison: The University of Wisconsin Press. 1991).

5. Rebecca Reichmann, "Introduction," in Rebecca Reichmann, ed., *Race in Contemporary Brazil: From Indifference to Inequality* (University Park: The Pennsylvania State University Press, 1999).

6. Rosana Heringer. "Mapeamento de ações e discursos de combate às desigualdades raciais no Brasil," *Estudos Afro-Asiáticos,* Vol. 23, No. 2 (2001).

7. "Issue networks" is a concept coined by Hugh Heclo in 1978 to describe "specialized subcultures of highly knowledgeable policy watchers."

8. See Luiz Claudio Barcelos, "Struggling in Paradise: Racial Mobilization and the Contemporary Black Movement in Brazil," in Rebecca Reichmann, ed., *Race in Contemporary Brazil: From Indifference to Inequality* (University Park: The Pennsylvania State University Press, 1999). Also. Michael George Hanchard, *Orpheus and Power: The Movimento Negro of Rio de Janeiro and São Paulo, Brazil, 1945–1988* (Princeton: Princeton University Press,1994).

9. Interview with Ricardo Henriques, Rio de Janeiro, July 4, 2002.

10. Interview, Rio de Janeiro, July 3, 2002.

11. Telles recently published an excellent book, *Race in Another America: The Significance of Skin Color in Brazil* (Princeton: Princeton University Press, 2004).

12. The PT has historically been committed to fighting against racial inequality and the party has a secretariat devoted to combating racism. Yet many in the party see race as subordinate to class. Believing that racism and racial inequality are largely a function of class inequality, they maintain that universal social policies will take care of the race problem. Thus, though party leaders lend support to anti-racist struggles. black activists see this as "support" (in rhetoric only). Interview with Deputy Paulo Paim, Brasília, June 19, 2002.

13. Ollie Johnson. "Racial Representation and Brazilian Politics: Black Members of the National Congress, 1983–1999," *Journal of Inter-American Studies and World Affairs,* Vol. 40, No. 4 (Winter, 1998).

14. Interview with Deputy Luis Alberto, November 12, 2002.

15. Nonetheless, Cardoso's decision to champion affirmative action. though consistent with his longstanding views, may also have stemmed from a desire to compensate for his inability to further a progressive social legacy in other areas. Unlike other social policies, affirmative action is relatively inexpensive and can be engineered by the executive branch without the need to broker deals with members of Congress.

16. Interview. Brasília, June 19, 2002.

17. Interview. Brasília, June 19, 2002.

18. At a Columbia University lecture on May 4, 2002, Pinheiro had similarly expressed his view of the importance of President Cardoso and the weakness of more pervasive institutional support for a human rights agenda. He exclaimed, "Everything we manage to do in this area is because of the personal support of the President. But it's institutionally very fragile. . . . I have no political support. In Congress, there is benign neglect . . . no political party really cares."

19. Gilberto Saboia and Alexandre José Vidal Porto, "The Durban World Conference and Brazil," unpublished paper, 2002.

20. Mala Htun and Mark Jones, "Engendering the Right to Participate in Decision-making: Electoral Quotas and Women's Leadership in Latin America." in Nikki Craske and Maxine Molyneux eds., *Gender and the Politics of Rights and Democracy in Latin America* (London: Palgrave, 2002).

21. Personal communication, October 30, 2002.

22. Interview. Brasília, June 19, 2002.

23. See Anthony Appiah, "Race, Culture. Identity: Misunderstood Connections." in Anthony Appiah and Amy Gutmann, eds., *Color Conscious: The Political Morality of Race* (Princeton: Princeton University Press, 1997); Stephen Jay Gould, The Mismeasure of Man (New York: Norton, 1996); Joseph L. Graves. *The Emperors New Clothes: Biological Theories of Race at the Millennium* (New Brunswick: Rutgers University Press, 2001).

Marisol de la Cadena

 **NO**

Reconstructing Race Racism, Culture and Mestizaje in Latin America

One of the most puzzling, disconcerting phenomena that the non-native visitor confronts while traveling in Latin America is the relative ease with which pervasive and very visible discriminatory practices coexist with the denial of racism. Although, of late, new social movements have challenged the "normality" of this practice, it has not subsided. The usual local explanation our traveler might receive—whether in metropolitan centers like Lima, Bogotá or Santiago, or in provincial cities like Cuzco, Cali or Temuco—is that the discriminatory behavior, practiced both by the elite and the dispossessed, is not racism because it is based on cultural differences and not on skin color or any other biological marker. Race is not important in Latin America, our foreign friend would also be told; it is ethnicity that matters.

These responses, far from whimsical or innocuous social conventions, are at the crux of Latin American racial formations. These modern practices that acquit discriminatory practices of racism, and legitimize them by appealing to culture, are expressions of the intellectual and political history through which, in most of Latin America, "culture" has been racialized and thus enabled to mark differences. Moreover, within this culturalist definition, race could be biology, but it could also be the soul of the people, their culture, their spirit and their language. Thus, within the Latin American racial field, phenotype (skin, hair, and eye color as well as facial features) could be subordinated to "culture" as a marker of difference. If our fellow traveler ignores this background, she will be puzzled upon the realization that brown-skinned individuals can be white and Indian-looking fellows do not self-identify as Indians.

To help our imaginary traveler understand the modern history of race in Latin America, I would invite her to start by reading the following dialogue (recreated by myself) between the French Anglophile Gustav Le Bon and the Mexican thinker José Vasconcelos.

Gustav Le Bon: The influence of race in the destiny of peoples appears plainly in the history of the perpetual revolutions of the Spanish republics in South America. Composed of individuals whose diverse heredities have dissociated their ancestral characteristics, these populations have no national soul and therefore no stability. A people of half-castes is often ungovernable.

From *NCLA Report on the Americas,* vol. 34, no. 6, May/June 2001, pp. 16-23. Copyright © 2001 by Marisol de la Cadena. Reprinted by permission.

José Vasconcelos: Hidalgo, Morelos, Bolívar, Petion the Haitian, the Argentines in Tucumán, Sucre all were concerned with the liberation of slaves, with the declaration of equality of all men by natural right, and with the civil and social equality of Whites, Blacks and Indians. In a moment of historical crisis, they formulated the transcendental mission assigned to that region of the globe: the mission of fusing all peoples ethnically and spiritually.[1]

Similar discussions were at the core of the creation of the scientific definition of race in the late nineteenth century. Although race was not questioned then, and disputes were not aimed at subverting its existence, Le Bon and Vasconcelos could not have disagreed more on their views of *mestizaje.* While North Atlantic thinkers, like Le Bon, imagined Latin Americans as hybrids and thus potentially—if not actually—degenerates, Latin American intellectuals tended to praise the benefits of racial mixture, and proposed "constructive miscegenation."[2] They thus reversed anti-hybrid arguments and, as illustrated in Vasconcelos' quote, placed the "spirit" at the center of their projects. Yet, since racial markers could include some biological aspects, physical characteristics were not canceled out. Rather, they were subordinated to the superior might of morality, which although innate, was perceived as susceptible of being improved through education. This brings me to a second invented dialogue—and intrinsic discrepancy—this time between Le Bon and the Limeño anarchist Manuel Gonzales Prada.

Gustav Le Bon: A Negro or a Japanese may easily take a university degree or become a lawyer; the sort of varnish he thus acquires is however quite superficial and has no influence in his mental constitution. What no education can give him, because they are created by heredity alone, are the forms of thought, the logic, and above all the character of the Western man. Our Negro or our Japanese may accumulate all possible certificates without ever attaining to the level of the average European. . . . It is only in appearance that a people suddenly transforms its language, its constitution, its beliefs or its arts.

Manuel Gonzales Prada: Whenever the Indian receives instruction in schools or becomes educated simply through contact with civilized individuals, he acquires the same moral and cultural level as the descendants of Spaniards.[3]

For the French thinker, racial essences were inalterable, fixed and determined by heredity; thus education could only polish external appearances. Most Peruvians, whether anarchists or conservatives, could not have disagreed more. "Thanks to education, man can today transform the physical milieu and even the race. It is his most glorious triumph," asserted the Peruvian aristocrat Javier Prado, thus coinciding with his political rival, the radical Gonzales Prada. And these beliefs could become state policies.[4]

◦⟨◉⟩◦

Culturalist definitions of race, which endowed education with almost eugenic might, were central to the invention and legislation of Latin American nations.

They were supported by ubiquitous images in which erratic combinations of heredity, nature, climate, culture, and history resulted in distinctively identifiable spirits or souls of the races that peopled the world. In Peru, the case I know best through personal experience and academic analyses, the culturalist tendencies of racial thought were reaffirmed and sharpened by *indigenismo*. At the turn of the century this was a nationalist doctrine that anchored the Peruvian nation in its pre-Hispanic past, and most specifically in the Inca legacy. Artists, literary writers, and politicians, *indigenistas* are usually identified only after their pro-Indian leanings. Yet they were especially explicit in defining race through culture. Luis Eduardo Valcárcel, a Cuzco resident historian and lawyer, and the undisputed intellectual leader of this nationalist movement, was exceptionally clear in this respect. Valcárcel believed that the essential peculiarities of a people were determined by what he called their history. In his view, culture was the imprecise concept, yet powerful force, that determined races:

> The universal relationship between human beings and the natural world is resolved through culture. We are the offspring, that is, the heirs, of a being that has been shaped by the interaction of Nature and Culture. We repudiate the idea that spontaneous generation, mutation, or any form of biological life determine history because they lack history.[5]

Referring to the interconnectedness of race and culture, the historian of anthropology George Stocking remarked that U.S. academics, used "race" as "a catchall that could be applied to various human groups whose sensible similarities of appearance, of manner, and of speech persisted over time, and therefore were to them, evidently hereditary." There was, he said "no clear line between cultural and physical elements or between social and biological heredity."[6] Peruvians therefore were not exceptional in conflating race and elements of what we now consider "culture." Neither were they the only ones to postulate the eugenic might of education to improve the races. In fact, this was common to other racial projects that optimistically rejected the dominance of heredity in determining race. What I find peculiar about Peruvian racial thought and racial relations during this period, is that there existed a tendency to subordinate manifest phenotypic markers to allegedly invisible racial characteristics such as "intelligence" and "morality." This attitude, in turn, was expressed through a certain dismissal of whiteness. For example, discarding European forms of whiteness as marks of racial status, the conservative writer Manuel Atanasio Fuentes reported: "In Lima, even those men who immediately descend from the European race have a *trigueño* color [literally 'like wheat,' light brown] which is pale and yellowed."[7]

Indeed, the Latin American academic ambivalence towards whiteness represented a significant difference with the experience of, for example, Franz Fanon, whose intellectual sophistication, he declared, did not remove the derogatory fact of his black skin: "No exception was made for my refined manners, or my knowledge of literature, or my understanding of the quantum theory."[8] In Peru instead, trigueño whiteness provided racial sanctuary to the mostly brown-skinned elites across the country. Yet, obviously, the sanctuary was not class-blind. Rather, it was couched in the ideology of decency, a racialized class practice, according to which an individual's skin color marked him or her depending on the moral standards reflected by his/her level of education. *Mestizos* started where decency ended; they were called "*cholos*" and were considered immoral and corrupted. Anti-mestizo daily life feelings were academically authorized by *indigenistas,* who borrowed from North Atlantic thinkers (those that they had otherwise contested) the idea that races degenerated if they were moved from their proper geographical places. "Every personality, every group is born within a culture and can only live within it," wrote Valcárcel, who finished his sentence: "the mixing of races only produces deformities." From this view, mestizos were ex-Indians who had abandoned their proper natural/cultural environment—the countryside—and migrated to the cities. There, Valcárcel claimed, they degenerated morally. The same author claimed: "The impure Indian woman finds refuge in the city. Flesh of the whorehouse, one day she will die in the hospital."[9]

Thus, while opposing terminal racial hierarchies, the culturalist definition of race had room for discrimination flowing from purist racial-cultural views and their dictum of sexual morality. Mestizaje was the impure consequence of rape or female sexual deviance. It had resulted in mestizos: sexually irrepressible, culturally chaotic, and therefore immoral social beings. Hence, cholos represented not biological, but moral degeneration, stirred by the alteration of the original order, by an inappropriate cultural environment, and furthered by a deficient education. The elite, regardless of skin color and of cultural mixture, were sheltered from the stains of mestizaje. They were educated, occupied their racial proper places—both geographically and socially—and thus lived within the dictum of moral order. They were *gente decente,* decent people, people of worth. Men were gentlemen, their women were ladies, and as such they displayed appropriate sexual behavior. *Caballeros* were responsible patriarchs and *damas* virtuous women, but more importantly *decencia* inspired them to fall in love with each other, thus preventing the transgression of racial boundaries. Sexual disorder was not normal among gente decente; it was the attribute of urban commoners, the mestizos. Being mestizo in Peru was a racialized class fact, where class was not only judged in terms of income but of education and origin.

None of the above means that mestizaje lacked supporters in Peru. On the contrary, it was championed by a broad array of politicians, from reactionary partisans of General Francisco Franco to anti-imperialist supporters of César Augusto Sandino. Yet it never became an official, state-led, nation-building project. This might have been the result of its exclusionary class nature, according to which only commoners were mestizos. But it could have also been one of the hidden legacies of *indigenismo.* Valcárcel became Minister of Education in the 1940s, and since then, either overtly or surreptitiously, *indigenismo* has inspired significant official educational policies. Key to *indigenista* success and relative consensus might have been Valcárcel's idea of "unity in diversity" which he presented as the context for his rural education program in a 1946 speech to the national Congress. Through this program, the Minister of Education expressed his desire to preserve Indians as agriculturalists, yet to offer them the benefits of civilization through bilingual Quechua and Spanish literacy programs, agricultural training, and hygiene lessons. While these policies might have prevented mestizaje from becoming official nationalist rhetoric, they did not invalidate it. Valcárcel's project could have been ambiguous enough as to bring consensus into the assortment of ideas proposed by the politically heterogeneous and even antagonistic champions of mestizaje.

In the years to come, and under such ambiguous slogans as "unity in diversity" the state promoted purist manifestations of indigenous folklore, emphatically discouraging those considered "inauthentic" or "mestizo," while at the same time "modernizing" the countryside through development programs. In the meantime, intellectuals faithful to the teachings of Valcárcel—most of them anthropologists—continued to blacklist pro-mestizaje efforts. For example, as late as 1965, in a conference entitled "Ideas and Processes of Mestizaje in Peru," the founder of the Institute of Peruvian Studies, José Matos Mar, defined mestizaje as "an imposition from the colonial past, an idea replete with racist prejudices, aimed at the extinction of indigenous cultures."[10] In the same conference, the celebrated Quechua writer José María Arguedas—who had worked with Valcárcel in the Ministry of Education—presented for the first time in public a version of what Peruvian anthropologists call "the myth of Inkarri," a story predicting the return of the Incas.[11] Three years later, in 1968, when the military regime issued the Agrarian Reform, they used the label "inkarri" to name a major annual event.

&⟨◉⟩⟩

In relative contrast, and during the same period, Mexico, Bolivia, Guatemala, and Ecuador implemented "assimilationist" policies that promoted Spanish literacy and explicitly or implicitly fostered the elimination of vernacular languages and indigenous cultures. Obviously, I do not think the Peruvian state represented the Latin American pro-Indian vanguard. Nevertheless, I want to link this Peruvian idiosyncrasy, to another one: While in the countries that I have just mentioned powerful ethnic social movements have emerged since the late 1970s, similar efforts in Peru are still very marginal.

Some analysts have interpreted the absence of "ethnic social movements" in present-day Peru to reflect indigenous "assimilation" and cultural loss. According to this perspective, Peruvian Indians are either behind in terms of ethnic consciousness or have yielded to dominant mestizaje projects. This perspective places indigenous Peruvians within the bounds of "an ethnic group," and forgets that ethnicity is only one among the host of social relations—race, gender, class, geography, generation (to name commonplaces)—that organize (and disorganize) indigenous and nonindigenous life processes. But, most importantly it disregards that "indigenous culture" exceeds the scope of Indianness. I know this sounds strange, but I will tell you what I mean and how I learned about it.

From the 1950s to the mid 1970s, indigenous peasant leaders from all over the country, but most specifically from Cuzco, led a long political insurrection against the traditional hacienda system. The conflict, organized in alliance with leftist parties and waged under the colors of class struggle, destabilized the political order and eventually forced a military coup and a radical Agrarian Reform in 1968. Blinded by the success of class rhetoric, leftist social scientists have ignored the indigenous cultural aspects of the struggle, which were abundant. Ardent insurrectional speeches were delivered in Quechua, and the massive demonstrations in the Plaza de Armas of Cuzco were attended by peasants wearing *ponchos* and woolen caps—*chullos*—clothes that express indigenous identity and which were specially and symbolically worn for those occasions.

THE MARKETING OF *EL CHOLO TOLEDO*

In 1990, the now infamous Alberto Fujimori ran for president against the renowned writer Mario Vargas Llosa calling upon *"chinitos"* (an allusion to himself) and *"cholitos"* (working class Peruvians) to join forces against *"blanquitos"* (Vargas Llosa and the elite circles surrounding him). *El Chino,* as he came to be known, promised a government that would promote "technology, honesty, and work." Once in power, he implemented a neoliberal economic plan and requested that the chinos and cholos forget their collective battles and instead struggle individually against poverty by becoming micro-entrepreneurs. The 2000 electoral campaign, the first act in the year-long drama that finally drove the increasingly corrupt and dictatorial Fujimori from office, pitted him against Alejandro Toledo, a Peruvian of working class origins, whose campaign evoked the complexity of Peruvian *mestizajes.*

Migration and education, like in most stories of mestizaje, play a crucial role in Toledo's public life story. This emphasizes his poor origins in an Andean village and his success in earning a Ph.D. from Stanford University. However, rather than using education to silence his origins, like the ideology of decency would have indicated, throughout his electoral campaigns, Toledo loudly claimed cholo identity. Yet, this identity is not simple. On the contrary, *"el Cholo Toledo"* is multifaceted; the images he uses to fashion his electoral persona draw—perhaps independently of his intentions—from the historical rhetoric of Peruvian mestizaje and its multiple meanings.

At the most obvious level, Toledo's electoral campaign connects with the Incanist, anti-mestizo tradition promoted by *Valcarcel's indigenismo.* As the symbol of his political party he chose the *"Chakana,"* described as an Inka symbol that signaled the dawn of a new era. Within the same script, very important political gatherings have been held in Cuzco, where the candidate opened the demonstrations with a ritual salute to the Andean deities that surround the city, and Eliane Karp, (his anthropologist wife) addressed the crowds in Quechua, the indigenous language. Not surprisingly, "et Cholo" has also been labeled Pachacutec, allegedly the most important Inca.

Less obviously, but summoning the attention of a crucial sector of the electorate, Alejandro Toledo's image wearing a *chullo* and a tie connects with indigenous views of mestizaje—those that, for example, see Quechua and vernacular Andean practices as compatible, even coming to fruition, with a university degree and economic success. However, and notwithstanding the candidate's reverberant claims to a working class cholo identity, he also connects with elite views of mestizaje. His university degree, his "studies abroad," (and of course his marriage to a foreign white woman) loom large, and thus "Alejandro"—as his elite peers familiarly call him—represents an "ironed" choloness, one that has been tamed by education and is a useful political strategy. Alvaro Vargas Llosa—the writer's son—praised Toledo's "cool calculating mind of a Stanford and Harvard academic" and his ability to "understand life from a viewpoint rooted in analytic rigor and scientific information." Coinciding with his son's opinion, Mario Vargas Llosa, expressed his support of Toledo by describing him as a "modern Indian, a cholo without grudges or inferiority complexes."

But Toledo's mestizo identities aside, and considering the historical trajectory of race (and racism) in Peru, a question remains: What happened at the end of the twentieth century that allowed for the profusion of racial images in a country used to silencing the racial identity of public figures and to the denial of racism? Attributing this effect to Alberto Fujimori would be too simple, and would have probably disappeared with the now fugitive ex-President. That this has not been the case obliges further explanation.

In 1998, in my annual summer visit to Peru, I was surprised by the outpouring of denunciations against racism set off when the employees of four separate night clubs and a coffee house in Lima barred entry to several persons seemingly because they perceived them to be nonwhite. The anti-racist saga was complex: The Institute for the Defense of the Consumer had taken on the denunciations and had leveled fines against the businesses accused of discrimination. Revealing that the state is not monolithic (and also making visible the corruption that affects its practices) several judges were bribed into revoking the Institute's sanctions. Against this backdrop, another state institution, the Human Rights Commission of the National Congress, organized a public audience to discuss the pros and cons of penalizing "racism" constitutionally. Throughout the process, I could not but think: Why denounce racism now? And the crucial response came from man named Alejandro Falla, a lawyer from the sanctioning Institute:

"People believe that the free market has no laws. But let me tell you, the free market has one law, and that law is that as consumers we are all equal. The free market does not tolerate any form of discrimination against consumers. Every individual, regardless of gender, religion, ethnic, or racial identity, has the right to participate in the free market."

And a law was passed unanimously in 1999 to legally sanction discriminatory actions for the first time in Peruvian history. The hegemony of Peruvian racism—its mute reign—was apparently over, and although this did not mean it would disappear, it did mean that it could be publicly censured. Racism's silent rule, however, was being challenged by the potential hegemony of neoliberalism and its embrace of the excluded as consumers, regardless of their self-identity.

Indeed, the cholo image that Toledo casts is highly compatible with the persona that neoliberalism requires: a solitary achiever, able to succeed without the intervention of the state. The public version of the candidate's life story describes him as a micro-entrepreneur since his childhood, working as a shoe shiner, a soda and popsicle vendor during Sunday soccer games, and a door-to-door peddler of the tamales his mother cooked. This boy, the story tells us, can become the President of Peru, and even if he does not, he lives a comfortable life. Thus, Toledo also plays into the hegemony of neoliberalism, and its promotion of a consumer who can come from any background, provided that he/she can buy and sell. The economic identity that neoliberalism requires, and the social success it offers, is not measured by the "refinement" standards imposed by "decency," because with globalization as one of its premises, identities can be multicultural.

Obviously, I do not think neoliberalism needs to raise anti-discriminatory banners, or to generalize the advocacy of multiculturalism. Yet I do think that in countries like Peru, neoliberalism has a certain amount of seductive room for selective class-blind multiculturalisms. Alejandro Toledo's "market economy with a human face" can also come with a cholo face. Thus, it potentially decouples the dominant identification of popular classes with immorality and perennial marginality. In so doing, it connects with popular mestizaje projects and promises an historically unprecedented possibility for the inclusion of the "unrefined" members of the "popular classes" in official politics.

Undoubtedly, the markers of indigenous mestizaje that Toledo used throughout both his campaigns represent an unprecedented public challenge to "decency," and this has provoked the explicit revulsion of the upper classes. Thus, while neoliberalism may appropriate multiculturalism, the practices of indigenous mestizaje are not for its consumption only. Insofar as they connote images that defy exclusion, they can be used by the new social movements to resignify the traditional cultural politics of race and class in Peru. Whether this resignification serves the market or the people is a historical matter. And by history I do not mean the past. I mean present-day people acting politically.

I would not have paid attention to the significance of these symbols without the help of Mariano Turpo, a self-identified indigenous leader, active since the 1930s, who took part in the 1960s–1980s struggle for land. From him I learned that indigenous utilization of class rhetoric was a political option that did not represent the loss of indigenous culture, but was rather a strategy towards its empowerment. The huge peasant meetings in the Plaza de Armas, and the struggle for land that they were part of, expressed a political practice that was not an either/or choice between ethnicity and class. Instead it coupled both. Don Mariano Turpo's personal experience illustrates this. He is a *paqo*—an Andean ritual specialist, somewhat like a diviner. During the years of the struggle, this role was crucial in his capacity as a regional politician. In his own words: "They did not follow anybody but me; they accepted me because I was the only one that knew. I consulted the Apu Ausangate [the regional Andean deity] before going on any strike, before signing any document."[12]

Don Mariano, who speaks Quechua and Spanish, has signed many documents. In one of them, written while imprisoned under the charges of being a Communist, he urged his compañeros to "learn how to read and write, as being illiterate, makes us more Indian, easy preys of the *hacendados* and their lawyers. We have to stop being Indians to defend ourselves." Indeed, I was surprised at this call for de-Indianization. Yet, I gradually learned from Don Mariano—and from many other indigenous *Cuzqueños*—that "not being Indians" did not mean shedding indigenous culture. Rather de-Indianization implied shedding a social condition entailing absolute denial of civil rights. This definition of Indianness was reinforced when, in the midst of the struggle for land, and while state cultural activists were busy promoting indigenous folklore, other state representatives—the police—used the label "Indian" to deny peasant leaders their rights to public speech while torturing people like Don Mariano. De-Indianization meant—as Don Mariano had urged in his letter—becoming literate, being able to live beyond the hacienda territory, in general obtaining civil rights. And none of this meant shedding indigenous culture. On the contrary it meant empowering it, and thus pushing it beyond the scope of disenfranchised Indianness.

After my lessons with Don Mariano, it was impossible for me to assume that "the loss of indigenous culture" explained the lack of ethnic movements in Peru. Don Mariano helped me realize that the absence of overt culturalist (or ethnic) political slogans during that period may have resulted instead from the need to distance the movement from state-sponsored *indigenismo* and its allegedly pro-Indian, and highly anti-mestizo language. I thus returned to the notion of mestizaje and found that it had had more than one trajectory, and more than one meaning. Indigenous Cuzqueños have appropriated the mestizo identity and given it an alternative meaning: They use it to identify literate and economically successful people who share indigenous cultural practices yet do not perceive themselves as miserable, a condition that they consider "Indian." Far from equating "indigenous culture" with "being Indian"—a colonial label that carries an historical stigma of inferiority—they perceive Indianness as a social condition that reflects an individual's failure to achieve educational improvement. As a result of this redefinition, "indigenous Andean culture" exceeds the scope of Indianness; it broadly includes Cuzqueño commoners who claim indigenous cultural heritage, yet refuse to be labeled Indians. They proudly call themselves "mestizo," without, however, agreeing to disappear in the cultural national homogeneity that the current dominant definition of mestizo conveys.

Thus, despised by prominent intellectuals, and lacking an overt official life, mestizaje was embraced by the working classes as an empowering identity project. Yet, adding to its multiple meanings, mestizaje in its popular version—what I have called "indigenous mestizaje"—may correspond to some of the demands for multiculturalism leveled by the Maya or Aymara social movements in Guatemala and Bolivia respectively. Indigenous mestizos in Peru use their vernacular languages along with Spanish; they combine formal education and indigenous practices; and they commute between city and countryside, and are versed in both ways of life. Most importantly, these grassroots forms of mestizaje cancel the immorality imputed to cholos, and they stress instead their proud endurance of, and struggle against poverty and adverse social conditions. Indigenous mestizaje is not meant to be resolved in "either Indian or mestizo" evolutionary choices imposed by modern concepts. Rather, as lived experiences, they distance themselves from conceptual abstractions and present alternatives that at first sight may seem oxymoronic to modern minds. "People can be different and similar at the same time. I practice indigenous culture but I am not an Indian," an indigenous woman in Cuzco told me. And many others echoed her.

❧

Obviously, dominant definitions of mestizaje, and the evolutionary racial-cultural projects those definitions entail, have not disappeared from the national political scene. They have remained latent both among leftist and conservative ideologues. The celebrated writer Mario Vargas Llosa revived them when he said:

> Indian peasants live in such a primitive way that communication is practically impossible. It is only when they move to the cities that they have the opportunity to mingle with the other Peru. The price they must pay for integration is high—renunciation of their culture, their language, their beliefs, their traditions, and customs, and the adoption of the culture of their ancient masters. After one generation they become mestizos. They are no longer Indians.[13]

Although used to promote mestizaje, Vargas Llosa's words illustrate the survival of earlier *indigenista* culturalist rhetoric, this time dressed in the evolutionary ethnic lexicon to which Peruvian anthropology resorted when race was evicted from scientific discourse. Within this new framework, Indians were an ethnic group that represented an earlier stage of development and were culturally different from mestizos. This allegedly nonracial yet evolutionary lexicon, which allows for images of "indigenous improvement" and speaks of hierarchies of reason, is facilitated by the "culture talk" provided by certain notions of ethnicity. It also gives a nonracist allure to images like those produced by Vargas Llosa, and leads to the current denials of racism in Peru.

A 1947 remark by the Argentine populist dictator Juan Domingo Perón prompts some final thoughts:

> For us race is not a biological concept. For us, it is something spiritual. It constitutes a sum of the imponderables that make us what we are and impel us to be what we should be, through our origins and through our destiny. It is what dissuades us from falling into the imitation of other communities whose natures are foreign to us. For us, race constitutes our personal seal, indefinable, and irrefutable.[14]

Culturalist visions of race have been pervasive among Latin American thinkers, and their efforts have not necessarily been aimed at separating race from culture. As the quote from Perón makes clear, the Latin American political contribution has consisted in emphasizing the "spiritual" aspects of race, and in privileging "culture" over "biology" as its defining essence. When the international scientific community rejected race as biology, it did not question the discriminatory potential of culture, let alone its power to naturalize difference. The Latin American tendency to explain and legitimate racial hierarchies through culture preserved its authority as a rhetoric of exclusion, discrimination and dominance framed in the apparent egalitarianism of culture talk. Unveiling the discriminatory potential of "culture" and its historical embeddedness in racial thought is important; it can shed light on Latin American culturalist forms of racism which are neither exclusive to rightist politicians nor limited to academia. This understanding goes a long way towards explaining the puzzle—racism accompanied by its denial—confronted by our innocent traveler in the Americas.

Notes

1. Gustav Le Bon, in Alice Widener, ed., *Gustave Le Bon: The Man and His Works* (Indianapolis: Liberty Press, 1979 [1913]) p. 240; and José Vasconcelos, *The Cosmic Race* (Baltimore: Johns Hopkins Press, 1997 [1925]), p. 16.

2. Nancy Leys Stepan, *The Hour of Eugenics: Race, Gender, and Nation in Latin America* (Ithaca: Cornell University Press, 1991).

3. Gustav Le Bon, *Gustave Le Bon: The Man and his Works*, p. 289 and Manuel Gonzales Prada in Jorge Ruedas de la Serna, ed., *Manuel Gonzales Prada: Una Antologia General* (Mexico City: SEP, 1904), pp. 173–174.

4. Javier Prado, "Memoria del Decano de letras del Ano 1908," in *Revista Universitaria de San Marcos* (Lima: Universidad de San Marcos, 1909), pp. 50–56.

5. Luis Eduardo Valcárcel, *Tempestad en los Andes* (Lima: Editorial Universo, 1978 [1927]), p. 109.

6. George Stocking, *"The Turn of the Century Concept of Race,"* Modernism/modernity, Vol. I, No. 1, 1994, pp. 4–16.

7. Manuel Atanasio Fuentes, *Lima: Esquisses historiques, statistiques, administratives, comerciales, et morales* (Paris: Fermin Didiot, 1867), p. 194.

8. Franz Fanon, *"The Fact of Blackness"* in *Black Skin, White Masks* (New York: Grove Press, 1968 [1952]), p. 117.

9. Valcárcel, *Tempestad en los Andes*, p. 45.

10. Jpsé Matos Mar, "Algunas consideraciones acerca del uso del vocablo mestizo," *Revista Historica* (Lima: Instituto Historico del Peru, 1975), Vol. 28, pp. 62–63.

11. Jpsé Maria Arguedas, "El mestizaje en la literatura oral," *Revista Historica* (Lima: Instituto Historico del Peru, 1975), Vol. 28, pp. 271–275.

12. Conversations with Mariano Turpo, Cuzco, 1990. Thanks to Eloy Neira for introducing me to Mariano Turpo.

13. Mario Vargas Llosa, "Questions of Conquest: What Columbus Wrote and What he Did Not," *Harper's*, December 1990, pp. 45–53.

14. Juan Domingo Peron, October 12, 1947, Dia de la Raza, Buenos Aires, Argentina; quoted in Ashley Montagu, *Man's Most Dangerous Myth: The Fallacy of Race* (Walnut Creek, CA.: Altamira Press, 1999), p. 54.

POSTSCRIPT

Does Race Matter?

de la Cadena's article explains how culturalist definitions defy common notions of "race." According to the many intellectuals and politicians she cites, race can and has been understood according to factors such as class, decency, morality, and education. At certain moments in Latin American history, de la Cadena notes, it was thought that the mixture of races or *mestizaje* was "a moral degeneration, stirred by the alteration of the original order." In the 1970s, however, "mestizaje was embraced by the working classes as an empowering identity project." Mala Htun's article details the Brazilian government's official recognition of the existence of racism. She points out that for many years Brazilians embraced the myth that racism did not exist in their country, but that today the government is implementing programs to address racism and its consequences.

Recently, the concept that all humans can be identified as being of a particular race has come under fire—from science. Through DNA sampling, geneticists have been able to trace ancestral lineage according to one's DNA code and comparing that to regional concentrations of genetic codes around the world. Ultimately, this new technology has led to many surprising results. People who previously viewed of themselves as members of a particular race have discovered that their DNA places them closer to a group that may not coincide with their phenotype (skin color, hair type, facial features). As a result, people who appear "black" based on skin color may actually have more links to Europe, which is generally considered to be predominantly "white." And, similarly, those who have viewed themselves as "white," such as lighter-skinned people who identify themselves as being of European decent, have often found that their DNA code matches more closely with those of African origin as opposed to European. Ultimately, DNA has challenged past definitions of what "race" is.

Despite these developments in science and although countries such as Brazil have taken steps to recognize the existence of racism, some contemporary governments in the region continue to uphold Latin America as an example of racial harmony. During the years of the U.S. civil rights movement, for example, Fidel Castro proclaimed that Cuba was a racial democracy. And, in 1994, a report by the Mexican government declared that "the Government of Mexico opposes any form of discrimination, institutionalized or otherwise, as well as the new forms of discrimination, xenophobia and other forms of intolerance that have emerged in several parts of the world, particularly in the developed countries" (quoted in Ariel E. Dulitzky's "A Region in Denial: Racial Discrimination and Racism in Latin America"). In a communiqué from a conference in 2000, South America's heads of state made the following statement: "The Presidents view with concern the resurgence of racism and of discriminatory manifestations and expressions in other parts of the world and state their commitment to preserve South America from the propagation of said phenomenon" ("The Brasilia Comuniqué," Meeting of the Presidents of South America, September 1, 2000 Andean Community General Secretariat). Decades before, the theorists who formulated the concept of racial equality had looked to other places, particularly to South Africa's apartheid or the racially discriminatory "Jim Crow" laws of the United States's South, to create their vision of racial harmony in Latin America. These statements by contemporary Latin American governments demonstrate a continuation of looking elsewhere to define the status of race at home.

The United Nation's Economic Commission for Latin America contradicts such contemporary claims to racial equality. According to a 2002 report by Álvaro Bello and Marta Rangel, "Discrimination and racism are an integral part of the problems afflicting Latin America and the Caribbean, and they have brought poverty, exclusion and inequality in their wake for millions of the region's inhabitants, mainly among Indigenous peoples and the Afrodescendant population" ("Equity and Exclusion in Latin America and the Caribbean: The Case of Indigenous and Afro-Descendant Peoples," *CEPAL Review* April 2002).

For many people inside and outside of Latin America, the question of racism may lie in differentiating between overt and covert racism. For example, in many Latin American countries, one needs only to look at the media—the faces of advertising campaigns, news anchors, and television personalities, as well as the composition of many state legislatures—to notice that a majority of the people in influential positions are light-skinned and possess more "European" features. Do darker-skinned peoples have equal access to the voting process? And if so, if a darker-skinned majority elects lighter-skinned political official or tends to buy products represented by someone of a different "race," who is accountable for whatever racism may exist? Ultimately, despite examples of covert racism, the central question remains: Do all types of people have an equal opportunity—void of discrimination—when looking for work, acquiring an education, or establishing their position within Latin American society?

For more information on the question of race in Latin America, see Álvaro Bello and Marta Rangel, "Equity and Exclusion in Latin America and the Caribbean: The Case of Indigenous and Afro-descendant peoples," *CEPAL Review* (April 2002); Ariel Dulitzky, "A Region in Denial: Racial Discrimination and Racism in Latin America," in Anani Dzidzienyo and Suzanne Oboler, eds., *Neither Enemies Nor Friends: Latinos, Blacks, Afro-Latinos* (Palgrave Macmillan, 2005); Peter Wade, "Race in Latin America," in Phillip Swanson, ed., *The Companion to Latin American Studies* (Arnold, 2003, 185–201); and Yesilernis Peña et al, "Racial Democracy in the Americas," *Journal of Cross-Cultural Psychology* (November 2004, 49–50).

ISSUE 10

Do Volunteer Border Patrol Groups Represent a Reasonable and Just Way to Address Immigration Across the Mexican-U.S. Border?

YES: Charlie Norwood, from "The Miracle on the Southwest Border: Illegal Immigration Smashed. A Direct Field Report on the Arizona-Mexico No-Man's Land," *This Week in Washington* (April 8, 2005)

NO: Editors of *Intelligence Report,* from "Vigilante Watch: A Newly Elected Congressman Discusses Anti-Immigrant Vigilantism and Racism in His Southern Arizona District," *Intelligence Report* (Spring 2003)

ISSUE SUMMARY

YES: Congressman Charlie Norwood argues that the presence of the Minutemen has reduced the flow of illegal immigrants into the United States.

NO: Congressman Raúl M. Grijalva contends that volunteer patrol groups on the Mexico-U.S. border are anti-immigrant, racist vigilantes. Instead of further militarizing the border, Grijalva advocates that more attention be paid to the economics, history, culture, and migration patterns of the border region.

From Tierra del Fuego in South America to the arctic regions of Canada and the United States, the movement of peoples to and within the Americas is one of the defining characteristics of the history of the Western hemisphere. Today, both internal migration and immigration across international borders continue to shape and challenge conceptions of cultural and national identity. In recent decades, waves of poor Ecuadorians have migrated from continental Ecuador to the Galapagos Islands in search of opportunities in the fishing and tourism industries. A record number of Colombians are fleeing to other regions in their country due to armed conflict and human rights violations. And, during the past century, urbanization has represented one of the most significant examples of migration in Latin America (David L. Clawson, *Latin America and the Caribbean: Lands and Peoples,* 2006, p. 368). In a variety of Latin American countries, immigration sparks heated debate that in some cases has motivated the creation of new legal restrictions. Controversy also frequently surrounds the U.S. immigration policy toward its Caribbean neighbors. Latin Americans and Caribbean people emigrate to destinations outside of the Western hemisphere as well, including France, Great Britain, Spain, and Japan (Clawson, p. 370).

Recently, illegal immigration into the United States across its southern boundary has generated fiery debate on both sides of the border. Nonetheless, the Hispanic presence and the movement of peoples across the U.S. border is not a new phenomenon. Before the conquest of the Americas, nomadic indigenous tribes moved freely through the region where the current border now exists. The border territory on the U.S. side now defined as Texas, New Mexico, Arizona, and California were territories of the Spanish viceroyalty of New Spain and later part of Mexico. With the signing of the Treaty of Guadalupe Hidalgo in 1848 and the Gadsden Purchase of 1853, those states—as well as parts of Colorado, Wyoming, and the entirety of Nevada and Utah—became part of the United States. In other words, some U.S. citizens of Hispanic descent trace their ancestral presence in the region to a time when the territory was part of Spain and, later, Mexico. In their case, it was the border—not people—that moved.

Along the border zone, the search for work has a long history. Facing a labor shortage in the agricultural sector during World War II, the United States established an agreement with Mexico called the Bracero Program (1942–1964) in which Mexican laborers could legally work in the United States on a temporary basis. The North American Free Trade Agreement has also generated an unprecedented movement of peoples and goods across the border in both directions, but citing economic, labor, social, and environmental issues, the treaty has many detractors in both Mexico and the United States.

Each year approximately 700,000 illegal immigrants enter the United States and the number of illegal immigrants currently living in the United States ranges from 7 to 20 million (*Christian Science Monitor*, May 16, 2006). Immigrants from Latin America and the Caribbean represent a significant percentage of these figures. As was the case during the years of the Bracero Program, the majority of these immigrants seek economic opportunity. And, the money they make is becoming increasingly more significant for their countries of origin. The Inter-American Development Bank reports that in 2005, of the $53.6 billion in remittances sent from abroad to Latin America and the Caribbean, almost 75 percent originated in the United States.

In geographic terms, the Mexico-U.S. border is 2,000 miles long, and 1,254 miles of this space is delineated by the Rio Grande. Due to augmented security on the U.S. side of the border, increasing numbers of immigrants attempt to cross the treacherous desert areas in Arizona and New Mexico. Currently there are small segments of fence along the border, however, where both official and unofficial efforts are underway within the United States to further extend a physical barrier.

Congressman Norwood contends that the United States needs to increase its border security and highlights the dedication and the patriotism of the Minutemen Project for their work to secure the border. Congressman Grijalva argues that volunteer patrol groups on the border are racist vigilantes whose activities should demand the legal attention of the federal government.

YES

Charlie Norwood

The Miracle on the Southwest Border: Illegal Immigration Smashed: A Direct Field Report on the Arizona-Mexico No-Man's Land

An on-going miracle is occurring this month in America's Southwest, a miracle with a direct impact on our district. After decades of being told that it is impossible to stop illegal immigration on the Arizona border, it has been all but halted since April 1 through the very means we were told wouldn't work—dedicated manpower and willpower.

This past Sunday, the Congressional Immigration Reform Caucus, of which I am a member, sent two senior staffers to investigate first-hand a chain of events beginning in late March which could force Congress and the Administration to dramatically rethink our approach to combating illegal immigration.

I insisted that John Stone from our Washington staff be a part of that first two-man team, so that we would have the most direct information on the situation possible. Stone is currently a Captain and public affairs officer with the Virginia Defense Force, the reserve to the Virginia National Guard, and a homeland security policy advisor. He partnered with retired Marine Colonel Fred Peterson, an expert on international homeland defense. They went into the border zone independently from any other federal agencies, with Caucus instructions to investigate every side of what is occurring in the zone, talk with any and all sources both on and off-the-record, and report those findings back to Congress. Their final and full report will be filed May 2, but their initial findings need to be known immediately.

The catalyst for the new focus on the border is a controversial movement by private citizens who are simply fed up with the ineffectiveness of federal efforts to combat the problem. They call their effort the "Minuteman Project", and have kicked off what they describe as a "Neighborhood Watch" effort to help our Border Patrol control illegal immigration through additional free, volunteer manpower.

Our Border Patrol has officially responded with less than open arms to the offer of free help, in spite of complaining for decades of not having enough officers to adequately cover the vast desert region. It is estimated that

From *This Week in Washington*, April 8, 2005.

more than half of the current 16 million illegal aliens in this country walked right through this same sector, yet the Border Patrol still says "no thanks."

Vigilantes or Patriotic Volunteers?

While that hasn't slowed the Minutemen down in bringing their 30-day project to reality, it has created an uncomfortable situation of armed civilian volunteers operating without first being sworn in by a lawfully authorized local, state, or federal agency.

That is a legitimate concern. One of the foundations of our Republic is that our military and law enforcement answers through an established chain-of-command to publicly elected officials. It is one of the key differences between the 200-year success of our nation and economy and the banana republics to our south that are the precise cause of so many folks wanting to flee to the United States.

Yet it is likewise an underlying principle of our Republic that elected officials faithfully act to defend and enforce the laws of the land, including our immigration laws. And our elected officials have repeatedly failed to take the necessary steps to do so.

Are the Minutemen vigilantes? That is a question for which Congress needed direct, unedited feedback from the field to attempt to answer.

President Bush has said he is against "vigilantes", while not directly calling the Minuteman volunteers by that name. But Mexican President Vincente Fox has directly referred to the Minutemen as "vigilantes." An interesting statement from a President with troops under his command who consistently violate our border. He obviously doesn't mind taking our law into his hands, he just has a problem with us doing the same with our own law.

So what is a vigilante? From a variety of sources, a vigilante is "One who takes *law enforcement* into one's own hands; vigilantes often operate in *secret*." The Caucus investigation has so far uncovered the following field evidence:

- **No Enforcement Efforts:** Project organizers are maintaining rigid rules that volunteers take no enforcement action whatsoever. They simply report the location of suspected illegal immigrants to the Border Patrol. Our team confirmed all volunteers are drilled on avoiding confrontation, even if provoked, and under instruction to allow all persons to pass unobstructed, and without verbal harassment. They are allowed to provide emergency aid to illegal immigrants if necessary, and our team investigated one incident of an illegal immigrant who fell behind his group, and was actually provided emergency food and water by Minutemen while Border Patrol agents were in transit. An illegal immigrant who claimed on Wednesday (6 APR) to have been detained by the Minutemen is likewise reported to have received food, water, and money from sympathetic volunteers before changing his story, reportedly after outside coaching.
- **Transparency:** The Minutemen organization has opened its operations 100% to media, government, and public inspection. Local, national, and international press, along with all government agencies, have access to all

Minutemen facilities in the area, as well as being offered the opportunity to observe all field operations. Our team accompanied newspaper reporters on an overnight observation of a high drug-trafficking area this week. Stone and Peterson confirm the reporters had full access to the entire operation, and the ability to talk to all members of the team. Some individual Minutemen team members chose not to talk or have their picture included in the story, which is within their rights, consistent with standard public affairs operations guidelines of state and federal agencies. By contrast, the U.S. Border Patrol did not allow our team to accompany their agents through ride-along requests that are traditionally provided as a courtesy to congressional fact-finding missions.

From these initial findings, if the Minutemen are "vigilantes", then so are all Neighborhood Watches that are not formally recognized by a law enforcement agency.

Elements at Play

The minutemen.　Leaders of the Minutemen Project say they currently have around 450 volunteers in the field. They have been in the field since Monday, April 4, and will be relieved over the coming weeks by another thousand or so volunteers. They estimate somewhere between 1000–1500 volunteers will participate before the project is over at the end of the month, with around 500 in the field at any given time.

The border patrol.　The Border Patrol has pulled in 534 seasoned agents from elsewhere in the country to reinforce the 2600 agents already in the sector. The Border Patrol says these reinforcements have nothing to do with the Minuteman Project, and are a planned step in the ongoing Arizona Border Patrol Initiative.

Coronado memorial national park.　The National Park Service has trucked in an undetermined number of tactical officers from other states. Coronado Memorial National Park covers nearly 5000 acres on the border with Mexico.

The media.　Our team identified the *Los Angeles Times,* the *San Antonio Express,* La Raza Radio News 97.9FM, NBC/MSNBC Crew West, the Associated Press, FOX News, and multiple European media outlets remaining on the scene long-term. Members of these and other media are constantly following the Minutemen, and have at times disrupted observation efforts.

Opposing groups.　The ACLU; La Raza; Hispanic separatist Dr. Armando Navarro; street gang MS-13; Mexican drug and human trafficking gangs, and Earth Liberation.

Fort huachuca.　The U.S. Army maintains its own security and patrols over the base area, frequently used by illegal immigrants. ROTC Cadets from Arizona

State University on training duty at the base apprehended and detained 16 illegal immigrants earlier this week; 513 illegals were apprehended on base in March.

Border Action to Date

Prior to the Minuteman Project observation posts becoming active on April 4, open-borders advocates protested and sent observers into the field, reportedly for the duration of the project. These groups included the ACLU, Earth Liberation, and others. Stone observed what is believed to be elements of these groups attempt to disrupt observation posts.

The Salvadoran street gang MS-13 along with Mexican human smuggling and drug rings has reportedly threatened armed attacks against the Minuteman volunteers. This MS-13 gang is the very one which is spreading so rapidly across our country, with a worldwide membership of 700,000, and a history of vicious machete attacks in the Washington, DC suburbs. It seems they object to having their illegal access to our country blocked.

The government-controlled Cuban press is telling the world that "armed racists" are standing by to shoot innocent migrant workers.

Mexican President Vincente Fox has ordered his military to mass on the U.S. border in higher numbers than usual, "just in case," of a confrontation. There won't be, as the Minutemen are under strict instructions to walk away from confrontation, but this policy position of Mexico is worth noting. This is the same Mexican military that provides water, aid, and traveler's advice to immigrants seeking to cross our border illegally, to help them do so. According to multiple reports, beginning April 1 the Mexican military has been blocking immigrants from attempting to cross the section of border patrolled by the Minutemen, and advising illegals to cross to the east and west of the Minutemen's area of operations. They are telling these immigrants that "crazed ranchers" are waiting to shoot them on sight on our side of the border if they cross in the wrong place.

The Minuteman volunteers, with a heavy percentage of armed former U.S. military members, have held firm to their project goals in spite of these threats and distortions.

Results—A Dramatic Decline in Illegal Immigration

Our team heard two conflicting stories on the results of these developments on the Southwest border. But both stories have the same ending: illegal activity in this, the heaviest illegal immigration border sector in America, has been brought to a screeching halt.

The U.S. Border Patrol attributes any and all decreases in illegal immigration this spring to their own efforts to increase enforcement, primarily their bringing in those 534 seasoned officers from other parts of the country the week before the Minuteman Project kicked off. They also credit the increased Mexican military presence on the other side of the border. Their official stance is that the Minutemen Project has had little or no effect, and was timed by its volunteer organizers to try to claim success for the efforts of the Border Patrol. A fascinating position when you think about it—a reverse conspiracy theory, in which federal bureaucrats suspect citizens of designing sophisticated plots against them. Interestingly, the Border Patrol had no knowledge of increased federal efforts elsewhere, such as the National Park Service team deployed to the state, or of whether U.S. Army enforcement efforts were increased.

Local law enforcement, and individual Border Patrol officers speaking off-the-record, say that illegal immigration has virtually stopped in the sector patrolled by the Minutemen as a direct result of Minutemen activity and publicity.

Regardless of the cause, a historic immigration reform myth has been exposed as a total travesty in just the first week of the Minuteman Project. That myth is that it is impossible to stop illegal immigrants from crossing the border with any reasonable amount of additional manpower, that controlling illegal immigration could only be accomplished through new technology still years away from implementation, and that a necessary ingredient is immigration "reform" that would allow most of those entering our nation illegally to just walk across the border with impunity.

That myth is now dead forever thanks to a remarkable first week of April on the Arizona-Sonora border. We can stop illegal immigration anytime we please by simply providing adequate and reasonable numbers of Border Patrol personnel, with Army or National Guard backup if necessary, to bring our national illegal immigration nightmare to an immediate end. We have the manpower. The only question left is whether we have the willpower.

Vigilante Watch

Elected in a landslide last Nov. 5, 55-year-old Raul Grijalva became one of 22 Hispanic members of the current U.S. Congress this January. Despite his freshman status, few people in Grijalva's district, which spans much of southern Arizona, expect him to sit at the back of the chamber and stay quiet. Grijalva's been an outspoken civil-rights advocate since the 1960s in Tucson, where he has run a series of winning campaigns—for county school board, board of supervisors and, now, Congress.

In January, Grijalva wrote to Attorney General John Ashcroft, inviting the nation's top law officer to come to southern Arizona and witness the threat of anti-immigrant vigilantes in person. He called on the FBI to investigate connections between Arizona militias and white supremacist groups, asked the U.S. Border Patrol to issue a "declarative condemnation" of citizens taking the law into their own hands along the border, and began rallying other members of Congress to the cause of border reform.

The *Intelligence Report* talked with Grijalva in December, the day after he took a helicopter tour of the border with Sens. John McCain and Jon Kyl and Congressman Jim Kolbe. The magazine followed up with Grijalva in February, asking about the progress of his anti-vigilante campaign.

INTELLIGENCE REPORT: Southeast Arizona has a long history of vigilantism and racist violence, but things were relatively calm for much of the 1980s and '90s. Did the recent resurgence of anti-immigrant vigilantism take you by surprise?

GRIJALVA: It looked like a dead issue for a while. But then you had the whole new U.S. border policy in the mid-'90s [when U.S. officials effectively shut down popular crossing routes in urban parts of California and Texas], which forced millions to cross the border through the Arizona desert, and it started again. I think what's happened in Southeast Arizona—mostly in Cochise County—is that there's been a kind of official tolerance of vigilantism, leading to the notion that it's OK. By tolerating it, you allow it to breed.

IR: Who is responsible for this official tolerance?

GRIJALVA: Local authorities, the sheriff of Cochise County primarily. Sheriff [Larry] Dever was on the helicopter ride yesterday, and I asked him, "Have there been no complaints about the vigilantes?" He said, "Zero." I said, "No complaints to the county attorney?" "Zero."

I said, "Hmm. You know, from [the anti-immigrant group] American [Border] Patrol's Web page and some other information that I've seen, you seem to be a supporter of theirs. Don't they tout you as being one of their supporters?" He said, "Well, they can claim all kinds of support. All you're doing is drawing attention to these people; you're making the issue bigger than it is."

IR: So are you approaching the federal government instead?

GRIJALVA: Yes, and I think it makes sense. If federal policy is driving this, causing these problems with immigration—and it is—then there has to be federal intervention.

The bottom line is this: You can't just allow vigilantes and hate groups to exist without a consequence. They need to know that they can't take the law into their own hands, they can't violate people's civil liberties, and they can't violate people's human rights. When there seems to be this official sanction by law enforcement authorities, this blind eye turned to it, it breeds.

IR: Like the kind of defiance that Chris Simcox, leader of the Civil Homeland Defense group, showed when he dared President Bush to come arrest his militia?

GRIJALVA: Yes. When he did that, there should have been an immediate response. Good, bad or indifferent on the immigration law, there are bona fide enforcers of that law: officers. No one else has the right to do that, nor should they have the right.

If Simcox's group or Ranch Rescue [a Texas-based paramilitary anti-immigration group] wants to call themselves "civilian patrols," that's a kind way to put it. The right term is vigilantes, and there's no place in this country for them. Vigilantes have never been successful, and their agenda has nothing to do with us trying to solve this issue on the border.

IR: Do you suspect these groups of any illegal activities?

GRIJALVA: There's a violation of federal law when you carry guns on national lands. There are issues of intimidation, violations of civil rights, and violations of the federal hate crime statute.

IR: Do you think the anti-immigrant groups operating in Cochise County have been encouraged by a lack of prosecutions in the past?

GRIJALVA: Prosecutions? There haven't been *investigations.* That's why I want an FBI investigation. Who are these groups? Who are they linked to? But really, the more light you shine on the cockroaches, the quicker they run for cover.

Besides, we're talking about hate crime issues. I'm asking federal investigators to follow our federal law and apply it to this region the way you'd apply it anywhere else. I don't think you'd tolerate this in Dade County, Fla. You wouldn't tolerate it in New York. You're not going to tolerate it on the East Coast or the Midwest.

These groups have had impunity, despite the fact that a lot of their leadership is driven by hate, not by any other reason. They use the excuse that "we're here defending the homeland," or "protecting private property," but that's not the basis of it.

IR: What do you think drives groups like American Border Patrol, Ranch Rescue, and Civil Homeland Defense then?

GRIJALVA: The strain that runs through these groups is anti-immigrant and downright racist. You look at their Web sites, their links—there's an ugly strain to these groups. They're intensifying and bringing considerable danger to an area that's already in the grip of a crisis, with the huge numbers of migrants being forced through the desert.

IR: There have been dozens of reported incidents in which private citizens have detained migrants at gunpoint, or even shot at them. At least some of these incidents clearly involved lawbreaking. Why has this been tolerated in southern Arizona?

GRIJALVA: Partly because of a double standard that is both racial and legal. The victims we're talking about are undocumented; they don't have the same rights as U.S. citizens. That has made it easy for the vigilantes. Among elected officials, I think there have been some political calculations about the support these groups might have; they're good at organizing letter-writing campaigns and making their support look greater than it is. Letters to the editor have been running six-to-one against me, for instance, since I started asking for investigations.

IR: That suggests some genuine support for these groups. Is that real?

GRIJALVA: I think it's pretty shallow, much more shallow than the numbers they boast about. But they are able to tap into a general feeling of anxiety in America. There's an economic downturn in this country, there's a recession approaching a depression, there's the threat of terrorism. In these historical cycles, there's always a scapegoat—an economic scapegoat, usually. Now it's Mexicans, "invading" and "taking our jobs."

So these groups, like American Patrol, very conveniently point to a target and say, "This is why we're in this situation. We have to keep them out of here, because look what they're doing to our jobs. We have to guard the borders, because of what happened on 9/11." They're appealing to that threatened feeling that Americans have right now, saying, "It's just them against us."

There is an appeal to that—the appeal of simple answers, and of having a target to point to. A lot of people don't buy their rhetoric, of course. There was an older gentleman in Douglas yesterday, where we were talking about terrorism and national security. When we broke, he came up to me and said, "You know, Raul, I haven't seen too many terrorists picking tomatoes in Willcox." What a perceptive way to put it. Almost all of the migrants are coming here for work, period.

IR: Why focus on vigilantism when there are hundreds of people dying as they try to cross the deserts of northern Mexico and southern Arizona?

GRIJALVA: The deaths in the desert are connected to the vigilante issue. Both are occurring as results of a failed border policy. One issue is the compassion and humanitarian support needed because of a failed policy; the other is defiance because of a failed policy. The reason for concentrating on the vigilantes is not just the threat they pose, but also the arrogance with which they're doing it. For us not to stand up to that arrogance would be a big mistake.

IR: If you were sitting here with Chris Simcox, the newspaper owner who started the armed Civil Homeland Defense patrols, what would you say?

GRIJALVA: I would tell him he's going to lose. Very directly. I would say, "You are an aberration, and you're going to lose."

I think there's a streak of decency in the American people. We can debate immigration, but there's a basic, fundamental streak of decency in Americans and this is not American. Simcox's group is the most un-American thing I've seen in a while, and I've seen a bunch. It goes to the basest part of people's character.

IR: How do you get people past that? How do you counter the rhetoric?

GRIJALVA: The whole border issue is being dealt with piecemeal, and that gives these groups—and their message—an opportunity to flourish. The border policy put in place in the 1990s is not working. It hasn't worked, and it won't work.

So what are we going to do? Instead of talking about "invasions" and using fear tactics and putting more military on the border, we need to talk about the root problems: How the Mexican economy has suffered after NAFTA, the historic patterns of migration that have been changed by U.S. policy, the history and culture of the border region.

And we need to explain that people are not running away from Latin America and Mexico because they want to flee their countries, or because there's some "invasion" going on. They're coming here for economic reasons.

IR: What makes it so hard to talk rationally about immigration?

GRIJALVA: Even within progressive ranks, the debate over immigration tends to float over into emotion. There's something unsettling for people about the changes in demographics. You get the English-only initiatives in California, the effort to ban bilingual education here in Tucson.

I'm not a conspiracy guy, but there seems to be an unsettled mood that the majority of Americans feel about what's going on around them. As much as we all preach diversity and inclusion and how we're a mosaic, that side of the American picture is not taking hold. And as you marginalize people more and more, you create the kind of breeding ground for racist violence that you have in Cochise County.

IR: Has your letter to Attorney General Ashcroft, requesting an investigation of vigilante groups and asking him to visit southern Arizona, gotten any response?

GRIJALVA: No. But we are going to meet with the U.S. attorney in Tucson, to talk about the vigilantes. The FBI has indicated they are looking at things. And I'm working to get more of my colleagues, especially in the Hispanic caucus, to sign on to the letter to Ashcroft, so I can forward it with more names than just my own.

I don't know where my complaints are going to go, to be quite honest with you. I don't know if they'll fall on deaf ears. But the point is making the complaint, energizing people and helping them focus on this issue.

IR: You've asked the Border Patrol to issue a "declarative condemnation" of vigilante groups. Has there been any response?

GRIJALVA: Not really. But the Tucson sector chief, David Aguilar, did say something that almost approached a condemnation—that these groups are not useful and that they're in the way.

IR: After your election, Glenn Spencer's American Patrol Web site accused you of supporting what he calls the *"reconquista"*—the reconquest of lands lost by Mexico to the U.S. in 1848. American Patrol also said you were "in cahoots" with a "Mexican government agent." Do you see these as racist attacks?

GRIJALVA: Yes, I think they are. They don't want to deal with the issues, don't want to confront the issues as equals, so they use all this other stuff. I basically ignore that. By virtue of the position I have now, I've been able to say something and people paid attention. That's how I became a target.

IR: Some local officials have gotten death threats for speaking out against the vigilantism. Does that include you?

GRIJALVA: Yes. We got five or six E-mails about my calling for an investigation of the groups. The subject line said, "VIGILANTES INVESTIGATED," and the message said, "If you do this, your family will be killed!" It was a pretty organized campaign, because they were all form letters.

IR: Were you surprised or scared?

GRIJALVA: Certainly not surprised. I knew this was going to happen. And when it did, it just told me that I was affecting them somehow.

IR: Hearing about vigilantism and the current anti-immigrant fervor in southern Arizona, many people probably assume that this area is more racist than other parts of the country. You've lived your whole life here. Is that true?

GRIJALVA: No, not necessarily. All the local communities' elected leadership, churches and other groups have rejected the vigilantes and anti-immigrant groups. But I think that because of the tolerance level of local authorities, they've had room to operate and to draw attention to themselves.

IR: After two migrants were gunned down in October at a remote spot outside Tucson, sheriff's investigators said they were looking at both vigilantes and Mexican smugglers as possible perpetrators. Now they seem to be blaming smugglers. Are you satisfied that the vigilante angle has been fully investigated?

GRIJALVA: No, no, no! I think that one required a much deeper investigation. It happened at a time when heightened tensions on the border were occurring, with Ranch Rescue patrolling and Civil Homeland Defense and American Border Patrol starting up, and I think the logical groups should have been investigated much more deeply. That includes the smugglers, but not only the smugglers.

IR: Aside from the decision to push illegal border-crossers inland to the desert, what aspects of U.S. border policy seem like particularly bad mistakes?

GRIJALVA: The fence along the border. It was built as a cattle barrier, you know; it was never meant as a human barrier. Those fences were put up in the '30s, '40s and '50s as a way to control livestock. Back then, seasonal migration from Mexico and back was a way of life. But now we've put up these horrendous walls.

There's a restaurant in Nogales/Sonora where I've been going since I was a kid. I actually avert my eyes when I cross the border there now, 'cause the wall's right in front of the restaurant I eat at. It makes me sick.

IR: What is your biggest challenge in trying to make others in Washington see the immigration problem—and the vigilante problem—the way you do?

GRIJALVA: Politicians are afraid of the immigration issue. Terribly afraid, because people are talking about how "they're coming over, they're taking our jobs, and what about the security risks?"

IR: Given the power of the anti-immigrant lobby in Washington, what can be done to overcome that political fear?

GRIJALVA: First, somebody's got to speak out about the real issues. Fortunately, I represent part of southern Arizona now, so I've got a way to speak out about it. Which is good, because we haven't heard the other side for a while. You also change minds by talking about things that haven't been talked about.

One of the things I read after 9/11, after that horrible thing happened, was that part of the problem they had in identifying victims was that many of them were undocumented, working as cleaning people and as restaurant people in the towers. Interesting commentary. They perished along with everybody else. The tragedy is the same.

IR: Are you afraid you'll be a lonely voice in Congress?

GRIJALVA: No. I think that other members of Congress are going to want to listen to the vigilante problem and hear about the deaths in the desert. If we create enough attention, then we're going to force some reactions on the part of the administration and the leadership of the Congress. The only way to do it is to create a burr. If we have a significant burr in the saddle, someone will have to react.

Like I said before, the more light, the better. Because there's something horrific going on. It's a tragedy. It should be an embarrassment to our government. The more people hear about it, the better off we're going to be.

There's a big place in this debate for organized labor, for communities of faith, for environmentalists. If we can create enough interest among those groups, I think we'll start drawing some real attention to the problems. That's going to be my little task.

POSTSCRIPT

Do Volunteer Border Patrol Groups Represent a Reasonable and Just Way to Address Immigration Across the Mexican-U.S. Border?

Raúl Grijalva and others fear that the volunteer groups currently patrolling the U.S.-Mexico border are modern vigilantes. These fears are based, in part, on historical examples of violence against Mexicans in the United States. As historians William D. Carrigan and Clive Webb explain, "between 1848 and 1928, mobs lynched at least 597 Mexicans" (*Journal of Social History,* Winter 2003, pp. 411–38). While this history informs one side of the border debate, the Minutemen Project rejects such accusations of vigilantism, stating that they are a peaceful organization that "has no affiliation with, nor will we accept any assistance by or interference from, separatists, racists, or supremacy groups or individuals" (http://www.minutemanproject.com).

Due to augmented security along the more densely populated areas of the U.S. side of the border, increasing numbers of illegal immigrants are attempting to cross at its most dangerous sections such as through the Sonora Desert. Many do not survive. According to the Latin America Working Group, 463 immigrants died crossing the border in 2005. Between 2000 and 2005, the average number of deaths per year was 361, and the total number of deaths was 2,167 (http://www.lawg.org/countries/mexico/death-stats.htm). There are volunteers who work along the border who provide humanitarian aide to migrants so that they do not suffer a similar fate. Border Angels, a non-profit organization led by Enrique Morones, maintains stations along the border where volunteers leave water, food, and clothing for individuals who pass through areas of extreme climatic conditions. And, despite their obvious resistance to illegal immigration, according to Chris Simcox, co-founder of the Minutemen Project, "Part of our training program ensures that Minutemen are prepared to assist with food and water while we wait for Border Patrol to respond." Simcox adds that "This is not the adversarial or racist operation the left media would like people to think it is. [. . .] Most of our missions are more search and rescue, as thousands of illegal immigrants get lost in the desert with no food or water." Simcox states that "more than 160 lives have been saved in three years" ("Minutemen Launch New Mission," *WorldNetDaily,* July 30, 2005).

In December 2005, the U.S. House of Representatives passed H.R. 4437: Border Protection, Antiterrorism, and Illegal Immigration Control Act. The bill includes a provision for the construction of an additional 700 miles of fence along the border. Two of the most controversial provisions are the criminalization of undocumented immigrants and of individuals or organizations who assist illegal immigrants to enter or remain in the United States. Opponents of the bill indicate that 1.6 million undocumented children currently living in the United States would have the status of aggravated felons. And, according to the language of the bill, medical personal, social services, or clergy who help illegal individuals would also be committing a federal crime. Coordinated in great part by Spanish-speaking television and radio, on May 1, 2006, more than 1 million Latinos across the United States protested the proposed bill. Groups that favor immigration reform in the United States organized counter-protests and critiqued the waving of the Mexican flag by immigrant protesters. Two weeks later, U.S. President George Bush ordered the deployment of U.S. National Guard troops to patrol the border.

The movement of people northward to the United States is clearly redefining the identity of the nations involved. Miguel Pickard reports that immigration to the United States has changed the cultural and economic landscape of rural Mexico: "This flight north is tearing apart Mexico, particularly in the countryside. [. . .] Thousands of rural communities have become ghost towns. In states with a decades-old tradition of heading 'up north,' the journey has become a rite of passage for young men, synonymous with reaching adulthood. The young leave and the majority will never return to reside permanently in their hometowns. Those who remain behind—the elderly, children and women, although women are migrating today more frequently—survive on remittances used to buy necessities of daily life and make improvements on their homes. Little is used for productive investment or savings" ("In the Crossfire: Mesoamerican Migrants Journey North," *International Relations Center,* March 18, 2005). Meanwhile, on the northern side of the border, critics of this "flight north" fear that without significant immigration reform, the future of the United States is grim. Without reform, according the Minutemen Project, "Future generations will inherit a tangle of rancorous, unassimilated, squabbling cultures with no common bond to hold them together, and a certain guarantee of the death of this nation as a harmonious 'melting pot.' The result: political, economic and social mayhem" (http://www.minutemanproject.com).

It would be incorrect to view all Latinos or Spanish-speakers who live in the United States as illegal immigrants. Many Latinos of Mexican ancestry (Mexican-Americans or Chicanos) trace their roots back to a time when the border was further north where it currently exists. They, like many Puerto Ricans, Cubans, Haitians, Jamaicans, Dominicans, and Central and South Americans are citizens of the United States. Today, it is interesting to note that the United States is the fifth-largest Spanish-speaking country in the world, after Mexico, Spain, Argentina, and Colombia. In addition, Los Angeles is the third-largest Spanish-speaking city in the world after Mexico City and Buenos Aires. Review the International Relations Center Americas Program Web site "Border Information Clearinghouse" for documents, statistics, and news: http://americas.irc-online.org/clearinghouse.html. Watch PBS's documentary "Beyond the Border/Más allá de la frontera" to learn about the lives of a family of immigrants who move from Mexico to the United States.

ISSUE 11

Is Latin America Becoming Protestant?

YES: Marcela A. Chaván de Matviuk, from "Latin American Pentecostal Growth: Culture, Orality and the Power of Testimonies," *Asian Journal of Pentecostal Studies* (July 2002)

NO: Edward L. Cleary, from "Shopping Around: Questions About Latin American Conversions," *International Bulletin of Missionary Research* (April 2004)

ISSUE SUMMARY

YES: Marcela A. Chaván de Matviuk from the Center for Latin American and Latino Leadership in the School of Leadership Studies at Regent University argues that the "relational character" of Latin American culture is a perfect fit for Pentecostal worship and that it directly contributes to the rise in Protestantism in the region.

NO: Edward L. Cleary, of the Dominican order, professor of political science and director of the Latin American studies program at Providence College, contends that the growth of Protestantism is not as profound as it might appear and that statistics on religion need to also consider the retention and dropout rates of Pentecostals.

$\mathbf{N}$early one-half of the world's one billion Roman Catholics live in Latin America, and, with 150 million followers, Brazil is the world's largest Catholic nation. Although statistics vary, a recent University of Notre Dame report estimated that today 70 percent of Latin Americans identify themselves as Catholic. The significance of Latin America within the global Roman Catholic Church was recently highlighted upon the death of Pope John Paul II in 2005 when many thought the next pope would be from Latin America (Harold Olmos and Peter Muello, "Next Pope Faces Loss of Latin American Faithful to Evangelical Churches," AP, April 16, 2005).

Religious conversion was one of many dramatic changes brought about by the European conquest of Latin America. Through royal patronage, the Vatican gave the Spanish monarchy the power to preside over the administration of the Catholic Church in their territories in the "New World." The Spanish monarchy was responsible for the conversion of the original peoples of the Americas to Catholicism, and colonial military expeditions were accompanied by representatives of the Church. When planning the layout of their new territories in Latin America, colonial powers clearly situated administrative and ecclesiastical buildings in the center of towns and cities as visible reminders of their power. When European conquistadors encountered indigenous peoples in their expeditions, they were required to read the "Requerimiento." Written and read in Latin, this paradoxical text "asked and required" its listeners to become Catholics, or they would be converted by the force of war. The *encomienda,* a feudal-based system in which Spanish colonizers were obliged to baptize, care for, and "civilize" their indigenous wards in exchange for land and forced native labor, was another indoctrination tool.

Whether through the encomienda, the requerimiento, or other forms of proselytization, conversions were often done en masse, and, consequently, many were incomplete. And, despite the violence of the conquest and the passage of time, to this day, pre-Columbian religions persist in Latin America, and native beliefs are often mixed with those of their conquerors. African slaves who survived the arduous passage across the Atlantic Ocean to the Americas were also forced to convert to Catholicism. Religious beliefs brought from Africa still exist today, primarily in the form of syncretism in and along the Caribbean and in Brazil.

The Catholic Church in Latin America no longer maintains the level of power it enjoyed during the conquest and colonial eras, and its authority has been challenged and often checked over time; however, it still holds significant cultural and political influence in the region. Yet, as anthropologist David Stoll asks in his book, *Is Latin America Turning Protestant?* (1990), perhaps the greatest threat to Catholicism in Latin America today is the growth of evangelical churches. In fact, as Haitian sociologist Laënnec Hurbon notes, "[since] the 1970s, religious movements have experienced spectacular success through the Caribbean and Latin America. Jehovah's Witnesses, Adventists, Mormons as well as Evangelicals, Baptists and Pentecostals have grown to the point of challenging the traditional hegemony of Catholicism" (*Between Babel and Pentecost,* 2001). According to Father James Fredericks, professor of theology at Loyola Marymount University, these changes in the religious landscape, and the rise of evangelical Protestantism in particular, are "perceived as a major threat" for Rome and Latin American Catholics. He adds, "The idea that you can simply presume that everybody in Latin America is Roman Catholic to one degree or another, that era is over" (PBS Newshour, June 14, 2005).

Marcela A. Chaván de Matviuk argues the growth of evangelical churches in Latin America represents "[one] of the most extraordinary religious transformations in history." Chaván de Matviuk contends that the "relational character" of Latin American culture is a perfect fit for Pentecostal worship and that it directly contributes to the rise in Protestantism in the region. Edward L. Cleary maintains that the terminology "used to refer the various Christian groups are often unsatisfactory" and that this confusion adds to the existing conflict over the statistics on the growth of Protestantism in Latin America. He argues that its growth is not as acute as it might appear and that statistics on religion should also take into account the retention and dropout rates of Pentecostals.

YES Marcela A. Chaván de Matviuk

Latin American Pentecostal Growth: Culture, Orality and the Power of Testimonies

Introduction

In recent decades Latin American societies have undergone a host of profound social, cultural, political, economic, and religious changes. This paper examines one of the most important aspects of these social transformations with special emphasis on the autochthonous religious characteristics of Pentecostalism, seeking to interpret them as well as envision future consequences. . . .

Latin American Scene

One of the most extraordinary religious transformations in history has taken place during the twentieth century in Latin America. In fact, in the 1900s almost all Latin Americans were Roman Catholics. However, more recently, as Valentín Gonzalez-Bohorquez claims, it is estimated that "11% of Latin Americans are evangelicals" and about "40% of all the members of Pentecostal denominations are in Latin America."[1] Although numbers may differ, the growth of Evangelicals within the Latin American population, particular the growth of Pentecostals, has been incredible. Manuel J. Gaxiola-Gaxiola colorfully describes Latin American Protestantism as being "in indeed a multicolored mosaic, a prism that reflects many hues and shades, a never-ending succession of peoples, places, and practices that gives Latin American Protestantism a special personality and color. And then . . . there are the Pentecostals."[2]

As some authors claim—not without facing counter-arguments—Pentecostalism was initially a North American export to the Latin American context. It was born out of the conviction that the baptism of the Holy Spirit, the miracles of divine healing and the supernatural gifts of the Spirit were designed by God "to empower his people for the task of world-wide evangelization."[3] Pentecostalism rapidly found in the Latin American context propitious conditions where it developed and grew to become the incredible force it is today. David Stoll claims that between 1960 and 1985 Pentecostalism doubled its size in Chile, Paraguay, Venezuela, Panama and Haiti. It tripled its size in Argentina, Nicaragua and the Dominican Republic. It quadrupled in Brazil and Puerto Rico, quintupled in El Salvador, Costa Rica, Peru and Bolivia, and sextupled in Guatemala, Honduras,

From *Asian Journal of Pentecostal Studies,* 5:2 July (2002), pp. 205–222. Copyright © 2002 by Marcela A. Chavan de Matviuk. Reprinted by permission.

Ecuador and Colombia.[4] Such a growth brought with it a variety of Pentecostal doctrine and practices and diversity among its members. David Barrett characterizes the world-wide Pentecostal/Charismatic movement as being more urban than rural, more female than male, more third world than western world, more impoverished than affluent, more family oriented than individualistic, and in general, comprised by people under eighteen years old and Latin American Pentecostalism is not the exception. It mainly includes a majority of females as well as young people who are generally poor and collectivistically oriented. According to Roger Cabezas, this can be viewed as a blessing and hope, or, as "a dangerous conspiracy undermining the processes of change and the search for solutions to the principal social, economic and political problems of Latin America and the Caribbean."[5] As we already find ourselves in a new century, it is appropriate to question what are the challenges related to distinguishing Pentecostal communication today. How did this growth happen and what were the elements involved in the process? What communication strategies and styles were used in bringing this change? These are questions that challenge us in times when, despite having such growth, the region "still operates in several self-destructive ways."[6] These questions are shaped by the necessity of having deeper impact on society as a whole and by the necessity of reclaiming, reinforcing, and challenging the distinctive characteristics of Pentecostals' communication.

Seeking the Voices of Our Identity

Faupel points out that Pentecostalism will define its identity and its mission "through the constructions of a historical narrative."[7] In constructing a historical narrative we have the elements present in the early expansion of the Pentecostal faith. In this regard, Robeck claims that Pentecostalism in our lands developed "with the aid of personal correspondence, early Pentecostal publications, personal testimonies, and missionary activity."[8] In other words communication in its different manifestations was at the core of the Pentecostal faith and its expansion. So what was so appealing in letters, testimonies, written material and the like in the communication of the Pentecostal message?

Principal Tenets of Pentecostalism

The appealing of the Pentecostal message it is found in the foundational beliefs of Pentecostalism. The early Pentecostals of the twentieth century considered themselves as God's end-time people, who by his grace, were 1) saved, 2) sanctified and 3) baptized in the Holy Spirit. They were people whose identity was profoundly shaped by an eschatological intensity and uttermost identification with the "full gospel" of the New Testament.

However it is not only what Pentecostals believed what made them attractive, but also their practices. In relation to the prominent practices of Pentecostalism, Harvey Cox points out five positive tendencies. He notes that Pentecostalism has: 1) spirituality centered on experience; 2) worship that is celebrative; 3) practicality in the way Christianity is lived; 4) impulse towards social criticism of convoluted values, beliefs, and practices that impoverish people's lives and systematically support oppressive structures and evil practices; and 5) power to generate the ideals of an inclusive Christian community (gender, ethnicity, and race). Bernardo Campos suggests almost the same characteristics when discussing Pentecostalism in Latin America. Campos says that Latin American Pentecostalism is: 1) a movement of spirituality, that is characterized by having a religious experience with the divine; 2) a movement of protest, which means that Pentecostal morals and ethics respond to social irregularities and accompany processes of immigration, industrialization, and urbanism; and 3) a movement of social change, since it is a movement opened to new social practices.[9]

Besides, it is not only what today's Pentecostals believe and practice that makes them revolutionaries of faith, but more importantly who they are. They are believers who identify themselves with the poor, the marginalized, and those who suffer, and a popular movement, that it is socially based on people.

From these characterizations, it is possible to understand Pentecostalism as a spiritual movement with a solid set of beliefs and a diverse social movement with a profound contact and sensitivity to the community.[10]

From a communication stand point, it is having people as central that partially accounts for the success of the Pentecostal message. This position does not ignore the Holy Spirit's work in Latin America but tries to offer a model for explaining Pentecostal growth in Latin America as well as pointing out issues that are relevant for the communication of the Pentecostal message in the twenty-first century.

Latin American Pentecostalism

If Pentecostalism can be characterized as a diverse social movement with a profound contact and sensitivity to the community,[11] its relationship with the local culture cannot be ignored. James Goff, Jr. says, "by default, Pentecostalism was allowed to adapt itself to local culture and worship patterns. It became the religion of the people wherever its message spread."[12] Pentecostalism in Latin America was and still is a popular movement, and, therefore, the communication of the Pentecostal message in this context is multicultural and popular in its essence. However as Sergio Matviuk argues, it is necessary to develop a "framework to understand what cultural dimensions of the local culture have been integrated with Pentecostal beliefs to foster the tremendous growth of Latin American Pentecostalism."[13]

Since Pentecostalism mainly is a popular movement, it is no surprise that researchers found Latin American Pentecostalism to be "autochthonous in its character."[14] Westmeier agrees with this affirmation and claims that "Latin American Pentecostalism is an expression of folk religion."[15] In other words, Pentecostalism is profoundly rooted in the essential aspects of local culture. . . .

Latin American Culture and Pentecostalism

The first element we have in common between Latin American culture and Pentecostalism is experience. Latin American culture has been characterized as an experience in which faith and life are inseparable. Joseph Fitzpatrick points out that this feature was "true of indigenous peoples before the time of Christianity in their elemental sense of the sacred."[16] In fact, life for indigenous people was essentially religious. With the conquest, the religious quality became "Christianized." Thus, Catholicism transferred this sense of the sacred into an official religion. In consequence, a fundamental concept within the Latin American world-view is that of God. "For Latinos, God is not so much a concept, as an experience."[17] Indeed the Spanish language reflects this enmeshment of religion and ordinary life with expressions that convey the collective belief in God and the acceptance of God's reality. Expressions such as "Vaya con Dios" (Go with God), "Que Dios se lo pague" (May God reward you), "Que sea la voluntad de Dios" (Let it be God's will), and "Si Dios quiere" (If God wants it) are examples of the pervasiveness religion. However, the mere use of these expressions does not mean that someone is a believer, rather that they are "bespeak to the religious sensitivity within the culture and to the collective consciousness of the people."[18] Therefore, Latin American Pentecostalism re-injected sacredness and transcendence of the religious experience. Sacredness and transcendence that were not related to the official religion. This is why, among other reasons, Latin American Pentecostalism embraced social change, since it is a movement opened to new social practices including rituals, liturgy, worshiping and to the involvement of the believer in these acts. The second element we find in common in the relationship Latin culture and Pentecostalism is the focus on the event. Marvin Mayer says that event is a value within the Latin American culture, and describes it as follows, "the event oriented person is interested in who's there, what's going on, and how one can embellish the event with sound, color, light, body movement, touch, etc. He [a Latin American] is less interested in time and schedule."[19] The elements included by Meyer as part of the "event orientation" take a very visible presence in the Pentecostal service.

> The gesture comes first. Later, the words. And one legitimizes the other in a constant reciprocity. Something new always happens. The expectation is fulfilled. Apparently nobody leaves the Pentecostal service frustrated, no matter how well they know the ritual, the songs, the altar calls the message, the offerings. What happens in the pulpit (on stage) is only the first act. Next the whole auditorium becomes a stage of action. The roles are switched momentarily: the pastor becomes the attendant, a spectator of the ecstasy that fills the souls and bodies of the crowed hall with personal and collective manifestations. . . .[20]

Pentecostal Communication

. . . [Religious communication deals] with intuition, imagination and emotion rather than with thinking, sensations or the will."[21] Pentecostal worship and liturgy constitute an excellent display of communication and within it, testimonies. . . .

As [Pentecostals] clap, sing, dance, praise and testify a feeling of solidarity arises among the participants creating a special ground for community, influencing the ways in which God is experienced. It is in the Pentecostal community "where learning about God directly and experiencing God perpetually inform and depend upon one another."[22] This dynamic of the Pentecostal worship and liturgy has a two-folded impact: first in the community of believers and second, in the broader community. In the community of believers because Pentecostal worship requires the full participation of every person, and this participation not only takes place in the event, but has the "intention of bestowing a capacity for action"[23] in the general community. . . .

Pentecostals Bridging with Outsiders: Narrative and Melodrama

How is the Pentecostal message delivered within the context of a collectivist culture? My hypothesis that it occurs through personal narrative.

Narrative has a rich history within the Christian tradition. Scripture itself is full of stories with nearly one-third of the Bible's books [N]arrative is universal and therefore it is liberating and empowering. It does not limit argumentation to those who have special skill or knowledge, because everyone intuitively knows how to use and evaluate narrative. Thus, narrative is an egalitarian form of discourse and a more holistic one since it incorporates experience. "Narrative appeals to all abilities, including reason, emotion, sensation, imagination, and values."[24]

As Bastian explains, while historical Protestantism has been a religion of literacy and education, Pentecostalism represents "religions of oral traditions, illiteracy and effervescence."[25] Although literacy levels in Latin American greatly diverge from one country to another, percentages vary between 95% to 55% of the population.[26] Reinforcing this second orality, are the new ways of perception brought by communications media technology that . . . give preponderance to the aural sense, permeates imagination and the affections.[27]

On the other hand, it is possible to link narrative with melodrama. Melodrama was born from "folk tales and fairy tales"[28] which were constitutional to the culture of orality. As Michael Roemer explains, popular stories have often assumed the form of melodrama, a genre that evolved during the industrial revolution, when large numbers of people moved from rural communities to the city. Since they were illiterate, their tradition could not survive in an urban environment and neither could their oral tradition, they turned to the stage.[29]. . .

Laurie Green says that narratives in oral cultures "can unify human groups, celebrate the clan, keep folklore alive and educate in a style interactive with the audience."[30] In short, stories create cohesiveness and are highly educative. . . . Moreover, in an oral culture, the oral performer and the live audience interact on occasions of public verbal performance, and this interaction shapes the verbal performance because the performer responds presently to the audience. Therefore, I contend that personal narratives, create an ethos in communion with the Spirit in which the speaker and the audience become one, reinforcing communal participation and testimony as a peculiarity of Pentecostal liturgy. In the light of this, a closer look at testimonies will follow.

The Role of Testimonies . . .

Although the general idea of testimony is a notion quite well known, it is also true that it is difficult for many to define. Despite these obstacles, all of us have testimonies. Testimonies are part of our lives. When persons share their testimonies they always have a story of how God acted. A more theological definition of testimony indicates that it "is a declaration, faith profession or public agreement and fundamentally an evidence given to God's actions."[31] In the New Testament testimony involves proclamation with words, works and suffering.

Throughout the last three centuries, testimonies have been the most popular way of communicating to others how one becomes saved. Land explains that "the [Pentecostal] church become a missionary fellowship where testimonies were given constantly in order to develop virtues, expectancy, attitudes and experiences of those testifying."[32]. . .

Relational Culture, Pentecostals and Testimonies

Cuando Cristo vino a mi corazón,
mi vida entera cambió.
Su paz y su amor alejaron de mí,
las dudas, las sombras y el temor.
Mi vida comezó cuando el Señor llegó
Y hoy puedo cantar yo de su amor
Hoy quiero que Cristo te transforme a tí,
Que cambie tu vida también,
Piensa en la cruz donde murió por tí
Y ábrele tu corazón.[33]

Since Jesus came to my heart
my whole life changed.
His peace and His love have taken away
my doubts, shadows and fears.
My live began when Jesus came to my heart
And now I'm singing about his love.
Today I want Him to transform you
That He may change your life as well
Just think in the cross where for you Jesus died
And open your heart to him.[34]

Latin American Pentecostals know about the transformation power in telling stories about what the living God has done and will do. Telling these stories involves the experiential and relational nature of narrative.[35] As a collectivist culture Latin Americans highly value relationships, and when a culture holds relationships as crucial, relationships are also hold the key to communication. In this context, the constitution and objective of communication "is not merely to pass on truth, but to establish, maintain, and enjoy the fruits of relationships."[36] Members of a collectivist culture develop into the relational foundations and implications of the message. "Truth or reality is not their starting point. The relational speaker is not chiefly concerned about reality. His goal is relationships."[37] Therefore, the western paradigm of communication of the gospel centered on reason and spotless speech falls short in a collectivist culture. This is why personal narratives are an effective way of presenting the message of salvation and hope. When surrounded by chaos, misery, sickness and hopeless, stories of salvation, healing, hope, and victory, are powerful and compelling stories that open the path for living the life in expectation of the miraculous, that is of "what God will do for me, because I heard, you told us, what he has done for you." . . .

Conclusions

. . . The relational character of Latin American culture was a perfect fit for Pentecostal worship and liturgy in which, personal narratives played a central role, as they recapitulated God's saving action. . . .

As we face the twenty-first century, technological advances affect cultural patterns. Therefore, storytelling and testimonies may be threatened if we overlook their importance in shaping an ethos in which faith, commitment, and walking with God is learned in a context of community and continuity. Paradoxically it is technology what can also make a great contribution to our narratives. The great challenge faced is to find creative ways in which we can present our testimonies, by using all media resources available, as well as understanding how can we use them effectively, in excellence. The challenge is also one of encouraging the younger generation to tell their stories finding ways others than verbalizing. We must be reminded that these are times dominated by the eye and the ear, and if appealing to these senses that testimonies can be used so pass the message on salvation and hope. Another challenge is the ethical use of the testimonies. Testimonies are not meant to foster a model of "come and see" but the incarnational narrative of Emmanuel, "God with us." Perhaps our great challenge will be to keep nurturing and encouraging the use of testimonies and within the community of believers. The explosion of growth in Latin American Pentecostalism has led to the mega church reality. Therefore, anonymity and lack of strong relationships may affect the construction of a solid communal identity, which is brought, in part, by the sharing of testimonies.

If in certain contexts storytelling is an art that is becoming more and more unusual,[38] and, if according to Fisher, "humans are essentially storytellers,"[39] it is urgent to reconsider how the stories are being told. Orality can much benefit with advances in technology, therefore, the need for quality content becomes more critical than ever, but content needs the context of community of faith.

Notes

1. Valentín Gonzalez-Bohorquez, *Latin America: A Continent on Fire* (www.ad2000 .org/gcowe95/gonz.html, May 7, 2001).

2. Manuel J. Gaxiola-Gaxiola, "Latin American Pentecostalism: A Mosaic within a Mosaic," *Pneuma* 13:2 (Fall, 1991), pp. 107–29 (114).

3. Murray W. Dempster, "The Search for Pentecostal Identity," *Pneuma* 15:1 (Spring, 1993), pp. 1–8 (1).

4. David Stoll, *Is Latin America Turning Protestant?* (Berkeley: University of California Press, 1990), pp. 8–9 and also review in pp. 189–90.

5. Roger Cabezas, "The experience of the Latin American Pentecostal Encuentro," *Pneuma* 13:2 (Fall, 1991), pp. 175–188 (175).

6. Pedro Moreno, "Rapture and Renewal in Latin America," *First Things* 74 (June/July 1997), pp. 31–34 (http://www.leaderu.com/ftissues/ft9706/articles/moreno.html, May 5, 2001).

7. William Faupel, "Whither Pentecostalism?" *Pneuma* 15:1 (Spring, 1993), pp. 9–27.

8. Cecil M. Robeck, Jr., "Southern Religion with a Latin Accent," *Pneuma* 13:2 (Fall, 1991), pp. 101–106 (101).

9. Bernado L. Campos, "El Pentecostalismo, En la Fuerza del Espíritu," *Cyberjournal for Pentecostal Charismatic Research* 9 (Feb, 2001) at http://pctii.org/cyberj/campos.html (March 23, 2001).

10. Douglas Petersen, *No Con Ejército, Ni Con Fuerza* [Not by Might Nor by Power] (Miami: Editorial Vida, 1996), p. 17.

11. Petersen, *No Con Ejército,* p. 17 argues that Pentecostalism has mostly acquired its strength among the weakest or unsatisfied sectors of Latin America, such as the peasants, urban poor, women, Indians, ethnic minorities, young adults and groups from the middle class. This reality is opposed to many Pentecostal stereotypes that describe Latin American Pentecostalism as a generator of passive attitudes among its followers, encouraging them to think only in eternity and to accept the status quo. What it is occurring demonstrates that Latin American Pentecostals are committed to social struggles in the here and now.

12. James R. Goff, Jr., "Closing out the Church Age: Pentecostals Face the Twenty-First Century," *Pneuma* 14 (Spring, 1992), pp. 7–21 (19).

13. Sergio Matviuk, "Pentecostal Leadership Development and Church Growth in Latin America," *Asian Journal of Pentecostal Studies* 5:1 (January 2002), pp. 155–72.

14. Luise Margolies, "The Paradoxical Growth of Pentecostalism," in *Perspectives on Pentecostalism: Case Studies from the Caribbean and Latin America,* ed. Stephen Glazier (Washington, DC: University Press of America, 1980), pp. 1–5 (1).

15. See K. Westmeier, "Themes of Pentecostal Expansion in Latin America," *International Bulletin of Missionary Research* 17:2 (1999), pp. 72–78.

16. Joseph Fitzpatrick, S.J., *One Church Many Cultures: The Challenge of Diversity* (Kansas City, MO: Sheed & Ward, 1987), p. 135.

17. Rosendo Urrabazo, "Therapeutic Sensitivity to the Latino Spiritual Soul," in *Family Therapy with Hispanics: Toward Appreciating Diversity,* eds. M. Flores and G. Carey (Needham Heights, MA: Allyn and Bacon, 2000), pp. 205–28 (213).

18. Urrabazo, "Therapeutic Sensitivity to the Latino Spiritual Soul," p. 213.

19. Marvin K. Meyers, *A Look at Latin American Lifestyles* (Summer Institute of Linguistics, Museum of Anthropology, 1976), p. 91.

20. Richard Shaull and Waldo Cesar, *Pentecostalism and the Future of the Christian Churches: Promises, Limitations, Challenges* (Grand Rapids, MI: Eerdmans, 2000), p. 16.

21. See Peter Roche de Coppens, *The Nature and Use of Ritual* (Washington, DC: University Press of America, 1979), p. 137.

22. Rick Dale Moore, "A Pentecostal Approach to Scripture," *Seminary Viewpoint* 8:1 (1987), pp. 1, 2.

23. Cheryl Bridges Johns, *Pentecostal Formation: A Pedagogy among the Oppressed* (Sheffield: Sheffield Academic Press, 1993), p. 100.

24. Stephen W. Littlejohn, *Theories of Human Communication* (Albuquerque, New Mexico: Wadsworth, 1999), p. 170.

25. Jean Pierre Bastian, "The New Religious Map of Latin America: Causes and Social Effects," *CrossCurrents* Fall 1998 (www.findarticles.com/cf_0/m2096/n3_v48/21202867/p1/article.jhtml?term=%22Bastian%22) (January 7, 2001).

26. See statistics provided by Patrick Johnstone, *Operation World: The Day-by-Day Guide to Praying for the World* (Grand Rapids, MI: Zondervan, 1993).

27. See Marshal McLuhan and Quentin Fiore, *The Medium Is the Message: An Inventory of Effects* (New York: Bantman Books, 1967).

28. Michael Roemer, *Telling Stories: Postmodernism and the Invalidation of Traditional Narrative* (London: Rowman & Littlefield, 1995), p. 271.

29. Roemer, *Telling Stories,* p. 271.

30. Laurie Green, "Oral Culture and the World of Words," *Theology* 102 (Sep-Oct, 1999), pp. 328–35 (333).

31. Richard Taylor, J. Kenneth Grider, and Willard H. Taylor, *Diccionario Teológico Beacon* (Kansas City, MO: Casa Nazarena de Publicaciones, 1995), p. 693.

32. Land, *Pentecostal Spirituality,* pp. 78–79.

33. A popular song throughout Latin American Protestant churches including those of the Pentecostal faith.

34. Translation is mine

35. Michael B. Dowd, "Contours of a Narrative Pentecostal Theology and Practice" (a paper presented at the annual meeting of the Society for Pentecostal Studies, Gaithersburg, MD, Nov 1985), p. 7.

36. Gary Sheer, "How to Communicate in a Relational Culture," *Evangelical Missions Quarterly* 31 (October 1995), pp. 470–74 (471).

37. Sheer, "How to Communicate," p. 471.

38. McCall, "Storytelling and Testimony," p. 139.

39. Fisher, *Human Communication as Narration,* p. 64.

Edward L. Cleary

 **NO**

Shopping Around: Questions About Latin American Conversions

When two noted anthropologists canvassed colonization projects in Bolivia's lowlands, they reached the last house on the new dirt road. The owner heard them coming and ran out of the house yelling as they approached, "*Soy católico. Nunca van a convertirme*" (I'm Catholic. You're never going to convert me.) He was the last and only Catholic left in the project.

This article focuses on the popular subject of conversion in Latin America, with the difficulties both of terminology and of actually counting the number of converts. At the center of the problem is the issue of how long these conversions last. It appears that, in Latin America at least, it is not prudent to study conversion without also studying dropping out, leaving religion as well as entering it. Following earlier usage, we may also refer to such leaving as apostasy.

Religious Conversions in Latin America

At times it does seem that the whole of Latin America is converting. Religious conversion is the single greatest social process changing Latin America and the Caribbean in the twentieth and twenty-first centuries. Conversions from and within religious groups have rocked the region and changed the face of religion. The process has taken place through a series of quiet explosions that are only now becoming clear.[1]

While the mainstream media in the United States and Great Britain has taken notice of this process, coverage has focused mainly on the challenge that Pentecostalism has represented to the dominance of the Catholic Church.[2] Far less attention has been paid to the role conversion and intensified religious practice have played in many other contexts, including the reinvigoration of Indian religions,[3] African religions,[4] and even of the Catholic Church itself. Indeed, the changes within religious denominations are as significant as those between denominations. While many Catholics are becoming Pentecostal, many mainstream Protestants and classic Pentecostals are also converting to "health and wealth" neo-Pentecostal groups. Traditional Catholics have converted to social Christianity by the millions. At the same time, many socially active Christians have joined more otherworldly Catholic and Protestant charismatic groups. Among the indigenous groups of the

From *International Bulletin of Missionary Research*, vol. 28, no. 2, April 2004, pp. 5–54. Copyright © 2004 by Overseas Ministries Studies Center. Reprinted by permission.

region, many persons who are officially Catholic now openly embrace Mayan or Andean spirituality.

Many historians and social scientists who have been looking at Latin American religion for the last twenty or thirty years agree, first, that the main religious shift in Latin America has been from Catholicism to evangelical religion, especially Pentecostalism or neo-Pentecostalism. Mainstream Protestants also, however, have suffered losses. While these Protestants have been overshadowed by the fast-growing Pentecostals, in countries like Costa Rica or Argentina they exercise an influence far beyond their numbers.

Second, the major sector of Catholicism affected by this shift has been that of nominal, indifferent Catholics, who have supplied most of the converts to Pentecostalism. This pool of nominal Catholics was very large. In 1960 probably two-thirds of the Catholic population seldom or never attended church. Starting in the late 1960s two trends occurred: large numbers of Catholics in many countries became active in church, and Protestants in two-thirds of Latin American countries gained large numbers of converts. Empirical studies and the long history of religious conversion have shown that the convinced and the committed are rarely converted to a different faith or group. Rather, it is typically the nominal Catholic or indifferent Protestant who becomes the engaged Pentecostal.

Scholars from various disciplines have begun looking more closely at conversion in Latin America, asking who the converts are and how they became converted. Beside the insight that Pentecostal converts typically come from the large indifferent sector of Catholicism, we have evidence that converts adopt and remain in another religion primarily because of networks of friends, job acquaintances, and neighbors who bring them into the church and help them remain faithful. We have begun to look more systematically at why so many Latin Americans have changed religion, both by studying the social context for change and by listening to the reasons converts give for their new (or renewed) commitment to a religion.

Conversion, Switching, and Indifference

Observers note that the rates of conversion to the new and changing religious groups are far greater in some countries than in others. Geographers studying the patterns of religion show some sections of the same country with much greater religious change than other sections. Reginald Prandi and other veteran Brazilian observers note that 25 percent of the population of São Paulo, one of the largest cities of the world, have converted to another religion. Respected Argentine researchers have also noted the incursion of both Pentecostalism and African religion into the extremely traditional religious grounds of their country.

For Latin American social scientists this moving between religions seems a new and especially Latin American characteristic. Some give explanations along the lines of switching religions being another Latin fad. Similar observations, however, were made of the United States, as newspapers in the 1990s spoke increasingly of a religious marketplace. The *Boston Globe* expressed some amazement at the blooming of black Pentecostal church buildings within its Puritan city, claiming that there were more Pentecostal churches in Boston than Catholic ones. Later the paper looked more closely and published another story, again with implied exclamation marks: 25 percent of the people in the Boston area had changed religious affiliation.

Changing religious groups is not a new story in the United States. People have been switching church affiliation for decades. About 40 percent of North Americans belong to a religion different from the one in which they were raised. Some observers have claimed, on the basis of new churches being built, that switching must be more common than it was. This is not true, however, for there has been little, if any, increase above the 40 percent norm.[5] Probably, then, Latin America lags behind the United States. I attribute this difference to Latin America's becoming a more open and diversified society, although lagging behind the United States in the process.

Religious switching raises questions about conversion. When much of the switching has been from denomination to denomination, it does not seem like a true biblical *metanoia* (repentance, or turning). Does the switching, at least in the United States, represent a trend toward a search for deeper spiritual decision making? Does switching represent an intensified religious sensibility on the part of persons seeking new (and better) messages and new messengers? Perhaps, but more common reasons for changing religious affiliation include changes in life conditions, such as religiously mixed marriages; moving into new neighborhoods, cities, and regions of the country; searching for social services, such as day care or self-help groups (as for addiction sufferers); and new friendship circles.[6]

Pentecostalism does seem to change the way one looks at religion in Latin America. While it is clear that the main Pentecostal growth in Latin America is not induced from the United States, still Latin American Pentecostalism shares characteristics of religion in the United States. Specifically, it places exceptional emphasis on congregational participation and worship attendance as a measure of religious involvement.

This emphasis is not true of all major and global religions. Islam, Hinduism, and Buddhism emphasize ritual and worship at home and with the family to a much greater extent than Latin American Pentecostalism. Nor did Latin American Catholicism give the same weighty emphasis that Pentecostalism did to congregational participation and worship attendance. Popular Catholicism was, at least until recently, the religion of most Catholics.[7] From their earliest years, practitioners of popular Catholicism learned from their parents that saints were somehow active in their lives and could be venerated in church, at home, or at strategic places in the city or country. Popular Catholics celebrated feasts, made promises, and prayed for blessings, in and outside of church.

The criterion to be established here for later reference is that indifference, or having no religion, is not measured the same for Pentecostals as it is for popular Catholics. Indifference, being *nada* (nothing), for Pentecostals means not attending church at least weekly. For cultural Catholics, in contrast, it means not participating in some ritual, in or outside of church, by which God is honored.

Conflict over Terminology and Statistics

The terms used to refer to the various Christian groups are often unsatisfactory. We seem to be stuck with the Spanish term *evangélico* for a wide range of Protestants, which is the usage of Latin American demographers and also the way many Latin American Protestants refer to themselves. Recent authors dealing with Latin American religion, such as Timothy Steigenga and Kurt Bowen, have used this word broadly to include all non-Catholics who are Protestant, and many professional colleagues seem to have adopted their usage without objection. Steigenga and Bowen also distinguish between historical Protestants and Pentecostal Protestants. This usage may be unfortunate, since classic Pentecostals are uncomfortable being under the same tent with "health and wealth" neo-Pentecostals. (For that matter, many Pentecostal pastors consider Catholics to be outside the number of true Christians.)

For statistics, recent academic publications continue to cite figures from Patrick Johnstone's *Operation World: The Day-by-Day Guide to Praying for the World* (1993). A recent example is Anne Hallum's citation in a key 2003 essay in the *Latin American Research Review*.[8] After some initial hesitation (could I obtain reliable statistics from a prayer book?), I obtained a copy of this work, which was reputed to be the best source available for statistics on religion in Latin America. That might have been true ten years ago, but no longer.

In *Operation World* (1993), Johnstone claimed that 27.9 percent of all Chileans were Protestant, with 25.4 percent Pentecostal/charismatic.[9] These figures, however, are much higher than those reported in the carefully and rigorously conducted national census of 1992, which showed only 12.4 percent *evangélicos*. According to preliminary indications, the national census of 2002 will reveal about 16 percent *evangélicos*.[10] Other systematic surveys of Chilean religion have confirmed the levels of the 1992 census.

The two other Latin American nations cited as the most Pentecostal or most Protestant are Brazil and Guatemala. For Brazil, no one doubts that Pentecostal growth there is impressive; probably half of Latin America's Pentecostals reside in Brazil. In 1993 Johnstone gave the Protestant population as 21.6 percent of the national population.[11] That stands in contrast with the national census of 2000, conducted by apparently competent demographers, that shows 15.4 percent *evangélicos*. Evangelicals themselves seem to be happy with the census's lower figure. The Web site (www.infobrasil.org) of Servicio Evangelizadora para América Latina, or SEPAL, an international missionary group in Brazil, provides information based on the national census, not on Johnstone.

An End to Evangelical Growth?

Latinamericanists consistently identify Guatemala as the most Protestant country in Latin America. In Guatemala, however, evangelical growth has leveled off. Some Protestant missionaries within the country are now willing to admit there has been no growth for a decade.

Since the early 1990s longtime experts on Guatemalan religion Virginia Garrard Burnett and Bruce Calder have reported their impressions that Protestant growth in Guatemala had leveled off. They observed that Protestant pastors and other observers of religion felt that Guatemalan Protestantism had reached a "kind of natural limit." "Some people," one pastor said in resignation, "will always be Catholic."

Surveys of Guatemalan religion, including those by SEPAL, have found that Protestant growth rates were indeed flat. One might think that this information would be important in mission and academic circles, but missiologists and academics have generally failed to take notice.

Only now is it clear from SEPAL and other sources that the growth of Pentecostalism and Protestantism leveled off in Guatemala some time ago at about 25 percent Protestant in the Guatemalan total population. The Gallup Organization's group in Guatemala began doing surveys in the country in the 1990s, including questions of religious affiliation. These surveys, repeated at various intervals and by now in the public domain for a number of years, consistently have showed Protestant affiliation to be in the 25 percent range.

One might note that though their number as a proportion of the Guatemalan population has remained constant, the conversion rate for neo-Pentecostals and others counted as *evangélicos* has continued to increase. How can that be? How can a rising rate of conversions be paired with a stagnant rate of growth? We shall see that conversion in only one part of the story.

Nonpractice Among Pentecostals

An initial observation is that many Pentecostals are not very observant. This is a fact that one would not easily learn, even from persons who conduct valuable studies. Two systematic surveys of Chilean religion were conducted by the Chilean Institute of Public Studies, an institute similar to that of the American Enterprise Institute in Washington and having close ties to eminent sociologist Peter Berger of Boston University. In 1991 this Chilean institute published studies that went beyond census data and asked about church attendance. It was quite a surprise to learn that less than half of Chile's Pentecostals attend church once a week, and more than a third hardly attend church at all.

One of the main researchers, Arturo Fontaine Talavera, barely alluded to the significance of nonpractice among Chilean Pentecostals.[12] But this finding was scandalous to Pentecostal pastors, since Pentecostals strongly stress attendance at weekly services and many Pentecostals go to church more than once a week. The results of the surveys were broadcast on Chilean television and threw pastors into a panic.[13]

By and large, Pentecostal pastors took up the challenge of religious nonpractice directly and honestly, searching their souls for reasons for the worrisome dropping out. They wondered whether a contributing factor might be the growing distance between the education and class background of the pastors versus that of the persons in the pews. At the time, 40 percent of Pentecostals were middle class in terms of education, which was a higher percentage than that of pastors.[14]

The same pattern of nonattendance is evident in Mexico. Bowen found that "fewer than half, forty-eight percent, continued to be active evangelicals who attended a church service at least once weekly."[15] The vast majority of the other 52 percent never or almost never attended services.

Leaving Protestantism

A further consideration is that leaving church or religion, dropping out, though seriously understudied in the United States, is even less well researched in Latin America.[16] Recent studies have found that not only is non-practice widespread but also many Protestants are leaving their churches altogether. Bowen found that 43 percent of those raised in Protestant churches were no longer Protestants as adults. Also, 68 percent of those baptized in Protestant churches in Mexico in the 1980s had left by 1990.[17] Steigenga believes the same rates of leaving may be true in Guatemala.[18]

As noted above, several Latin American countries exhibit a rather high rate of evangelical conversion, but not much of a rise or none at all in the percentage of Protestants. Retention is thus clearly a factor. In terms of conversion, when 40 percent or so do not continue in their commitment, does the conversion itself have to be doubted? In Latin America, one common response is to say that only God knows. But in social science and missiology, when a religion displays such a high dropout rate, to discuss conversion without also looking at apostasy seems partial and misleading.

One reason researchers have overlooked the significance of church leaving may be that they believed they were looking at *nomadismo*: people shopping around for religion. In typical patterns, people shifted from indifferent Catholic to Pentecostal, from Pentecostal to neo-Pentecostal, from Catholic to Afro-Brazilian religions. Sometimes they seemed to convert to these religions all in the same day.

Why They Leave

One can learn a lot from delving into church leaving. Here we are discussing mainly Pentecostals who have departed. Not only are Pentecostals the largest non-Catholic group in Latin America, but also, judging by Mexico, they may have the highest dropout rates. But why? The responses are complex, but years of interviewing Pentecostals and of observing Pentecostal churches in most Latin American countries convinces me that living up to the perfectionist character of Pentecostalism is extremely difficult. Over the long haul, most people simply tire of trying to follow the heavy moral and social demands that many Pentecostal churches impose.

Entry into Pentecostalism takes seriously the turning that early Christians thought necessary. Men and women are expected to change their behavior to include not only the familiar rules of no smoking, no drinking, and no dancing and the giving of 10 percent of one's income to the church, but also marital fidelity and a wholehearted embrace of communal life and frequent prayer.

The Assemblies of God churches that flourished in Central America have had pastors who preach observance of the *Reglamento local,* the stated rules for doctrine and practice by which the communicants are expected to live.

Members of Assemblies churches, as classic Pentecostals, have a gritty sense of living counterculturally, an acute awareness of evil in persons and institutions, and a humility born from watching their own and others' minor slips and major failures. Many Central American pastors confided to Everett Wilson, recent president of Bethany College (Scotts Valley, California) and longtime resident in Central America, that over a long period of time only about 15 percent of congregants showed fidelity to the *Reglamento local.*[19]

There is another side to the Pentecostal churches' high dropout rate that needs to be explored, an aspect that few have emphasized. Do Pentecostal churches keep key members and attract many new ones because, directly or indirectly, they effectively cast off their faltering members? After he had walked along Mexican dirt roads and byways for years, listening to Pentecostal pastors and communicants, it occurred to Bowen that Latin American Pentecostal churches actually cast off the less committed among their members so that those more committed might continue unimpeded in the pursuit of their high goals. Less committed members would tend to pull the more committed down to a common denominator of laxer practice. The churches keep the luster of their religion bright precisely by shedding the nonobservant and the unrepentant.

Moving to No Religion

Until recently, Latin America stood out, at least from Europe and Canada, in having relatively few persons in the category "no religion." Manuel Marzal, a respected expert in religious research in Latin America, says that this kind of person was hardly representative of Latin Americans.[20] His argument is based not only on forty years of looking at religion in the region but also on a global study of religion in 2000. Marzal's view is challenged, however, by new evidence that shows a widening pool of "no religion" in Guatemala, Costa Rica, and Chile. This new fact lends significance to the question, Where are the church leavers going?

Much anecdotal evidence exists indicating that many Pentecostal dropouts return to the Catholic Church. James Scanlon, a Maryknoll priest, said that he and his activist parish members brought 1,800 persons in his Guatemala City neighborhood back to the Catholic Church.[21] Somewhat similar stories were heard by others in Guatemala.[22] But Steigenga, who conducted surveys in Costa Rica and Guatemala in 1992 and 1993, took a careful look at the persons who said they had no religious affiliation and found evidence that many had practiced, some rather profoundly, evangelical religion. Of this group, 13 percent said they had spoken in tongues, 37 percent said they had experienced a personal conversion, and 57 percent said they had experienced a miraculous healing. In general he found that few former evangelicals turned (one cannot say returned, because many were born Protestants) to Catholicism. Polls in Guatemala since 1990 show a group of about 12 percent of the national population that identify themselves as having no religion.

In Mexico Bowen's grassroots questioning of evangelical pastors and lay Mexicans found that 43 percent of those raised in the second generation of evangelicals no longer claimed any religious affiliation. Within that group, the rate for Pentecostal dropouts in the second generation was even higher: 48 percent. He found that hardly any of the leavers chose to practice Catholicism or any other faith. In terms of Mexican evangelicalism, they were *nada* (nothing).[23] This conclusion repeated what Steigenga found in Guatemala and Costa Rica, where leavers from evangelical, mostly Pentecostal, backgrounds may be going into a dark pool of "no religion."

This is a new category, one virtually unknown previously in Guatemala and much of Latin America. But what is it like to be without religion in this hotly religious country? Would one feel relief to be on an island of calm away from the heat of religious passion? Do people who say they have no religion still believe in God? Are they hurting and in need of help? We know almost nothing about this category.

In Conclusion

By looking at both conversion and dropping away, it becomes possible to ask whether evangelicals are destined to remain a small but vibrant minority, or whether they are capable of embracing sufficient numbers of Latin Americans for Latin American society as a whole to be transformed. It is clear that the capacity of the vibrant community of evangelicals to change the face of Latin American religion is severely curtailed by its inability to retain many of its members. The Mexican churches are losing many new members. The older Chilean churches are also losing members, perhaps third- and fourth-generation ones. It is also clear that there is a growing pool of Latin Americans with no religion. This is no surprise to those who look at the challenge of conversion. We still stand in amazement at Paul, Augustine, and Latin Americans who persevered in their Christian commitment.

Notes

1. Manuel Marzal has a valuable discussion of conversion in Latin America in his *Tierra encantada* (Madrid: Editorial Trotta, 2002), pp. 497–530.

2. Recent works on Pentecostalism in Latin America include Brian H. Smith, *Religious Politics in Latin America: Pentecostal Versus Catholic* (Notre Dame, Ind.: Univ. of Notre Dame Press, 1998); Edward L. Cleary and Hannah Stewart-Gambino, eds., *Power, Politics, and Pentecostals in Latin America* (Boulder, Colo.: Westview, 1997); Timothy J. Steigenga, *The Politics of the Spirit: The Political Implications of Pentecostalized Religion in Costa Rica and Guatemala* (Lanham, Md.: Lexington, 2001); and Daniel R. Miller, ed., *Coming of Age: Protestantism in Contemporary Latin America* (Lanham, Md.: Univ. Press of America, 1994).

3. Edward L. Cleary and Timothy J. Steigenga, eds., *Resurgent Voice* (New Brunswick, N.J.: Rutgers Univ. Press, forthcoming), and Alison Brysk, *From Tribal Village to Global Village: Indian Rights and International Relations in Latin America* (Stanford, Calif.: Stanford Univ. Press, 2000).

4. See, for example, John Burdick, *Blessed Anastacia: Women, Race, and Popular Christianity in Brazil* (New York: Routledge, 1998), and Ari Pedro Oro, *Axé Mercosul: As religiões Afro-Brasileiras nos países do Prata* (Petrópolis: Vozes, 1999).

5. N. J. Demerath III *Crossing the Gods: Worldly Religions, Worldly Politics* (New Brunswick, N.J.: Rutgers Univ. Press, 2001), pp. 221–22.

6. N. J. Demerath III and Yonghe Yang, "What American 'Culture War'? A View from the Trenches, as Opposed to the Command Posts and the Press Corps," in *Culture Wars in American Politics: Critical Views of a Popular Thesis,* ed. Rys Williams (Chicago: Aldine de Gruyter, 1997).

7. Marzal, *Tierra encantada,* p. 336.

8. Anne Motley Hallum, "Taking Stock and Building Bridges: Feminism, Women's Movements, and Pentecostalism in Latin America," *Latin America Research Review* 338, no. 1 (2003): 169–86.

9. Patrick Johnstone, *Operation World: The Day-by-Day Guide to Praying for the World* (Grand Rapids: Zondervan, 1993), p. 160.

10. *El Mercurio,* April 10, 2002.

11. Johnstone, *Operation World* (1993), 128.

12. Arturo Fontaine Talavera, "Trends Toward Globalization in Chile," in *Many Globalizations: Cultural Diversity in the Contemporary World,* ed. Peter L. Berger and Samuel P. Huntington (New York: Oxford Univ. Press, 2002), pp. 263–95, comments on the remarkable growth of Pentecostals in Chile but does not mention obvious signs of aging and decline in the fourth generation of Pentecostals.

13. See Edward L. Cleary and Juan Sepúlveda, "Chilean Pentecostalism: Coming of Age," in *Power, Politics, and Pentecostals,* ed. Cleary and Stewart-Gambino, p. 110.

14. Ibid., p. 111.

15. Kurt Bowen, *Evangelism and Apostasy: The Evolution and Impact of Evangelicals in Modern Mexico* (Montreal: McGill-Queen's Univ. Press, 1996), p. 71.

16. Exceptions are provided by Leslie J. Francis and Yaacov J. Katz, eds., *Joining and Leaving Religion: Research Perspectives* (Leominster, Eng.: Gracewing, 2000), and Stan L. Albrecht and Howard M. Bahr, "Patterns of Religious Disaffiliation: A Study of Lifelong Mormons, Mormon Converts, and Former Mormons," *Journal for the Scientific Study of Religion* 22, no. 4 (1983): 366–79.

17. Bowen, *Evangelism and Apostasy,* pp. 218, 224.

18. Steigenga, *Politics of the Spirit,* p. 48.

19. For description of Assemblies of God discipline, see Everett W. I Wilson, "Guatemalan Pentecostals: Something of Their Own," in *Power, Politics, and Pentecostals,* ed. Cleary and Stewart-Gambino, pp. 147–49.

20. Marzal, *Tierra encantada,* p. 227.

21. Interviews with Carroll Quinn, July 19 and October 3, 1990.

22. Steigenga, *Politics of the Spirit,* p. 38.

23. Bowen, *Evangelism and Apostasy,* pp. 70–71.

POSTSCRIPT

Is Latin America Becoming Protestant?

As Professor Cleary explains, it is difficult to establish concrete statistics for determining the current religious composition of Latin America. And, while statistics and the actual number of Protestants may not be exact, Protestantism has clearly gained a strong visible and audible presence in Latin America. Chaván de Matviuk mentions the phenomenon of mega-churches in the region. As their name suggests, these congregations number in the thousands. From its sermons and testimonies to its music, the format of their services is meant to evoke the active participation of its members. This is perhaps the feature of evangelical Protestantism that, at least temporarily, draws Latin Americans away from Catholicism; people who may not feel included or significant in the religious environment in which they grew up seek a sense of inclusion in other spiritual settings.

Charismatic leaders like the evangelical preacher Alberto Mottesi, known as the "Latin America's Billy Graham," have international recognition for their dynamic presence on the television and radio. Colossal revival events like the "March of Glory" in 2003 in Mexico City exemplify the visible presence of evangelical christianity in the region and the celebratory atmosphere that its leaders seek to promote. The event drew a million attendees from different parts of Mexico. Shutting down four lanes of traffic—coupled with a 10-mile procession down one of the city's core thoroughfares to Mexico City's physical, cultural, and historical center, the Zócalo square—the event took place in front of the National (Catholic) Cathedral. Complete with sermons and prayers by Mottesi, a "praise band," 400 dancers in uniforms, balloons, banners, all-night vigils, the 17-hour event, according to an evangelical attendee, "rivaled the excitement and atmosphere of a Latin American championship soccer game" (Eric Tiansay, *Charisma*, September 2003, pp. 40–44, 84).

In addition to analyzing the changing number of Catholics and Protestants, Chaván de Matviuk, Cleary, and other scholars have taken note of the political and social changes that have accompanied the rise of Protestantism over the past century. A number of scholars note the new leadership roles afforded to women and the poor in Protestantism. Interestingly, one aspect that Mottesi defines as his spiritual work is challenging *machismo* in Latin American society: "I believe that in this Latin American revival, there is a great freedom for women in ministry taking place. [. . .] I have asked for forgiveness from the Latin American women for *machismo*. . . . I asked forgiveness of the sins of my people" (*Charisma*, September 2003, pp. 40–44, 84). Of course, there are those who argue that some evangelical churches further restrict the role of women in society by highlighting a more traditional role of women.

Significant changes have also taken place within the Catholic Church in Latin America over the past few decades. In addition to the "opening up" of the Roman Catholic Church worldwide with the changes brought about with the Second Vatican Council (1962–65), liberation theology has pushed for a closer application of the Bible's gospel since its beginnings in the late 1960s and early 1970s. According to this school of thought, Christians should work to "liberate" people from poverty and oppression. Liberation theology's focus on social justice and human rights has at times brought its leaders into conflict with the Vatican. Today, scholars disagree as to the strength of liberation theology's Base Christian Communities (CEBs). R. Andrew Chesnut, however, suggests that CEBs have lost their "popular appeal" in the region, but that "[at] the beginning of the twenty-first century, the Catholic Charismatic Renewal (CCR) stands as the largest and most dynamic movement in the Latin American church." Rivaling the mega-churches of the evangelicals, this "Catholic movement easily fills soccer stadiums in the major cities of the region with tens of thousands of fervent believers." He adds that "[if] the perennial shortage of priests has eased somewhat in the last two decades and if the Catholic church is finally employing mass media, especially television, as a tool for evangelization, it is because of the Charismatics, whose missionary zeal rivals that of their chief competitors in the religious marketplace, the Pentecostals" ("Opting for the Spirit in Latin America: The Catholic Charismatic Renewal as a Response to Pentecostal Competition").

While noting that Catholicism is "in decline" in the region, Cristián Parker, for his part, reframes the Catholic-Protestant question asserting that "[we] have have passed from being a 'Catholic continent' to being an increasing pluralist religious continent." In addition to noting the presence of nonbelievers and atheists, he offers a number of examples of this religious plurality: Judaism, Umbanda, Santería, Candomblé, the Theology of Prosperity, Mother Angelica, New Age spiritualities, and popular saints like Sarita Colonia and Romualdito ("On the Social and Cultural Roots of Increasing Religious Pluralism in Latin America: Some Hypotheses from the Chilean Experience," 2005). Offering another perspective on the religious landscape of Latin America, in 2004 Professor Cleary and Timothy J. Steigenga edited *Resurgent Voices in Latin America: Indigenous Peoples, Political Mobilization, and Religious Change,* which discusses the role of religion in indigenous activism.

For more information on Catholic, Protestant, Pentecostal, Evangelical, indigenous, and Afro-Latin American religions, see the "Religion in Latin America" Web site: http://lanic.utexas.edu/project/rla/index.htm. For more information on the relationship between the growth of Protestantism and social and political change in Latin America, read *Rethinking Protestantism in Latin America,* edited by Virginia Garrard-Burnett and David Stoll (1993). For more information on Pentecostalism, see *Between Babel and Pentecost: Transnational Pentecostalism in Africa and Latin America,* edited by Andre Corten and Ruth Marshall-Fratani (2001).

On the Internet . . .

United Nations Environment Programme (UNEP): Regional Office for Latin America and the Caribbean

The UNEP's Regional Office for Latin America and the Caribbean's home page includes news and information on environmental law, national resources, environmental training, and industry, technology, and economics. It offers materials in English, Spanish, and Portuguese.

http://www.pnuma.org/ing/index.php

Tierramérica

Tierramérica is an information service that provides news on the environment and development. Produced by Inter Press Service and supported by the UNEP and UNDP, its purpose is to offer a "space for debate, drawing a wide range of social actors from Latin America and the world." Tierramérica's Web site is in English, Spanish, and Portuguese.

http://tierramerica.net/english/2006/0318/index.shtml

The Land Research Action Network (LRAN)

The LRAN is a network of researchers and social movements who work toward "land reform and agrarian change around the world." Its home page provides news, country studies, a topic library, research on human rights, and links to other organizations. It is available in English, Spanish, and Portuguese.

http://www.landaction.org/

Amazon Watch

Amazon Watch is a non-profit organization that works "with indigenous and environmental organizations in the Amazon Basin to defend the environment and advance indigenous peoples' rights in the face of large-scale industrial development-oil and gas pipelines, power lines, roads, and other mega-projects." Its home page includes links for news, reports, photos, and videos on the Amazon region.

http://www.amazonwatch.org/

PART 3

People, Land, and the Environment

*S*ince *living beings first appeared on Earth, both plants and animals have affected and attempted to control their environments in order to better survive. Although humans cannot exist without impacting the environment in some manner, the issue of humankind's relationship to land and long-term environmental sustainability is the flash point for many controversies. In analyzing the relationships between humans and the natural world, however, one must also consider conflicting philosophical perspectives, the basic needs, and the economic differences among human beings.*

- Should DDT Be Given Another Chance?

- Do the Economic Benefits of a "Dry Canal" in Nicaragua Outweigh the Financial, Human, and Environmental Costs?

- Is Plant Biotechnology the Solution to Hunger in Latin America and the Caribbean?

- Is Expropriating Land and Giving It to the Poor a Good Economic and Cultural Policy?

ISSUE 12

Should DDT Be Given Another Chance?

YES: Paul Driessen, from *Eco-Imperialism: Green Power, Black Death* (Merril Press, 2003)

NO: Michelle Allsopp and Bea Erry, from "POPs in Latin America: A Review of Persistent Organic Pollutant Levels in Latin America," Greenpeace Research Laboratories (October 2000)

ISSUE SUMMARY

YES: Mr. Driessen, senior fellow with the Committee for a Constructive Tomorrow, believes that the ban prohibiting the usage of the pesticide DDT (dichloro-diphenyl-trichloroethane) has created more problems than solutions since a greater number people have died related to the spread of malaria than would have died from exposure to DDT.

NO: Greenpeace researchers Michelle Allsopp and Bea Erry contend that the group of chemicals known as POPs (persistent organic pollutants), which include the pesticide DDT, represent a significant global contamination problem because they are resistant to natural breakdown processes and are highly toxic. They argue that DDT and other POPs should be phased out of use in Latin American countries.

In low-lying humid areas of Latin America, most notably in the Caribbean, Central America, Colombia, Venezuela, the Guyanas, and Brazil, complications due to malaria cause many deaths, especially among young children. The disease is spread through contact with the female *Anopheles* mosquito that serves as a host to a parasite that lives and develops inside the mosquito. Symptoms of the illness are high fevers, shaking, chills, and flu-like illnesses. These symptoms can last anywhere from 10 days to 4 weeks and, if not treated immediately, may lead to death.

Due to the rapid proliferation of the disease, both the treatment of the symptoms and the cost of death can become a drain on the many financially strapped nations of Latin America. Although there has been much research in the prevention of malaria, as of 2005 there was no vaccine to prevent contracting the disease—only to treat it once a person has contracted it. Yet, despite the lack of development of an adequate preventive measure, malaria can be reasonably controlled and treated, but appropriate action and medication must be used in a timely and effective manner. However, anti-malarial treatments are often expensive or unavailable in certain regions of Latin America. As a result, victims of the disease are frequently treated with inappropriate and/ or ineffective medications, making the disease difficult to stop. And, when people are not promptly treated for the disease, particularly *P. falciparum*—the deadliest form of malaria—complications may lead to kidney failure, seizures, mental confusion, coma, and ultimately death. According to the arguments presented in Driessen's article and also due to the fact that the *Anopheles* mosquito is present throughout many Latin American countries, some advocate the usage of pesticides such as dichloro-diphenyl-trichloroethane—or DDT, as it is commonly recognized—to eliminate the mosquito.

All pesticides have varying degrees of toxicity to each living organism. Chemical insecticides function by poisoning the nervous system of the intended insect, therefore leading to its resultant death. However, effects related to the infiltration of these toxins may also manifest themselves in mammals. It is this toxic effect on plants and animal life that creates concern about the application of DDT. According to Michelle Allsopp and Bea Erry, the danger of DDT is that it is a persistent organic pollutant (POP). POPs are defined as "a group of chemicals which are very resistant to natural breakdown processes and are therefore extremely stable and long-lived." Because DDT is resistant to natural breakdown processes, some people fear the effects of DDT are interminable, therefore raising concerns about its long-term and concentrated applications in particular regions of Latin America.

DDT was first created in 1874. However, its use as an insecticide was not realized until 1939 by a Swiss scientist, Paul Hermann Müller, who in 1948 was awarded the Nobel Prize in medicine for his discovery that DDT kills the *Anopheles* mosquito and consequently prevents malaria. In 1962, environmental biologist Rachel Carson wrote *Silent Spring*, identifying DDT as a carcinogen and a pesticide that was extremely harmful to the environment. Carson's actions, in part, led to the 1972 ban on the usage of DDT for agricultural purposes in the United States and subsequently many other countries including several in Latin America. Twenty years later, the Stockholm Convention treaty to protect human health and the environment from POPs was signed, stating POPs "accumulate in the fatty tissue of living organisms and are toxic to humans and wildlife. . . . In implementing the Convention, Governments will take measures to eliminate or reduce the release of POPs into the environment" (http://www.pops.int/). In addition, as part of the terms of the agreement, any countries receiving monetary aid related to the Stockholm Convention are also forbidden from using DDT, or their international aid may be terminated.

Today, there are those, such as Paul Driessen, who believe that more damage has been caused as a result of the ban of DDT, as opposed to its usage. He argues that more deaths are caused due to complications related to malaria than deaths due to exposure to DDT. Others, however, such as Michelle Allsopp and Bea Erry, affirm that DDT presents a global contamination problem and is a harmful pesticide that should be banned from all countries of the world, including Latin America.

YES

Paul Driessen

Eco-Imperialism:
Green Power, Black Death

Sustainable Mosquitoes—Expendable People

Fiona "Fifi" Kobusingye is a 34-year-old designer and businesswoman from Kampala, Uganda. In early November 2002, she saw her doctor because she felt fatigued—and discovered she had malaria. Her year-old niece was shivering and crying all night, and suffering from impending kidney failure, because of malaria. Her sister was critically ill and hospitalized with malaria, and her mother came to Kampala to help tend everyone—but ended up in the hospital herself with malaria.

"Our family and community are suffering and dying from this disease, and too many Europeans and environmentalists only talk about protecting the environment," Kobusingye says. "But what about the people? The mosquitoes are everywhere. You think you're safe, and you're not. Europeans and Americans can afford to deceive themselves about malaria and pesticides. But we can't."[1]

Compared to many others, though, her family is lucky—so far. It can afford medical treatment, and everyone is feeling better, for now at least. But other families aren't so fortunate.

In 2000, say World Health Organization and other studies, malaria infected over 300 million people. It killed nearly 2,000,000—most of them in sub-Saharan Africa. Over half of the victims are children, who die at the rate of two per minute or 3,000 per day—the equivalent of 80 fully loaded school buses plunging over a cliff every day of the year. Since 1972, over 50 million people have died from this dreaded disease. Many are weakened by AIDS or dysentery, but actually die of malaria.[2]

In addition to these needless deaths, malaria also saps economies and health care resources. It keeps millions home from work and school every day. Chronic anemia can sap people's strength for years and leave victims with severe liver and kidney damage, while cerebral malaria can cause lifelong learning and memory problems, followed by early death.

The disease drains the Indian economy of as much as $737 million every year, in lost wages due to deaths and absence from work, reduced productivity due to fatigue, and money spent on insecticides, medicines and malaria research, New Delhi's Liberty Institute has calculated.[3]

Africa's gross national product would be $400 billion a year—instead of its current $300 billion annually—if malaria had been wiped out in 1965, when it was eliminated in most of the developed world. Malaria control costs Africa $12 billion annually, depleting budgets for other health, environmental, economic and social programs. It particularly afflicts poor families, who must use up to 25 percent or more of their income on prevention and treatment.[4]

Uganda alone spends nearly $350 million a year on malaria, and devotes up to 40 percent of its outpatient care to malaria patients. In 2002, 80,000 Ugandans died of the disease, and again half of them were children.[5] "Most families can't even afford to get proper treatment. Where do you get the money to go back to the hospital again and again," asks Kobusingye, "when your family needs food and so many other things?"

These are real deaths and real impacts—not just theoretical deaths, based on extrapolations from rodent studies (as in the case of Alar, the growth-regulating chemical that was the subject of a vitriolic attack and fund-raising campaign by the Natural Resources Defense Council and Fenton Communications in 1989[6]), or hypothetical catastrophes (like flood and drought scenarios generated by certain climate change computer models).

They are due in large part to near-global restrictions on the production, export and use of DDT. Originally imposed in the United States by EPA Administrator William Ruckelshaus in 1972,[7] the DDT prohibitions have been expanded and enforced by NGO pressure, coercive treaties, and threats of economic sanctions by foundations, nations and international aid agencies.

❧

Where DDT is used, malaria deaths plummet. Where it is not used, they skyrocket. For example, in South Africa, the most developed nation on the continent, the incidence of malaria had been kept very low (below 10,000 cases annually) by the careful use of DDT. But in 1996 environmentalist pressure convinced program directors to cease using DDT. One of the worst epidemics in the country's history ensued, with almost 62,000 cases in 2000.

Shortly after this peak, South Africa reintroduced DDT. In one year, malaria cases plummeted 80 percent; with the introduction of Artemesinin-based Combination Therapy drugs, in three years they were down by 93 percent! Next door, in Mozambique, which uses pyrethroids but not DDT, malaria rates remain high. Similar experiences have been recorded in Zambia, other African countries, Sri Lanka, Bangladesh and elsewhere.[8]

DDT likewise helped to eradicate malaria from vast areas of South America, though not in Central America, and to control the disease in additional areas via indoor spraying. Control continued as long as the centralized spray programs were maintained. However, as environmental groups and the World Health Organization succeeded in eliminating both outdoor and indoor uses of DDT, the number of malaria cases spiraled upward. Manaus, Brazil, and many other areas are now enduring the return of endemic malaria to pre-DDT levels.

"The re-emergence of this devastating disease," says Donald Roberts, Professor of Tropical Public Health at the Uniformed Services University of

Health Sciences, "is clear and unambiguous testimony to the falsehoods of environmentalists and the failed policies of the WHO."

No other chemical comes close to DDT as an affordable, effective way to *repel* mosquitoes from homes, *exterminate* any that land on walls, and *disorient* any that are not killed or repelled, largely eliminating their urge to bite in homes that are treated once or twice a year with tiny amounts of this miracle insecticide. For impoverished countries, many of which are struggling to rebuild economies wracked by decades of disease and civil war, cost and effectiveness are critical considerations.

Substitute pesticides help but are problemmatical. While carbamates work well, they are four to six times more expensive than DDT and must be sprayed much more often. Organophosphates are dangerous and thus not appropriate in homes. And mosquitoes have built up a huge resistance to synthetic pyrethroids, because they are used so extensively in agriculture.

For poor African, Asian and Latin American countries, cost alone can be determinative. Not only do they need their limited funds for other public health priorities, like safe drinking water, but they have minimal health and medical infrastructures. Every dollar spent trying to control malaria is a dollar that's unavailable for other public health needs. "DDT is long-acting; the alternatives are not," says Professor Roberts. "DDT is cheap; the alternatives are not. End of story."[9]

DDT is not a panacea, or a "super weapon" that can replace all others. Nor is it suitable in all situations. However, it is a vital weapon—often the "best available technology"—in a war that must be fought against a number of mosquito species (vectors) and constantly changing malaria parasites, in different terrains and cultures, and under a wide variety of housing and other conditions. Like any army, healthcare workers need to have access to every available weapon. To saddle them with one-size-fits-all solutions (tanks and pistols, bed nets and drug therapies) is unconscionable.

The chemical is no longer used in agriculture (which accounted for 99 percent of its use at the time Rachel Carson wrote *Silent Spring*). Today it is used almost entirely, and very selectively, in malaria control, via spraying in tiny quantities on the insides of the traditional huts and houses that are common in areas of Africa most threatened by the disease.

It is not carcinogenic or harmful to humans; used in accord with these modern practices, it is safe for the environment; and malaria-carrying mosquitoes are far less likely to build immunities to DDT than to other pesticides that environmentalists and US, EU and UN agencies tolerate only as a last resort. Rare cases of immunity in decades past have since been linked to gross overuse in agriculture during the 1950s and 1960s. DDT's alleged toxicity to wildlife may have been due to faulty lab studies, its being mixed with dangerous petroleum distillates, or rampant discharges of other chemicals into waterways. "In the 60 years since DDT was first introduced," notes South African Richard Tren, president of Africa Fighting Malaria, "not a single scientific paper has been able to replicate even one case of actual human harm from its use."[10]

During World War II, DDT was actually classified as a secret weapon, because of its unparalleled ability to prevent malaria and typhus among Allied troops. After the war, virtually every concentration camp survivor and many other Europeans were also doused multiple times with DDT to prevent typhus, with no ill effects reported. The widespread use of DDT in Europe and the United States played vital roles in eradicating malaria and typhus on both continents.

In 1979, a World Health Organization (WHO) review of DDT use failed to find "any possible adverse effects of DDT" and deemed it to be the "safest pesticide used for residual spraying in vector control programs." Estimates by reputable scientists and scientific organizations have gone as high as five hundred million lives saved by the use of DDT.[11]

Nevertheless, the WHO, United Nations Environmental Program (UNEP), World Bank, Greenpeace, Pesticide Action Network, World Wildlife Fund, Physicians for Social Responsibility and other groups remain adamantly opposed to the use of DDT—and other pesticides. Their stance angers many who must live with malaria's consequences every day. However, these organizations ignore the victims' growing anger and the rising body count. Instead, they continue to advocate steps that, while helpful, simply cannot be the sole solution to this widespread and complex disease.

- Insecticide-treated mosquito bed nets do help at night, if used properly and regularly. But they are not foolproof, or repellant, must be re-treated regularly, and are hardly appropriate during the day, at work, in school or at play.
- Drug therapies are extremely expensive for poor families and poor countries. They also depend on public health facilities that are lacking in most malarial regions, and on committed patients and parents treating themselves and their children on a regular basis. Moreover, the parasite that causes malaria has become increasingly resistant to chloroquine and other drugs, the cheapest and most common medical treatments.
- Fish that eat mosquito larvae at best offer a haphazard approach that helps under certain, limited circumstances.

But the government and donor agencies and environmental activists still do not support the use of pesticides, and certainly not DDT. Indeed, they are trying to phase out all pesticides, via international treaties and other means.

A principal argument against DDT is that its use is not "sustainable." This claim has frequently been made by Gro Harlem Brundtland, who was instrumental in promoting the sustainable development concept when she was Norway's prime minister—and headed the World Health Organization between 1998 and 2003. However, without DDT, the lives of millions in developing countries are certainly not sustainable.

"My friend's four-year-old child hasn't been able to walk for months, because of malaria," Fifi Kobusingye says softly, her voice breaking. "She crawls around on the floor. Her eyes bulge out like a chameleon, her hair is dried up, and her stomach is all swollen because the parasites have taken over her liver. Her family doesn't have the money to help her, and neither does the Ugandan government. All they can do is take care of her the best they can, and wait for her to die."[12]

Professor Roberts has heard many stories like this, and seen similar tragedies unfold right before his eyes. He is outraged at the "high pressure tactics" that have forced many countries to abandon public-health uses of DDT—and watch their disease and death tolls soar. He is not alone.

"If we don't use DDT, the results will be measured in loss of life," David Nabarro, director of Roll Back Malaria, says bluntly. "The cost of the alternatives tend to run six times that of DDT."[13] That fact, however, appears to be irrelevant to many activist groups and aid agencies.

Activists like actor Ed Begley, Jr. and the Pesticide Action Network like to say there is no global ban on DDT. But they are playing semantic games. Increasing restrictions on the production, storage, transportation and use of DDT and other pesticides, lengthy delays in getting approvals to use them, mounds of costly red tape, and the refusal of donor agencies and foundations to fund indoor residual spraying programs all add up to one thing: sickness and death for millions of Africans every year. From the activists' perspective, says Richard Tren, that's just "bad luck for the people who have to die, so that über bureaucrats in Geneva can dot their i's and cross their t's."

"The US Agency for International Development will not fund any indoor residual spraying and neither will most of the other donors," Tren notes. "This means that most African countries have to use whatever [these donors] are willing to fund (bed nets), which may not be the most appropriate tool." Belize and Bolivia have both admitted that they stopped using DDT in the face of USAID pressure, and many other developing countries refrain from using DDT because "they don't want to damage their chances of exporting agricultural produce to the North." Mozambique beats around the bush, in giving absurd reasons why it won't use DDT, even as tens of thousands of its citizens are dying.[14]

USAID director Andrew Natsios' pointed comments about GM corn and starvation thus stand in sharp contrast to the agency's position on the use of DDT to combat malaria. The agency refuses to fund DDT programs, because the WHO does not support its use, and the insecticide is not permitted in the United States, where malaria and West Nile virus problems pale in comparison to mosquito-borne diseases in developing countries. Its current stance also contrasts sharply with its previous support for DDT and other chemicals between 1950 and 1972, when it contributed $1.2 billion to the Global Malaria Eradication Campaign. German, Swedish, Norwegian and other aid agencies take a similar position.[15]

All these donor agencies, suggests Tren, "need to decide whether they are in Africa to save lives, or to be politically correct and please the Greens at home."[16]

·◄◉►·

What is permitted today in risk-averse countries that have already conquered malaria should simply be irrelevant for nations that are suffering massive epidemics today. As Tren and Roger Bate ask, would Sweden really refuse to fund hospital nurses in Africa if they worked under conditions that do not fulfill Swedish health and safety requirements?[17] Would donor agencies refuse to fund immunization programs, because some people have allergic reactions to vaccines?

India's Department of Trade and Industry worries that the country's agricultural produce will be turned away from Europe if any traces of DDT are found, Tren notes. And in a truly bizarre example of misplaced priorities and concerns, Zimbabwe's department of health was told to stop using DDT because growers were worried that their *carcinogenic* tobacco would get rejected by the USA and EU if any DDT were found on it.[18]

Domestic US laws also prevent the import of produce with residues of pesticides and other chemicals that have been banned in the United States. This has forced growers to spray more often with non-persistent pesticides that are more expensive and more toxic to workers, resulting in more cases of pesticide poisonings, especially in poor countries where hand spraying is the norm. Whether it will also result in bans on the import of fish and agricultural products from South Africa, Uganda and other countries that dare to use DDT is an open question.[19]

Ugandan Health Minister Jim Muhwezi summed the matter up succinctly, when he announced in late 2002 that his country would begin using DDT to control mosquitoes. Uganda did so despite warnings by environmentalists and the European Union that it risks having a boycott launched against its coffee and having its fish and agricultural exports banned in EU and other foreign markets, if it goes forward with its plan. Kenya is also considering the use of DDT to combat its growing epidemic; that would make it only the eighth African nation to do so.

In Muhwezi's view, the cost of treating malaria, and the burden it places on the country, outweigh any environmental repercussions, which indeed are almost nil. He cited the successful use of DDT in Mauritius and South Africa to slash malaria disease and death rates and said, "Our people's lives are of primary importance. The West is concerned about the environment because we share it with them. But it is not concerned about malaria because it is not a problem there. In Europe, they used DDT to kill anopheles mosquitoes that cause malaria. Why can't we use DDT to kill the enemy in our camp?"[20]

The United States and Europe successfully used DDT to eradicate malaria. For them to downplay the lethal effects of this disease on developing nations— while obsessing about theoretical health problems from trace chemicals in food and drinking water—strikes Tren, Muhwezi and others as hypocritical, paternalistic and callous. It is hardly ethical or socially responsible.

New insecticides, chemicals and drugs are clearly needed. However their development and use are hampered by insufficient funding (in Africa), excessive reliance on the precautionary principle (particularly in Europe), and drug approval delays and the ever-present threat of multi-billion-dollar liability judgments (especially in the United States). Even if they might someday be a reliable substitute for DDT, tens of millions are likely to die in the meantime.

Simply put, the suggestion that alternatives to DDT exist now or are "just around the corner" is little more than wishful thinking in its deadliest form—promoted by people who have staked out an ideological position against DDT anywhere, anytime and under any circumstances, and cling to their position like limpets to a rock.

As author, film producer and PhD molecular biologist Michael Crichton put it: "Banning DDT is one of the most disgraceful episodes in the twentieth century history of America. We knew better, and we did it anyway, and we let people around the world die, and we didn't give a damn."[21]

Even the *New York Times* (which usually sides with radical environmental groups) now says the developed world "has been unconscionably stingy in financing the fight against malaria or research into alternatives to DDT. Until one is found, wealthy nations should be helping poor countries with all available means—including DDT."[22]

And still anti-pesticide activists like Greenpeace and the World Wildlife Fund are unmoved.

Many Africans, Asians and Latin Americans are understandably outraged. They view the intense pressure on countries not to use DDT as a lethal form of eco-imperialism, imposed by nations that eradicated malaria, dengue fever and typhus decades ago—against nations that continue to be devastated by these deadly diseases. The restrictions on pesticides are also a grotesque abuse of the precautionary principle, akin to telling terminally ill cancer patients they may not use morphine to ease their pain, because *you* are concerned about the use of addictive drugs by well-to-do high school students.

The United States death toll from West Nile virus (260 people in 2001 and 2002 and 2002 combined) is a mere 0.007 percent of Africa's annual death toll from malaria. And yet, Americans are again using pesticide spraying programs to control mosquitoes that spread the virus. They would never tolerate being told they had to protect their children solely by using bed nets, larvae-eating fish and medicinal treatments. But they have been silent about conditions in Africa, and about the intolerable attitudes of environmental groups, aid agencies and their own government.

"Corporate social responsibility ought not be used to impose policies that kill people," says Kenya's James Shikwati. "It should not be used to render poor populations sick, unproductive and perpetually destitute. For rich countries to tell poor nations to . . . ban chemicals that help control disease-carrying insects—and then claim to be responsible, humanitarian and compassionate—is to engage in hypocrisy of the most lethal kind."[23]

Niger Innis, national spokesman for the Congress of Racial Equality, is equally blunt. "There is no more basic human right," he emphasizes, "than to live—to not be murdered by design, indifference or callous disregard. And yet, [civil rights leaders] and Amnesty International are missing in action. So are the CEOs of BP, Shell Oil, Ford Motors and other members of the World Business Council for Sustainable Development.

"Surely, sustaining, improving and saving lives is the most fundamental form of corporate social responsibility," Innis continues. "Why have they not challenged the radicals who set the Council's agenda and promote these lethal policies? Aren't they just a little uncomfortable being complacent accessories to what many Africans view as eco-manslaughter?"[24]

The anti-pesticide activists and donor groups know full well the consequences of their actions—just as a driver knows full well what is likely to happen if he takes his car at full throttle the wrong way down a busy street. But still the radicals persist in their deadly "game" with people's lives.

And yet, for their intense opposition to DDT use—and despite their blatant lack of concern for people—companies, politicos, NGOs, Hollywood celebrities, foundations and government bureaucrats are frequently hailed as "socially responsible," concerned about people's health and well-being, and "passionate about the environment."

It would be laughable, if it weren't so tragic.

Notes

1. Fifi Kobusingye, personal interview with Paul Driessen, May 6, 2003.

2. See www.FightingMalaria.org and extensive studies and articles cited and linked by that website, including "Malaria and the DDT Story," by Dr. Kelvin Kemm of Stratek Technology Strategy Consultants, in *Environment Health* (Lorraine Mooney and Roger Bate, editors). See also Walter Williams, "Killing people," *The Washington Times,* October 17, 2002; Deroy Murdock, "Nutritional Schizophrenia," NationalReviewOnline, June 25, 2002.

3. Barun Mitra and Richard Tren, *The Burden of Malaria,* Delhi, India: Liberty Institute, Occasional Paper 12, November 2002.

4. John Gallup and Jeffrey Sachs, *The Economic Burden of* Malaria, Harvard University Center for International Development, London School for Hygiene and Tropical Medicine, for the World Health Organization, 2000. For a detailed examination of the health, social and economic impacts of malaria—especially on African countries—see Richard Tren and Roger Bate, *When Politics Kills: Malaria and the DDT Story,* Sandton, South Africa: Africa Fighting Malaria (2000). A more recent version of *Malaria and the DDT story* can be downloaded from the Institute of Economic Affairs website at http://www.iea.org.uk/record.php?type=publicationsID=11

5. Alexander Gourevitch, "Should the DDT ban be lifted?" *Washington Monthly,* April 9, 2003.

6. The chemical Alar was used to regulate the growth and ripening of apples, until it became the subject of an attack launched by Fenton Communications, the NRDC and CBS's "60 Minutes." In a later interview, David Fenton admitted that "the PR campaign was designed so that revenue would flow back to NRDC from the public." See Bonner Cohen, John Carlisle, *et al., The Fear Profiteers: Do "socially responsible" businesses sow health scares to reap monetary rewards?* Arlington, VA: Lexington Institute (2000).

7. In so doing, Ruckelshaus ignored thousands of pages of scientific evidence attesting to the pesticide's safety, as well as expert recommendations that its use be continued for malaria control.

8. Richard Tren, president, Africa Fighting Malaria, personal communication, December 20,2002; Brian Sharp, P. van Wyk, et al., "Malaria control by residual insecticide spraying in Chingola and Chililabombwe, Copperbelt Province, Zambia," *Journal of Tropical Medicine and International Health,* pages 732-736, September 2002. Richard Tren and Roger Bate, "Relief South Africans found for malaria is spelled DDT," *Investors Business Daily,* March 25, 2004. Indoor residual spraying programs pose virtually no environmental risks.

9. Alexander Gourevitch, "Should the DDT ban be lifted?" and Donald Roberts, personal communication to Paul Driessen, April 29, 2003.

10. Richard Tren, "DDT still saving lives," a UPI Outside View commentary, November 11, 2002. See also Bjorn Lomborg, *The Skeptical Environmentalist: Measuring the real state of the world,* Cambridge, UK: Cambridge University Press (2001), pages 233–235, 237, 243–244.

11. See Thomas R. DeGregori, *Bountiful Harvest: Technology, food safety and the environment,* Washington, DC: Cato Institute, 2002, page 132.

12. Fifi Kobusingye, personal interview with Paul Driessen, May 6, 2003.

13. David Nabarro, director, Roll Back Malaria; quoted in "Malaria Meeting: Africans Discuss a Disease Biting Into Lives and Economies," ABCNews.com, April 2000.

14. Richard Tren, personal communication, December 17, 2002; Roger Bate, "Without DDT, malaria bites back," www.spiked-online.com, April 24, 2001.

15. Richard Tren and Roger Bate, *When Politics Kills: Malaria and the DDT story,* page 24. All other countries combined contributed only $2.8 million, via the World Health Organization, they note.

16. Personal email to Paul Driessen, April 7, 2003.

17. Richard Tren and Roger Bate, *Malaria and the DDT Story,* London: Institute of Economic Affairs, 2001, page 58.

18. Richard Tren, president, Africa Fighting Malaria, personal communication, December 17, 2002.

19. DeGregori, page 147, citing Matt Crenson, "Thousands of Children Jeopardized by Pesticide Use," Associated Press, Nando.net online, December 18, 1997. Amazingly, the 1996 Food Quality Protection Act specifically forbids the USEPA from considering occupational exposures to pesticides on the part of the children and adults who grow and pick the produce Americans eat.

20. David Kaiza, "Uganda to use DDT despite ban," *The East African,* Nairobi, Kenya, December 2, 2002; Tom Carter, "Kenyan research center favors DDT use: Malaria toll trumps ecological threat," *Washington Times,* May 9, 2003.

21. Michael Crichton, "Our Greatest Challenge," Remarks to the Commonwealth Club of San Francisco, September 15, 2003.

22. *New York Times* editorial, December 23, 2002. *See also* Tina Rosenberg, "What the world needs now is DDT," *New York Times Magazine,* April 10, 2004, chronicling the virtues of this repellant-pesticide.

23. James Shikwati, "How Europe is killing Africans," *The Day* (New London, CT), February 3, 2003.

24. Niger Innis, "Jesse and Al: Missing in action," Congress of Racial Equality commentary, July 2003.

**Michelle Allsopp and
Bea Erry**

 **NO**

POPs in Latin America: A Review of Persistent Organic Pollutant Levels in Latin America

Executive Summary

Persistent organic pollutants (POPs) are a group of chemicals which are very resistant to natural breakdown processes and are therefore extremely stable and long-lived. POPs are not only persistent in the environment but many are also highly toxic and build up (bioaccumulate) in the tissues of animals and humans. Most do not occur in nature but are synthetic chemicals released as a result of anthropogenic activities. Vast amounts of POPs have been released into the environment and due to long-distance transport on air currents, POPs have become widespread pollutants and now represent a global contamination problem. Certain POPs have been responsible for some catastrophic effects in wildlife, ranging from interference with sexual characteristics to dramatic population losses. POPs are suspected of causing a broad range of adverse health impacts in humans and there is evidence that current levels of POPs in women in the general population of some countries is sufficient to cause subtle undesirable effects in their babies due to transfer of these contaminants across the placenta and via breast milk.

In recent decades, numerous POPs have been produced in large quantities worldwide and many are still in production and use. Some POPs, such as dioxins and furans, are not produced intentionally but are generated as by-products of many industrial processes, particularly combustion processes. Several POPs, notably certain organochlorine pesticides such as DDT and technical grade HCH, have been completely banned in industrialised countries and banned from agricultural use in most less industrialised countries. However, due to the persistence of these pesticides, high levels remain in many regions of the globe. Moreover, in some less industrialised countries, including Latin America, organochlorine pesticides, particularly DDT, are still used in sanitation campaigns against vector borne diseases such as malaria. In addition, illegal use of organochlorine pesticides often cannot be ruled out.

This report draws together published scientific literature on levels of POPs in the environment and in animals and humans of Latin America. The report reveals that there is a great lack of research on levels of POPs in Latin

From POPs in Latin America: A Review of Persistent Organic Pollutant Levels in Latin America, October 2000. Copyright © 2000 by Greenpeace Research Laboratories. Reprinted by permission. The full report is available at http://www.greenpeace.to/publications_pdf/popsinla.pdf

America in comparison to countries of the Northern Hemisphere. An overall insight into the state of contamination of Latin America is therefore impossible. However, available research does at least highlight the state of POPs contamination in some regions of Latin America.

What Are POPs?

POPs encompass many different and varied groups of man-made chemicals. Some POPs have been listed by national and international organisations as being chemicals of concern. For instance, the United Nations Environment Program (UNEP) has listed certain POPs, which are organochlorines, as being chemicals of clear concern. Organochlorines are substances containing chemically combined chlorine and carbon. They are a huge group of chemicals that include many POPs. The UNEP list notes 12 organochlorines. They are:

- dioxins and furans chemicals that are formed as unintentional by-products of combustion and processes involving the manufacture, use and disposal of organochlorines. For example, they are produced as by-products of municipal waste incineration and other types of incineration, open burning, landfill fires and during the production of PVC.
- PCBs industrial chemicals that have been banned but are still released to the environment in significant amounts from old sources and as unintentional by products of combustion and processes involving the manufacture, use and disposal of organochlorines.
- HCB a chemical used as a pesticide and in the manufacture of pesticides and produced as an unwanted by-product of various industrial processes involving organochlorines.
- Organochlorine pesticides, including DDT, chlordane, toxaphene, dieldrin, aldrin, endrin, heptachlor and mirex. Use of these organochlorine pesticides is banned or is severely restricted in most countries, but not in all.

POPs included in the above list are of immense concern given that they contaminate the global environment and are toxic. Most research on POPs is limited to a few of these chemicals only. There are however numerous other POPs which are also environmental contaminants and are of great concern. These include pentachlorophenol, brominated flame retardants, HCH isomers such as the organochlorine pesticide lindane, organotin compounds (for example, used as anti-fouling agents for ships), short chained chlorinated paraffins (for example, used in cutting oils and lubricants) and certain phthalates DBP and DEHP, which are somewhat less persistent but are none the less hazardous (main uses as plastic softeners, especially in PVC).

Where Are They Found?

All environmental media can become contaminated by POPs once they are released into the environment. For instance, spraying pesticides that are POPs on crops can contaminate vegetation and soils, direct discharges from POPs manufacturing facilities may contaminate rivers and releases of POPs from the stacks of incinerators and industrial facilities contaminate air. Consequently, POPs can contaminate local areas close to where they are released. However, some POPs are volatile/semivolatile and may evaporate from soil or water to air. Subsequently they may be transported for thousands of kilometers on air currents and contaminate regions remote from their source. These POPs migrate on air currents from warmer regions of the globe towards colder polar regions. Once they reach colder temperatures they condense and are deposited again on the Earth's surface. POPs may also be transported for long distances by rivers, ocean currents and as contaminants in wildlife. Due to the extensive releases of POPs and long distance transport they have become global contaminants and even attain high levels in remote regions, such as the arctic.

POPs in Food Webs

Many POPs which pollute the environment become incorporated into food webs. They accumulate and persist in the fatty tissues of animals and humans because they are soluble in fats and are not easily broken down in the body. Even low environmental levels of POPs can lead to high levels in the body tissues of animals and humans. For many POPs, the levels in fat increase as one animal eats another, so that the highest levels are found in predator animals at the top of food webs, such as polar bears, seals, toothed whales, birds of prey and humans. Marine mammals accumulate particularly high levels of POPs because of their large quantities of fatty blubber and a reduced capacity to break down some POPs compared to other species.

POPs in Latin America

Persistent organochlorine pesticides have been used for agriculture in Latin America over the past few decades although agricultural use is generally now illegal. Particularly large quantities have been used in Mexico for growing cash crops. In more recent years, the use of organochlorine pesticides has been restricted to public health programs against diseases such as malaria. In this regard, Mexico is by far the biggest user of the pesticide DDT in Latin America followed by Brazil with other countries using lower quantities.

This report reviews data on POPs in Latin America from the scientific literature, (mainly that published in the english language). Literature was identified mainly from the BIDS ISI scientific database. The studies that are reviewed can only be seen to be representative of the particular region studied and can by no means be considered to be representative of each country as a whole since so little research is available.

Detailed comparisons between POPs levels found in a study with other studies is difficult because of inconsistencies in laboratory methods used and different laboratory quality control standards. Nevertheless, comparison between studies can give insight into the state of contamination of an area and whether levels of POPs are considered to be high or low. Current levels of organochlorine pesticides in Latin America reflect both past and current uses.

Coastal Environment

Several studies reported on POPs levels in coastal lagoons, water and sediments and fish/shellfish. The majority of this research was limited to assessment of DDT levels in Mexico and the Gulf of Mexico.

Sediments in the aquatic and marine environment act as an ultimate sink for POPs. Notably high levels of DDT in estuarine or lagoon sediments were found in certain regions of northwest Mexico (16,600 ppb, dry weight), in northern Gulf of Mexico (1600 ppb), and in Nicaragua (270 ppb). In Mexico, the high levels of DDT were a consequence of its use for vector control and in Nicaragua it was due to extensive DDT use for cotton production over many years. Lower levels of DDT were reported for sediments in Brazil, Argentina, El Salvador, and other regions of Nicaragua, Mexico and the Gulf of Mexico. For fish and shellfish, comparatively high levels of DDT (>100 ppb wet weight) were again evident in certain regions of northwest Mexico, the Gulf of Mexico and Nicaragua.

PCBs were detected in estuarine and lagoon sediments from several Latin American countries. Particularly high levels were found in estuarine sediments in El Salvador (1137 ppb). Levels of PCBs in fish/shellfish were comparatively high (>100 ppb wet weight) in the Gulf of Mexico, Nicaragua, Argentina and Chile. The levels in fish/shellfish were within a similar range to those reported for marine fish from Australia (range 0.22 to 720 ppb) and were generally higher than those reported for Southeast Asian countries (0.38 to 110 ppb).

Oceanic Environment

A global survey of oceanic air and seawater in 1993 detected several organochlorines in the Caribbean Sea and Gulf of Mexico. In general, organochlorine concentrations in air in northern and southern oceans have remained constant in recent years despite bans on their use in many regions. In seawater, DDT was detected at comparatively low concentrations from the Caribbean Sea and the Gulf of Mexico.

Fish and Shellfish

Few data was available on levels of POPs in marine biota from the open oceans. DDT was found to be the most common contaminant in fish and shellfish taken from the Gulf of Mexico. Levels of PCBs in squid were considerably lower in animals taken from waters of the Southern Hemisphere compared with the Northern Hemisphere. Similarly organotin levels were also considerably lower in squid from Southern Hemisphere waters, including waters off Peru and Argentina.

Marine Mammals

Only a few studies were found in the literature on levels of POPs in marine mammals of Latin America. Research on bottlenose dolphins from the Gulf of Mexico revealed high concentrations of chlordane compounds and dieldrin in blubber of these animals. Levels of DDT were similar to levels in dolphins from the Atlantic coast of the US and were in the same range as levels in

Burmeister's porpoises from Argentine waters. A study on brominated flame retardants in marine mammals showed that levels found in dolphins from the Gulf of Mexico were similar to levels found in marine mammals in the Northern Hemisphere.

Aquatic Environment

A limited number of studies reported that several organochlorine pesticides were detectable in surface water, sediments and/or fish and shellfish in aquatic environments of Brazil, Mexico, Honduras, Argentina, Uruguay and Chile. Chemicals included DDT, heptachlor and heptachlor epoxide, dieldrin, aldrin and lindane.

Comparison of POPs levels in the aquatic environment of Latin America with other countries showed that levels were in general not considered to be high in most regions that were studied. However, there were some very notable exceptions:

- In the Ipojuca river basin in Brazil, extremely high levels of heptachlor were evident in river water (up to 57.8 ppb) in 1995/6 which clearly exceeded legal limits (10 ppb). It was inferred that the cause of this was the use of heptachlor in public health programmes. Levels of total HCH (maximum of 3760 ppt) in water also exceeded legal limits in this region.
- In an intensive agricultural region of the Choluteca river Basin in Honduras, very high levels of dieldrin were found (40 ppb) that according to the study exceeded US EPA water standards.
- In the Biobio river basin in Chile, notably high concentration of DDT (up to 2788 ppb) and lindane (up to 773 ppb wet weight) were detected in fish. The lindane levels were among the highest values ever reported in the world and reflected the massive use of lindane-based pesticides in the area.
- In the Rio de La Plata in Argentina, comparatively high levels of PCBs were evident in water and fish. Levels were similar to those reported for the Great Lakes.

Assessment of the concentration of POPs in drinking water in Latin America was almost non-existent in the scientific literature. Researchers expressed concern about the lack of information on levels of POPs in groundwater of Mexico that is used for drinking water. Serious groundwater contamination with the organochlorine pesticides 2,4-D and 2,4,5-T was found in Mexico at the Yucatan peninsula. At La Lima, Honduras, high levels of lindane and chlordane were found in drinking water that were above WHO standards.

Terrestrial Environment

Air, Soil and Vegetation
The scientific literature was almost devoid of studies on levels of POPs in air, vegetation and soil of Latin America. One study was available for Mendoza, Argentina which monitored levels of organochlorine pesticides in pine needles from urban parks as an indirect way of assessing air pollution. High levels

of DDT and HCH were found in comparison to rural areas of Argentina and to levels found in Germany. This implied that localised air pollution from insecticide spraying had occurred where the high levels in pine needles were detected. A study on municipal compost from different regions of Brazil found that levels of dioxins were similar to levels in German compost, while levels of PCBs were lower.

Birds
Several studies were published on levels of POPs in birds for Mexico, one study for Chile and none for other Latin American countries. Evidence of egg shell thinning due to high levels of DDE was found in Mexican birds of prey from the 1950s to the 1980s. No studies on this subject were available for the 1990s, but a recent study warned that birds in Chiapas state in Mexico may be at significant risk of DDT accumulation due to its continued use in this region. A range of other organochlorine pesticides were detectable in resident and migratory birds of Mexico in the 1980s and 90s and birds from central Chile in the 1990s.

Food
POPs are detectable in foodstuffs from all over the world. In Latin America, research on POPs in food was scarce and was limited to research in Argentina and Mexico. Limits set by the World Health Organisation (WHO) and Food and Agricultural Organisation (FAO) as "safe" levels for POPs in food were exceeded for DDT in cheese samples taken in Mexico and milk in Argentina. Milk from Mexico and Argentina also greatly exceeded regulatory limits for heptachlor. In Mexico, total HCH levels in milk exceeded the recently set limit for HCH and meat samples exceeded regulatory limits for DDT and HCH. These results imply that exposure to POPs via food in Mexico and Argentina may be high, but far more research is needed to clarify whether this is the case in general since current research is so limited.

Humans
Measurable quantities of POPs are present in human tissues worldwide. In Latin America, research on POPs in human tissues over the past 15 years or so are limited to a handful of studies, most of which focused on DDT in Mexico and Brazil.

One study in Rio de Janeiro, Brazil, 1992 found levels of dioxins and PCBs in breast milk were at the lower end of the range of those found in Western countries.

For DDT and its breakdown product DDE, the highest levels in human milk have been reported for Asia, Africa and Latin America. In various regions of Mexico and Brazil, DDE levels found in human milk were high (>2.5 ppm lipid) compared to most countries. This was almost certainly due to the continued use of DDT in these countries. In addition, very high levels of DDT have been found in pesticide sprayers from Brazil, Mexico and Venezuela. Levels of total DDT in adipose tissue of pesticide sprayers from Mexico were 6-fold higher than the general population while blood levels of Brazilian sprayers were 4.7-fold greater than levels in non-exposed workers.

Other organochlorine pesticides including dieldrin, HCB and heptachlor epoxide were found in human milk from Mexico and Brazil at concentrations that were within the range of those found in other countries. However, this gives no room for complacency because these chemicals are persistent, bioaccumulative and toxic. In addition, the developing young are particularly vulnerable to the impacts of such chemicals and they are passed from the mothers body to the developing foetus in the womb and to the nursing infant via breast milk.

Regulatory authorities use the concept of acceptable daily intakes of chemicals in food in an attempt to protect public health. The ADI is the amount of a chemical that can be taken in on a daily basis in the diet that is considered to be safe. If the ADI is applied to human milk taken in by the nursing infant, calculations showed that the ADI is exceeded for several POPs in many countries. In Latin America, calculations show that the ADI for the breast-fed infant was exceeded for DDT in two regions of Mexico and for dieldrin in two regions of Brazil. It is, of course, questionable how the ADI is applicable to the nursing infant because ADIs are calculated for a 70 kg adult taking in food over a whole lifetime. However, since the infant is more vulnerable than the adult to chemical exposure, it has been argued that the ADI should definitely not be exceeded for infants. It is therefore of great concern that the ADI is exceeded through intake of human milk in Latin America. Nevertheless, it is very important to note that breastfeeding is highly recommended by experts because of the many advantages it conveys.

Conclusions

- Published scientific studies clearly show that POPs contaminate terrestrial, aquatic and marine environmental media throughout Latin America. However, published research on levels of POPs in Latin America is extremely limited. This is both in terms of the quantity of research that is available and the number of POPs that have been researched. The majority of research has been generated in Mexico and secondarily in Brazil with little or no research in other countries. Data are mainly limited to investigations of levels of a few organochlorine pesticides. Only a few studies on dioxins are available in the whole of Latin America and research on brominated flame retardants is limited to one study on marine mammals.
- Notably high levels of some organochlorine pesticides are evident in some regions of Latin American countries which relate to past and/or present uses. Levels of DDE in human milk in Mexico and Brazil indicated that exposure of the general population is high in some regions.
- It is almost certain that POPs which are released in tropical Latin America not only cause local contamination problems but may also contribute to pollution in areas of the world far away from their source. For instance, studies on rivers and sediments in other tropical areas (Asia) indicate that because of high temperatures in the tropics, the residence time of POPs is shorter in water bodies and transfer to the atmosphere is greater. Transfer to air has wider implications for the global environment. Semi-volatile and persistent POPs such as HCB and HCH appear to be redistributed from tropical point sources to colder regions on a global scale.

POPs—A Global Problem

The problem of global POPs contamination is set to continue because the majority of POPs from anthropogenic activities are still being released into the environment. Decreases in the levels of POPs which are banned in some countries gives no room for optimism or complacency. Levels of POPs are still high enough to be of concern, and moreover, levels of other POPs which are still widely produced, such as the brominated flame retardants and organotins, add to the already heavy burden of POPs. Because the release of POPs into the environment is continuing, there is a potential for further severe impacts on the health of wildlife and humans. Given the persistent nature of POPs there is only one way forward to safeguard the environment and future generations. This is to phase out the production and use of all POPs, and the processes that lead to the unintentional generation of POPs as by-products, on an international/global basis and implement clean production technologies. Action must be taken now to address the existing POPs problems, prevent new problems and start on the road to a Toxics-Free Future.

Greenpeace Demands

- The production and use of all POPs, and human activities that lead to the generation of POPs, must be phased out at a national, international and, ultimately, at a global level.
- This must be achieved through the substitution of POPs (or the processes and materials which generate them) with non-hazardous alternatives. Strict timelines must be applied to achieve this goal.
- Industry and agriculture must pursue clean production technologies and manufacture clean products, recognising that the only way to prevent releases of POPs into the environment is to avoid their production and use.
- As a matter of urgency, action must be taken to stop production, and eliminate all discharges, emissions and losses of those chemicals prioritised for action by UNEP.
- Community Right to Know legislation provides a means to give citizens and the general public the tools to prevent and reduce industrial pollution, and protect themselves and their environment. Public access to information must exist at all levels of industrial production from production processes to food and product ingredient labelling.
- Presume that all chemicals are hazardous until demonstrated otherwise, i.e. until hazard identification is completed, or in those instances where hazard identification is limited by lack of information, chemicals must be assumed to present hazards of unknown proportions.
- Ultimately, measures to eliminate releases of all POPs and all other hazardous substances to the environment will need to be taken both at a regional level and on a global basis, because chemical contamination of the environment is a global problem and chemicals do not respect national boundaries.

POSTSCRIPT

Should DDT Be Given Another Chance?

The authors of both of these essays are ultimately concerned about people's lives; however, the question at stake is which of the two evils—DDT or malaria—is the lesser. Driessen believes that if governments were authorized to use DDT to reduce the number of mosquitoes, there would be fewer people, particularly children, dying in underdeveloped countries such as Latin America. However, Allsopp and Erry assert that because of DDT's resistance to the natural breakdown processes, it is extremely toxic and long-lived and, therefore, will "contaminate terrestrial, aquatic, and marine environmental media throughout Latin America." Their notion is, of course, that people who eat foods sprayed with DDT or eat fish from pesticide-laden waters are vulnerable to those toxins, just like the insects that the pesticide is intended to destroy. Allsopp and Erry also point out that not enough studies have been conducted to fully understand the short- and long-term effects of DDT in those regions of Latin America where its usage is most prevalent.

However, several organizations have conducted studies in various parts of the world, including Latin America, to better understand the effectiveness of DDT. One study conducted by the Pan-American Health Organization from 1993 to 1995 found that the number of malaria cases increased by 90 percent when DDT spraying had stopped after 1993. And, overall, where there was an increased use of DDT after 1993, the malaria cases decreased considerably. Furthermore, Dr. Deborah Winn, head of the extramural epidemiology program at the National Cancer Institute, points out that in several studies where women were subjected to varying levels of DDT, no connection was evident between exposure to the pesticide and the onset of breast cancer (August 12, 2002, http://www.susanlovemd.com/community/flashes/in-the-news/news020812.htm).

However, other scientific studies have shown that breast milk registered a high level of contamination when DDT is present in the environment. 1989 data from Brazil reveals that "Levels of DDT found in breast milk are not always higher in rural areas than in urban areas. This study showed that urban areas had approximately twice the level of contamination as rural populations, likely the result of DDT applications for mosquito abatement in Brazil, particularly in urban areas" (L.S. Sant'Ana, I. Vassilieff, and L. Jokl, "Levels of Organochlorine Insecticides in Milk of Mothers from Urban and Rural Areas of Botucatu," *Bulletin of Environmental Contamination and Toxicology,* vol. 42, 1989, pp. 911–18).

The Stockholm Convention on Persistent Organic Pollutants met for its first meeting in Uruguay in 2005. As Diego Cevallos reports, the "United Nations Environment Program (UNEP), the driving force behind the Convention, called for caution on the DDT question." Klaus Toepfer, UNEP executive director, offered his perspective on the future use of DDT: "Unless more ambitious investments are made in the search for better vaccines against the malaria parasite and better pesticides and methods for fighting against the mosquitoes that serve as vectors, it will be many years before the complete elimination of DDT is achieved" ("Much-Maligned DDT Still Has Supporters" *Tierramérica,* May 3, 2005). In its 2006 meeting, the Stockholm Convention recognized the importance of cost-effective alternatives to DDT. The convention called for further evaluation of "the comparative efficacy and environmental and human health safety of alternative insecticides to DDT" (http://www.pops.int/documents/meetings/).

Given the varying results of these tests and others, it is apparent that more research is needed to determine whether or not DDT is as harmful as was previously suspected. Of course, DDT may not be the only solution capable of fighting malaria. In addition to determining the full impact of DDT, scientists are also trying to develop other pesticides, herbicides, and natural defenses that may be as effective as DDT in combating malaria without the potentially dangerous side effects.

To learn more about the status of the use of DDT in a variety of Latin American nations, read "Much-Maligned DDT Still Has Supporters" by Diego Cevallos (*Tierramérica,* May 3, 2005). For information on alternatives to pesticide use, see Pesticide Action Network International, a network of nongovernmental organizations, institutions, and individuals from around the globe: http://www.pan-international.org/. In "Bolivia: Dengue Fever and Malaria Useless Campaign," biochemist Sylvia Pasquier advocates the use of DDT to combat malaria and dengue fever, another tropic disease transmitted by the mosquito. Find Pasquier's article at the Hispanic American Center for Economic Research's Web site: http://www.hacer.org/current/Boli044.php.

ISSUE 13

Do the Economic Benefits of a "Dry Canal" in Nicaragua Outweigh the Financial, Human, and Environmental Costs?

YES: CINN, from "The Dream of a Nicaraguan Canal," http://www.drycanal.com/overview.htm (2005)

NO: Jerry Mueller, from "Nicaragua's Proposed Dry Canal," *Nicaragua Network* (2001)

ISSUE SUMMARY

YES: CINN (Canal Interoceanico de Nicaragua), a multinational corporation that is the leading candidate to construct a canal across Nicaragua, argues that the construction of a canal through Nicaragua will provide major long-term economic benefits to Nicaragua by distinguishing it as the nexus of global commerce.

NO: Nicaragua Network's Environmental Committee, who seek to strengthen environmental protection in Nicaragua by working with Nicaraguan non-governmental organizations and attracting international support, believe that the construction of a canal through Nicaragua will only benefit a few elites and cause major environmental destruction.

T he Panama Canal is one of the greatest transportation projects ever built. It is a testament to the engineers, builders, and laborers that the Panama Canal has remained largely unchanged for nearly an entire century since it first opened in 1914. The idea to construct a canal through Central America has existed since Christopher Columbus first landed in the Americas in 1492. Less than 40 years after Columbus' arrival, Charles V, the Holy Roman Emperor and King of Spain, considered building a canal to shorten the route to Spanish territories located on the western coast of South America, such as Ecuador and Peru.

Prior to the construction of a canal, however, the first "modern" transportation route across the Panamanian Isthmus was built—the Panama Railway. In 1885, Colombia, who at that time ruled the land that is now Panama, gave exclusive rights to the United States to construct, manage, and use the railway. Travel times across the isthmus were shortened from 5 days to a matter of hours. In addition, major volumes of cargo could be quickly unloaded at one port, shipped overland, and reloaded onto a ship heading out to sea in less than a day.

Although the Panama Railway was considered an engineering marvel in its time and possessed the highest volume of cargo per mile of track anywhere in the world, the desire to eliminate the time spent unloading and reloading spurred the construction of what came to be the Panama Canal. The width and depth of the canal was calculated based on the size of ships of that era. However, modern watercraft are too large for the canal and were designed beyond the limited width and depth capacities of the canal. Contrasting the tremendous increase in the size of ships against the limitations of a canal designed to the specifications of early twentieth-century shipping needs, the need for a canal with modern capabilities is paramount to the shipping industry. It is estimated that by the year 2011, over one-third of all container ships will be too large to pass through the canal.

Given the costs associated with dredging and widening the current canal in Panama—estimated at over $5 billion—a number of other governments, including Mexico, Costa Rica and Nicaragua, have been developing more economical options. The leading alternative, spearheaded by CINN (Canal Interoceánico de Nicaragua), is the construction of a railway or "dry canal" across Nicaragua. The dry canal would require less than one-half the costs of expanding the Panama Canal and would greatly increase the annual volume ships that can pass through the Panama Canal, currently at 14,000 vessels per year. CINN also identifies the economic benefits that Nicaraguans will receive through the construction, traffic, and tolls related to the canal, including up to 50,000 new jobs for a country where over half its citizens live below the poverty line.

However, not all Nicaraguans are convinced of CINN's claims. Citing corporate and political special interests, environmental destruction, disruption of habitats, displacement of native societies, and the potential exploitation of cheap Nicaraguan labor with the bulk of the revenues going to politicians and big business, groups like the Nicaragua Network Environmental Committee fear a lack of public input and participation will hinder the potential gains of the canal from reaching the tens of thousands of the people impacted by its construction. In addition, the historical legacy of neoliberal economic policies in Nicaragua has created significant distrust of the government's management of major investments.

CINN focuses on the potentially huge economic boon that the dry canal could have, including job creation for a country that is one of the poorest in Latin America, as well as the benefits of placing Nicaragua at the hub of global trade. However, environmental groups such as the Nicaragua Network Environmental Committee remain skeptical that many of the dry canal's possible financial gains will end up in the hands of the powerful and wealthy, while the native peoples and the environment in which they live may endure significant devastation for economic benefits that may never appear.

The Dream of a Nicaraguan Canal

The history of Nicaragua has been marked by the old dream of an interoceanic canal. Several historians point to 1567, when King Felipe II of Spain ordered the study of a canal through Nicaragua. In 1850, when "gold fever" was all the rage in the United States, efforts to transport cargo from one coast of the USA to the other became focused on the San Juan River and Lake Nicaragua, encouraging the US military to construct a channel through that route.

Nonetheless, the dream of such a canal evaporated, at least temporarily, when in 1902 the US Senate decided to construct the Panama Canal. Dr. Carlos Argüello G. mentioned an exhibition in the Nicaraguan Historical Institute, that as late as 1913, the US Ambassador to Nicaragua, George Weitzel, said: *"In all cases of controversies between Nicaragua and Europe, Mexico, and Columbia, the true cause of the problem was the desire to control the interoceanic canal route."*

Later, Dr. Argüello stated that although the historic dispute between the Nicaraguan cities of León and Granada was in part fueled by the idea of a canal, the planned canal was to utilize Lake Nicaragua, which is more a lake of Grenada than a lake of León. Ambassador Weitzel said, *"In summary, it can be said that the question of the canal is the principal theme of disturbances of the affairs of Nicaragua, whether they be international [or] internal, and this is not less certain by the fact that the route through Panama was chosen years ago . . ."*

In the same statement, Dr. Argüello mentions several interesting and not well-known anecdotes about the canal, including:

- As early as 1797, several of the fathers of Latin American independence—Francisco de Miranda among them—tried to obtain British support to change the special transit rights for the proposed canal;
- In 1830 a Nicaraguan canal concession was granted to a group of businessmen from the Netherlands, headed by the King of Holland;
- In 1848, Prince Louis Napoleon accepted a concession to construct the "Napoleon Canal of Nicaragua" and said, *"In the New World there exists a country as superbly situated as Constantinople . . . We refer to the State of Nicaragua . . . which is destined to reach an extraordinary level of prosperity and greatness."*

All through the second half of the 19th century there were many developments and false starts for a Nicaraguan canal, but in 1902 everything appeared to end with the decision to build the canal in Panama.

Fast forward to the 1990s, when the Panama Canal had been in operation for eight decades, but was rapidly reaching the point of saturation. A group of U.S. investors led by New York attorney and entrepreneur Don M. Bosco, had the foresight to pursue that early dream of an international trade route across Nicaragua in a modern form. Rather than the expense and environmental jeopardy that a water canal would incur, Mr. Bosco and the late Juan Manuel Rodriguez conceived the all container railroad service, since East-West container movements had grown at an average annual rate of 8% in the decade of the 1980's and continued such growth into the 1990s. Other groups have tried to copy and modify this new approach. Since then, much has been said and written about various proposals to build and operate interoceanic canals through Nicaragua—both so-called "wet" canals, and "dry" canals. This information is at times confusing, with arguments both for and against the idea being advanced—sometimes backed by legitimate research, sometimes not.

Among these proposals, the Nicaraguan Interoceanic Railroad and Ports Project, being developed by the Canal Interoceanico de Nicaragua, S.A., (CINN), was first to appear with a concrete plan, officially termed the Nicaragua International Railroad and Ports Project, but known popularly as the "Dry Canal." CINN has pursued this proposal quietly but determinedly during the past 10 years, working with Nicaraguans to advance the proposal and create the legal foundation for such a large foreign investment in Nicaragua, amid a swirl of disinformation and efforts to undermine or stop the project from within and outside of Nicaragua.

CINN's proposal consists of the construction of two deep-water ports, one in the Caribbean and the other in the Pacific, united by a railway to transport ocean freight containers along the approximately 377 km-long route.

CINN: Some Background

In view of the fact that CINN has spent over ten years developing this project, a review the chronology of the principal developments during that period is in order.

In the early 1990s, a group of private investors including Mr. Bosco investigated the possibility of building an interoceanic canal in Costa Rica to provide a viable alternative to the Panama Canal, which, according to international shipping industry experts, would soon reach saturation levels and, because of inherent design limitations, would be unable to accommodate the largest, newest generation of container vessels which Asian shipping companies had under construction (the "Post-Panamax" size vessels).

Moreover, it was thought that a *"Dry Canal"*—an overland rail route connecting two ports for the transport of containers—represented the most efficient use of land, resources, funds and modern technology. In addition to providing the most economical way to transport cargo containers across the Central American isthmus, the Dry Canal would have a much less deleterious impact on the local environment and indigenous inhabitants than a highway or water canal, and would present far less complex engineering and construction issues.

However, while the Costa Rican effort was thwarted by senior advisors to then-President Jose Maria Figueres, by the early 1990s the political environment in Nicaragua had stabilized and foreign investors were encouraged to see the new opportunities in Nicaragua for business and investment during the administration of President Violeta Chamorro.

The Bosco group of investors decided to investigate the natural conditions and business conditions in Nicaragua in June 1994 and proposed were invited to move their Dry Canal project to Nicaraguan in late 1994.

In February 1995, . . . CINN was formed by the same group of investors who had developed the project in Costa Rica led by Mr. Bosco. CINN, formed under the laws of Nicaragua, set out to develop, build, and operate the Dry Canal of Nicaragua.

From the start, CINN committed itself to respecting Nicaragua's sovereignty, environment and economy. Over the past ten years, CINN became a joint effort between the early nucleus U.S. investors who provided the initial funds and conceptual planning, and a larger international consortium of engineers, port designers, consulting and construction firms representing a diverse group of countries (Belgium, Canada, U.K., USA, Hong Kong and China) which conducted studies and developed more detailed plans.

In 1995, the Nicaraguan government created a Joint Executive-Legislative Commission (Comisión Mixta), which formally received CINN's proposal and signed an accord in March 1995. This event was significant in that it was the first incidence of Liberals and Sandinistas to jointly act and sign an agreement with foreign investors since the end of the civil war.

In October 1996 the Nicaraguan Government approved CINN's Terms of Reference for the Feasibility Study of the Dry Canal Project.

In 1997, after a change in government, formal discussions took place to establish procedures for a Viability Study (Pre-Feasibility Study) which the new government asked CINN to conduct prior to the Feasibility Study in order to demonstrate that the Project could be realized.

On January 16, 1998, the Ministry of Transporation and Infrastructure directed a letter to the President of CINN, which stated that the Nicaraguan government recognized *"that CINN has created and developed, in its view, a project that was worthy of being given the first option for construction."*

The same letter gave CINN a timeline for the completion of the Viability Study, which was completed by CINN on time, with the promise by the Government that upon successful completion of the Viability Study, the negotiations for CINN's private concession contract would take place simultaneously with the Study and would be signed between the Government and CINN.

In January 1998, the Minister of Transportation and Infrastructure stated, *". . . CINN will continue to have the first option for the concession if the results of the Study determine the viability [of the Project] and the interests of the nation are preserved in all aspects."*

With these assurances CINN began the Viability Study, and at the end of March 1998, sent an international team of experts and planners representing engineering and construction firms from around the world, to Nicaragua. The plan was to ascertain the level of information available, meet with various

Nicaraguan agency officials, and perform on-site surveys of the relevant sites. On return of this group to their respective countries, the process of writing and finalizing the Viability Study began. Unfortunately, the Government did not act on the draft concession contract CINN provided and negotiations did not start until after the completion of the Viability Study.

Meanwhile, Presidential Order No. 68-98, promulgated in Gazette No. 63 of April 1998, provided for the establishment of the Multi-Sectorial Commission, "to study the contract of concession of the Canal Interoceánico de Nicaragua (CINN) project. . . ."

On August 27, 1998, CINN presented the results of the Viability Study to the President, the Vice President, and the Economic Cabinet of Nicaragua, four days before the established deadline. At the same time, CINN presented the document to the Minister of Transportation and Infrastructure, who chaired the Multi-Sectorial Commission, pursuant to the Presidential Order of April 1998.

With this, CINN preserved its primary option to develop the Dry Canal, and received clearance to move to the next stages of the project.

On October 26, 1998, in the Confrerence Hall of the Ministry of Transportation and Infrastructure, the Multi-Sectorial Commission was officially installed.

CINN continued negotiating the concession contract with the President's Legal Advisors Office, and the President of the Republic approved and transmitted the contract and implementing legislation to the National Assembly recommending approval in July, 1998. Public hearings were held by the Commission on Transport and Infrastructure and the Commission on the Environment and Natural Resources, and both Commissions approved the President's proposed legislation and accompanying concession contract. . . .

Since that time, CINN has undertaken the preliminary work to prepare the final TORs for the Feasibility Study, negotiated more detailed terms with the Nicaraguan Government and is waiting for the Nicaraguan Government to act in accordance with the law and regulations. CINN has continued to send engineers and environmental experts to the field and the port sites to gather information and continue with design and engineering work.

The Project

The fundamental objective of the Dry Canal project is to provide a new route for the transshipment of commercial container cargo between a deep water port on the Caribbean coast, and a second deep water port on the Atlantic coast, connected by high-speed rail.

The Dry Canal will initially support the movement of 730,000 containers/ year, a number which will increase incrementally over time.

The projected cost of the Dry Canal project as conceived in the Viability Study is $2.64 Billion.

Two Port Complexes

CINN is developing plans for two port complexes: one on the Caribbean coast, in the vicinity of Monkey Point, Municipality of Bluefields, in the South Atlantic Autonomous Region (RAAS), and one on the Pacific coast, in the vicinity of Pié de Gigante, in the western Department of Rivas.

Both port complexes will be constructed to accommodate the latest and biggest generation of container vessels—the Post-Panamax class. To that end, the ports will be built to a depth of 16 meters, and initially, with a docking span of 810 meters. Each will be served by five cranes and a system of breakwaters to permit safe docking maneuvers.

Each port complex will be fitted with platforms for the surveillance and classification of containers and facilities for temporary storage. State-of-the-art security systems for the inspection and tracking of cargo containers will assure compliance with the highest precautionary standards in an age of heightened vigilance for terrorist and narco-trafficking activities.

In cooperation with international law enforcement agencies, including the U.S. Department of Homeland Security and its Nicaraguan counterparts, CINN is prepared to deploy the latest anti-terrorist technologies, including container screening, radio-frequency identification (RFID) and satellite tracking of container ships, to assure the transport of cargo safely to its destination—and to identify, isolate, and neutralize potential threats before they can reenter the stream of global commerce or enter US ports.

All basic port services, including water treatment plants and power plants, will form part of each port complex, as well as adjacent Free Trade Zone activities and businesses. Both port complexes will be self-contained mini-communities, served by administrative and operations offices, residential developments, information technology and telecommunications infrastructure, shopping, commissary, and restaurant facilities, medical clinics, commuter airports, and roadway access. To the extent possible, environmentally-conscious and "green" construction, engineering, waste-disposal and power-generation methods will be utilized, including the use of solar power, recycling, and renewable resources.

As part of its commitment to supporting Nicaragua's economic development, CINN intends to using Nicaraguan personnel wherever possible, and will provide for the training of Nicaraguans to perform specialized jobs in port administration, surveillance and security, information technology, civil engineering, maintenance, logistics, and other areas vital to the operation of the port complexes and railway. In cooperation with Nicaraguan technical schools and universities, CINN will establish a Training Center, staffed by the most qualified instructors from Nicaragua and around the world, to ensure that Nicaraguans participate and qualify for technical and administrative positions in the Dry Canal operations.

A Maintenance and Repair Facility will serve each port complex, to perform safety inspections and equipment maintenance, and to supply logistics, parts, and expertise for both Dry Canal infrastructure and for docking vessels and their crews.

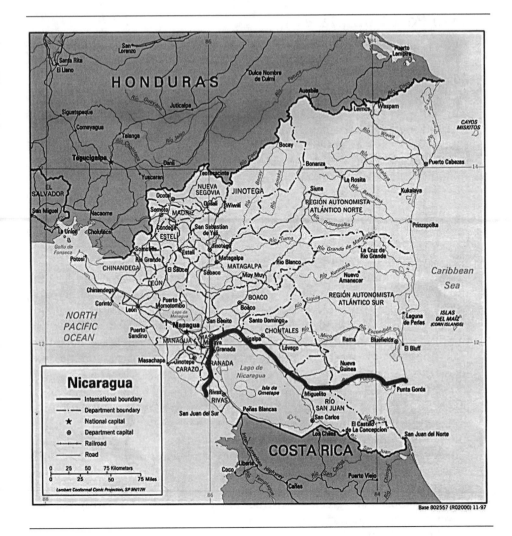

Base 802557 (R02000) 11-97

Interoceanic Railway

Spanning 377 kilometers from coast-to-coast, the CINN Interoceanic Railway (the "Railway") will provide a fast, safe, and cost-effective link between the Atlantic and Pacific port complexes. In the first stage of construction, the Railway will be a single-track railroad route, with switching stations and lateral bypasses to accommodate the simultaneous movement of trains in both the east-west and west-east directions. Later expansion of the Railway will supplement the route with additional parallel tracks to serve the increased traffic levels expected after the first 2–3 years of operation of the Dry Canal.

Electro-diesel locomotive trains, designed to haul approximately 200 fully-loaded shipping containers, with an average speed of 70 miles/hr, will provide rapid and convenient transit of containers between the port complexes. . . .

Environmental Considerations

The Viability Study concluded in 1998 included a look at important environmental considerations. Currently, a more complex investigation of environmental issues is being performed in an in-depth Environmental Impact Study.

Significantly, the environmental questions under review are not exclusively restricted to the impact of the Project on the natural environment, but also its potential social, economic, cultural, historic, and archeological impacts. This strategy, worked out cooperatively by CINN, the Nicaraguan government, and representatives of indigenous populations of the impacted regions, takes into account the fact that every human activity, however insignificant it appears, has both positive and negative impacts on the environment as broadly conceived. What is critical is that the necessary measures are taken to mitigate the negative impacts, and that countervailing benefits are provided to the affected populations, with a view to promoting their development and economic well-being now and in the future.

In the Feasibility Study and Environmental Impact Study phases of the project, the following objectives are being pursued:

- Identification of all significant impacts which could be financially very difficult or impossible to mitigate;
- Development of a broad socio-economic overview of the project's impacts, and a process for data collection and analysis;
- Assessment of natural threats such as seismic activity and geo-engineering strategies for their mitigation;

Taking into account these broad objectives, the Environmental Impact Study is considering the following factors:

General Environmental Assessment

- Physical and geological positioning of railway and other facilities
- Climate considerations
- Hydrological and water quality considerations
- Maritime ecosystems
- Coastal terrestrial ecosystems
- Forests
- Farmlands and agricultural issues
- Wetlands

Additional Considerations

- Protected areas and endangered species
- Air quality
- Noise and vibrations
- Historical and archeological sites
- Indigenous peoples
- Cities, towns and population centers potentially impacted by the project

Natural Threats

- Hurricanes and floods
- Seismic disturbances
- Volcanic activity
- Forest fires

General Considerations

The Dry Canal project, as conceived by CINN, will provide great benefits to the economic development of Nicaragua and its population, as well as to the Nicaraguan state. CINN sees the following facts as important:

- During the construction phase (approximately 5 years), about 20,000 new jobs will be created *directly* by the project;
- An additional 60,000 new *indirect* jobs will be created to service and supply the project, the port complexes, and the Railway;
- During the operation phase, some 6,000 permanent jobs will be directly provided by the CINN Dry Canal and its local subsidiaries;
- The study, design, construction, and operation of the Dry Canal system will demand the participation of a large number of graduates of Nicaraguan technical schools and universities, and will contribute to building of Nicaragua's competitive workforce of the future, as well as its resources in engineering, design and construction companies;
- CINN expects the establishment of an International Financial Center in Nicaragua, which would promote global trade through the Dry Canal and facilitate international financial and import-export transaction worldwide.

With these considerations in mind, CINN expects the Dry Canal to provide substantial, lasting and far-reaching benefits to Nicaragua and, in general, to global trade and the international shipping industry. The Nicaraguan Dry Canal will be a new, efficient and cost-effective center of international trade, providing a viable and attractive alternative to both the Panama Canal and overland USA rail and trucking routes, and will at last fulfill the dream of so many forward-thinking leaders, navigators and merchants of centuries past—to make Nicaragua a hub of global commerce.

 **NO**

Nicaragua's Proposed Dry Canal

Alternatives to the Panama Canal: Globalization and the Meso-American Megaprojects

In the Central American nation of Nicaragua, plans are quietly being hatched for new interoceanic transportation routes, both water routes and rail lines, that would compete with the Panama Canal. While the proponents of these routes claim that their development projects will provide economic salvation for the people of Nicaragua (the second poorest nation in the hemisphere after Haiti), voices from within Nicaragua are asking: Who will truly profit from the proposed megaprojects, and what will the real costs be?

Genesis of a Mega-Project

Throughout most of the twentieth century the canal across Panama has served the needs of interoceanic traders and travelers well. Yet as a new century is dawning, the Panama Canal is no longer considered sufficient to satisfy the growing demand for shipment of goods between the Atlantic and Pacific Oceans. This is true for a number of reasons, including:

- The Panama Canal has been increasingly unable to meet the growing quantity of interoceanic trade. The container trade between Asia, North America, and Europe has been increasing by between 6% and 8% annually since 1990. As a result the Panama Canal has lost a large share of its potential trade to overland rail and truck routes in the U.S. In addition, congestion in the canal area is increasing, causing frequent bottlenecks and delays. For as long [as] the global economy continues to grow, the canal will be increasingly unable to meet the demand for trade between the continents.[1]
- In the modern transport industry, the largest ships are considered the most economical, but the Panama Canal is too small to allow passage of the "post-Panamax" supertankers. It has been predicted that "in less than 20 years more than half of the world's ocean-going cargo vessels may be too large to pass through the canal's locks."[2] . . .

Based on the political uncertainties and technical shortcomings of the Panama Canal, in recent years a number of proposals have surfaced for alternative routes from sea to sea. Several of these proposals have targeted Nicaragua for interoceanic routes, [including] . . . a "Dry Canal," a rail line that would extend between Caribbean and Pacific ports.

Of all the proposals made for alternatives to the Panama Canal, the proposal for a Dry Canal in Nicaragua appears to be among the most feasible. . . . [If] one wished to take a shortcut across the Americas, from the Atlantic Ocean or Caribbean Sea to the Pacific Ocean, . . . the best possible route . . . would be across southern Nicaragua. . . . The first feasibility study for an interoceanic route in Nicaragua dates back to 1567 and the reign of King Philip II of Spain. Since then Spain, Britain, and the United States have tried to maintain influence in Nicaragua and thereby control over the many proposed interoceanic rail and water routes. This multinational power grab has made Nicaragua the country most invaded by the United States.

Present Day Canal Proposals

Considering the history of grand plans for a canal or railway across Nicaragua, any new proposals may be looked upon with suspicion as just the latest in a long litany of dead-end schemes. Yet currently the proposals for a Nicaragua Route are being promoted and debated with as much earnestness as ever. Given the potential impacts that a canal megaproject could have on Nicaragua's natural environment, indigenous people, and national sovereignty, the latest proposals need to be taken seriously. In the recent dialogue on potential routes across Nicaragua, any proposals for construction of a traditional all-water route like the Panama Canal, in which large ships traverse the isthmus entirely by water, have been discounted as being prohibitively expensive. The leading recent proposals in Nicaragua have been variations on the old theme of a coast-to-coast railway. . . .

The Dry Canal

During the 1990s various companies came forth with proposals to build a Dry Canal across Nicaragua. All of the proposals were variations on the old theme of a cross-country railway with ports at either end. The railways would be modern high-speed lines, and would be used only for shipping standard cargo containers. The Hong Kong–style ports would be able to accommodate the largest "post-Panamax" ocean vessels, and would be fully-equipped with machinery for loading and unloading cargo containers to and from trains and ships. The modern proposals would also utilize the natural deepwater harbor at Monkey Point on Nicaragua's Caribbean Coast. Monkey Point is located on an isolated stretch of coastline in a region inhabited by Rama Indians and longtime Creole residents. . . . From the Caribbean rainforest the railway would ascend into the hills that lie to the east of Lake Nicaragua, and would then pass to the north of the lake. . . .

The [Canal Interoceanico de Nicaragua] (C.I.N.N.) proposal was widely reported to have the support of Nicaraguan President Arnoldo Aleman, as well as the Nicaraguan Army, whose officials were "rumored to hold at least 15 percent of the company's shares." The retired commander-in-chief of the Nicaraguan armed forces, General Joaquin Cuadra Lacayo, stated in the Nicaraguan press that his father, the prominent Nicaraguan lawyer Joaquin Cuadra, owned a number of shares in C.I.N.N.[3]. . . . The U.S. government has also gotten involved, in support of the CINN group. . . .

Like many of the multinational corporations that operate in Nicaragua, C.I.N.N. is officially based in Managua, and has a small office there, but the money and decision-making power lie abroad. The companies that comprise the consortium are said to be mainly from Asia and Europe. The president of the consortium is a New York lawyer named Donald Mario Bosco. . . . Bosco has prior experience in China, and the greater part of the funding for the project would reportedly come from investors from China, Taiwan, Japan and South Korea.[4]. . .

Concessions Granted

On March 27, 2001, the Nicaraguan National Assembly approved two decrees that 1) authorized a concession for exploration, and 2) established the conditions for a future concession for construction and operation of the high-speed inter-oceanic railroad across Nicaragua. . . . The National Assembly's Communication, Transportation, Energy and Construction Committee noted that between 20 and 50 thousand jobs would be created but many of these would be temporary jobs that would only last until the construction is completed. Supporters maintain that the "canal" would serve as a catalyst for further investment, especially maquiladoras in the free trade zones that would be established at either end of the railroad line. But, maquiladora jobs have yet to pay workers enough to feed their families so it is hard to say if those jobs are better than the subsistence agriculture to which rural families have until now dedicated their working lives.

Other critics of the dry canal are skeptical about its viability. According to Costa Rica–based transport economist Warren Crowther, for example, "These same outfits came here with the idea of selling the Costa Ricans big on this," he said. "My own hypothesis is that these guys are really more interested in getting feasibility studies done and getting consulting fees than in getting any dry canal done."[5] A 1995 report noted that "even if Nicaragua's landbridge could capture all of Panama's $64 million in container traffic, it would not cover half of the annual finance charges on the investment nor operating costs."[6]. . .

Potential Impacts of the "Dry Canal" on Nicaragua's Environment: Industrial Corridor or Biological Corridor?

All along the proposed route, and especially at the two ends on the Pacific and Caribbean coasts, the Dry Canal would cause unavoidable ecological impacts. On the Caribbean side, the associated industrial development would occur on the Miskito Coast, the juncture of two of the most biologically-rich habitats in the world, rainforests and coral reefs. On the Pacific side, the railway and port facilities would threaten one of the largest areas of intact tropical dry forest remaining in Central America, as well as rich coastal areas including sea turtle nesting grounds. Any realistic assessment of the Dry Canal proposal needs to carefully consider these impacts.

Impacts on Nicaragua's Atlantic Coast Rainforest

Nicaragua's Atlantic Coast region contains the largest remaining relatively pristine rainforest in Central America. The Indio-Maiz Biosphere Reserve in southeastern Nicaragua along with the Bosawas Biosphere Reserve in northeastern Nicaragua and adjacent forests in Honduras represent one of the best opportunities in the Americas to protect large intact rainforest habitats north of Amazonia. The proposed Dry Canal would only exacerbate the deforestation that is already rampant on Nicaragua's Atlantic Coast due to commercial logging and the spread of the nation's agricultural frontier. Both from the direct need to deforest land for construction of the rail line, port facilities, and associated factories and buildings of the proposed free trade zone, and from the secondary wave of deforestation that would be caused by the influx of settlers that would surely follow, it is realistic to assume that the Dry Canal would lead to deforestation of a large portion of southeastern Nicaragua.

Construction of the Dry Canal would strike a severe blow against efforts to protect a Central American biological corridor. . . . Without north-south natural corridors, many species will be stranded in islands of habitat that may no longer be hospitable.

Proposed Dry Canal and Protected Sites

A north-south corridor of protected natural habitat and an east-west corridor of industrial development would seem to be mutually exclusive. Without even considering the secondary development which would be certain to occur along much of the length of the proposed rail corridor, the minimum 500-meter right-of-way through the forest preserve would in itself compromise the natural corridor and inhibit movement of some wildlife species.

In addition to impacting southeastern Nicaragua's biological diversity, deforestation caused by the Dry Canal would also lead to severe soil erosion. Parts of the area are hilly and are dissected by many tiny streams that flow through steep ravines. The deforestation that would occur during and after construction of the Dry Canal would leave the shallow soils of these steep slopes exposed to the region's torrential rainfall and vulnerable to severe erosion. The resulting soil erosion would not only degrade the landscape, but would also degrade the aquatic environment by burdening the region's streams and rivers (such as Cane Creek, Monte Cristo Creek, and the Rio Punta Gorda) with sediment. . . .

Proposed Port at Monkey Point

The impacts of the proposed Dry Canal on the coastal resources of Caribbean Nicaragua are . . . enormous. . . . In order to construct a port that could handle the largest post-Panamax vessels, dredging would be needed to deepen the waters off Monkey Point. In addition, the C.I.N.N. proposal calls for construction of a breakwater that would extend from Monkey Point over a mile into the sea, and would be necessary to protect the port area from the Caribbean surf that normally pounds Monkey Point. The combined effects of the breakwater, dredging, and pollution from ships and port facilities would degrade southeastern Nicaragua's coastal habitats.

An even larger threat to the region's coastal habitats is posed by the potential for shipping accidents at or near the Monkey Point port, such as an oil spill. The impacts of oil spills on western Caribbean habitats have been demonstrated by repeated spills at Bahia las Minas in Panama. Following the spills, reefs, sea grass beds and mangroves in the vicinity immediately died. Further damage ensued when oil was absorbed into the soil beneath the mangroves, and was slowly released into surrounding waters for several years. To date, "there has been virtually no recovery of corals, sea urchins, or oysters at any of the most affected sites."[7] The prevailing nearshore current along Nicaragua's southeastern coast flows from north to south.[8] Thus if an oil spill was to happen at or near Monkey Point, the areas most likely to be affected would be the beaches of the Rio Indio-Maiz Biosphere Reserve and farther down the coast of the beaches of Tortuguero in Costa Rica. The beaches at Tortuguero are protected as the most important nesting site for green turtles in all of the Caribbean, and contamination of this vital stretch of coastline would drive the endangered turtles closer to extinction. . . .

Ecological Impacts of the Dry Canal in the Pacific Coast Region

The proposal promoted by C.I.N.N. and favored by the Nicaraguan government calls for construction of a brand new port and free trade zone at a relatively isolated spot on the Pacific Coast called Pie de Gigante. As with Monkey Point on the Caribbean coast, the site of the proposed Pacific port is in an ecologically sensitive area, both with regards to land and sea. To an even greater extent than the proposed Caribbean port at Monkey Point, a port built at Pie de Gigante would cause direct harm to endangered sea turtles. Pie de Gigante lies at the heart of a stretch of coastline that is used by sea turtles for nesting. Female turtles visit the region's beaches every year to lay their eggs in the sand. Most of the turtles land at a stretch of beach that lies within the Chacocente Wildlife Refuge approximately 20 miles north of Pie de Gigante. "The Chacocente beach is the third most important olive ridley sea turtle nesting beach in Central America. From June to December the female turtles come to Chacocente in synchronized arrivals called "arribadas," where as many as 10,000 turtles arrive within a few days to lay their eggs. Over 20,000 olive ridley turtles come there each year. The beach is also important for nesting of globally endangered leatherback turtles."[9] . . .

Efforts are currently underway to protect a forested corridor between the . . . protected areas. The Dry Canal would sever this connection. The extent of the damage incurred would depend largely on what type of additional development occurs along the route. If the route remained an "express," with no intermediate stops, then the impacts would be largely limited to those caused by the rail corridor itself. If, however, "exit ramps" were provided all along the route, the resulting development and settlement of previously natural areas would likely proceed unchecked. In fact, the Dry Canal consortium C.I.N.N. has claimed that a free trade zone with user and shipper services will be established "along the route," and the consortium's president Donald Bosco has described the railroad as a "kind of a spinal cord across the country," along which development will occur.[10] In its eagerness to entice investors into the Dry Canal's free trade zones, it is difficult to believe that the Nicaraguan government, at least in anything resembling its present form, would make environmental protection a top priority.

Impact on Nicaragua's Indigenous Peoples and on Atlantic Coast Autonomy

If built, the proposed Dry Canal would fundamentally change the lives of Nicaragua's Rama Indians. . . .

The Rama have traditionally lived a subsistence lifestyle rooted in the rich coastal and rain forest habitats of southeastern Nicaragua. Depending on the season, fish, shrimp, sea turtle, and other foods are harvested from the coastal lagoons and near-shore marine waters. In the forest the Rama hunt a variety of animals including peccary, deer, tapir, and currasow. . . .

There will be radical changes for the Rama if the Dry Canal is approved and built. The proposed site for the eastern terminus of the Dry Canal, Monkey Point, lies 30 miles south of Bluefields, and is right in the heart of the Ramas' traditional lands. The likely route of the Dry Canal would cross Cane Creek, a quiet forest-lined stream where Rama families maintain a traditional lifestyle. The potential impacts of such a mega-development project to the landscape and marine environment, and thus the Rama culture, are hard to underestimate. . . .

For many years, . . . a mixed community of black Creoles, Mestizos, and Rama Indians has lived at Monkey Point. Along with the Rama, the Creoles and Mestizos are concerned about what will happen to their community as plans for the Dry Canal move forward. Recent events have demonstrated that these concerns are valid.[11] These communities are under attack as titles surface from a railroad proposed one hundred years ago. . . . One of the old titles materialized in early 1999 when a former Atlantic Coast government official named Percy Spencer suddenly claimed to hold the title for 500 acres (200 ha.) of land at Monkey Point. Spencer in turn sold the land to U.S. businessman John Vogel. Vogel's hired hands have proceeded to begin clearing the land of its forest, planting citrus trees, and trying to evict the inhabitants of Monkey Point from their lands.[12] . . .

Having received a glimpse of what will likely lie ahead if the Dry Canal is approved, the Ramas and the community at Monkey Point are fighting back. In fact, they have gone right to the top and filed a lawsuit against none other than Nicaraguan President Aleman himself, as well as Nicaragua's Attorney General, Julio Centeño Gomez, who in his official capacity would actually be the one to sign any concession granted for construction of the Dry Canal. According to the Ramas' lawyer, the Nicaraguan indigenous rights expert and public advocate Maria Luisa Acosta, given the potential of the Dry Canal to profoundly impact the Ramas' traditional lands and culture, it is reprehensible that they have been excluded from the planning process. . . .

The Response of Nicaraguan Civil Society

. . . Nicaraguan NGOs, cooperatives, and indigenous communities, in addition to local and regional governments, have several demands in regard to the proposed Dry Canal. . . .

Information

So far only a sketchy outline has been provided to the Nicaraguan public (via the media) of what the Dry Canal and or water canal would actually entail. These megaprojects hold the potential to transform Nicaragua in profound ways, and it is unacceptable that the project details should be known only by the heads of the canal companies and the nation's highest government officials. On the other hand, it is likely that detailed analyses of the potential environmental and social impacts of the megaprojects simply do not exist.

Respect of the Nation's Laws

So far President Aleman and the Dry Canal entrepreneurs have seemed far more concerned with personal benefit than with respecting the nation's laws regarding the environment, indigenous rights, Atlantic Coast autonomy, and property rights in general. . . .

Sustainable Development

Civil society is calling for the adoption of economic, social, and environmental policies that promote long-term stability and social equity within the nation, rather than huge engineering works that obliterate all in their path and potentially carry large unintended consequences.

Summary: The Dry Canal, Nicaragua, and the Global Economy

There can be little doubt that some portion of Nicaragua's population would derive economic benefit from the nation's proposed rail and canal schemes. The question remains, however, of who would truly reap the profits from the megaprojects, and who would suffer. While Nicaraguans are unanimous in their desire for improvement of the nation's overall living standards, many in the country have become skeptical of development strategies that claim to be for the benefit of all but ultimately enrich only a select few, often foreigners, while degrading the nation's resource base. This pattern has characterized Nicaragua's development over most of the past 500 years, and there is reason to believe that the proposed transportation megaprojects might continue the trend, especially the Dry Canal. The sentiment expressed by Hector Mairena of the Nicaraguan organization MAN (Movimiento Ambiental Nicaraguense or Nicaraguan Environmental Movement) is representative of many Nicaraguans' critiques of the Dry Canal: "Poverty is Nicaragua's principal environmental problem. . . . Neither the Suez Canal nor the Panama Canal solved the problems of poverty in those countries. Poverty plus the resulting destruction of the environment and natural resources to survive equals more poverty. So it turns into a vicious circle, which we have to break."

Does the Dry Canal really offer Nicaragua's "Economic Salvation"? . . .

It is unlikely that any megaproject scheme such as the Dry Canal will suddenly launch Nicaragua into the small group of "winners". Thus, a better question still may be, "How can a nation such as Nicaragua best insulate itself from the profoundly exploitative, unequal, and unsustainable global economy?" . . . If Nicaragua's central government chooses a development strategy that prioritizes pursuing dreams of affluence above meeting the basic needs of the nation's citizens, most Nicaraguans will surely remain clinging to the lowest rungs of the global socioeconomic ladder. . . .

An International Campaign of Action

Given the powerful external forces that influence the course of political and economic affairs in Nicaragua, clearly Nicaraguan activists and their allies abroad need to be working in unison. With respect to the proposed canal projects in Nicaragua, an international action campaign is warranted that will:

- Help spread the word about the canal proposals for Nicaragua and stimulate discussion of the likely implications of such projects. . . .
- Provide Nicaraguans with an independent perspective on the potential social and environmental impacts of the proposed megaprojects. . . .

The proposed dry canal may never materialize. . . . However, we cannot rely on past scrapped canal plans to guarantee the failure of this proposal, for on the slim chance that . . . the proposed project may move forward, the potential impacts are too immense to not take the proposal seriously. If nothing else, the time and energy devoted to considering the canal proposals is well-spent if it helps us to realize how rich Nicaragua truly is, and what stands to be lost if not valued and protected.

Notes

1. Hernandez (1998, July 22).
2. *Economist* (1999, June 12).
3. Fonseca, Roberto (1998, August 6).
4. Canal Interoceanico de Nicaragua, S.A. (1996).
5. Costantini, Peter (1996).
6. Coone, Tim (1995).
7. Jackson, Jeremy B. and Luis D'Croz (1997) pp. 67–68.
8. See Murray, S.P. and Young, M. (1985).
9. Furchgott, Jane (1999, Spring).
10. Costantini, Peter. (1996, October).
11. Mairena Martinez, Mario (1999, May 7).
12. Monterrey, Carlos Eddy (1999, August 8).

POSTSCRIPT

Do the Economic Benefits of a "Dry Canal" in Nicaragua Outweigh the Financial, Human, and Environmental Costs?

The desire to build a canal through Nicaragua is not a new idea. In 1825, the United States hired surveyors to determine the most feasible location for a canal through Central America. In 1849, Cornelius Vanderbilt constructed a rail line across Nicaragua that efficiently functioned for 6 years. And again, in 1895 the U.S. Nicaraguan Canal Commission convened regularly to discuss the merits of a canal through Nicaragua. However, due to political concerns and fears of volcanic activity, plans for the canal moved to Panama, arguably creating an economic disparity between the two countries that remains evident today.

Because the Panama Canal is quickly fading into obsolescence, primarily due to the increased size of container ships, Nicaragua may now have an opportunity to address decades of impoverishment and underdevelopment. With the backing of foreign investors, including significant contributions from the United States as well as from Central American countries and Mexico, Nicaragua may have the greatest potential to be chosen as the dry canal construction site. However, reminiscent of past ills that prevented Nicaragua from winning the bid for the interoceanic canal at the turn of the past century, political and environmental issues may once again inhibit investment— for better or for worse.

Of particular interest is the reemergence of Daniel Ortega, former president of Nicaragua from 1985 to 1990 and principal leader of the Sandinistas or FSLN (Sandinista National Liberation Front), a revolutionary political party of the left that was in power in Nicaragua from 1979 to 1990. Some political scientists and analysts predict Ortega will be reelected president of Nicaragua in the fall of 2006, which may spark animosity and political confrontation similar to what occurred in the 1980s. If these political issues resurface, it would not be unrealistic to anticipate a complete withdrawal of U.S. support and funding for the canal. Yet, other countries with large export economies such as Japan, China, and South Korea are also keenly interested in the expansion of the canal and might not have as much concern regarding Ortega's political history as the United States would. However, both Ortega and his rival, Herty Lewites, support the plan for a dry canal through Nicaragua.

Regardless of the many differing points of view on the dry canal, the debate regarding its construction across Nicaragua will persist until either the

Panama Canal is widened or groundbreaking begins elsewhere. To better understand environmental concerns and indigenous land rights issues that the dry canal proposal may involve, view *Our Land, Our Future*, a 2006 documentary film by Ed Schehl and Katherine Knight and read Gerald Riverstone's *Living in the Land of Our Ancestors: Rama and Creole Territory in Caribbean Nicaragua.* For background and current news related to Daniel Ortega, see "Remember Daniel Ortega? He's Back," (*Christian Science Monitor,* September 15, 2005). To understand the economic benefits that the dry canal would potentially bring, visit the CINN Web site at http://www.drycanal.com. For an environmental perspective, visit http://environment.nicanet.org. For historical information, publications, and interactive activities on how the Panama Canal works, see the "Research and Students" page on the canal's official Web site: http://www.pancanal.com/eng/persona/ed/index.html.

ISSUE 14

Is Plant Biotechnology the Solution to Hunger in Latin America and the Caribbean?

YES: Juan Izquierdo and Gustavo A. de la Riva, from "Plant Biotechnology and Food Security in Latin America and the Caribbean," *Electronic Journal of Biotechnology* (April 15, 2000)

NO: Silvia Ribeiro, from "The Day the Sun Dies: Contamination and Resistance in Mexico," *Seedling* (July 2004)

ISSUE SUMMARY

YES: Juan Izquierdo, from the Food and Agriculture Organization of the United Nations, and Gustavo A. de la Riva, from the Centre of Genetic Engineering and Biotechnology, Havana, Cuba, maintain that plant biotechnology, if properly implemented, offers a responsible means to increase agricultural productivity and the possibility to feed future generations in Latin American and Caribbean countries.

NO: Silvia Ribeiro, a researcher with the Action Group on Erosion, Technology and Concentration, argues that genetically modified maize has contaminated native crops and is a potential threat to agrobiodiversity, small-scale farming, and cultural identity.

$\mathbf{F}$or millennia, humans have used biotechnology to alter their world. The selective breeding of animals and livestock domestication and the use of yeast to create beer and wine are all examples of humankind's use of technology to affect their biological environment. Two of the world's most important crops originated in pre-Columbian Latin America: Corn (maize) was invented in Mexico and Central America, and the potato was domesticated in the Andean region of South America. Over the course of the past few decades, however, a fierce debate in developing countries, and Latin America in particular, has inspired a host of polarized descriptors ranging from "hope," "solution," and "life-saving" to "invasion," "contamination," and "frankenfoods."

Biotechology is "any technological application that uses biological systems, living organisms, or derivatives thereof, to make or modify products or processes for specific use" (United Nations, Convention of Biological

Diversity). Genetically modified organisms (GMOs), genetically modified foods (GMFs), genetically modified plants (GMPs) and transgenic foods are terms often associated with developments in modern biotechnology. The technological process behind these terms refers to the act of altering genetic material to produce animals, bacteria, and plants with new characteristics. The advent of modern genetic engineering in the 1970s has inspired mixed reactions; some scientists celebrate biotechnology's potential to improve the lives of humankind, while others argue that genetic engineering is morally reprehensible and that it may unleash unwanted and dangerous consequences like new "super-bugs," "super-weeds," or new strains of diseases.

According to the United Nations, the world's population reached 6.5 billion in 2005 and is projected to reach 9.1 billion in 2050 (Population Challenges and Development Goals, 2005). Normal Borlaug—Nobel Prize Laureate for Peace and pioneer of the Green Revolution of the 1960s—notes that the "majority of agricultural scientists, including myself, anticipate great benefits from biotechnology in the coming decades to help meet our future needs for food and fiber." "First World" critics of GM foods, he argues, do harm to people in developing countries by limiting their access to new technologies (*Plant Physiology*, October 2000). Plant geneticists, Luis Herrera-Estrella and Ariel Alvarez-Morales, share Borlaug's concerns and add that restricting biotechnology in developing countries will exasperate environmental degradation: "Tropical forests are irreplaceable regional and global ecosystems that contain more than 90% of plant and animal species. But more than 11 million hectares of forest are cleared every year by farmers searching for more productive land."

Opponents of the use of modern biotechnology in Latin America note that it will not reduce hunger or poverty but rather lead to monoculture farming, the contamination of native crops, and the production of new allergies and toxins. Professor of agroecology Miguel Altieri further explains that the root of hunger in Latin America is poverty and an unequal distribution of resources: "80 percent of the agricultural land is in the hands of 20 percent of the farmers; and this is the best agricultural land" (Russell Schoch, "A Conversation with Miguel Altieri," *California Monthly*, 2001). Altieri contends that GM seeds will not benefit poor farmers because "[g]enetically modified seeds are under corporate control and patent protection, consequently they are very expensive. Since many developing countries still lack the institutional infrastructure and low-interest credit necessary to deliver these new seeds to poor farmers, biotechnology will only exacerbate marginalisation" ("The Case Against Agricultural Biotechnology," 2002). Opponents of biotechnology also question the ethics of taking and patenting the DNA of plants and other living things ("bioprospecting" or "biopiracy") for commercial use.

Juan Izquierdo and Gustavo A. de la Riva maintain that agricultural biotechnology will reduce Latin America's growing dependence on food imports and help fight malnutrition and poverty while offering the benefit of environmental sustainability. The second selection by Silvia Ribeiro examines the social, religious, historical, and economic impact of the introduction of GM seeds in Mexico and the resistance it has inspired in indigenous communities.

YES

**Juan Izquierdo and
Gustavo A. de la Riva**

Plant Biotechnology and Food Security in Latin America and the Caribbean

Agriculture is expected to feed an increasing population, forecasted to reach 8 billion by 2020, out of whom 6.7 billion will be in developing countries where the carrying capacity of agricultural lands will soon be reached given the current technology and the on-going environmental degradation (FAO, 1999). New technologies, if properly focused, offer a responsible way to enhance agricultural productivity at present and for the future. As suggested by the Nobel Peace Laureate, Norman Bourlag (1997), biotechnology and genetic plant engineering, complemented with conventional plant breeding, are needed to boost crop yields to feed the world.

Today, nearly 800 million people suffer from malnutrition; 1100 million do not receive appropriate nutrition while subsisting below the levels of poverty (FAO, 1996a). In the case of the Latin American and the Caribbean (LAC) countries, in spite of the abundance of natural resources and continued investments in development, rural poverty and food insecurity have persistently affected more than 55 percent of the rural population with one third of the latter being below the extreme poverty line (income below a basic food basket). Furthermore, in six out of eleven countries for which there was information for several years, extreme poverty increased between the beginning of the eighties and the mid nineties. These elements establish the magnitude of the poverty and food insecurity to which research in agricultural production, comprising the application and complement of plant biotechnology, has to find a way to alleviate.

The food sector in the LAC Region is characterised, among other factors, by the growing dependence on food imports, primarily cereals, the decelerated growth of the agricultural production and poverty affecting wide sectors, especially the rural population. Within this context, the increasing frequency of adverse environmental and climatic factors [such] as drought and desertification, soil erosion, floods and hurricanes, and on-going changes in land use regarding other economic activities, are producing a significant reduction of the agricultural areas (James, 1996, 1997). Under these conditions, the use of sustainable technologies, traditional or modern, focusing on those with less input demands as well as emphasis on product quality and productivity are important factors for employment and income generation.

Juan Izquierdo, Per. Plant Biotechnology and Food Security in Latin America and the Caribbean. *Electronic Journal of Biotechnology* [online]. vol. 3, no. 1, April 15, 2000. Available from: http://www.ejbiotechnology.info/author/iautor.html. ISSN 0717-3458. Reprinted by permission.

Fifteen years ago, plant biotechnology comprised only a few applications of tissue culture, recombinant DNA technology and monoclonal antibodies. Today, genetic transformation, and marker-aided selection and breeding are just a few examples of applications in crop improvement with profound implications for the LAC Region (Izquierdo, 1999). Plant biotechnology applications must respond to increasing demands in terms of food security, socio-economic development and promote the conservation, diversification and sustainable use of plant genetic resources as basic inputs for the future agriculture of the Region (FAO, 1999).

The scientific results obtained in the last two decades substantiate biotechnology as an option to increase food production. Some of the imperative reasons to use new biotechnology in an upward form reside in the fact that the benefits of the Green Revolution have already been surpassed and cannot guarantee the success of sustained food programs including their inability in terms of economic and environmental costs. Although the objective of the Green Revolution was to promote the production and the trade of cereals and other agricultural commodities, the majority of the developing countries have become net importers of basic cereal foods for daily human consumption and for livestock feeding (FAO, 1996b; Rosendal, 1992; Asiema, 1994).

The LAC agricultural sector needs a strong input of new knowledge and technologies to successfully confront the food insecurity challenge coupled with a realistic interpretation of the global environmental and economic situation (Commandeur, 1994; Vunne, 1995). It is in this complex food security context where biotechnology is called to play a growing role to contribute toward a safer world.

The Food Security Concept

Food security is defined by FAO as the access by all people at all times to the food needed for a healthy and active life. The concept means the achievement of the food self-sufficiency, and guarantees that this condition will be sustained in the future. Food security also implies reaching a productive growth, compatible with the economic status of the producers and the preservation of the environment. The factors that determine the degree of food security, in any Region, country or zone in particular, are food availability, production stability and access to food by all members of the community (FAO, 1998).

Food availability is a factor directly related to the productivity of raw food supplies, as grains, root and tubers, oil and molasses. Variations in yield due to limitations of the crop genetic potential for a given environment and losses due to biotic, abiotic and postharvest factors, greatly affects this issue.

Stability is related to the conditions of the productive process, including the sustained handling of natural resources, an appropriate policy for environmental protection, and the creation of an adequate rural infrastructure and political dynamics of rural development.

Access to food is a factor directly related to the prevailing socio-economic conditions in a particular zone or country. The lack of access to food is often exacerbated by the fact that producers try to keep higher prices by destroying large amounts of stocked foods or livestock. In addition, some countries that generate food surplus deny their access to others countries as a measure of political pressure. The causes and consequences of food insecurity and poverty are inextricably linked (FAO, http://www.fao.org/spfs/).

The per capita world food supply was equivalent to 2300 daily calories as an average in 1970. This figure included data from developed countries, whose average was 3030 calories, as well as those from developing countries, where this indicator hardly reached 1960 calories per capita, showing the enormous disproportion existing between both groups. 75% of the population of the developing countries, around 1600 million, corresponds to countries whose daily average per capita was nearly 1850 calories. The situation is even more precarious for the poorest sectors in the population due to the existing inequalities in each country (FAO, 1996c; Garett, 1997).

Chronic undernutrition and food insecurity are principally caused by: low productivity in agriculture, frequently caused in part by policy, institutional and technological constraints; high seasonal and year-to-year variability in food supplies, often the result of unreliable rainfall and insufficient water for crop and livestock production; lack of off-farm employment opportunities, contributing to low and uncertain incomes in urban and rural areas.

Food Security in the Latin American and Caribbean Region

According to the countries' technical documents prepared for the Food World Summit, in the decade of the 70 the per capita food supply in the Region increased from 2360 to 2510 calories, while in the world it varied from 2300 to 2440 calories, compared with a global increase from 1960 to 2130 calories in the developing countries altogether (FAO, 1996a, b and c). This growing tendency was observed until the decade of the 80 when the per capita daily food supply went up to 2720 calories for the LAC Region, 2330 for the developing countries and 2580 for the world.

Unfortunately, these indexes did not represent a significant improvement in food security and remained practically unaltered (14% in 1980 and 15% in 1992). Considering the growth of the LAC population (279 million in 1970, 354 million in 1980, 443 million in 1992, 593 million estimated for 2010) malnutrition embraced 53 million people in 1970, 48 million in 1980 and 64 million in 1992. Today, it affects 15% of the population in Mexico, Central America and the Caribbean and 13% of the population in South America (FAO, 1996c and d) while the Region represents nearly 23% of the arable lands, 12% of the world cultivated areas, 46% of the forests, 31% of the world's fresh water reserves, and a rich ecosystem, with 50% of the plant and animal species of the biosphere representing an immense wealth in genetic resources.

Within the above context, food production growth should be sustained as a guarantee of food security (FAO, 1996a; Trigo, 1995) considering the differences among the LAC Region countries and internally among the different social sectors. This inequality is increasing and a society under such conditions cannot have food security. The levels of food security in the LAC Region have not increased and this situation should be reverted without delay.

To improve the levels of food security in countries with low income and food deficit, FAO has implemented the Special Program for Food Security (SPFS) as an assistance program to increase the food production and productivity on those countries less able to meet their food needs with imports. The objective is to reduce the present number of malnourished people in the world to one half, by the year 2015. Although in many of the LAC countries the demographic pressure is less than in other developing regions due to lower birth rate and better educational and health facilities (James, 1996; FAO, 1996; Garett, 1997; Trigo, 1995), a strong revitalisation of the agricultural sector is needed to secure food and rural income. Agriculture is a fundamental sector for the establishment of an appropriate food production system. It has a marked multiplier effect in the general economic growth, generating employment and involving, besides its own activities, important economic sectors like transport, storage, processing and trade. The sector demands additional services beyond those already mentioned. Consequently, appropriate agricultural development can generate increased food availability, improving social development and providing better access to food.

Biotechnology and Agriculture

Plant biotechnology offers several possibilities for increasing productivity, diversification and production, while developing a more sustainable agriculture (Izquierdo, 1999). This technology includes biopesticide production, plant tissue culture techniques, and the use of advanced molecular biology techniques for plant transformation, genomic analysis coupled with breeding and plant-disease diagnoses. It can be an effective instrument to mitigate the consequences of climatic change and can offer cropping alternatives in lands degraded by erosion and desertification or by careless agricultural use (FAO, 1999). Agricultural biotechnology has different levels of implementation and development according to its degree of complexity, infrastructure costs and investment.

The first level includes technologies of low complexity and cost, like handmade and semi-industrial production of biological products, like bio-inoculants for leguminous crops, reproduction of pest antagonist and pest predators and production of bio-pesticides. The transfer of these simple technologies to the small producers has proven feasible and it can offer remarkable results quickly.

The second level comprises the application of cell and tissue culture techniques, cell culture for production of secondary metabolites, disease diagnostic systems based on polyclonal antibodies and other technologies with medium complexity. This stage can also include investments to implement semi-industrial production of biological products. The results of these technologies can be seen in the medium term (three to five years), depending on the complexity of the projects and the degree of organisation for extending the results to the field or laboratory. The first two stages do not require many resources but an efficient organisation for the transfer of technology to extend the results to the producers in a brief period of time.

The third level considers the use of molecular biology, genetic engineering, large-scale industrial production of biological products and complex plant cell and tissue culture techniques like liquid-bioreactors. This level is characterised by its complexity and high costs of research and development. The short term impact of this advanced biotechnology is limited because, as in any novel technology, it needs a starting phase corresponding to the innovation of its own research methods, analytical techniques and a semi-industrial base to supply the needed inputs and equipment. To create such conditions it is compulsory to build a framework of institutional support by public and private investment sectors.

Basic knowledge on the complexity of the molecular organisation of living organisms and their interrelationships is far from its complete elucidation and limits the number of characters that can be manipulated by genetic engineering. Identification techniques, isolation and characterisation of new genes to be transferred to different crops to produce genetically modified plants (GMP) are subjected to constant research. Plant genetic engineering now permits manipulating monogenic characters while the productive characteristics of the crop species of a quantitative nature result in the expression of multiple genes (polygenic). Often, one isolated gene does not have a great influence in the complete genome expression and this reinforces the importance of conventional plant breeding assisted by molecular markers (Robentson, 1989).

The above issues are related to proprietary rights and institutional capacity building. The right of farmers to freely reuse a genetically modified food crop variety to strengthen food security and the patenting and marketing of GMP seeds, is under dispute.

Biotechnology has begun to have an economic impact in the productivity of crops and in the decrease of production costs. In 1996 in the United States 15 novel GMP products existed in the market whose initial sales totalled about 380 million dollars. It is considered that this emergent market will increase 20% annually during the next decade (Persley, 1997). In that year, GMP were planted for the first time in Latin America comprising commercial fields, among which are herbicide tolerant soybean and insect resistant corn and cotton (Woodson, 1997) introduced by transnational companies after a case-to-case approval by national authorities. In 1999, 39.9 million hectares were globally planted, 6.7 in Argentina alone (James, 1999), resulting in a 44% increase in the adoption of such a technology by the medium and large farms.

The release of genetically modified organisms is a matter of growing concern and requires the evaluation of biological risks and their environmental and socio-economic impact together with appropriate technological packages (FAO, 1999). . . .

Opportunities and Scenarios for Plant Biotechnology Applications

Plant biotechnology represents one of a number of competing technological approaches to address any agronomic problem in a particular ecosystem but, as an example, a pest problem might equally be addressed through conventional plant breeding, through a transgenic approach, by the use of bio-pesticides, through an integrated crop management (ICM) approach or by any combination of these.

Andean agricultural scenarios in Bolivia, Chile, Peru, Ecuador and Venezuela, for instance, are depositories of important genetic resources that could constitute inputs to food security and sustainable development. Andean "orphan" food crops such as arracacha (Arracacia xanthorrhiza), achira (Canna edulis), yacon (Polymnia sonchifolia), mashua (Tropaeolum tuberosum), oca (Oxalis tuberosa), ulluco (Ullucus tuberosus), quinoa (Chenopodium quinoa), amaranto o kiwicha (Amaranthus caudatus), popping beans . . . (Phaseolus vulgaris), tarwi (Lupinus mutabilis), goldenberry . . . (Physalis peruviana), cherimoya (Annona cherimola) and passion-fruit (Passiflora sp.) are highly under-utilised. The use of modern plant biotechnology for the conservation and sustainable agricultural use of those essential genetic resources needs to be strengthened. For this purpose, biotechnologies such as cell and tissue culture, molecular genome analysis, plant genetic transformation, molecular plant disease diagnosis and gerplasm cryo-conservation coupled with plant breeding and physiological integrated crop management, can be successfully used to cope with genetic erosion. This can reinforce ex-situ collections and in-situ conservation, to upgrade the supply of improved and healthy seeds and planting materials for farmers and to integrate a new approach into the development programmes for food production and food security in mountain lands (Izquierdo and Roca, 1998). In the meantime, the population of the Andes suffer severely from the effects of poverty, food insecurity, malnutrition and derived health problems.

The Amazon Basin is one of the richest areas in the world. The high plant and animal biodiversity gives this area a real potential to be sustainable in terms of food security, nutrition, and economy. However, the Amazon area in all of the countries where this very special humid forest exists, has security and malnutrition problems, as well as increasing poverty, specially in areas near the biggest cities of the Amazon (Izquierdo et al. 1999). The biggest problem in the Amazon has been the colonisation path. The countries in the Amazon have a very intense migration and have been penetrated with culture systems, especially animal production, that have caused a severe impact in this very fragile bio-system. The management of Amazon soils, their poor structure, low fertility and acidity, is one of the most important subjects to be studied and this is the principal concern of several R&D institutions in the Amazon countries. The gradual conversion of the on-going "extractivism" to sustainable fruit crop-agroforestry management, where all the productivity factors are considered, requires plant biotechnology applications for fruits, vegetables, medicinales, and forestry species including micropropagation and biotechnology-enhanced breeding.

Biotechnology is a powerful tool in agricultural development with great potential—both positive and negative. Coupled with other technologies, biotechnology can surely provide new solutions for some of the old problems hindering sustainable rural development and achievement of food security (FAO, 1999; Ortiz, 1998). Biotechnology also offers unique opportunities to solve environmental problems, some of which derive from unsustainable agricultural and industrial practices. . . .

References

Asiema, J. (1994). Africa's Green Revolution. *Biotechnology and Development Monitor.* 19:17–18.

Bourlag, N.E. (1997). Feeding a world of 10 billion people: the miracle ahead. *Plant Tissue Culture and Biotechnology* 3:119. 127.

Commandeur, P. (1994). REDBIO and FAO's Global Programme on Plant Biotechnology. *Biotechnology and Development Monitor.* 21:20–22.

FAO (1996a). Documentos técnicos de la Referencia. *Cumbre Mundial sobre la Alimentación.* Volumen 1:3–28.

FAO (1996b). Documentos Técnicos de Referencia. *Cumbre Mundial sobre la Alimentación.* Volumen 1:1–3.

FAO (1996c). Documentos técnicos de referencia. *Cumbre Mundial sobre la Alimentación.* Volumen 2:1–22.

FAO Yearbook (1996d). Volume 50.

FAO. (1998). Regional Development Partnerships Programme (RDPP).

FAO, 1999, Committee on Agriculture: Biotechnology. 25–29 January. COAG. http://www.fao.org.unfao/bodies/coag/coag15/x00074e.htm

Garett, J. (1997). Challenges to the 2020 Vision for Latin America: Food and Agriculture Since 1970. Food, Agriculture and the Environment Discussion Paper 21. International Food Policy Research Institute. Washington D.C.

Izquierdo J., Ciampi, L. and García, E. (1995). Biotecnología apropiable: racionalidad de su desarrollo y aplicación en América Latina y el Caribe. Red de Cooperación Técnica en Biotecnología Vegetal (REDBIO). Oficina Regional FAO para América Latina y el Caribe, Santiago, Chile.

Izquierdo, J. (1995) New varieties for sustainable agriculture: genetic improvement assisted by biotechnology. In *Seed of Conflict: Biodiversity and Food Security US Comm.* World/Food Day.

Izquierdo, J. and Roca, W. (1998). Under-utilized Andean food crops: status and prospects of plant biotechnology for the conservation and sustainable agricultural use of genetic resources. *Acta Horticulturae* 457:157–172. http://www.rlc.fao.org/prior/recnat/recursos/biodiv/andinos.pdf.

Izquierdo, J. (1999). Biotechnology can help crop production to feed and increasing world population?: positive and negative aspects need to be balanced, a perspective from FAO. Presented at International Symposium on Plant Genetic Engineering, 6–10 Dec. 1999, Cuba (in print, Elsevier).

Izquierdo, J., Schejtman, A. and Figuerola. F. (1999). Heterogeneity poverty scenarios as a factor of technology demand in Latin America and the Caribbean. Presented at International workshop on research impact on poverty alleviation, San Jose, Costa Rica, CIAT, 14-16 Sept. 1999.

James, C. (1996). Agricultural Research and Development: The Need for Public-Private Sector Partnerships. *Issues in Agriculture* 9:1–2. CGIAR. Washington D.C.

James, C. (1997). Progressing Public-Private Sector Partnerships in International Agricultural Research and Development. ISAAA Briefs No. 4 ISAAA, Ithaca, NY. pp. 31.

James, C. 1999. Preview: global review of commercialized transgenic crops,1999. ISAA report, No.12.

Ortiz, R. 1998. Critical role of plant biotechnology for the genetic improvement of food crops—perspective for the next millenuim. *Electronic Journal of Biotechnology* at http://www.ejb.ucv.cl/content/vol1/issue3/full/7/

Persley, G. J. (1997). Global Concerns and Issues in Biotechnology. *HortScience* 32:977–979.

Robentson, D.S. (1989). Understanding the relationship between quantitative genetics. Development and Application of Molecular Markers to Problems in Plant Genetics, Helentjaris T and Burn D. (Eds). Cold Spring Habour Press.

Rosendal, K. (1992). Blue Revolution could avoid failures of green predecessor. *Biotechnology and Development Monitor.* 12:10.

Trigo, E.J. (1995). Agricultura Cambio Tecnológico y Medio Ambiente en América Latina: Una perspectiva para el año 2000. Documentos de Discusión sobre Alimentación, Agricultura y Medio Ambiente 9. Instituto Internacional de Investigaciones sobre Políticas Alimentarias. Washington D.C.

Vunne, L. (1995). Biotechnology: the impact on food and nutrition in developing countries. *Food Nutrition and Agriculture.* 1:32–36.

Woodson, W.R. (1997). Biotechnology and Horticulture, *HortScience* 32:1021–1023.

Silvia Ribeiro

The Day the Sun Dies: Contamination and Resistance in Mexico

Mexican peasant maize, the origin of life and culture, the essence of the flesh of peoples who create and cultivate it, has been contaminated by genetically modified (GM) maize. As described earlier in *Seedling*[1], this was an intentional crime. The 'scientists' who created transgenic maize were aware that maize plants cross openly with other maize plants, and that insects and the wind carry its pollen over long distances. Contamination is inherent to the presence of GM crops and is inevitable once they reach the field.

Maize is not the only crop to have been contaminated. In 2002, Agrifood Canada announced that Canada's canola foundation seeds had been contaminated. Earlier this year, the Union of Concerned Scientists released a report on the transgenic contamination of conventional seed varieties in the United States,[2] which showed that at least 50% of maize seeds, 50% of cotton seeds and 80% of canola seeds contain transgenic DNA. The report warns of the risk of the future disappearance of GM-free seeds and of the threat of contamination of the food chain with plants modified to produce pharmaceuticals and industrial chemicals.

Industry's strategy is clearer than ever: deliberately contaminate our fields and our food, and then hope that when the damage becomes obvious, it will be too widespread and people too impotent to overcome contamination. To make things even worse, the same companies, now with support from governments, have launched a new stage in their attack in the legal field. In Canada, where transgenic canola—which cross pollinates even more readily than maize—has contaminated most canola crops, farmers are being warned not to use their own seeds or to save any for the next planting season, because companies may sue them for 'abuse' of their patented genes.

In Mexico, the centre of origin for maize and many other crops, the situation is even worse and more complex. The potential impact of contamination is multiplied by the huge number of local maize varieties, as well as wild and semi-domesticated relatives, plus many other species of fauna and flora in ecosystems and agro-ecosystems. But most serious is the profound cultural significance—in the broadest sense—of maize that is at stake.

From *Seedling*, July 2004, pp. 4–10. Copyright © 2004 by Silvia Ribeiro, researcher at ETC Group, Mexico, www.etcgroup.org. Reprinted by permission.

The Maize People

Maize is the most important agronomic achievement in the history of humanity. From a mere grass (*teocintle*), indigenous peasant peoples in Meso-America created a very nutritious and tremendously adaptable plant which could be grown in many different ecosystems and for multiple uses. It does not grow wild, and it is always linked to its creators, whom—according to foundational myths throughout Meso-America—it also created, in a process of mutual care.

Among the hundreds of traditional maize varieties used every day by peasants and indigenous people in Mexico, there is a large diversity of colors (white, red, yellow, blue, black, spotted), with ears ranging from a few centimetres up to 30 centimetres, with different shaped ears and varying numbers of kernels. . . .

Maize in Mexico is much more than a crop. It is a central element in rural and urban culinary habits and lies at the heart of the history and the daily lives of the peoples of Mexico, their economy, their religions and their worldview. The cycles and the uses of maize give rise to festivals and to aesthetics, they create furniture and specific utensils, they influence architecture. For indigenous and peasant peoples, it is the basis for their identity and for their autonomy. So the transgenic contamination of the peasants' maize is no small event. As Alvaro Salgado, from the Centre for Indigenous Missions (CENAMI) put it, *"This is an act of aggression against the deepest identity of Mexico and of its original peoples. Our communities and organisations have therefore decided to take this problem into our own hands."*[3]

Civil Society Responses

GM contamination in Mexico gave rise to a collective discussion on the issue, involving indigenous and peasant communities and organisations as well as civil society organisations, which has brought out the complexities of the problem as well as the complexities of the resistance against contamination. In clear contrast to the resignation and *"surrender"*[4] the industry hoped for, Mexico's people have risen to the challenge.

Once the contamination had been demonstrated, many civil society organisations protested in Mexico and internationally. Amongst the demands raised were stopping the causes of contamination, for governments and international agencies to step in to monitor contamination, for impact studies to be done and contingency plans prepared, and for liability suits to be drawn up against the multinationals. Some also raised the need for national and international biosafety regulations. We demanded transparent proof from the Food and Agriculture Organisation and the Consultative Group on International Agricultural Research that they had not been contaminated as well, nor could be in the future, and called for a moratorium on planting GM crops. Mexico's indigenous and peasant communities, meanwhile, have gone much further and deeper. Their experience is invaluable to understanding the issue of contamination and to go on building resistance in other parts of the world.

Causes of Contamination

The primary cause of contamination of maize in Mexico is the importing of unsegregated maize from the US. From being self-sufficient in maize till the late 1980s, the birthplace of maize has become an importer, because of national farm policies that discourage small-scale production. These policies were intensified with the signing of the North American Free Trade Agreement (NAFTA) in 1992. Today Mexico imports about a third of the maize it consumes from the US, and has placed no restrictions in relation to GM imports. Since over 40% of US maize output is genetically engineered and authorities refuse to segregate GM and non-GM maize, at least that percentage is flowing into Mexico. The percentage is likely to be even higher, since other major importers (like the EU and Japan) have refused US maize, creating a glut.

Meanwhile, Mexico disassembled its public system for supplying and marketing nationally-produced maize. It used to buy the maize from farmers and then sell it country-wide through a system of 23,000 rural stores known as DICONSA. Spread through the most remote corners of the Mexican countryside, these stores are often the only point of sale for cereals and other supplies. After dismantling the national supply system, the market was taken over by a handful of companies dominated by a few multinationals like Cargill, ADM and Maseca, which prefer to import their maize from the US (where prices are kept artificially low) and sell it through the DICONSA system, in competition with Mexican maize growers. Although the great majority of Mexican peasants do not plant store-bought maize seeds, distortions in the economy mean that it is cheaper to buy maize than grow it, thus reducing and depleting their own seed supply. Moreover, out of normal peasant curiosity— which has been critical for the development of the world's agrobiodiversity— they plant some of what they buy, just to see what happens. They also buy at the DICONSA stores when they lack seed for other reasons, such as floods or droughts that leave them with no harvest. Even when that maize grows out poorly, as is often the case because it is not adapted to the peasants' fields, they grow enough to produce pollen to contaminate their and their neighbours' fields.

Another cause of contamination has come from farmers replanting some of the grain provided as food aid from the World Food Program and foreign NGOs. In addition, field trials were undertaken in Mexico with GM maize without adequate supervision to ensure that contamination could not take place prior to the establishment of a moratorium in 1999. And finally, while there has never been any authorisation in Mexico for the commercial planting of GM maize crops, given that even much of the seed considered non-GM in the US is actually contaminated, large-scale Mexican maize growers may also have become unwitting vectors of contamination, just like their peasant compatriots. There are many ways in which GM maize has infiltrated the country, but the main cause is that a few huge transnational companies saw no problem in genetically modifying an open-pollinated crop of great economic and cultural importance and had no concern for the many and diverse impacts this would have.

The Official Response

When the contamination of Mexican maize came to light, Mexican government officials with few exceptions[5] first denied the facts, then played them down and threw a blanket of silence over the subject. The government maintained imports and even suspended the moratorium on growing or importing GM maize. NAFTA stripped the country of any rights it might have had to refuse GM imports under the Cartagena Protocol on Biosafety. Under one NAFTA accord signed in November 2003, Mexico agreed to allow shipments from Canada and the US to dispense with identifying contamination by GM grain when its presence is *"adventitious"* or does not comprise more than 5% of the grain. This is an arbitrary and absurdly high threshold, whose supervision is the responsibility of the companies themselves.

Meanwhile, representatives of the Mexican Academy of Science drew up a bill of law on 'biosafety', which ignores the precautionary principle and offers a clear framework to promote GM crops and to legalise contamination in Mexico. Based on the argument that the bill is *"science-based,"* it was approved by all parties in the Senate and is now under discussion in the Chamber of Deputies. Indigenous and peasant communities describe it as *"shameful and offensive to peasants and indigenous people and to all citizens of Mexico in general."* They say that *"We are not asking for a 'better' law. We believe that Mexico, centre of origin of maize, does not need to take on the social, economic and environmental risks posed by transgenic crops. It should simply forbid them."*[6]

Attacks on the Maize People

In sharp contrast with the official position, the news of contamination of Mexico's maize shocked the country as a whole, and raised tremendous concerns for millions of peasants and indigenous people. Just months after the discovery of the contamination of maize made by Ignacio Chapela and David Quist, in January 2002, more than 300 indigenous, peasant, civil society, academic and religious representatives met in Mexico City at the First Forum in Defence of Maize. The meeting's conclusions included a declaration, policy demands and proposals, strategies for action and an analysis of the context for understanding the contamination.

> *"Maize is the heritage of mankind, the fruit of domestication done by Meso-American indigenous and peasant peoples for over 10,000 years, not by transnational corporations. The transgenic contamination of native maize varieties is a loss of genetic memory of traditional Mexican agriculture, and it may be irreparable. Agricultural and trade policies undermine national maize production, which is the core of the peasant economy and organisation, as well as food sovereignty. Maize represents more than 10,000 years of culture and is the legacy of Mexico's Indian and peasant peoples. Maize growing is the heart of community resistance."*[7]

From the outset, it was clear that this was more than an isolated event of contaminated maize, an environmental or a health problem, or even just a 'genetic engineering' issue. It was part of a broader phenomenon, which became known as *"the attack on maize people"* in the Second Forum in Defence of Maize. One key realisation at the First Forum was that we did not need a campaign as such, but a process. This process would neither be linear nor short-term, but would be defined through a broad, diverse, collective and horizontal effort. Its objectives, methodologies and norms would change continuously, as a result of the self-managed and culturally diverse nature of the process.

Without Maize We Are Nothing

As Ramón Vera Herrera expressed in an excellent reflection on the various aspects of the process unleashed by the contamination of maize,[8]

> *"The first steps involved information and analyses, marches and protest letters, lobbying activities and many regional workshops. There was and still is a real concern at the very idea of contaminating the most sacred element of their lives and the foremost source of their food, what makes them be and provides the identity that has been forged for millennia. When the Wixaritari (or Huichole) community members found out, one of them immediately and incisively observed that 'Without maize, we are nothing; we would not just be dead, we would cease to exist'."*

All around the country, people found a voice. This contribution from Aldo González, from UNOSJO, summarises the concerns of many:

> *"Native seeds are a very important part of our culture. The pyramids may have been destroyed, but a handful of maize seed is the legacy we can leave to our children and grandchildren. Today they are denying us this possibility. The process of globalisation that our country is going through and the undermining of governmental authority are keeping indigenous communities from being able to pass on this age-old legacy, which represents more than 10,000 years of culture. For 10,000 years our seeds have proven they don't harm anyone. Today they're telling us that transgenic seeds are harmless. What proof do they have of this? Five or six years of planting transgenic maize seeds in the world gives no indication that the seeds or this grain are harmless to humanity. We have every reason to doubt their seeds."[9]*

. . . With indigenous meetings held around the entire country, a strong, invisible movement began to emerge to defend maize and to understand the implications of its contamination. For example, at the National Indigenous Congress (CNI) Assembly for the Central Pacific Region held in Jalisco in July 2002, contamination became such an issue that the delegates from the Wixárika, Purépecha, Ñahñú, Huachichil, Chichimeca, Nahua and Amuzgo peoples from various states of Mexico, stressed among their final resolutions that:

> *"We demand that the Federal Government cease the introduction into our country of maize that is transgenic or of doubtful origin. We call on all indigenous and peasant peoples, and on maize consumers throughout the country, to defend our seeds and to unite behind our demand."*

Interestingly, the CNI made the direct link between the defence of maize and the importance of maintaining biodiversity and their traditional knowledge, and of preventing biopiracy. They further extrapolated this issue to the protection of traditional medicine. Two months later, the communities and organisations that make up the CNI held a National Forum to Defend Traditional Medicine, which drew together countless traditional medicine practitioners, authorities and delegates from indigenous communities and organisations from 20 different states. Those present represented the following peopels: the Tohono O'odham, Mayo, RaráMuri, Cora, Wixaritari, Nahua, Huachichil, Tenek, Chichimeca, Purhépecha, Mazahua, Tlahuica, Matlatzinca, Hñahñu, Tepehua, Amuzgo, Tlapaneco, Mixteco, Huave, Zapoteco, Mixe, Mazateco, Maya Peninsular, Tzeltal, Tzotzil, C'hol, Tojolabal, Mame, Zoque, Chuj and Mochó peoples, along with civil society organisations.

After demanding respect for indigenous territories, natural resources, biodiversity, and both the ancient and modern knowledge of indigenous peoples; after refusing to submit to the validation of traditional medical practices by public health authorities; after demanding autonomy and self-government; after declaring a moratorium on bioprospecting in the territories of the peoples signing the document, those present at the conference also made a striking call on the issue of transgenic contamination:

> *"As part of our defence of Mother Earth and of everything to which she gives birth, we repudiate the introduction into our country of transgenic maize, because Mother Maize is the first foundation of our peoples. To this end, we demand that the federal government declare an open-ended moratorium on the introduction of transgenic maize, regardless of the use which it may be given."*. . .

Notes

1. GRAIN, "Poisoning the Well: the genetic pollution of maize," *Seedling*, January 2003, p 4: http://www.grain.org/seedling/?id=219; GRAIN, "Confronting Contamination: Five reasons to reject co-existence," *Seedling*, April 2004, p1; http://www.grain.org/seedling/?id=280

2. Margaret Mellon and Jane Rissler, *Gone to Seed: Transgenic contaminants in the traditional seed supply*, Union of Concerned Scientists, Washington DC, 2004. http://www.ucsusa.org/food_and_environment/biotechnology/page.cfm?pageID=1315

3. "Contaminación transgénica del maíz en México: mucho más grave" Collective press release by indigenous and peasant communities with civil-society organisations. Oct. 9, 2003, Mexico. http://www.etcgroup.org/article.asp?newsid=407

4. Don Westfall, a consultant to biotechnology companies, said in 2001: "The hope of the industry is that over time the market is so flooded [with genetically modified organisms] that there's nothing you can do about it. You just sort of surrender." *Toronto Star*, Canada, Jan. 9, 2001.

5. With the minority exception of the Institute of Ecology and the National Biodiversity Commission, which took samples that confirmed the contamination, released the results and held dialogue with peasants and with civil-society organisations.

6. Collective document by indigenous communities from Oaxaca, Puebla, Chihuahua and Veracruz, CECCAM, CENAMI, ETC Group, CASIFOP, UNOSJO y AJAGI, October 2003, Mexico. http://www.etcgroup.org/article.asp?newsid=408

7. Conclusions from the First Forum In Defense of Maize (*En Defensa del Maíz*): http://www.ceccam.org.mx/ConclusionesDefensa.htm

8. Ramón Vera Herrera, "En defensa del maíz (y el futuro)—una autogestión invisible." May 2004, IRC, http://www.americaspolicy.org/

9. *Ojarasca,* in *La Jornada* 58, February 2002.

POSTSCRIPT

Is Plant Biotechnology the Solution to Hunger in Latin America and the Caribbean?

According to Clive James of the International Service for the Acquisition of Agri-biotech Applications (ISAAA), in 2005 there were 21 countries growing biotech crops and, of those countries, seven were in Latin America: Argentina, Brazil, Paraguay, Uruguay, Mexico, Colombia, and Honduras. The number is eight when one includes Puerto Rico. James also states that in 2005, "the US, followed by Argentina, Brazil, Canada and China continued to be the principal adopters of biotech crops globally, with 49.8 million hectares planed in the US (55% of the global biotech area)" (http://www.isaaa.org/kc/CBTNews/2006_Issues/Jan/CBT_Jan_11.htm).

Modern applications of biotechnology continue to be supported by many Latin American and Caribbean scientists. Working in conjunction with scientists from around the world, in 2000 the Brazilian, Mexican, and Third World Academies of Sciences produced a report entitled "Transgenic Plants and World Agriculture." The report details the agricultural, health, and environmental benefits of GM technology and its potential to feed the world (Royal Society of London et al., July 2000). During the Fifth Latin American and Caribbean Meeting on Agricultural Biotechnology in 2004, scientists composed the "Boca Chica Declaration." The declaration situates Latin American development within a global and historical perspective: "Significant challenges faced by humanity over the last one hundred years still persist in Latin America and the Caribbean. These limit attainment of the degree of development and social equity that we all desire in this new century for our peoples." The persistence of poverty, food insecurity, and environmental devastation, the document contests, requires a shift in focus in the development models for Latin America. A new model must "advocate for human welfare above any other political or economic cause. Undoubtedly, a development model to achieve collective prosperity and equity can be boosted by the development and sustainable use of biotechnology" (Technical Cooperation Network on Plant Biotechnology (REDBIO/FAO) and International REDBIO Foundation Government of the Dominican Republic, http://www.ejbiotechnology.info/feedback/declarations/09/index.html).

Agri-business is also an important player in discussions on biotechnology. In "The Public Debate on Agrobiotechnology: A Biotech Company's Perspective," Roger W. Krueger, a representative of one of the largest seed corporations in the world, affirms: "We at Monsanto believe that biotechnology provides an important tool for agricultural sustainability." Yet, he recognizes that "bioengineered crops face a mixed regulatory and public acceptance environment in certain parts of the world." Krueger acknowledges that the past years for Monsanto have been "turbulent" and that the company is taking steps to improve its public image (*AgBioForum,* vol. 4, no. 3&4, 2001, pp. 209–220).

Despite agri-business' efforts, many are not convinced of the benefits of GM seeds. The backlash against GM foods has been particularly marked in Europe. Due to consumers' concern about the potential negative health implications of biotech foods, the European Union instituted a moratorium against them (1998 to 2004). As a result, Latin American countries interested in producing and exporting GM crops take careful note of the changing political climate and trade regulations. As Diego Cevallos reports in "Wanted—Labels for Genetically Engineered Products," Latin American consumers are also concerned about the safety of GM foods. According to Cevallos, "In Brazil, 74 percent of those surveyed in 2001 by the Brazilian Institute of Public Opinion and Statistics said they preferred non-transgenic foods [. . .] in Chile, 58.5 percent of consumers prefer foods that have not been genetically modified [and in Mexico] 98 percent of the people consulted said they distrust transgenic products and that food companies should inform consumers about whether they use them or not" (*Inter Press Service News Agency,* February 21, 2006).

Many environmentalists consider the application of modern biotechnology in agriculture as a threat to biodiversity. (For more information, see Haider Rizvi's "Biodiversity: Don't Sell 'Suicide Seeds,' Activists Warn," *Inter Press Service News Agency,* March 21, 2006). Due to concerns about the risks of living GMOs, in 2000 United Nation's Convention of Biological Diversity adopted a supplementary agreement called the Cartagena Protocol on Biosafety (http://www.biodiv.org/biosafety/background.asp).

As is suggested in Ribeiro's article, there are indigenous groups that protest the patenting and commercial sale of germplasm of crops they have cultivated for centuries. Joann Kawell discusses this question in "Who Owns Knowledge?" *(NACLA Report on the Americas,* March/April 2002).

For the World Health Organization's assessment on GM foods, see "20 questions on Genetically Modified Foods" (http://www.who.int/foodsafety/publications/biotech/20questions/en/). Carmelo Ruiz Marrero discusses the "invasion" of GM seeds in Argentina, Brazil, Paraguay, Mexico, and Puerto Rico in "Biotech Crops Invade Latin America" (http://americas.irc-online.org/articles/2005/0503gmo.html). For Norman Borlaug's critique of the opponents of biotechnology, read "Ending World Hunger: The Promise of Biotechnology and the Threat of Antiscience Zealotry" (*Plant Physiology,* October 2000, pp. 487–490). Miguel Altieri offers an agroecological perspective on GM foods in "The Myths of Agricultural Biotechnology: Some ethical questions" (http://agro-eco.org/doc/the_myths.html). During the World Social Forum held in Caracas, Venezuela in 2006, the World Social Forum passed a resolution on small farmers, patents, food sovereignty, and holistic agrarian reform. To read the resolution, see: http://www.alternatives.ca/article2395.html.

ISSUE 15

Is Expropriating Land and Giving It to the Poor a Good Economic and Cultural Policy?

YES: James Petras and Henry Veltmeyer, from "Dynamics of Peasant Organizing in Latin America," *Social Policy* (Summer 2003)

NO: LulaWatch, from "Focusing on Latin America's New 'Axis of Evil'," *The American Society for the Defense of Tradition, Family and Property* (May 23, 2003)

ISSUE SUMMARY

YES: Professors Petras and Veltmeyer maintain that peasant-based social movements are dynamic agents for social change in Latin America.

NO: The LulaWatch group points out that although land reform is not new to Brazil, it has always been an economic and social failure. LulaWatch believes that the Brazilian government should halt its "draconian" land reform program.

Landless movements are not new in Latin America. With roots in the unequal distribution of land put in place by the European conquest of the Americas, land redistribution is an issue of paramount significance and controversy in Latin America. The uneven access to land in Latin America has inspired a host of revolutions and movements throughout the centuries, and land reform is often viewed as key to addressing existing socioeconomic disparity. Yet, the results of twentieth-century land movements in Latin America have been varied. Some land reforms were implemented soon after the conclusion of the various campaigns and conflicts, whereas others were never addressed, oftentimes as a result of governmental instability, perpetual squabbles over rightful ownership, native land rights, and regular U.S. military intervention with intentions to restore a previously removed regime, among others.

Throughout Latin America, landless farmers and peasants have been waiting, negotiating, and fighting for what they feel is their right to own land. Meanwhile, the proportionately fewer, wealthy landowners who own an overwhelming majority of the land prefer to maintain the status quo arguing their right to own private property. Concerned that governments are not distributing land in an equitable manner, some groups of landless people have illegally settled on disputed lands and claimed these parcels for themselves.

Many landless groups have garnered attention both in and outside of Latin America. Perhaps the most well-known is the MST, otherwise known as the Landless Rural Workers Movement, which was founded in Brazil in 1984. Its slogan of "occupy, resist and produce" reflects it objectives. Other similar movements have arisen throughout Latin America. For example, the Revolutionary Armed Forces of Colombia (FARC), was founded in 1964 "as an overwhelming peasant movement, largely of subsistence farmers" (Petras and Veltmeyer). In Ecuador, there is CONAIE (Confederation of Indigenous Nationalities of Ecuador). And in Mexico, the EZLN (Zapatista Army of National Liberation) has also been active in the struggle for lands.

The primary issues surrounding this controversy are judicial concerning the legality of the activities of the various movements and also relate to human rights. Why should governments expropriate legally owned land, pay a low price to its owners, and divide the land among poor farmers who may not have the means to make the land productive? On the other hand, why should large landholdings owned by one or only a few individuals lie unused if hundreds of people could benefit from making the land productive and improving their lives?

The circumstances and historical legacy surrounding the questions have been highly visible. In Brazil in 1996, the Eldorado dos Carajás massacre took place when military police killed 19 landless workers who were participating in a march. Nine years later, 12,000 landless Brazilian peasants completed a 150-mile, 17-day march across the country to raise awareness regarding land reform (*CommonDreams.org*, "Landless Peasants March in Brazil, Build a New Road by Walking"). In response to these and other demonstrations along with public outcry, the government has stood by its claim that land reform is under way. However, many feel that the government has no intention of redistributing the land and is deliberately stalling.

Of course, land reform is not without their detractors. Luiz Antonio Nabhan, a third-generation cattle and crop farmer from the state of Goiás in Brazil, criticizes Brazil's federal government for its recognition of MST as a "social movement": "With that, the MST gained strength and began to invade and pillage productive private farm properties, in organized rampages that include theft, destruction and torching of buildings and infrastructure, the killing of farm animals, physical aggression and the illegal capture and holding of individuals in isolation against their will" ("Brazil's Ideology-Based Land Grab: A Pointless, Wasteful Exercise . . ." *InfoBrazil*, April 17–23, 2004).

In their article, James Petras and Henry Veltmeyer discuss the importance of peasant-based social movements in implementing land reform. And, although the *LulaWatch* article primarily focuses on the MST landless movement in Brazil, much of its argument can apply to other regions in Latin America where landless movements exist. LulaWatch contends that governments should not invoke land redistribution practices as a response to pressures by landless movements such as MST.

YES

**James Petras and
Henry Veltmeyer**

Dynamics of Peasant Organizing
in Latin America

Introduction

How are we to understand the change agents and social forces and processes
involved in the sweeping changes taking place in Latin America? In particular,
how do we view contemporary peasant and landless workers' movements? Are
they hopelessly romantic, 21st century versions of the early Industrial Revolution
Luddites who destroyed machines to preserve their crafts? Or, are they realisti-
cally fighting an expression of the multinational corporation-western dominated
international financial institutions-neo-liberal ideology/industry complex?

Our study of peasant-based social movements contradicts dismissive
attitudes towards the peasantry as a significant social and political force.
These rural efforts respond to oppressive social and economic structures and
to the specific neo-liberal policies of domestic and international elites. The
peasantry, which in a number of contexts (Bolivia, Ecuador, Mexico, Peru) has
a decidedly ethnic or indigenous character, is an important part of the rural
social structure in many Latin American societies and an equally important
agency for social change and development.

The peasantry are constrained by both economic and political structures
which shape how they view themselves—their consciousness. They are a
highly modern social class, a catalyst for systemic change and a dynamic force
in an ongoing modernization process. They seek a more just and participatory
society, free from oppression, in which the direct producers of the society
democratically control the economy and realize a decent standard of living.

The intensification of rural conflicts between landowners and peasants/
rural workers is best understood by placing contemporary rural capitalism in
the larger urban-industrial economy context. Some analysts believe a displaced rural population will be incorporated into the industrial-urban economy. Since at least the 1960s, Latin America's urban centers experienced
explosive in-migration of displaced rural people. Over the last five years, for
example, Brazil's cities drew five to eight million from rural areas; over the
next five years, another eight million are anticipated.

But another tendency is at work as well. As of the early 1980s, Latin
American economies tended to stagnate, drastically reducing the absorptive

From *Social Policy,* vol. 33, no. 4, Summer 2003, pp. 33–38. Copyright © 2003 by Thomson-Gale.
Reprinted by permission.

capacity of urban economies. In this situation, urban migration is more problematic and the decision to stay and fight for change in the rural areas becomes more plausible. Lack of opportunity in the cities and increased opportunities to engage in successful social movements in the countryside have increased recruits for rural social movements. These new activists are willing to engage in mass direct action. Over the past 20 years, they have become increasingly radicalized and a new leadership with solid roots in the peasantry has emerged.

Rural movements have won land, developed productive agricultural cooperatives, built decent and affordable housing and achieved significant education and health care reforms. In so doing, they created a new momentum that attracts new activist households. Even where concrete achievements have been minimal, the movements have attracted new followers because they promise a better future, solidarity in resisting further evictions and strength to negotiate with established powers.

Large-scale rural social movements are sources of power that have a major impact on urban and national politics, converting the peasantry and indigenous peoples into an active force for broad social and political change. The Rural Landless Workers Movement in Brazil (MST), the Revolutionary Armed Forces in Colombia (FARC), and the National Confederation of Indigenous Nationalities (CONAIE) in Ecuador have all shaped national policies and become major challengers of state power. MST has built coalitions with urban trade unions, urban shantytown organizations, and church and human rights groups. It has made agrarian reform a major national political issue. FARC is a rural-based guerrilla group with 15-20,000 armed supporters, overwhelmingly peasant or landless rural workers. It controls or has influence in half the municipalities of the country and is in off-again/on-again negotiations with the government on a possible peace accord with agrarian reform one of the centerpieces. CONAIE, the major Ecuador Indian-peasant confederation, paralysed the country with general strikes and highway blockages, occupied Parliament in January 2000, and in May 2000 swept highland state and local elections.

Today's agrarian reform proposals are not a simple replay of traditional demands for "land to the tiller" and opposition to capitalist "modernization" associated with large-scale corporate export farming. Rather, they comprise an alternative modernization strategy built around modern social classes and positively disposed toward the possibility of significant, even transformative, change. Peasants/farm workers or at least their cadres/leaders view land distribution as only the first step in agrarian reform. Their ideas of reform are vastly different from past images of atomized subsistence farmers, relying solely on traditional farming know-how, barely aware of markets, alternative cropping and non-traditional marketable crops, and resistant to technological innovation. It is precisely the emergence of a different peasantry and different rural workers that accounts for the resistance to being displaced to join the urban reserve army of unemployed or the underground economy selling Chicklets to wealthy tourists.

The formation of a rural landless working class is derived from several processes. Large families of small farmers, for example, create a surplus of sons and daughters who do not have access to land. In other cases, sharecrop-pers, renters and tenant farmers are displaced by larger farmers converting to new crops and introducing mechanization. In many cases, government neo-liberal trade policies result in the importation of cheap food stuffs that drive small farmers bankrupt. Cutbacks in agricultural credits and loans and high interest rates also force large numbers of small family farmers to migrate to cities or to become a rural proletariat. Those who remain in the countryside are formally "propertyless rural workers," but their ties to the land are recent and relatively strong, their "lineage" and extended family networks are "rural" and their "class consciousness" is still tied to access to land, particularly cultivatable land in regions familiar to them.

Each of these three movements is unique and, as we shall see, all of them share important characteristics.

The Rural Landless Workers Movement (MST) in Brazil

MST is directed toward modernizing agriculture, converting fallow estates into productive units that incorporate credits, technical assistance and inno-vative marketing strategies. MST's slogan is "occupy, resist and produce." Over 300,000 families have been settled in co-ops since MST's 1984 founding. The great majority have increased cultivation of land, raised living standards (improved health, education and housing) and produced a marketable sur-plus, including significant coffee exports to overseas markets. MST's national and regional leadership have passed through advanced training programs (many MST-sponsored), where invited lecturers, including university profes-sors and technical experts, teach courses on modern farming techniques, cooperative management and contemporary political economy.

MST activities, tactics and strategies are expressed in a highly sophisti-cated organizational structure. Between May 1–7, 2000 over 400 land occupa-tions were organized throughout the country, relaying information via the Internet to Brazilian and international supporters. The land occupation strat-egy is based on an elaborate structure of self-governance dealing with food, security and negotiations with the state. During the 1999–2000 period, MST engaged in direct action protests demanding greater credits and financing to stem the outflow to urban centers of bankrupt small holders and impover-ished landless rural workers.

MST has been a leading force organizing urban alliances to counteract the neo-liberal agenda of privatization and budget cuts. It mobilized trade unions, political parties, university and religious groups through a campaign called "Consulta Popular." In the late 1990s, MST led a march of over 100,000 urban and rural workers to Brasilia, the nation's capitol, drawing urban support along the cross-country parade route. Lula's recent electoral victory, supported by the MST, led many to believe that a new era in agrarian reform was at hand. Unfortunately, Lula has embraced the entire austerity program of the International Monetary Fund (IMF), and the MST is reluctantly returning to direct action.

MST TACTICS & STRATEGY

- Through mass group actions, organizers and militants press the government to redistribute unused productive land to landless workers and farmers.
- Grassroots activists raise awareness of landless farmers and workers, explaining their rights under the Constitution, and they coordinate land occupations.
- National leaders lobby government to improve credit and agriculture support services for family-based farms, [and] to accelerate land reform.
- Banks and government buildings are occupied to raise awareness of agrarian reform and pressure the government to fulfill its promises of support for poor farmers.
- National campaigns are conducted to educate the country's population abut the possible effects of free trade accords and downside of genetically modified organisms.
- International partnerships are established through structures such as the Via Campesina and World Social Forum to share experiences and build a common front against domination by multinational companies.

MST's organization, leadership, productive units and activities aim toward modernizing agriculture and opposing unproductive landlords and land speculators, both of whom invest little to increase productivity and create a marketable surplus. MST also counterposes its modernization strategy to large agribusiness enterprises that have expelled small holders and farm workers. In this context MST juxtaposes a "modernization from below with equity" strategy to the elite modernization strategy favored by the recent Cardoso regime and its World Bank sponsors. A key difference between the two approaches is the social and ecological foundations from which the contrasting modernization strategies are organized. The elite modernization strategy is based on a small group of large capitalist farmers, tied to chemically intensive agriculture and almost exclusively linked to overseas foreign export. MST's modernization from below strategy is built on the inclusion of a large contingent of former landless laborers in agricultural co-ops and pursues a sustainable agricultural strategy that produces food for local markets and includes a social agenda incorporating gender and racial equality.

Within the dominant capitalist system's institutional framework, MST has widened its agenda from agrarian reform to include banking and credit reform, foreign debt moratorium, conservation of the Amazon, protection of domestic producers and organic farming. It has called for greater social spending for public health and education as part of efforts toward greater national autonomy within the international economy. It has been an active participant in many of the most important national and international conferences dealing with globalisation, environmental issues and gender and minority rights. MST's effectiveness and prominence in national and Third World politics is based precisely on its capacity to build a modern program and adapt it to the primary demands of the landless rural worker and impoverished small landholder.

The Revolutionary Armed Forces of Columbia (FARC)—Columbia

FARC was founded in 1964 as an overwhelmingly peasant movement, largely of subsistence farmers, in the relatively underdeveloped region of Marquetalia. The guerrilla movement was based on peasant land settlements that had developed a degree of autonomy from the national government, and were therefore seen as a threat to its control. The Armed Forces' attempt to exterminate the peasant communities led to the formation of FARC, which evolved from an armed formation dedicated to defending peasantry from the depredations of the national government and landlords into a national political-military force of 15–20,000 active fighters with influence in half the municipalities of the country. The centerpiece of FARC's program has been Agrarian Reform, although it has grown into a national political force with a political program that embraces other political and economic issues, including reform of state institutions, welfare state expansion and increased national control over domestic markets, energy and communications.

FARC is a complex organization whose main constituency includes subsistence farmers, displaced peasants, landless rural workers and a sector of urban workers and employees; its national and regional leadership and rural cadres embrace modern values. According to FARC, about 65% of the organization is peasant and 35% is "urban"—including rural towns. While FARC leadership includes the legendary Manuel Marulanda and others who are formally members of the Communist Party of Colombia, in fact, FARC has its own leadership, program, strategy and tactics, with a decidedly distinct social base. Even in its origins FARC developed a modern program of agrarian reform based on land distribution and government financing, credits and technical assistance. Its political program called for break-up of the political monopoly exercised by the century-old traditional two parties (Liberals and Conservatives)—both rooted in urban and rural oligarchies.

Though FARC continues to defend underdeveloped rural producers tied to small scale production, its leaders and program propose introducing modern agricultural techniques and marketing strategies to benefit the rural poor. During the 1999–2000 peace talks, FARC organized a national forum on issues including projects for alternative development, illicit crops, unemployment, privatization versus nationalization, free trade versus protection, etc. FARC position papers reflect a sophisticated understanding of contemporary debates. FARC-organized forums held in the "liberated zones" were attended by the whole gamut of social organizations, including trade unions and employer associations, Wall Street investment bankers, government officials, etc.

FARC's military organization is highly structured, strategically sophisticated and equipped with light modern arms. It is a modern guerrilla army linked to a mass peasant base. FARC leadership envisions a mixed economy and strong state welfare and regulation of the private economy. What began as a rural defensive movement based on pre-capitalist rural producers has been transformed into a modern guerrilla army linked to a modernization-through-equity vision of political transformation. While the setting for much of FARC's

KEY MST CHALLENGES

- Brazil land ownership is highly concentrated; under 3% of the population owns two-thirds of the country's arable land.
- Small producers can't afford rural credit because of recent neoliberal interest-rate hikes.
- Agricultural subsidies have been eliminated while northern countries continue large subsidies to their agricultural sectors.
- Cheap agricultural imports flood the market, depressing domestic prices, while costs of farm inputs and capital have increased.
- Agriculture sector technical assistance programs have been gutted.
- Small farms disappear and land cultivated diminishes because of increased bankruptcy and default on debt.
- Large export-oriented agribusinesses tied to multinational commodity traders have benefited from recent government policies, crowding out small farmers.
- Falling per-capita grain production, decreasing incomes, and rising rural unemployment have forced millions to move to the country's poor, crowded urban peripheries.

activity is the most underdeveloped and impoverished regions, its organization, leadership and program are oriented toward opening Colombia's political system, eliminating para-military forces and creating a more dynamic domestic market via redistributive policies. The juxtaposition of democratic political values to vertical military organization, the elaboration of a modernist development agenda to a largely subsistence rural base, the promotion of the home market in the context of deepening international integration are some of the formidable contradictory elements now confronting FARC.

The major challenge facing FARC and other democratic popular movements and human rights groups is massive military intervention by the US via Plan Colombia which, despite claims to the contrary, and like its US-backed counterparts elsewhere in Latin America, supports death squads. To fulfill Colombia's economic obligations to foreign debt holders and conform to Washington's terrorist/anti-terrorist strategy, President Alvaro Uribe has slashed public funding, cut social services, lowered wages and attacked protective labor legislation. In September 2002, more than 150,000 demonstrated in Bogota; and in late October 2002, major labor, peasant and civic organizations led a general strike of workers and peasants. Uribe and his US backers, cornered by the mass peaceful protesters and the armed guerrillas, have struck back with a "total war" strategy. The question arises whether in the future the trade unions and the rural based guerrilla forces can combine forces against this war.

US media highlight FARC's expulsion of elected local officials who refuse to resign, kidnappings and, in one case, murder of hostages. No doubt there have been excesses, but they must be placed in this context: in the mid-1980s, a modern multiparty system was the basis of peace negotiations with then-President Betancourt. The FARC-supported Patriotic Union Party was soon decimated. Three

AGENDA OF THE LANDLESS WORKERS' MOVEMENT (MST) (EXCERPTS)

- Timely implementation of agrarian reform that would redistribute unproductive estates to landless families.
- Orientation of agricultural production towards the internal market in order to assure Brazilian food security and boost employment.
- Application of policies aimed at strengthening small-scale and family-based farms, including policies regarding prices, subsidies, rural credits, and food security.
- Promotion of agro-industrial cooperatives in order to improve access to the market and boost farmers' income.
- Creation of programs to stimulate rural employment, both in the agricultural and non-agricultural sectors, and establishment of mechanisms that secure the rights of workers.
- Guaranteed access to primary education for all residents of rural areas, as well as improved curriculums and conditions in schools.
- Development of policies to protect the environment and natural resources in a manner that is compatible with farm production and that promotes rational use of both solar and hydroelectric power.
- Implementation of a special development plan for the semi-arid northeast.
- Restoration and reorganization of the various agencies that make up the agricultural public sector in order to focus their work on supporting small-scale producers.
- Research into and development of agricultural technology that is appropriate for Brazilian soil conditions, climate and resources and that promotes an equilibrium between increased productivity and environmental preservation.
- Promotion of labor-intensive industry, particularly agro-industries in municipalities around the country.
- Suspension of payments on Brazil's foreign debt and the reorientation of the country's involvement in multilateral organizations and regional trade agreements to favor the interests of small family-run farms, not just large agribusinesses.

of its presidential candidates were killed, as well as more than 4,000 activistsists and sympathizers—often with the complicity of local pro-regime officials. The renewal and intensification of the civil war that followed led to massive displacements of millions of peasants, largely the result of Armed Forces' and their paramilitary progeny's scorched earth policies. It should also be noted that FARC has unilaterally released prisoners without regime reciprocity and offered to negotiate a total prisoner exchange with the government.

Confederation of Indigenous Nationalities (CONAIE)—Ecuador

In 1990, a significant sector of Ecuador's indigenous peasants launched an uprising against the government and its neoliberal policies. Over the subsequent decade the conditions that led to this uprising generated an anti-system social movement of significant proportions, with a series of concerted actions that included storming Congress in 2000 and a brief take-over of the presidency. At issue are a significantly deteriorating economic situation and drastic economic reforms and policies of adjustment that include a serious proposal to adopt the US dollar as the country's currency. Another major issue is permit concessions to transnational corporations to construct oil pipelines and engage in economic development projects to the detriment of the country's indigenous peoples, their communities, the environment and the local economy. Behind the mass actions can be found well-organized indigenous communities from across the highlands that are politically represented by CONAIE. By the turn of the new millennium this peasant-based indigenous movement had clearly taken the lead of a nation-wide social movement against the government's IMF-mandated policies and for social transformation, aimed at changing not only the relationship of the country's indigenous peasants to the country's state and economy but at overthrowing the whole system. Peasant communities are the most dynamic grouping favoring systemic social change for the country as a whole.

The beliefs and ideas used to mobilize collective action by Ecuador's peasant and indigenous peoples are clearly articulated in a series of programmatic statements by the movement's leaders and spokespeople. Although often couched in the language of identity politics, including a"return to the good times" and "reaffirmation of our historical roots," the series of uprisings and the overall movement of the country's indigenous peoples and peasants are based on clearly modernist development ideas: democracy, radical change in existing forms of class domination and social justice.

CONAIE addresses issues of national economic development and the need for a new politics centered on community-based relations and forms of power. It seeks an alternative development that is constructed from below, participatory, people-led and centered, inclusive, equitable, just and empowering. CONAIE has committed itself to a process of non-capitalist modernization rooted in both the indigenous peasant economy and equitable participation in the country's resources and national development process. CONAIE sees itself as a means to convert the country's indigenous peoples from a "passive object" into ". . . active social and political subject(s)" and, in the process, bring about a state of development, democracy and justice.

Zapatista Army of National Liberation (EZLN)—Mexico

Because the Zapatistas are so much better known we have not included them in our analysis. However, the major principles examined above apply to Mexico and its national economic and political system. The armed rebellion and uprising of indigenous peasants in Chiapas was directed against the Mexican State and the capitalist system supported by it. As far as Subcommandante Marcos and the EZLN are concerned, the enemy is imperialism and the Mexican State that sustains the neo-liberal project.

The Zapatista uprising coincided with the inception of NAFTA, viewed as "the death knell of the peasant economy." In a series of communiques, reflections and calls for solidarity, the Zapatistas speak consistently of the need to combat (structural and political) relations of oppression and exploitation; and to establish new economic and political power relations based on "independence, democracy and justice."

Major Signs of Hope

Far from being irrelevant romantics seeking a return to the unreturnable, these movements formulate analyses, strategies and policies that are realistic, responsive to existing relations of power in their respective countries and that envision transformation of their social order. In each case, economic justice, creation of new forms of local economic organization, recognition of global economic forces, participatory democracy and celebration of the richness of their nation's cultural diversity are part of their programs. These peasant and landless workers' movements are engaged in a struggle to secure socio-economic improvements within a modern economy dominated by capital. Their enduring presence and increasing importance are based precisely on their modernity. They tend to resist the pressures and demands of financial and commercial capital whose free market policies and world market orientation undermine the livelihood of small local producers, rural workers and their communities.

The resurgence of peasant and rural movements in Latin America combines: traditional forms of cohesion based on kinship, community and in many cases class and ethnic identity; modern goals and techniques; a strategic understanding of the levers of power in the national and international system; and the quest for an alternative form of development—either socialist or non-capitalist (cooperatives), including small holders who join in marketing or other cooperative forms.

In each case, whether with or without a strong emphasis on ethnic or racial identity, these movements struggle for an alternative to the prevailing capitalist system in its world-wide operations. Whether explicitly socialist or more limited in its objectives, all of these and other peasant-based social movements, particularly at the level of leadership, have exhibited a consistent orientation towards egalitarian and communitarian values as well as a capacity to transcend the traditionally narrow (almost parochial) focus of agrarian mobilizations in Latin America.

In general, Latin American peasants tend to see themselves as combatants in a class war unleashed by the capitalist class and its state apparatus. These movements present diverse ideological and political positions, depending on the circumstances. In every case, the state is confronted as "the enemy," a depository of the most reactionary social and political forces as well as the agent of antipeasant neo-liberal reforms. The movements continue to exhibit dynamic and diverse forms of struggle. They enter cross-class civic alliances to form or participate in a broad coalition of oppositional forces while maintaining clear autonomy in relation to political parties and nongovernmental organizations on the Left. These movements are a major sign of the radicalization of Latin American politics. Together with the growth of leftist electoral power in Brazil, Bolivia and Ecuador, Latin America is moving toward basic changes. The question is how costly in human suffering will they be—a question that can be answered in part by the degree to which US activists can stay the hand of Washington decision-makers.

Focusing on Latin America's New "Axis of Evil"

Implementing an agrarian land reform in Brazil is a major goal of President Luiz Inácio Lula da Silva's administration. To do this, the President chose Trotskyite-leaning Miguel Rossetto, the most radical member in his cabinet, as Land Reform Minister. This issue of *LulaWatch* will deal with the present status of land reform in Brazil.

1. Brazilian Land Reform before 2003

The left has always been obsessed with land reform. They cannot conceive a platform without a land reform plank which would deeply undermine and eventually destroy rural private property. French sociologist Alain Touraine, a well-known Brazilianist, says "the ideological share in the land reform plan is very heavy, while the economic projections of its effectiveness are relatively weak" (*O Estado de S. Paulo*, 4-20-03).

As in the ex- Soviet Union and today's Cuba, the pretext for land reform is to favor poor farmers. However, such farmers have actually been victims, rather than beneficiaries of land reform.

Over the last few decades, the media have saturated the Brazilian public with reports favoring land reform. However, the public has not jumped on the bandwagon. A recent Ibope/CNI survey shows that land reform holds a modest 11th place among the 18 main concerns of the population.

Land reform is hardly new to Brazil. The government started implementing it in 1960. It later gained momentum in 1985 with the end of the military regime, and was carried out on a large scale during the eight years of President Fernando Henrique Cardoso just prior to Lula's election.

Thus, Brazil has plenty of experience when it comes to land reform. The problem is that all of that experience has turned out to be bad. Wherever it has been tried, land reform has been a monumental failure.

In theory, Brazilian land reform is supposed to follow the following procedure:

    a. Expropriation of "large unproductive farms." This is a misnomer since such farms are usually not unproductive lands. Actually, they often are quite productive but deemed "unproductive" because they fail to meet the high degree of productivity set by government agencies. Expropriations are not paid in cash but with long-term government-issued bonds of low market value;

b. Once in possession of the land, the government divides it up in settlements (small plots) that are given to landless peasants for cultivation. The new owners are also given financing to set up operations, tend to their basic needs, and start planting;

c. These settlements or plots are usually brought together in cooperatives that administer the money coming from the government, buy machinery, seeds and other materials and turn over the land to the settler families as soon as they can function on their own.

This is the land reform theory in Brazil. What happens in the real world is quite different. Even the theory has a very strong dose of statism, as in socialist countries. Nothing is done naturally. The state is omnipresent at every stage. It expropriates the land, divides up the plots, inspects cooperatives, and decides when people can function on their own. It is the real owner. The great loser is the right of private property, which is profoundly weakened and even tends to disappear.

Today Brazil is one of the world's largest agricultural producers, particularly of grain and meat. However, this ever-increasing production comes from lands unaffected by land reform. Where land reform is implemented, production grinds to a halt. In the best of cases, settlement plots produce only enough for subsistence farming.

2. The Landless Movement (MST)

Land reform in practice is even more draconian than in theory. Pressure groups like the Landless Movement (MST) and similar organizations frequently invade and occupy lands in the hopes of forcing expropriations and hastening implementation of land reform policies.

The MST is a highly revolutionary movement whose writings explicitly call for seizing power and imposing socialism in Brazil. It has always been closely linked with the Workers Party (PT) of President Lula. Furthermore, many publications highlight MST links with Colombia's FARC and Mexico's Zapatista movement.

> "MST's armed clashes with police, the Army and security guards on farms invaded or under threat can lead Brazil to a bloody armed conflict like the one plaguing Colombia for more than three decades." This warning comes from none other than a member of the Central Staff of FARC-EP (Revolutionary Armed Forces of Colombia—People's Army). 'Open your eyes! That's how it started here,' advised Comandante Iván Rios in an exclusive interview with Jornal da Tarde (JT) in the village of Los Pozos in the demilitarized zone of Southern Colombia. . . . JT has learned from a well-placed source in the high command of FARC-EP that the organization 'maintains relations, in Brazil, with MST and Lula's party" (*Jornal da Tarde*, 5-24-2000).

The MST also foments unrest in the country. One of the MST's most conspicuous leaders, José Rainha Jr., speaks about freeing criminals as a stage to achieve social revolution. The press reports on drug-trafficking and cannabis production and consumption on land reform settlements. Illegal weapons have also been seized in the settlements with some frequency.

The MST was born from, and is driven by, the so-called Catholic left. The latter is made up by bishops, priests and laity who discarded traditional Catholic doctrine and adopted Marxism, though still cloaked in religion. This brand of "religious Marxism" is also known as Liberation Theology.

The Pastoral Commission on the Land (CPT) is one of the most active arms of the Brazilian National Bishops Conference (CNBB) and the main organization of the "Catholic left" active in rural areas. It encourages MST and participates in land invasions. CPT President, Bishop Tomás Balduíno, in an interview with *Jornal dos Sem-Terra* (translated as "Landless People's Newspaper") said "the name agrarian land reform is only barely acceptable; in fact what we seek is an agrarian revolution."

The MST breaks the law by invading farms, killing cattle, demolishing homes, destroying crops, taking hostages and fomenting violence even to the point of killing people. On occasion, they have clashed with or attacked the police. However, the leftist government and media have designated the MST as a "social movement," which puts it in a privileged position where it can break the law of the land with impunity.

The MST is an extremely useful vehicle for social revolution. It pressures and threatens landowners and thus facilitates government confiscation of farms. Many landowners are intimidated by the possibility of a MST invasion and destruction of their farms. They resign themselves to government expropriation under the law. Thus, land reform moves with a pincer-like movement. On one hand, the MST uses violent and threatening methods; on the other hand, the government implements legal and peaceful legislation. Both favor the same socialist and confiscatory goals.

The MST also controls settlers' cooperatives and (illegally) takes a cut in the government monies. Accusations of corruption are rife.

Finally, the MST constantly carries out other political activities unrelated to land reform. Its members, for example, can be seen demonstrating in front of American consulates against the Iraq war, the Free Trade Association of the Americas, and other issues. Its leaders admire Venezuelan president Hugo Chávez.

3. The Failure of Brazilian Land Reform

Prof. Plinio Corrêa de Oliveira, founder of the Brazilian TFP and its president for several decades, often emphasized the communist aspect of the land reform process and the fact that it was destined to fail. Yet, Brazilian governments shunned his warning and allowed land reform to be adopted as an untouchable myth. Today the fiasco of land reform is recognized by economists and journalists from all ideological hues. Even the PT, an ardently pro-agrarian reform party, and the government itself are forced to admit the failure.

It has failed economically. Settlements now cover an impressive 20 million hectares (the size of Panama and Nicaragua combined). Almost all of this area is completely unproductive. Only a few units produce enough for subsistence. Nearly a third of the settlements have been abandoned by their occupants. Other settlers linger on but find other jobs to survive. Finally, some settlers merely wander from one invasion to the next.

Socially, the failure is even greater. Without production, the settler cannot progress. He becomes dependent on the state and almost its slave. Without hope or future, he receives everything from the government in order to survive in his rural slum. He spends his life at protests begging for credit and benefits. He can do nothing by himself.

Financially, land reform has been an almost unbearable burden. The Fernando Henrique administration (1996–2002), settled 600,000 families at a cost of $12 billion, a hefty drag on Brazil's coffers, with no practical result (save to maintain the MST and its land invasion program).

The socialist left, nevertheless, has reaped some fruits from land reform. in its quest to implant a Marxist, Cuban-style government. To a certain extent it has wrought havoc to Brazilian farming and broken the traditional agricultural structures that have made Brazil great.

4. An Even More Socialist Land Reform under Lula

After so many resounding failures, now would seem the worst possible time to force land reform upon Brazil. Reflection about the issue is required. Brazilian TFP experts and other specialists claim not land reform but incentives to generate more jobs in the farm sector and to improve farm worker conditions are what can bring peace to rural areas and well-being for farmers.

Unfortunately, this is not happening. The Lula da Silva government seeks to carry land reform even further and throw even more good tax money after bad. Here are some of the proposals being debated:

a. A disastrous bill is already well advanced in Congress that would further relax the norms for land expropriation. Until now, the National Institute for Colonization and Agrarian Reform (INCRA), which implements land reform, offers farmers much less than market value for their farms and immediately takes possession of them. All the legitimate owner can do is fight that figure in court in suits that often take years. Presently, the owner can claim the interest due to him during the years at court. The proposed bill would deny payment of interest to the owners of expropriated areas. It also excludes from compensation areas of natural forest that the law obliges owners to maintain.

b. There is talk of a draconian application of a previous law without great concern for legal recourse that would revoke titles of property given by the government in the distant past in all areas within 100 miles of the country's borders. This strip of land involves some 30,000 rural properties. The new application would extend this measure not only to the distant past but to all those who later received the land in good faith. These could be stripped of their property.

c. Another crucial development is the ongoing legislative efforts to approve a law limiting the size of rural property. PT deputy Luci Choinaki proposed a constitutional amendment limiting the size of rural properties in Brazil to 35 rural modules (in Southern Brazil, a module is about 20 hectares). This attack against the principle of private property can have disastrous consequences on farming and cattle ranching.

d. Legislators want to review productivity requirements so that properties presently meeting productivity criteria can be labeled "unproductive" and thus expropriated by a land-grabbing Big Brother.

e. President Lula declared he would launch a great program extending credit to cooperatives so farm workers can organize. The organization of settlers in cooperatives has been often done by MST, which uses them as a means to socialize the land-reformed area. Such measures could eventually lead to the implantation of a new type of Soviet kolkhoz system.

f. One goal of Minister Rossetto is to withhold property titles from settlers. The government would own the land while settlers would have neither property nor possession but only a right to use the land. This would amount to a type of collectivization of lands similar to that carried out by communist governments.

5. The 'Zero Hunger' Program at the Service of the MST

The Zero Hunger Program of the Lula administration provides yet more support for the MST by supplying the 'landless' agitators with a large quantity of basic 'food baskets.' This may reduce poverty but, above all, it keeps the MST actively invading lands. According to INCRA's superintendent in the State of Piauí, Fr. Ladislau João da Silva, distributing food baskets "helps the men and women workers to resist in their struggle for land" (*Meio Norte*, Teresina, 4-30-03).

INCRA president Marcelo Resende claimed that "the question of resources [for land reform] will be linked to the Zero Hunger Program. We will tie it in with Zero Hunger in order to optimize the actions of INCRA" ("Zero para otimizar as ações do INCRA," *Zero Hora*, 1-16-03).

Brazilian sociologist Prof. Zander Navarro teaches the post-graduate program on rural development at Rio Grande do Sul's Federal University. He is a specialist on rural social movements. He also has a doctorate from Sussex University in England and a post-doctorate at the Massachusetts Institute of Technology. He states: "MST is actually the Party [PT] founder in dozens of municipalities and its leading militants are active in Party life. . . . We can affirm, with no margin of error, that it is presently an organization that survives mainly from public funds and is therefore a quasi-state organization" (*O Estado de S. Paulo*, 5-5-03).

The government is quick to disregard MST's illegal actions like land invasions. The Minister for Agrarian Development, Miguel Rossetto, said: "Repressing demonstrations is not the ministry's business."

It is no wonder that Pará State's main newspaper, *O Liberal*, commented: "The landless peasants have arrived in power with their weapons, luggage and tents. There is no question that we will see a scenario where the tendency is an advance of illegality and criminal daring that translates into [land] invasions" (4-14-03).

6. MST Has Now Become Government

In the Lula da Silva administration, members of MST and CPT have been placed in strategic posts where they can implement land reform in accordance with their own socialist-communist imaginings.

Members of the MST and CPT now hold the posts of state supervisors of INCRA. The presidency of INCRA was given to Marcelo Resende, a CPT member. When asked if the federal government has means to prevent land invasions, Mr. Resende was peremptory: "Absolutely not. There is no instrument for that" (*Zero Hora*, 1-16-03).

"Under Luiz Inácio Lula da Silva," comments the Folha de S. Paulo (2-19-03), "INCRA has been turned into an extension of MST, CUT, the left wing of PT and the progressive current of the Catholic Church. . . . The lottery of posts [of INCRA state supervisors] was guided by ideological criteria." According to O Globo (5-6-03) the Ministry of Land Reform gave "the state apparatus over to one of the litigants [MST]."

Faithful to its socialist principles that produce equality in misery, the MST is against large scale agricultural production for export. The movement's leaders are already studying the launching of a campaign to combat the capitalist agricultural model now in force, a vigorous and enterprising agribusiness with a highly positive impact on the Brazilian balance of trade.

Friar Betto, a special aide to the President, is a key man of the "Catholic left" both because of his past links with communist guerrillas, terrorists and Nicaragua's Sandinistas, and his present close connections with Fidel Castro. This Dominican friar believes nothing can shake the "partnership" between MST and the government, not even the recent invasions and vandalizing of public buildings (*Jornal do Brasil*, 3-8-03).

Landowners say that they "can no longer put up" with the MST and that "the goal of farmers is to demonstrate publicly their indignation with the position of the Lula da Silva government in the land dispute" (*Folha de S. Paulo*, 5-5-03).

All indications are that if the Lula government maintains its orientation on land reform, the failures of this program will be aggravated even further and can cause the terrible traumas it produced in communist countries.

POSTSCRIPT

Is Expropriating Land and Giving It to the Poor a Good Economic and Cultural Policy?

James Petras and Henry Veltmeyer assert that peasant and landless movements in a variety of countries are working to combat a "class war unleashed by the capitalist class and its state apparatus." The "class war" that Petras and Veltmeyer refer to is the great disparity in Latin America between the wealthy and the poor, which leads to a number of issues related to inequity and imbalance. Oftentimes, the poor and landless express a frustration of feeling voiceless, claiming that issues related to justice and the rule of law are precluded by special interests and cronyism among powerful political figures, corporate magnates, members of law enforcement, and wealthy landowners. Therefore, when questions of land ownership arise, many feel that they are at a disadvantage in trying to reclaim their right to land they believe is theirs. For indigenous peoples whose land was taken centuries ago at the time of the Conquest or even in recent years, for example, establishing the rightful ownership of a piece of land is extremely complicated. Of course, twenty-first-century native populations are not alone in their seeking land reform as other impoverished populations have begun attempts to reclaim what they feel are injustices, particularly revolving around land reform.

However, LulaWatch maintains that when governments expropriate lands that are legitimately owned, it undermines the rule of law. In addition, when land is redistributed to landless farmers, they may not have the means to make the land productive or profitable. LulaWatch also argues that governments that succumb to law-breaking groups such MST subvert their own ability to govern effectively and that conceding to these movements only exacerbates the problem by encouraging other similar groups to appeal to the government for more land reform.

Brazil's uneven distribution of land is among the world's most pronounced, and it is estimated that approximately two-thirds of Brazil's land is owned by roughly 3 percent of its citizens. Given the historical legacy of injustice, abuse, and a lack of continuity in the application of land reform policy in Latin America, many feel that these movements are justified in their causes. For example, many priests, nuns, and Christian communities that identify themselves with "Liberation Theology" support the notion of land reform. Although the Vatican has asked the Catholic Church and its representatives to remain impartial regarding political alliances, some clergy in the Latin American Catholic church believe groups like MST act in support of the dispossessed and are willing to march in support of the movement or provide dissenters with asylum, if needed. The involvement of the clergy has not been without controversy. In 2005, Dorothy Stang, a U.S.-born Catholic nun and an activist in peasants' and environmental rights, was violently killed by a Brazilian landowner because of her position on land reform (http://www .mstbrazil.org/?q=openlettertolula).

A principle commonly associated with Mahatma Gandhi and Martin Luther King Jr., MST identifies the strategy of non-violent rebellion as the method through which it wishes to exact land reform. Nonetheless, detractors of the mission and/or the tactics of organizations like MST point to the violence, intimidation, and kidnappings that many of these movements have fostered—intentionally or not. And, due to violence sparked by MST's strategies and landowners' reaction to them, in 2005, a "congressional inquiry in Brazil has called for land invasions to be declared acts of terrorism" ("Brazil Land Invasion 'Terrorism'," *BBC News*, November 30, 2005). One of the most criticized movements associated with land reform is FARC. Although Petras and Veltmeyer view this movement as "a complex organization whose main constituency includes subsistence farmers, displaced peasants, landless rural workers and a sector of urban workers and employees," LulaWatch sees FARC—a group that many consider to be a terrorist organization—as an example of how the land reform movement is not what it purports itself to be and fears that FARC currently "maintains relations, in Brazil, with MST and Lula's party."

In a move that "some fear could inflame the divisions between rich and poor," the recently elected President Morales of Boliva announced in June 2006 that the government will redistribute plots of idle land to the poor. The government will "start by redistributing about 12 million acres of state-owned land to indigenous rural workers." The move could affect one-fourth of the population ("Bolivia Plans to Redistribute Idle Farmland," *Washington Post*, May 18, 2006). Through this plan, "Morales hopes to speed up a process that has dragged on for more than a decade due to an inefficient justice system and tangled title disputes. The targeted state land was set aside for redistribution before Morales took office in January" ("Two Shot and Injured in Bolivian Land Conflicts," *Jamaica Observer*, June 9, 2006).

For information on Chile's indigenous land reform movement, read "The Autonomous Mapuche Movement in Chile" by Jed Kinnison and Sebastián Guzmán (LeftTurn.org). To learn about agrarian reform in Guatemala, see Lisa Viscidi's "La Plataforma Agraria: Land Reform and Conflict in Guatemala" (September 8, 2004). In "Land Reforms in Latin America: Ten Lessons toward a Contemporary Agenda" (2002), Alain de Janvry and Elisabeth Sadoulet offer guidelines for future programs of access to land. Luiz Antonio Nabhan Garcia, president of Brazil's national association of agricultural landowners, offers his perspective on MST and land reform in "Brazil's Ideology-Based Land Grab: A Pointless, Wasteful Exercise" (April 17–23, 2004).

On the Internet . . .

United Nations Development Programme (UNDP): Latin America and the Caribbean

The UNDP's regional office for Latin America and the Caribbean "offers policy advice on sensitive socio-economic and political development issues." It seeks to help governments in the region in "planning and managing development programmes." UNDP's home page contains country and thematic reports on Millennium Development Goals and information on its programs on poverty reduction, energy and the environment, democratic governance, and HIV/AIDS.

http://www.undp.org/regions/latinamerica/

World Bank Group: Latin America and Caribbean

The World Bank's purpose is to be a "source of financial and technical assistance to developing countries around the world." Its regional office for Latin America and the Caribbean seeks to reduce poverty through "higher competitiveness) employment and growth" and "support to institutions to enhance equity, inclusion and sustainability." This site offers data and statistics as well as links for information on gender, poverty, civil society, public sector governance, and economic policy.

http://www.worldbank.org/lac

Economy/Development in Latin America (Latin American Network Information Center)

Economy in Latin America and Development in Latin America are resource pages of the Latin American Network Information Center (LANIC) at the University of Texas at Austin. LANIC's economy page includes content areas on business, economy, finance, internet, economy and E-commerce, management, statistics, and trade. Its development page includes links for country, regional, and international resources.

http://lanic.utexas.edu/la/region/development/

http://lanic.utexas.edu/subject/economy/

Choike: International Financial Institutions Latin American Monitor

Choike's International Financial Institution (IFI) Latin American Monitor seeks "reform of the Bretton Woods institutions." IFI's Latin American Monitor home page includes articles that critique the policies of the World Bank, the International Monetary Fund, the World Trade Organization, and General Agreement on Trade in Services (GATS).

http://ifis.choike.org/

PART 4

Economics and Development

*A*lthough not new to the region, Latin America has recently witnessed heated discussions on economics and development. Underlying these debates is the very definition of development as well as competing visions on the best way to improve the standard of living of the people of the region.

Some feel economic and developmental actions and policies only exacerbate existing problems in Latin America; others believe that if the practices of countries like the United States were adopted, similar prosperity would emerge throughout Latin America. However, with the investment and direction often originating outside of Latin America, the question continues to linger—is it unwanted meddling or developmental assistance?

- Do the Social and Economic Costs of Privatization Outweigh Its Benefits?

- Is the Free Trade Area of the Americas (FTAA) Good for Latin America?

- Is International Aid Successfully Promoting Development and Stability in Latin America?

ISSUE 16

Do the Social and Economic Costs of Privatization Outweigh Its Benefits?

YES: Raúl Zibechi, from "Privatizations: The End of a Cycle of Plundering," *Americas Program, Interhemispheric Resource Center* (November 1, 2004)

NO: Naomi Adelson, from "Water Woes: Private Investment Plugs Leaks in Water Sector," *Business Mexico* (March 2000)

ISSUE SUMMARY

YES: Raúl Zibechi, professor, journalist, and researcher at the Universidad Fransicana de América Latina, details the history behind neoliberal economic policy in Latin America and contends that one of its cornerstones, the privatization of state-owned enterprises, imposes financial and human hardship in the region and is a new form of plundering and conquest.

NO: Naomi Adelson, a Mexico City–based freelance reporter, explains that the Mexican government is financially unable to manage its colossal water-related concerns including sanitation, variable population distribution, and high levels of leakage. Privatization ventures, she contends, offer efficiency and the financial resources necessary to improve water services and infrastructure.

$\mathbf{F}$rom water and power plants to telecommunication systems and rail lines, over the past two decades Latin America has experienced waves of privatizations of previously state-owned entities. The opposite of nationalization, privatization is the process by which ownership is transferred from the public to the private sphere. For example, in 1990 ownership of Argentina's telecommunications firm ENTEL was transferred to the Spanish firm Telefónica and the French company, Telecom. From the end of the World War II to the mid-1980s, these and other services were primarily state-owned (George R.G. Clarke, et. al., World Bank, 2004). As the first of the following selections explains in detail, the privatization of publicly owned entities in Latin America is part of the economic structural readjustment policies overseen by the World Bank and the International Monetary Fund. Under these policies, public entities are sold to private companies to reduce the government's external debt. Privatization is considered one of the cornerstones of neoliberal economic policies. In Latin America, privatization and neoliberalism are often associated with the fiscal policies that have come to be defined as the Washington Consensus.

Proponents maintain that, in addition to reducing public debt, privatization increases tax revenues for the state, boosts competition of business, and offers more choice of services to the consumer. Those who favor decentralization also underscore that privately owned utilities are more efficient because it is in the interest of the private owner to invest in services to generate a profit. Because of corruption and a lack of resources, it is argued, state-owned entities are not able to offer the quality of services that private companies offer. After privatization in "Mexico, the waiting time for new telephone connection dropped from 890 to 30 days" and in "Argentina, the number of phone lines more than doubled, from 3.1 million to 6.85 million" (John Nellis, et al, "Privatization in Latin America," *Center for Global Development,* 2004). A study by Sebastian Galiani, Paul Gertler, and Ernesto Schargrodsky in 2002 also showed that since the privatization of the local water companies in Argentina during the 1990s, "child mortality fell 5 to 7 percent in areas that privatized their water services overall; and that the effect was largest in the poorest areas" ("Water for Life: The Impact of the Privatization of Water Services on Child Mortality," unpublished).

Despite these positive results from privatization, *Latinobarámetro's* 2004 opinion polls indicted that a clear majority of Latin Americans surveyed believed that privatization had not been beneficial. From a global perspective, "privatization has provoked more popular discontent and criticism in Latin America than in other parts of the world" (John Nellis, et al, *CGD,* 2004). Latin Americans have severely criticized the privatization of utilities like water, electricity, and transportation services. In the 2000 Water War in Cochabamba, Bolivia, thousands participated in general strikes and transportation blockages to protest rising water prices that resulted from the sale of Bolivia's water services to foreign investors. In Paraguay in 2002, the Democratic People's Congress mobilized the participation of thousands of citizens to protest and eventually halt the passage of their nation's privatizations law.

According to the Center for Global Development, "[it] is incontestable that a number of Latin American privatizations have resulted in job losses." In Nicaragua, for example, "privatization resulted in the dismissal of 15 percent of the total labor force," and "[approximately] 50 percent of all employees in firms privatized in Mexico lost their jobs" (John Nellis, et al, 2004). In addition to job losses, some Latin Americans reject the idea of selling their utilities to foreign corporations. The word "privatization" has become such a politically charged term that, for its critics, it is a perceived threat.

Raúl Zibechi details the history and effects of privatization in a variety of Latin American countries. Zibechi contends that this cornerstone of neoliberal economic policy imposes financial and human hardship in the region and represents a new form of conquest and plunder. Naomi Adelson argues that the Mexican government does not have the financial resources to manage its enormous water-related concerns and that privatization will offer efficiency of services and improvements in infrastructure.

YES

Raúl Zibechi

Privatizations: The End of a Cycle of Plundering

One of the cornerstones of the neoliberal policies adopted by most Latin American governments in the 1990s was the privatization of state-owned enterprises. This process of passing national wealth on to the private sector has been so injurious that it could soon render entire countries unviable. On occasion, citizen organization has succeeded in halting privatizations through public demonstrations that at times have turned into outright insurrections.

The public has almost always viewed state-owned enterprises as "its own," and to a certain extent these companies have served public or national interests. Many state-owned enterprises were created following the economic crisis of 1929 and especially during and after World War II. During those years, the decline of Great Britain as the hegemonic power in Latin America and its replacement by the United States encouraged tentative development based on a more active role for nation-states in economic management through import-substitution industrialization.

State-owned enterprises—generally services, transport providers, or manufacturers—were part of the national wealth, although they were known to be mismanaged and to primarily benefit the political elite. Though state-owned companies were necessary for countries attempting to industrialize, many governments used them to perpetuate their power by doling out favors and privileges. These practices, along with inefficient management, undermined state enterprises by unnecessarily bloating employee rosters, thereby reducing efficiency and raising costs.

Consequently, in varying degrees from one country to the next services provided by state-owned enterprises deteriorated for three decades following the end of WWII. Many had fallen into serious financial crisis. This state of affairs greatly facilitated the work of the privatizers of the eighties. Promising efficiency to consumers fed up with shoddy goods and second-rate services, this first wave of privatization encountered little effective resistance.

The Debt Crisis

Broadly speaking, "the privatization of state enterprises is always linked to the renegotiation of a country's foreign debt," notes Belgian economist Eric Toussaint, president of the Committee for the Abolition of Third World Debt.[1]

The roots of privatization policy can therefore be traced back to the so-called "debt crisis" ignited by Mexico's payment moratorium in August 1982.

At that time, Washington was facing a crisis in its global hegemony caused by the United States' military defeat in Vietnam, domestic antiwar protests allied with the black civil rights movement, and the demands of Third World countries. This erosion of power culminated when the Iranian Revolution of 1979 sparked the hostage crisis the following year.

The convergence of these multiple challenges laid bare the declining hegemony of the world's most powerful nation and *ushered in a long-term shift: "Domestic and global New Deals* were abandoned, and the United States tried to restore its military prestige. To pay for increased military expenses for the Second Cold War, it raised interest rates and began to compete actively for international capital in search of investment. During the 1980s, it attracted the global surplus and precipitated the 'debt crisis,' signaling the abandonment of the promise of 'development.'"[2] As the U.S. Federal Reserve hiked interest rates, loans to poor countries were drastically curtailed, preventing them from obtaining new loans to repay their debts. As a result, Third World debt became unpayable.

Until the 1980s, Third World indebtedness had several objectives: to create an outlet for Eurodollars accumulated in financial markets, to encourage arms purchases, and to lubricate the corruption mechanisms of pro-U.S. governments. By design, Third World debt did not affect the balance of payments of the lending countries. To give just one example, two-thirds of all debt assumed by the Argentine military dictatorship (1976–83) was deposited in bank accounts in the North.[3] Needless to say, the money lent—largely as "aid" to poor countries—often never arrived or arrived piecemeal to the economies of the recipient countries and their constituencies.

The Brady Plan, devised in the 1980s, required bilateral accords between Latin American countries and U.S. authorities on the reduction or staggering of debt payments.[4] One of the linchpins of the Brady Plan was the privatization of state-owned enterprises. In 1985, after a conference on foreign debt in Berne, Henry Kissinger was characteristically blunt: "There is no painless solution to their critical situation, but we must promote some corrections to the IMF's adjustment program. The solution will entail sacrifice; I prefer that debtor nations ensure their external obligations vis-à-vis their creditors rather than receive aid in the form of real assets, by surrendering the assets of state companies."[5]

To ensure their ability to repay their debts, countries adopted structural adjustment policies promoted by the International Monetary Fund (IMF) and the World Bank (WB). As far back as the early 1980s, those two bodies became the debt crisis managers and were put in charge of implementing adjustment policies and collecting debt payments. IMF- and WB-promoted adjustments touted macroeconomic stabilization (devaluation, lifting of price controls, and fiscal austerity) as a first step on the path to structural reforms based on trade opening, deregulation of banks and financial activities, greater labor-market flexibility, and privatization.

This set of policies clearly entails a loss of economic sovereignty for countries applying them. In addition, debtor nations had to forfeit their political sovereignty, either beforehand or simultaneously. As dictatorships and corrupt democracies did the "dirty work" of applying the reforms, foreign debt in Latin America multiplied eightfold between 1971 and 1980.

In nearly every Latin American country, state-owned companies were already heavily indebted, since governments used them to contract debt as a way of obtaining loans from private banks. In 1976, at the beginning of military rule, Argentina's state-owned petroleum company, YPF, had a debt of only $372 million. Seven years later it owed $6 billion, and nearly all of the money borrowed remained in the hands of the dictatorship without entering the coffers of the company. YPF was forced to send its petroleum to private refineries, since it was not permitted to acquire its own refinery. In 1982, when the dictatorship ended, nearly all of the company's assets had been collateralized for debts.[6] As a result, when the company was privatized the sale price did not even cover outstanding debts. The debt merely served to enrich those in charge of implementing the policies of dependence and subordination.

A Gangster Style of Operating

Joseph Stiglitz, 2001 Nobel Prize winner in economics, former chairman of the Council of Economic Advisers for the Clinton administration, and former vice president of the World Bank, argues that one of the main problems with the IMF- and WB-promoted privatization policy was that it "had to be carried out quickly." Thus countries that "privatized more quickly received the highest scores."[7] Stiglitz, a proponent of privatization, complains that the privatizations were carried out without the proper controls, that they replaced public monopolies with private monopolies so burdening consumers, and that they were shrouded in corruption and bribes.

In Latin America, privatization has not only decimated countries such as Argentina and Peru, but has also exacted a high human cost. Consider, for example, the October 2003 massacre during the "gas war," in which Bolivians attempted to recover control of their main natural resource that a succession of neoliberal governments had surrendered to Repsol-YPF, Shell, Enron, and Petrobras.

Several significant cases reveal the *modus operandi* employed in the rush to privatize. In Argentina, a privatizer's paradise, the first company to be put on the auction block was ENTEL, a telecommunications firm. Although its appraised value was $3.1 billion, the government set the minimum bid at $214 million. The sale needed the approval of the company's creditors. After several delays and numerous irregularities, ENTEL was sold to a joint bid by the Spanish firm Telefónica and France Telecom. The companies paid a total of only $214 million in cash; the remainder consisted of the acquisition of foreign debt. At the time of privatization, ENTEL's debt totaled $1.9 billion—$1.4 billion to foreign creditors and $500 million to Argentine contractors.

Although the government had promised to invest the privatization proceeds in health and education, 60% was used for foreign debt payments, and the remaining 40%, according to researcher Daniel Muchnik, "was lost in the back alleys of public administration accounting."[8]

Carlos Menem's government merely continued the corrupt ways of the Argentine military dictatorship. Between 1990 and 1992 the Menem government privatized much of the nation's wealth, precipitating $60 billion in losses. In the privatization of YPF, U.S.-based Merrill Lynch was given the task of assessing the company's value. But Merrill Lynch deliberately underestimated the company's oil reserves by 30% to reduce YPF's appraised value. Once the privatization had concluded, the hidden reserves reappeared on the books, and the purchasers thus reaped fabulous profits, thanks to the immediate increase in the stock market valuation of YPF shares.

In what might seem like a bad joke, "Argentina's Central Bank stated that because it had no record of public foreign debt, the Argentine authorities that succeeded the dictatorship had to rely on declarations from foreign creditors and contracts signed by the members of the dictatorship, without these contracts having been verified by the Central Bank."[9] Moreover, the military government nationalized private debt contracted by the affiliates of Renault, Mercedes-Benz, Ford, IBM, Citibank, Chase Manhattan Bank, and Bank of America, among others. In 1981 and 1982, exchange risk insurance regimes were established—the state ensured a preferential exchange rate for these companies—through which a large part of the debts of those economic groups was transferred to the state. . . .

In Bolivia, the October 20, 1999, passage of Law 2029 privatizing drinking water services took place with no public consultation whatsoever. To avoid a debate on water resources, Bolivia's ruling coalition entered into a temporary alliance with its main political opponent, the MNR. The MNR is the party of former president Gonzalo Sánchez de Lozada, under whose administration the current economic model was designed. Law 2029 enacted regulations regarding the provision of drinking water and access to water sources for any use, granting exclusive rights to the licensee without taking into account the practices and customs of communities and social organizations, which were to become mere consumers of the services provided by the concession holder. The law pegged rate increases to the U.S. Consumer Price Index and gave legal status to contracts held by companies such as Aguas del Tunari, a subsidiary of the London-based International Water Limited, owned by Bechtel Enterprises of San Francisco, California, and Edison of Milan, Italy.

[In] Bolivia (as well as in [Peru,] Paraguay and Uruguay), . . . privatizations sparked strong social opposition, leading to popular uprisings in several cases.

A Shocking Failure

Not only did the privatizations take place against a backdrop of rampant corruption and plundering of national resources; they were also a commercial failure, and the population of the countries involved ended up footing the bill. Meanwhile, poorer-quality services, higher rates, and a deterioration in infrastructure due to a lack of investment resulted in fabulous profits for multinational corporations.

A recent book by the American geographer David Harvey explains the logic of privatization.[10] Given the growing difficulty of obtaining profits, due to an overabundance of capital and a dearth of opportunities to profitably invest it, global elites developed what Harvey calls "accumulation by dispossession." This term refers to the fencing of communal land in Victorian England, which served as the catalyst for capitalist expansion.

But unlike the expropriation of communal lands—and the entire process of plunder, war, and colonial conquest through which capitalism established its ascendancy—the accumulation by dispossession currently under way combines brutal forms with more subtle "legal" types of dispossession: biopiracy, intellectual property rights, the pillaging of humanity's genetic resources by a half dozen pharmaceutical companies, and privatization. Indeed, in capitalism's current phase, neoliberalism "internalizes cannibalistic, predatory, and fraudulent practices" that once seemed eradicated.[11] Most importantly, Harvey's analysis shows that in the current economic era, corruption is the system's "habitual" way of operating.

In response to the large number of irregularities in Argentina's privatized companies, Néstor Kirchner's minister of economy, Roberto Lavagna, requested a report from the General Auditing Office of the Nation. The agency compiled 40 studies on privatizations conducted since 1993, and found that companies do not comply with investment commitments, modify work plans, amounts and time schedules without authorization; do not comply with minimum asset requirements set forth in contracts to ensure solvency; resort to borrowing to finance operations; owe payments to the pension system; modify stock-options packages, despite contract prohibitions against this practice; and fail to protect assets.

Moreover, privatized companies fail to take out insurance or allow their policies to expire, adjust rates in violation of their contracts, neglect to pay fines imposed by regulators, lack complaint-reception procedures, and fail to submit government-required documentation. Several of the studies recommend that many privatization contracts be rescinded.[12]

A recent report by FLASCO (Latin American Faculty of Social Sciences) asserts that privatized companies in Argentina reap profits unparalleled anywhere else in the world. From 1993 to 1999, the country's 200 largest businesses generated 25.9 billion dollars in profits; 54% of these profits accrued to 26 companies, which grossed $2 billion a year. The study concludes that in the 1990s, "the average profitability of privatized companies was between seven and eight times higher than the rest of the country's largest firms." The study also notes that illegal rate increases were levied, the quality of services worsened, and employee rosters were cut, resulting in a "transfer of resources, first, from wage-earning and low-income sectors to business sectors, and, second, within businesses, from small and medium enterprises to large ones."[13] Though the Argentine and Peruvian cases are among the most extreme, they illustrate how privatization has contributed to the concentration of wealth, eroding economic security for most people, polarizing countries, and undermining social harmony.

Resistance: From Opposition to Insurrection

In the final decades of the past century, broad popular struggles in Latin America took aim at fiscal adjustment policies (the "Caracazo" in 1989) or at the corruption endemic to neoliberal governments (the "impeachment" of

Brazilian President Fernando Collor de Melo in 1992) or at neoliberal policies generally, in nearly every country. This resistance intensified beginning in about 2000.

A series of struggles against privatizations succeeded in imposing bottom-up changes in neoliberal policies vis-à-vis state-owned enterprises. Most notable are the early-2000 uprising in Cochabamba over control of aquifer resources, the broad-based struggles in Peru and Paraguay in 2002, and the 2003 referendum in Uruguay on the privatization of the state oil company.

As the failure of privatization became evident, opposition grew more radical. Protests and referendums gave way to direct action in a process that accelerated toward the end of the 1990s from the revolts in Arequipa, Cochabamba, and Paraguay to the events of December 19 and 20, 2001, in Argentina and the gas war in Bolivia in September and October 2003. Neoliberal policies—especially privatizations—catalyzed opposition forces, uniting diverse social sectors including workers, the unemployed, and the middle class and triggering unprecedented crises.

[Two] examples illustrate this radicalizing transition. In Uruguay the grassroots movement has often used legal mechanisms to repeal laws. By submitting the signatures of 25% of registered voters, activists can force the executive branch to call a referendum. In December 1992, during the term of Luís Alberto Lacalle, a broad social, trade-union, and political movement succeeded in blocking the State Companies Law (which called for several privatizations), when 72% of the votes cast in a referendum favored repeal. In 2002, the union of the state-owned oil company, ANCAP, the trade-union movement, and the political left obtained enough signatures to force another referendum. An overwhelming 62% of the voters favored repeal, while 35% voted in favor of leaving it on the books.

In countries without legal safeguards to prevent privatization, people have resorted to direct action. . . .

An entire book could be written about Bolivia's "water war" in the city of Cochabamba. This was the first victorious large-scale street battle with specific objectives in many years and succeeded in coalescing very diverse social actors: workers, peasants, Indians, housewives, professionals, and young people. In early 2000, the Coordinadora por el Agua y por la Vida (Coordinating Group for Water and Life) was created as an umbrella group comprising a Water Defense Committee; Irrigators Federations; unions of factory workers, teachers, merchants, and peasants; and associations of professionals, including engineers, lawyers, and economists. The Coordinadora convened a popular consultation for Sunday, March 26, after marches, town meetings, and mobilizations were severely repressed by military deployments in the city. Fifty thousand persons expressed their opinion at more than 140 polling stations in every neighborhood in the city.

Based on the outcome of the consultation, starting April 4, calls were made for a general shutdown of the city and key roads. Appeals were issued for the government to find a definitive solution to the water problem, amid warnings that the "final battle" was beginning. Demands were made for the privatizing company, Aguas del Tunari, to leave the region, for water rates to be frozen, and for water privatization to be repealed. Starting April 4, the Coordinadora began its strike by closing local roads. It was joined by the Campesino Federation (CSUTCB), which blocked roads throughout the country. Workers of one airline (LAB) even delayed flights in support of the struggle in Cochabamba. Four days into the general strike, military and police forces seized Cochabamba's main plaza, which was packed with protestors, arrested the Coordinadora leaders, and declared a state of siege.

In the rural areas of the department of La Paz, three town meetings were held (the most important, in Achacachi near Lake Titicaca, was attended by 15,000 Indians) ratifying proposals to continue with the highway blockages. On April 7, Cochabamba was once again taken over by thousands of protestors, who regained the plaza and faced down the forces of repression. The mayor announced that Aguas del Tunari would leave, and a grassroots celebration broke out. Members of the military and police were cowed into returning to their barracks by the massive presence of the street protestors. In this climate, on April 10, the government acquiesced, signed an agreement with peasant groups, and confirmed that Aguas del Tunari would depart.

The Cochabamba insurrection witnessed "unprecedented forms of organization, capable of harboring a modern, hybrid proletarization of the urban population and the expansion of discursive constructs firmly anchored in a self-recognition of want, suffering, and laboriousness." Marches and strikes—usually deemed appropriate for moments of upsurge—were eschewed as the main form of struggle in favor of the occupation of spaces. Grassroots opinion was polled through town meetings, and traditional representation gave way to self-representation. Such representation, exemplified by the multitudes in the street, was "an all-out expression of local self-organization," a powerful network of power, mobilization, and territorial and regional self-control.[14]

An analysis of how opposition to privatization moved from disarray to militancy potency reveals its intense mobilization and the changes away from the centrality of the worker as the main social actor. "Each neighborhood, each water committee, began to arrive at the plaza with its leaders and banners at the fore of compact formations of young people, of men and women brandishing sticks, bottles, Molotov cocktails, rocks, and knives. Each neighborhood, agrarian union, and water committee had decided to wage war and was willing to do so. . . . The militarization of local structures of mobilization later led to the emergence of water warriors who entrenched themselves in Plaza 14 de Septiembre for the three following days."[15] . . .

Tentative Balance: Social and Political Crisis

Seen through the prism of grassroots struggle, the victorious campaigns against privatizations in . . . Uruguay and Bolivia reveal how new social actors have evolved in the wake of changes promoted through two decades of neoliberalism. [Zibechi also critiques privatizations in Brazil, Peru, and Paraguay. He details events related to resistance against privatization in Peru and Paraguay. —Ed.] These conflicts also reveal the fragility of nation-states, the emergence of new forms of struggle, and the maturing of relations between social and political stakeholders.

Since 2000 the social sector has regrouped—as manifested in the struggles against privatizations—following setbacks in the 1980s and 1990s. However, this offensive occurred within a social landscape modified by the neoliberal model. The most obvious tactical adaptations embraced by grassroots activists are related to the nonexistence of a central stakeholder comparable to workers in the previous period. In their stead a diverse ensemble of protagonists (from informally employed and unemployed laborers to technicians and professionals) has emerged, establishing de facto alliances responding to concrete situations. In all cases, there has been a tendency for distinct relations to be established between social forces and political ones. The vitality of the mobilizations has been provided by the former, while the latter seek to reshape old structures on the left (as in the Bolivian case) or are excluded offstage (as in Peru).

The South American struggles against privatization also reveal the increasing weakness of nation-states. Except in Uruguay, where the state has maintained discipline over civil society, governments have exhibited a striking inability to resolve social conflict without resorting to repression. This undermining of social contracts is directly related to neoliberal policies and to the further weakening of the traditional left throughout most of the continent.

Sociocultural changes are reflected in changing forms of struggle, closely linked to the crisis of representation experienced in most Latin American countries. Road closings and insurrectional mobilizations have nudged into the political space once occupied by the labor movement's strikes and work stoppages. These innovative forms of struggle have two noteworthy characteristics: they represent the emergence of geographically delimited stakeholders with a new configuration and spatial relationship in which shantytown dwellers, peasants, the unemployed, women, and young people all play a significant role. Grassroots movements seize public spaces, because they reject representation. By organizing independently, they give life to a new grassroots force that has characterized the most important civic battles in recent years in Latin America.

Same Old Problems, New Questions

Lastly, a new debate is taking shape that is intimately related both to the failure of privatizations and to the success of struggles against neoliberalism: What is to be done with the privatized companies? How are they to be recovered? And, above all, how are they to be managed, and who is to manage them?

The recent referendum in Bolivia may provide some insights. First, the social movement, which appeared very united in its opposition to privatization, fragmented when solutions were sought. The Bolivian people's solidarity in defending the gas nationalization with their lives evaporated when Carlos Mesa's government called for the July 18 consultation.

The problem, in the end, is the state. An increasing number of social sectors are suspicious of governments' capacity to properly manage national resources. The memory of corruption in the managing of companies that were later privatized undermines the option of state ownership. Nevertheless, the debate is still alive. In Bolivia, since both the water war in Cochabamba and the October 2003 uprising over the gas issue, as well as in Argentina and in many other countries, these issues are being hotly debated.

The choice is no longer reduced to public vs. private ownership. The Argentine economist Julio Gambina, echoing the sentiment of popular assemblies and piquetero (unemployed) groups, recognizes that the outright nationalization of the privatized companies is not the answer, "because [nationalized companies] end up being bureaucratic and subjugated to the political group that happens to run the state at a given moment."[16] No one has ready-made alternatives, but the ongoing debates reveal possibilities for state-run or, at least, mixed management: cooperative companies run by users by users, with the possible participation of the state, and for creating a flexible social space capable of accommodating non-state-run companies, mutuals, cooperatives, and community organizations.

All of these options can be open to joint management by consumers, workers, and perhaps the state. This still-inchoate debate has an enormous virtue: it channels the concerns of common people in a new direction—toward resolving how to achieve empowerment vis-à-vis public assets without blindly handing over their management to some outside expert. If this direction is strengthened and clarified, the terrible history of privatizations might yet have a happy ending.

Notes

1. Eric Toussaint, *Deuda externa en el Tercer Mundo: las finanzas contra los pueblos,* (Caracas: Nueva Sociedad, 1998), p. 141.

2. Giovanni Arrighi and Beverly Silver, *Chaos and Governance in the Modern World System* (Minneapolis: University of Minnesota Press, 1999). Quote taken from *Caos y orden en el sistema-mundo moderno* (Madrid: Akal, 2001), p. 219.

3. Toussaint, *Dueda externa,* p. 86.

4. Nicholas Brady was then secretary of the treasury.

5. Quoted by Toussaint, *Dueda externa,* p. 79.

6. Toussaint, *Dueda externa,* p. 189.

7. Joseph Stiglitz, *Globalization and Its Discontents.* Quotes taken from Spanish translation: *El malestar en la globalización* (Buenos Aires: Taurus, 2002), p. 90.

8. Daniel Muchnik, *Plata fácil. Los empresarios y el poder en la Argentina* (Buenos Aires: Norma, 2001), p. 227.

9. Toussaint, *Dueda externa,* p. 191.

10. David Harvey, *New Imperialism* (Oxford University Press, 2003). Quotes from the Spanish edition: *El nuevo imperialismo,* (Madrid: Akal, 2004).

11. Harvey, *New Imperialism,* p. 121.

12. For more information, please see www.agn.gov.ar.

13. A summary of the FLASCO report "El modus operandi" can be found at www.lavaca.com.

14. Alvaro García Linera, Raquel Gutierrez, and Luis Tapia, "La forma multitud de la política de las necesidades vitales," in *El retorno de la Bolivia plebeya* (La Paz: Muela del diablo, 2000), p. 148.

15. Ibid., p. 157.

16. Julio Gambina, "Cómo recuperar las empresas privatizadas," at www.lavaca.org.

Water Woes

Dr. Leopoldo Rodarte Ramón, general director of the Federal District Water Commission, has a tough job. He is responsible for supplying an ever-growing population with water, draining thousands of tons of rain and wastewater, and treating huge discharges of industrial and domestic waste. To complicate matters, the Mexico City's water infrastructure is no longer able to carry away the torrential rains that lash it during the summer months, making the capital prone to extensive flooding. Furthermore, the over-exploitation of aquifers is causing the city to sink.

Why, then, does Rodarte act so calm and relaxed?

Rodarte takes his daunting responsibilities in stride, probably because he manages Mexico's largest and most modern water project—the Valley of Mexico Sanitation Project—putting him at an advantage when compared to the rest of the country. Not only are private interests salivating as they wait for the bidding process to begin, the venture promises to solve some of the colossal sanitation and water-transport problems that affect the area.

Too Much or Too Little?

While Mexico is a water-rich country—receiving approximately 30 inches of rainwater annually, which provides residents with more than 4,800 cubic meters per capita, according to National Water Commission (CNA) statistics—rainfall is not regular. The country receives most of its precipitation during only four months of the year, making it difficult to provide a regular supply to the population. Additionally, a mere 4 percent of the nation's rain falls on the northern 30 percent of the country, while the southeast and the coasts receive over half of the total.

The distribution of the population has also put pressure on the water supply. The central region, where 60 percent of the population lives—and where 70 percent of the gross national product is generated—receives only 25 percent of the country's precipitation, says César Herrera Toledo, vice director of the National Water Commission's General Program.

The use of this precious resource is also highly uneven. According to Herrera, approximately 76 percent of the water consumed in Mexico is used for irrigation, 17 percent for residential use, and 5 percent for industry.

From *Business Mexico,* March 2000, pp. 26–30. Copyright © 2000 by Naomi Adelson, PhD.

High levels of leakage also plague various regions of the country. The largest user—irrigation—is responsible for more leakage than total residential and industrial demand combined, according to the CNA.

Scaling Back the State

Given the mounting problems faced by the water sector, the federal government began a restructuring of both its water entities and strategies at the end of the 1980s. Government policy had focused on building large public works, but it could no longer finance such large projects alone.

"Water is one of the most capital-intensive businesses around, so sooner or later private sector investment will have to enter," says Michael Phillips Jones, chief operating officer of Latin America North/Caribbean for Industrias de Agua de la Ciudad de México (IACM).

And the private sector is exactly who the government turned to. Since neither states, municipalities, or the federal government could make the colossal investments necessary to resolve the nation's water problems, a new emphasis was placed on "private sector participation," says Herrera. The operation of irrigation districts was transferred to users, while municipalities (through their own water companies) were given the responsibility of providing potable water services, treatment, and drainage.

Mexico turned out to be at the forefront of what would soon become a developing national trend: attracting private-sector investment for water. According to the World Bank, between 1984 and 1990, developing countries awarded water and wastewater contracts totaling US$297 million. Seven years later, private-sector investment in developing countries' water had skyrocketed to US$25 billion.

Private Party

Mexico's current water policies continue to encourage private-sector participation. According to the national Hydraulic Plan 1995–2001, "addressing underdevelopment requires huge investments that in turn require private-sector participation, together with public-sector participation." As a result, private-public sector partnerships have now become common throughout the country.

Most states and municipalities—now obligated to provide water services—opted to contract out services or grant full concessions to the private sector. The cities of Cancún, Aguascalientes, Navajoa, and Nogales later decided to fully privatize their water services. U.S.-based water company Azurix, through its affiliate Azurix Cancún, entered into a partnership with Grupo Mexicano de Desarrollo (GMD)—one of the country's largest construction companies—to operate the Cancún water and wastewater concession. Azurix acquired a 49.9-percent interest from GMD, paying US$13.5 million in cash and assuming approximately US$25 million in financing and operational commitments, according to company reports.

"We have a 30-year concession for all water services (potable water, wastewater, and infrastructure) in Cancún. In fact, we are now *the* water company, though we are regulated by the water company of Quintana Roo," says Michael Wood, chief executive officer for Latin America North/ Caribbean at Azurix.

"We feel that (full concessions) are better because you are a total provider. You become more efficient when you run the whole water company. You can manage capital costs, and it's easier to get financing because you are actually controlling the whole system," he says.

In Aguascalientes, French-based Vivendi—the world's largest water company—joined with Ingenieros Civiles Asociados (ICA) to form a joint venture called Operación y Mantenimiento de Sistemas de Agua (OMSA). The joint venture now holds the full concession for water services in that city.

Nevertheless, Azurix's Wood doubts that more cities will follow suit with full concessions.

"People don't like to think of a private company owning the water," he says, adding that that sentiment won't change "until people see concessions really operating well."

"Here, the wave of the future is going to be public-private sector partnerships," says Wood. And so far, his assessment is correct: While Cancún and Aguascalientes opted to open their doors to private investment, other cities— like the Federal District—are only providing service contracts, due to local resistance to the privatization of what citizens here often view as a public good. Last April, in fact, locals gathered outside the local Congress of Chilpancingo, Guerrero to protest after a legislator suggested that the district's water supply be privatized.

The government is also encouraging private investment in what Wood calls "Mexico's biggest need": wastewater treatment plants. Azurix itself particpates in a joint venture with FYPASA Construcciónes, and holds a 49-percent interest in a US$25-million wastewater treatment plant currently under construction in León, Guanajuato. The firm also holds an interest in a US$20-million treatment plant in Torreón, Coahuila, and is building another for the city of Cancún.

"There will probably be three to four other plants put up for bid this year in Mexico," says Wood, adding that his company will bid on the upcoming Gómez Palacio, Durango plant. But Azurix faces stiff competition from the subsidiaries of French-based firms Lyonnaise des Eaux and Vivendi. The two hold Federal District service contracts, and Lyonnaise des Eaux, through its subsidiary, Degremont, has a number of waste and cleanwater treatment plants spread throughout the country. Vivendi also holds the service contract for Acapulco and Puebla. Proagua Potosí is building a wastewater treatment plant in the capital city of San Luis Potosí.

Such plants are usually built under Build-Operate-Transfer (B-O-T) schemes that last from 10 to 15 years. Since large investments of this nature are highly risky, Mexico is providing government guarantees to assuage private-sector fears of instability. The nation's public-works bank, BANOBRAS, guarantees the transparency of bidding and state and municipal payments in all B-O-T agreements.

Rethinking Water

Yet it is the Valley of Mexico where the most significant investments are needed. The valley covers 9,000 square kilometers, at the bottom of which is located the Federal District and part of the State of Mexico. The valley is completely closed in by the surrounding mountains, and has no natural drainage. The area was originally composed of several lakes, among which the Aztecs created a system of canals to release water from the valley. The Spanish, however, drained most of the lakes, leaving today's city managers with the burden of enormous flood risks and infrastructure needs.

Inter-American Development Bank (IDB) statistics demonstrate that the Valley of Mexico's aquifers are now over-exploited. While the aquifers are recharged with approximately 700 million cubic meters annually, nearly double that amount is extracted. Yet the valley still counts on them to obtain 66 percent of its water. The groundwater over-exploitation is the root of recent water shortages, as well as the cause of the city's sinking.

"The sinking of the city is a problem that we have been living with for a century," says the city's Water Chief Rodarte. "What we are doing to reduce the effects is to transfer wells to zones where they provoke minimal sinking—at the edges of the valley."

The Great Drainage Canal—one of the city's two large canals that artificially drain the city—now rises and falls distances of up to 10 meters (due to differential sinking). And in several areas where deep drainage pipes used to flow downhill, they are now inclined. The city has had to install pumps to push the water through the Great Canal, as well as move water through urban drainage networks.

That situation has left the Great Canal operating at 10 percent of its original capacity. But the fact that the city is sinking is not its only problem. Since the world's largest metropolitan zone can no longer get residual and rainwater out of the city, flooding risks are a paramount concern. The IDB says that if the Great Canal is not rehabilitated, it will be inoperable in just a few years, leaving the Central Collector to extract all of the city's water. If the Central Collector were to fail, 210 square kilometers of the city would find itself under several meters of water, necessitating the evacuation of nearly 4 million people. Worse still, 90 percent of the subway system is located within the prospective flood zone.

The Valley of Mexico's water problems have also spilled over to surrounding areas. Mexico City has the capacity to treat 7 cubic meters of residual water per second, but operates at 4 cubic meters per second. Yet the city discharges 35 square meters of water per second, leaving 28 cubic meters untreated, says Rodarte. The IDB places that figure at 41 cubic meters per second.

Mexico City's wastewater has traditionally been discharged in the nearby irrigation district of Tula, Hidalgo, causing great environmental damage. In a 1992 study, the National Health Institute and the National Nutrition Institute found that the incidence of intestinal worms (*Ascaris Lumbricoides*) is between 10 and 20 times higher in the Tula Irrigation District than in areas where water is treated at least once. The IDB estimates that 400,000 people are negatively affected by untreated water from the Federal District.

Yet the governments of the Federal District and the State of Mexico—most of whose population lives in the so-called conurban zone surrounding and attached to the Federal District—are too fiscally strained to revamp the water, drainage, and treatment systems in such a large metropolitan area alone. In 1996, the IDB approved a US$1.035-billion project to clean up the mess. Mexico City and the State of Mexico government will invest US$2.6 million, the IDB will loan US$365 million, and the Overseas Economic Cooperation Fund of Japan will provide US$410 million in what is called the Valley of Mexico Sanitation Project.

"There will be three types of works: wastewater treatment plants, drainage, and an increase in the amount of water available to the Valley of Mexico," says Rodarte. A new water highway, known as the *acuiférico,* will bring four more meters of water per second into the zone, which will allow the Federal District to close wells within the city to reduce sinking and provide more water to the State of Mexico.

The IDB views private-sector participation in the water sector as an "important factor for development in the sector," and it will "continue to assist these types of initiatives in the project." The design, construction, and operation of the wastewater treatment plants, as well as drainage works, will be conducted by private companies, according to Bank documents.

"The bidding will be open to businesses from any country," says Rodarte, adding that it is expected to begin sometime this year.

The private sector is quite aware of the size of the IDB project and is awaiting the bidding anxiously.

"We certainly are interested in that project. In fact, one of the treatment plants will be one of the largest in the world, treating 45 cubic meters of water per second," says IACM's Phillips.

Population Problems

Mexico City officials also have to contend with providing water services to its population of 16 million, according to IDB estimates. In the mid-1990s, the city created the Federal District Water Commission to restructure the sector. Service contracts were to be awarded to an unknown number of pre-qualified companies in a transparent bidding process.

"That was the first time that water services were concessioned in the Federal District," says Rodarte.

Seven international consortia entered bids.

"At bidding time, no one knew how many contracts there would be. We only knew that there would be a minimum of two," says Phillips.

The Federal District Water Commission ended up dividing the contracts among four companies with four districts each. Each winning consortium now holds a 10-year contract that began in 1994. The firms must be 51 percent Mexican-owned, so foreign companies formed local partnerships to tap into the market.

THE BIG DRAIN

Mexico City officials must provide water services for 16 million people. Here are just a few of their most pressing issues:

- **Water leakage** accounted for a 37-percent loss of water in 1997. By 1998, leakage had been reduced to 34.2 percent, and in 1999, leakage is estimated to have fallen to 32 percent.

- **Mexico City facilities** can treat 7 cubic meters of residual water per second, but operate at only 4 cubic meters per second. The capital discharges 35 square meters of water per second, leaving 41 cubic meters untreated. Every year, more than 400,000 people are negatively affected by untreated water from the Federal District.

- **The aquifers** are recharged with approximately 700 million cubic meters annually, but nearly double that amount is extracted. Nevertheless, the Valley still relies on aquifers to obtain 66 percent of its water. Groundwater over-exploitation is the root of recent water shortages, as well as the cause of the city's sinking.

- **The Great Drainage Canal**—one of the city's two large canals that artificially drain the city—now rises and falls up to 10 meters due to differential sinking. That situation has left the Great Canal operating at 10 percent of its original capacity, and if it is not rehabilitated, it will be inoperable in just a few years.

- **The Inter-American Development Bank (IDB)** approved in 1996 a US$1 billion project to clean up the water mess in the capital. In the near future, Mexico City and the State of Mexico government will invest US$2.6 million, the IDB will loan US$365 million, and the Overseas Economic Cooperation Fund of Japan will provide US$410 million in what is called the Valley of Mexico Sanitation Project.

- **Mexico's annual rainfall distribution**
  - Mexico receives around 30 inches of rainwater annually
  - Rainwater provides more than 4,800 cubic meters per capita
  - Only four percent of the annual rainfall reaches the northern 30 percent of the country
  - The southeast and the coastal regions receive more than half of the total annual rainfall
  - The central region, where 60 percent of the population lives, receives only 25 percent of the total annual rainfall

Two of the world's largest water companies, Vivendi and Lyonnaise des Eaux, won one district each through joint ventures with ICA and Grupo Bufete Industrial, respectively. Agua de México, the joint venture of U.K.-based United Utilities and Grupo Gutsa, was also awarded a contract. Azurix recently aquired a 49-percent interest in Industrias del Agua (IASA), a water and wastewater service joint venture based in Monterrey, Nuevo León, which held the fourth concession with U.K.-based Severn Trent and the Mexican company Samsa. Today, through its subsidiary Industrias del Agua de la Ciudad de México, Azurix is providing the water services.

So far, the private-public sector partnership in Mexico City has been fruitful for both sides. Rodarte says the concessions "are going well," while the government continues to be the owner of the water system.

The service providers are now responsible for leak detection and have significantly reduced leakage. According to Rodarte, in 1997, the city was losing 37 percent of its water to leaks. By 1998, leakage had been reduced to 34.2 percent, and in 1999, leakage is estimated to have fallen to 32 percent.

Perhaps the greatest gift the private sector has given Mexico City is technology. Azurix has been replacing sewer mains without excavations, using technology developed in the United Kingdom that avoids having to tear up sidewalks and streets to reach the pipes. They are also replacing asbestos cement pipes with polyethelene ones.

"Asbestos cement is a rigid material, which is not ideal for a city that suffers from earth tremors and sinking," says Phillips. Polyethelene, in contrast, is flexible.

To obtain the US$365-million loan from the IDB, Mexico City had to increase its operating efficiency significantly. With the participation of private firms, the city was able to reach the level required for the fourth year of the project in the first year, according to Rodarte.

Nevertheless, the project is a bit behind schedule. In the initial stage of the contract, the companies were to take a census of users within their designated zone, install meters, and map the infrastructure. Then, the firms were to enter the commercial stage: reading and maintaining meters, calculating and billing consumption. In the third stage, the companies were to begin the operation and maintenance of secondary networks. According to Phillips, however, "that is only being partially implemented. And the day-to-day operation of the sewage lines and water distribution continues to be the responsibility of the delegations."

Here to Stay

"The quality of life and commerical development of the country in many ways will be dependent on having a water infrastructure to meet commercial growth needs," says Phillips, adding that, though some authorities are still resistant to the idea of giving up their water responsibilities, private investment will eventually become imperative.

"The government just doesn't have the capital to do the work here," says Azurix's Wood. So that leaves a lot on the private sector's plate. "We think that Mexico affords firms the best opportunities (for investment) at this time. It's a good country to do business in."

POSTSCRIPT

Do the Social and Economic Costs of Privatization Outweigh Its Benefits?

The word "privatization" has become such a politically charged term that, for its critics, it is categorized along with a number of other perceived threats to national sovereignty: globalization, neoliberalism, the World Trade Organization (WTO), the Free Trade Area of the Americas (FTAA), and regional trade agreements like CAFTA. Privatization was one of the topics discussed by the International Social Movements Assembly during the World Social Forum in Caracas, Venezuela, in January 2006. The assembly produced a document that, in addition to condemning the FTAA and WTO, rejects privatization by saying that "water, genetic resources and biodiversity belong to the people; we will not allow their privatization nor their commercialization" (http://www.alternatives.ca/article2395.html).

Álvaro Vargas Llosa, political analyst and senior fellow at the Independent Institute, explains in "Populism in Latin America" (2005) that the "backlash" against privatization will have dramatic and dangerous political implications in the region. While he supports free market reform, he asserts that in many cases privatization contracts were made "under monopoly arrangements." He argues that "if privatization means simply high tariffs and high prices, you're going to be vulnerable to the populist message" and, consequently, Latin Americans will vote for populist figures like Hugo Chávez. The successful 2005 presidential campaign of Evo Morales in Bolivia points to the validity of Vargas Llosa's assertion; Morales campaigned on the promise that he would nationalize his nation's energy industry. In fact, Monte Reel from the *Washington Post* sees a trend toward the re-nationalization of utilities. In March 2006, "Argentina announced it was rescinding its 30-year contract with the French company Suez and reinstating government control of the water supply." Reel explains that President Kirchner's move "is not without precedent," as in "2003, he took the nation's postal service out of private hands, and it has since turned a profit" ("Turning the Taps Back to the States: Privatization of Utilities Falls Out of Favor in Latin America," March 27, 2006). In May 2006, Evo Morales announced that he would renegotiate contracts with foreign investors to partially nationalize Bolivia's energy resources. A Bolivian flag was hung over the gas installations, and Morales announced: "It is time to put an end to the auctioneers and to recover our natural resources. Today we are nationalising our energy resources, 10 years after they were privatized" (Franz Chávez, "Morales Plays Hardball," *Inter Press Service News Agency*, May 2, 2006).

The privatization of water continues to ignite debate throughout Latin America. Profound differences of opinion on this topic became clear during the Fourth World Water Forum held in Mexico City in 2006. As Laura Carlson asserts in "World Water Forum not the Place to Solve Global Water Crisis," discussions on water revealed a "clash of worldviews." On the one side, "forum officials expressed their view that water cannot be valued properly until it is assigned a market price that reflects costs, and that private participation is necessary for investment in infrastructure." Carlson explains that that this "is the vision pushed by the World Bank and others since they created the Water Council in the mid-nineties." Other forum attendees held a quite different perspective: "members of the urban popular movement, small farmers' organizations, and indigenous peoples asserted that access to water is a right and a public good" (Americas Program, International Relations Center, http://americas.irc-online.org/am/3168).

In "Bright Spots in Water Privatization," Luis Alberto Moreno outlines the successes of recent private ventures and maintains that innovations within the private sector have improved public utilities. He also highlights the significance of small-scale providers working in the water sector who primarily work in remote rural areas: "Small-scale water companies thrive in almost every Latin American country. [. . .] Paraguay and Bolivia have dozens of water entrepreneurs who use their own capital to build networks in communities not reached by public utilities. These providers are succeeding because they offer reliable services at competitive prices with the support of local governments and citizens." For more information on the successes of private ventures, see: http://psdblog.worldbank.org/psdblog/2006/ 03/bright_spots_ in .html.

Some argue that the conflict over national resources, services, and utilities could be avoided, at least in part, if the external debt owed by developing or Third World nations was forgiven. Inspired by the Jewish and Christian concept of jubilee—a special year that came every 50 years when slaves were freed and debts were forgiven—efforts like the Jubilee Debt Campaign contend that rich countries should forgive the debt of impoverished countries. If their debt were cancelled, indebted countries would not be forced to privatize services and utilizes (Jubilee Debt Campaign, http://www. jubileedebtcampaign.org.uk/).

For articles on the World Water Forum and the water crisis, see Choike (http://www.choike.org/nuevo_eng/informes/730.html). Carmelo Ruiz Marrero reviews new developments on water privatization discussed during an alternative forum on water issues in "First People's Workshop in Defense of Water: Water Privatization in Latin America" (http://americas.irc-online.org/am/2885). To learn more about the origin and goals of what has come to be called the Washington Consensus, see John Williamson's "What Should the Bank Think about the Washington Consensus?" (Institute for International Economics, 1999, http://www.iie.com/publications/papers/paper.cfm?ResearchID=351).

ISSUE 17

Is the Free Trade Area of the Americas (FTAA) Good for Latin America?

YES: Tehsin Faruk et al., from "FTAA—Why It's Beneficial," http://www.umassd.edu/iba/reports/ftaa-tehshin.pdf (2003)

NO: Oxfam Canada, from "Let's Harness Trade for Development: Why Oxfam Opposes the FTAA," http://www.oxfam.ca/news/Peoples_Summit/Opposes_FTAA.htm (February 24, 2005)

ISSUE SUMMARY

YES: Tehsin Faruk and her colleagues at the University of Massachusetts–Dartmouth attest that the FTAA will break down existing trade barriers and promote free trade to the benefit of the 34 participating countries in the Western hemisphere.

NO: Oxfam Canada, a non-profit international development organization that supports community programs in food security, health, nutrition, and democratic development, argues that the FTAA is driven by the narrow commercial self-interest of business elites.

Globalization is a new word with old ideas. The journey of Venetian explorer and merchant Marco Polo to Asia in the thirteenth century and Christopher Columbus' first voyage to the Americas in 1492 provide two of the more widely recognized historical examples of globalization. Both moments triggered an increased interdependence and interconnectedness of people and places on Earth. Although "globalization" did not become a part of the English lexicon until the last decade, it is important to remember that goods and services have been traded between cultures, empires, and tribes since the beginning of humankind.

However, in contemporary society, oftentimes a value judgment is placed on globalization—is it good, or is it bad? In addition to understanding more complex issues such as free trade agreements, common markets, and other economic agreements that exist between countries, it is necessary to recognize that globalization, itself, is neither good nor bad. A more representative and accurate evaluation of globalization would be to analyze the systems, mechanics, and structures that are employed in global trade. Understanding questions such as which people stand to gain or lose as a result of a particular agreement, whose interests is a particular system designed to suit, and how certain economic tools—such as the usage of tariffs, taxes, and specific trading statuses—affect the concerned parties offers a much clearer picture as to whether or not globalization is good or bad for any given participant in global trade.

The FTAA is an example of one of these economic mechanisms—a free trade agreement—that is used to increase trade between its member countries. A number of free trade agreements exist around the world, including ASEAN (Association of Southeast Asian Nations), the Agadir Agreement (Egypt, Jordan, Morocco, and Tunisia) and the largest of the free trade agreements, NAFTA (North America Free Trade Agreement), which is comprised of the United States, Canada, and Mexico. The FTAA would greatly expand NAFTA, removing trade barriers across the Western hemisphere and involve 34 member nations, excluding Cuba, Venezuela, and Bolivia, who recently entered into their own trade agreement known as the Bolivarian Alternative for the Americas.

Proponents of the FTAA, including the governments of the participating countries as well as major multinational corporations, view the FTAA as a natural next step that builds upon the successes of NAFTA. Since NAFTA went into effect on January 1, 1994, its supporters refer to statistics that suggest NAFTA has been a great success, relying on indicators such as a significant decline in the unemployment rates, increased gross domestic product per capita, and economic growth rates of over 30 percent for all three countries. Based on this data, the notion is that if a free trade agreement like NAFTA creates beneficial economic results, then the expansion of this agreement to include more nations would allow even more people to reap these financial rewards.

However, many feel that NAFTA, and therefore the FTAA, exists only for benefit of the elites. Since NAFTA began, thousands of small farmers in the United States, Canada, and Mexico can no longer compete with highly subsidized industrial farms and have been forced to look for a means of income elsewhere—often migrating to places where they find their skills are not compatible with the hi-tech world of modern business. In addition, the United States has seen a huge increase in the number of Mexican laborers who illegally enter the United States primarily looking for work in agriculture due to higher wages largely influenced by governmental subsidies. The small farmers who have stayed to work their land have been forced to cut their prices, decreasing their annual income by roughly 20 percent. In addition, many claim that environmental, social justice, and human health issues are often the casualties of similar trade agreements.

Due the controversy surrounding the FTAA, only cursory progress has been made in pushing the agreement forward. The team of academic economists of Tehsin Faruk, Bryan Kofton, Dhruv Nag, Christina Dos Reis, and Kartik Subramanian support the argument that the FTAA would be a huge benefit to nearly the entire Western hemisphere and would provide even greater economic growth than what members have experienced through NAFTA. However, non-governmental organizations like OxFam-Canada feel the current format of FTAA contains narrowly focused mechanisms that benefit only major corporations and will lead to continued economic disparity, environmental degradation, social justice issues, and fewer opportunities for small farmers and agricultural laborers.

YES

Tehsin Faruk et al.

FTAA—Why It's Beneficial

FTAA—An Introduction

What is FTAA?

FTAA stands for "Free Trade Area of the Americas". The FTAA was first proposed by the United States in 1994 as an extension of NAFTA. NAFTA, also known as the North American Free Trade Agreement, is an agreement between Mexico, the United States, and Canada to dissolve trade boundaries and promote free trade. FTAA attempts to bring down the barriers of trade between 34 countries in the Western Hemisphere to make it the largest free trade zone in the world. The free trade zone market encompasses just under 800 million people in a $13 trillion market[i], which is double the size of the European Union. . . .

The scope of the paper will attempt to delineate the background of FTAA and offer detailed discussions on the merits of implementing FTAA and its future benefits. We feel that the FTAA will benefit both the United States and the Latin American countries to a great extent and strongly opine that it is the right direction for both. . . .

Objectives

According to the preamble of the FTAA draft, there are over 23 statements concerning the goals and objectives of the FTAA. These statements can be grouped into four distinct areas of focus: individual economies, foster globalization, environmental concerns, and employment issues.

The FTAA will be committed to promote healthy economies and to foster the growth of those economies. According to the preamble, this will promote stronger bonds between economies and promote social development as well as bring economic stability to weaker economies. Every effort will be taken to ensure that all countries, strong and weak, are represented fairly and equally in the organization [and] to create opportunities for all involved.

Globalization is another major theme within the framework of the FTAA. The parties of the FTAA seek to achieve globalization through free trade, integration of economies, and fair competitive practices. The importance of market openness and trade liberalization is designed to enhance competition and foster a stronger, more stable global market.

The last major areas of focus for the FTAA are environmental concerns and labor concerns. The FTAA seeks to better support the environment and recognizes that a healthy environment promotes sustained development and growth. Workers rights are also addressed by empowering the International Labor Organization to establish and manage workplace and worker standards. Through better management of labor, the FTAA will . . . promote better working conditions and higher standards of living.

Brief History and Background

Trade agreements eliminate barriers to trade like tariffs, quotas and subsidies, making it easier for the movement of goods and services across international borders. . . .

The General Agreement on Tariffs and Trade (GATT), which was established in 1947 after World War II, was the first major global trade agreement. . . . There have been [many] trade agreements since then, the most notable fcbeing . . . NAFTA.

The FTAA is the extension of the North American Free Trade Agreement (NAFTA) to the entire Western Hemisphere with the exception of Cuba. In December of 1994, 34 countries committed to the FTAA at the Summit of the Americas. The preparatory phase began in January 1995 and formal negotiations were launched in April 1998. The creation of an FTAA would . . . be the most important chapter in the history of regional cooperation in the Western Hemisphere and mark a fitting culmination to a fast maturing trade policy framework in Latin America and the Caribbean. . . . The FTAA will expand NAFTA, not only geographically, but is also likely to include new rules and policies designed to give investors (corporations) rights and freedoms that are more extensive than the ones they enjoy under NAFTA. . . .

The Foreseeable Effects

[Critics] argue that essential social services will be endangered. . . . [However,] the FTAA will include commitments to liberalize trade in services such as education, health care and environmental services, [such as the] removal of national licensing standards for medical, legal and other key professionals, allowing doctors licensed in one country to practice in any country. . . . [Although this] may [lead to] . . . difference in [the standards] of professional services, . . . the free movement of professional services can enhance the transfer . . . [and] quality of services at the same time[ii].

[Many critics, including those in the U.S.,] do not support the privatization of public schools and prisons, . . . which they feel would open the door to greater corporate control, corruption and the cutting of critical corners to increase profits, and privatization of postal services by transferring U.S. Postal Service functions to a few delivery companies like FedEx, which would then send postal rates through the roof. Some also reckon that the Free Trade Area of the Americas will only increase the flow of trade and make others earn their own living by trampling the environment, such as [increasing] the rate of timbering. Nevertheless, the President of [the United States] still insists that the Free Trade Area of [the Americas will be a boon to] global trade. . . . FTAA will [maintain positive aspects] of the North American Free Trade Agreement. The flow of trade would increase and [any side] effects would be [resolved through] negotiation and cooperation among different states.

FTAA: A New NAFTA?

. . . Proclaimed in 1998 as a landmark accord for greater economic coopera-tion and prosperity, the North American Free Trade Agreement . . . , according to many, has failed to benefit average Americans, Canadians and Mexicans. . . .

Though NAFTA has been under [much] criticism, . . . the United States, Canada and Mexico have benefited [from] their trade agreement to a great extent. NAFTA has improved the competitiveness of all three countries in other global markets. Not only are [these] countries enjoying greater produc-tivity and efficiency, public officials and corporate leaders alike are looking at the three-nation region as a single market, sharing manufacturing roles and responsibilities.

Canada After NAFTA

[Due to NAFTA, exports] of U.S. goods to Canada amounted to $178.8 billion, rising 7.32 percent over the previous year. Nearly 86 percent of Canada's mer-chandise exports are shipped to the United States, representing 33 percent of the country's GDP. As a result, Canada's relationship with the United States is an overwhelming factor [in] determining [their] economic progress. Huge investments from U.S. companies in such sectors as automotive assembly, telecom equipment and electronics have helped bridge the gap between the somewhat lower productivity of Canadian industry and that of U.S. industry. Productivity growth is also accelerating in Canada in large measures because of the expansion of Canada's information technology sector.

Mexico After NAFTA

Last year, trade between the United States and Mexico [totalled] $263 billion, more than three times the amount achieved in 1993, the year before NAFTA was enacted. Trade with Mexico has grown faster than with any other major U.S. trading partner, including China, Germany, Korea and the United Kingdom. From 1993 to 2000, [trade] expanded at an annual average rate of 16 percent. Even more positive for Mexico's long-range growth, U.S. manufactur-ers are now turning to Mexico's research and development facilities to play a greater role in designing their next generation of products.

U.S. Trade Representative Robert Zoellick, briefing at the White House April 19, said that between 1993 and 2000 U.S. exports to Canada and Mexico rose 104 percent, while exports with the rest of the world advanced at half that rate. (Source: Bilateral Trade Reports, 2003)[iii]. That kind of performance has inspired hope . . . that the FTAA will lead to comparable growth in U.S. trade with the rest of the Western Hemisphere. Currently, U.S. exports to . . . NAFTA partners are about four times as great as exports to the rest of the hemisphere, and imports from . . . NAFTA partners [are] five and a half times as great. But given the magnitude of trade among . . . NAFTA partners, that means that trade with the rest of the hemisphere is still substantial. Therefore, the lobbyists of FTAA are making considerable arguments that this extension of . . . NAFTA will make every endeavor not to repeat their mistakes[1] and ensure that the full potential of FTAA is achieved.

Important Issues

Does FTAA only Favor the US?

For the U.S. the FTAA means opening up a very promising market in the Americas for its [services and technology-based industry. As the U.S.] is primarily a service-based economy, its service sector would grow rapidly. The FTAA could . . . establish stronger economic, political, security, and foreign policy ties with Latin American countries, . . . enhance U.S. market access to Latin American markets, . . . offer the U.S. a better platform to negotiate greater access to goods, services, and capital movements throughout the region, . . . put U.S. trade and investment in an advantageous position vis-à-vis European and Asian countries doing business in the region, and increasing trade between the two economic regions would help prevent future attempts at protectionist measures, and market-oriented reforms such as privatization. . . .

Hence, it is recognized that the FTAA favors the United States, but the U.S. believes it will benefit all countries involved. Even without the FTAA, there would still be inequalities, poverty, political instability and human right violations in these countries. Prosperity needs to begin somewhere and the U.S. has offered much to these other countries in order to make the FTAA the starting point. In April 2001, during the Summit of the Americas, United States President George Bush declared "We have a great vision before us: a fully democratic hemisphere, bound together by good will and free trade. That is a tall order. It is also a chance of a lifetime. And it is the responsibility we share."

Opportunities and Benefits

As stated before, the FTAA, if implemented, will be the largest free trade region in the world. The combined GDP (Gross Domestic Product) of the 34 nations would be an estimated $13 trillion dollars. . . . The FTAA would represent more than 800 million people and $800 billion dollars in trade. This is over two times that of the European Union, which only consists of 375 million individuals in 15 countries. The European Union has benefited greatly from their trade agreement with greater access to large markets and economies of scale, [yet] only half the size of the proposed FTAA. This would mean twice the benefits for the members of the FTAA. These benefits would include the removal of restrictions on the trade of goods and services, developmental and technological advances, implementing of common food standards, [and] enhancing protection of intellectual properties. Other benefits would be the removal of current tariffs, preventing new tariffs, providing protection against expropriation, [and] promoting honest government and initiating social/ political reforms. . . .

The Richer Families

[Over] 1/3 of Latin Americans workers earn $2 dollars a day. If they can spend $2 dollars less on one commodity, they [will save an entire day's income.] Trade can make this possible. It will give . . . families greater purchasing power. The poorest of . . . nations would benefit by being able to buy more with their money due to cheaper imports from elsewhere. These nations will also benefit from being able to export . . . excess [crop production in larger quantities. Other] countries will be more likely to buy more imported goods if tariffs were removed. . . .

The Smaller Economies

With the larger economies investing in the smaller economies, there [are] bound to be [additional] opportunities. [The] FTAA will produce a tremendous [surge in] interregional trade and a great deal of aggregate job creation. The working class will benefit from new and higher paying jobs. New types of business and service sectors will form with financial investments. [Farmers will also] benefit from access to [these] new markets and the implementation of new technologies to help them [reach] their total capacity. Many countries only [reach] their total capacity. Many countries only produce . . . a fraction of their potential due to a lack of equipment and technology. . . .

Positive Effect on Small Businesses

One major sector that will . . . greatly benefit is the small business sector— businesses . . . with less than 500 employees. Only an estimated 1% of all American small businesses export. Out of the 63% percent of those who do export, they only export to one other country. Ninety-one percent of the businesses that export to South America are small or medium sized. This number tripled from 1987 to 1997. Smaller businesses worldwide [recognize that] exporting would be beneficial but do not have the means to do so. This is an enormous opportunity for smaller businesses to grow by expanding sales and their target markets. The FTAA is [establishing] guidelines, procedures, and strategies for those smaller firms (in all 34 nations) that . . . are ready [to] expand overseas.

A Brazilian Outlook

From a Brazilian point of view, the FTAA could potentially facilitate access to the U.S. market, lower the costs of inputs and [outputs,] facilitate and induce technology transfer, and [increase the flow] of U.S. investment [into] Latin American economies. In 2000, US-Brazil merchandise trade . . . exceeded $29 billion, but a free-trade agreement could double or triple that figure.

Brazil is MERCOSUR's main economy, accounting for close to 70% of MERCOSUR's GDP. In 2001, the Brazilian economy [shifted] its attention

[away] from domestic stabilization efforts towards the external sector [and] is more . . . dependent on increasing exports for continued growth and development. . . .

Forming Ties and Ending Political Tensions

. . . [The 2002 United Nations Human Development Report] said the countries that are most likely to overcome poverty are those that are most integrated with the global economy. The main reason being countries can rely [on] and learn from one another. They can share their [assets] with other countries to help them overcome weaknesses, [helping to sustain they through the] weaker stages of their economic cycles, [as well] as corruption, inflation or any political changes that may occur. The countries will eventually form close ties [with] one another, [resulting] in diminished political tensions and conflicts. In case of a dispute, the FTAA has [formulated] policies to resolve differences among the 34 countries and promote uniform values and democracy across all the nations. President George Bush, during his speech at the signing of the Trade Act of 2002, stated "Free trade is also a proven strategy for building global prosperity and adding the momentum of political freedom. Trade is the engine of economic growth. In our lifetime, trade has helped lift millions of people, and whole nations, and entire regions out of poverty and put them on the path to prosperity."

Central America and the FTAA

Central America has already benefited greatly from trade. . . . The average tariff rate in Central America has taken an enormous drop from 20 percent to 7 percent from 1990 to 2000. The United States, in [promoting] the FTAA, is preparing a new trade agreement with Central America called the Opportunity Alliance for Central America and Mexico. [This plan will] sponsor regional integration by helping remove existing tariffs. [This] alliance will also assist in creating a lawful environment—free of corruption—that will help attract trade and investment. The last step of the alliance is to launch a new . . . program [designed] to help local coffee producers . . . improve . . . quality and [competitively] market its product . . . on a national and overseas level.[2]

FTAA and the Caribbean

The FTAA [also favors] the Caribbean. . . . The Caribbean's closest ties are with the United States and they have already received funding from the United States in hopes to promote the FTAA. Between 2002 and 2003, The Caribbean economies will [have received] $1.5 million dollars in support funds to help them with [educational] costs and to reform the telecommunications sector. In 2004, the United States plans to provide even more funding [of a] yet to be [determined amount.]

How will [the] Andean Region Be Affected?

The Andean Region also has a trade agreement with the United States called the ATPA (Andean Trade Preferences Act), which was recently renewed. This [agreement] allows the Andean region to export flowers and textiles without duties. In addition, [the] US government [will] have donated over $3 million dollars to the Andean Equity Investment Fund by the end of 2003 . . . to help provide currency to small businesses. The United States is also contributing an estimated $1 million dollars a year to build public and private sector support of the FTAA by expanding regional trading capacity. An estimated $13 million dollars will also be donated by the end of the year to enhance business developments and regional market access [helping] farmers in rural areas . . . get their products into large cities regionally and even overseas.

Human Rights Issues

Human rights violations have also been a key argument in the FTAA negotiations. The United States recognizes that Human Rights are top priority and have made the following contributions since December 2000:

- The United States Agency for International Development (USAID) has formed eleven dispute centers throughout the 34 countries. These centers were established to [treat issues regarding] human right violations.
- The United States government contributed to the Organization of American States (OAS) $500,000 dollars to sponsor the expansion of the Arias Foundation for Peace and Human Progress.
- The U.S. publicly [stated they were proud financial] supporters of the Inter-American Institute of Human Rights and the Inter-American Commission on Human Rights (IACHR). They also supported the IACHR study of the Belem do Para Convention . . . to eliminate violence and [inequity toward] women. . . .

The Environment

There are many concerns as to what the FTAA may [do] to the environment. Free trade across the borders would involve shipping goods over huge distances, which means increased burning of large quantities of fossil fuels. It also involves packaging and repackaging of goods for different segments of their voyage causing considerable negative environmental impact through the waste of paper and other materials. The U.S., [in response] has backed numerous Latin American and Caribbean environmental programs and donates over $60 million dollars a year to such programs. The U.S. has [also] formed regional offices in the American Embassies in both Costa Rica and Brazil to first-handedly [oversee] any environmental issues that may arise. The United States [assigned] Peace Corps members to 10 of the 34 nations to work solely on environmental projects. The U.S. has also financially sponsored the UNEP Caribbean Environment Program, which currently funds sewage treatments in St. Lucia, Venezuela, Colombia, and Belize, [and] will soon expand to Nicaragua, Honduras and Guatemala. . . .

The Trade-Democracy Link

It can be said . . . that as the United States moves forward with trade liberalization in Latin America under the Free Trade Area of the Americas, it should work with like-minded countries in the Western Hemisphere to adopt an explicit "democracy clause," . . . modeled [after] other regional economic agreements, such as the European Union and the Southern Cone Common Market (MERCOSUR), but . . . stronger. [The] definition of democracy could be elaborated, institutional mechanisms for responding to problem cases could be specified, and actors other than national governments could be given [authority] to bring cases.

However, [this] connection between free trade and democracy [is] neither linear nor guaranteed. [Yet, fragile] and young democracies [have benefitted] greatly from the "carrot" of support, advice, and assistance offered by mature democracies. There are also instances when coordinated external pressure and action—[working in conjunction] with like-minded domestic forces—can help protect democracy when it is threatened. Nowhere is this truer than in Latin America—a region that has faced strong challenges to its nascent democracies over the past two decades. In the 1990s alone, the United States joined with other Western Hemisphere countries and the Organization of American States to deflect numerous challenges to democratic governance, including . . . Guatemala, Haiti, Paraguay, Ecuador, and Peru. . . .

While the relationship between free trade and democracy is not a simple one of cause and effect, trade liberalization can help . . . promote democratization. In heavily regulated and state-controlled economies, trade liberalization encourages the removal of [governmental intervention] and stimulates the private sector. The removal of barriers to foreign trade and investment also spurs competition, challenging domestic monopolies and entrenched interests. More broadly, increased contact with the rest of the world, encouraged by trade, fosters international awareness and understanding of democratic norms. The equations between modernity and democracy, between legitimacy and the rule of law, are strengthened. [Economic] growth and prosperity supported by increased trade and investment promotes the expansion of a substantial middle class, with both increased interest in democratic structures and the power to maintain and reform them.[3] . . .

The FTAA is a suitable and appropriate forum for explicitly dealing with the promotion of democracy for three reasons. First, while there are reasons for optimism based on recent progress, Latin America has a long history of political cycles of democracy alternating with authoritarianism, such that there is reason to fear backsliding away from democratic rule. Many countries still have weak and underdeveloped democratic systems. Public opinion polls show that many people are dissatisfied with the ability of their young democracies to deliver social progress so far, and authoritarian political impulses remain strong. Indeed, other regional treaties have included commitments to democracy for precisely this reason. Second, a democracy clause is possible in the Western Hemisphere because the current democratic wave is at a crest, and all . . . but Cuba are, at least in form, [freely elected] democracies.

Finally, a democracy clause . . . will form the cornerstone of a wider concept of a community of democracies in the Western Hemisphere. The FTAA is a genuinely multilateral process, being driven by all of the nations in the region, and aims to deepen economic integration beyond simple tariff elimination. Indeed, the primary benefit of the FTAA to the United States is arguably not economic (such as increased exports) but political—the building of stable, democratic, and prosperous neighbors to the south that are willing to work with the United States on a wide range of important issues of mutual concern, from combating narcotics trafficking and other international crimes, to better controlling migratory flows and protecting the environment, [as well as] harnessing the advantages of electronic commerce, telecommunications, and air travel. In effect, for a hemisphere largely at peace and devoid of major interstate [conflicts, the FTAA can become the cornerstone] hemispheric security alliance for the 21st century. . . .

Overcoming the Skepticism

There is no doubt that the FTAA has many challenges and obstacles to overcome [and many countries remain] skeptical. The FTAA needs to show the smaller less-fortunate nations that the agreement is not a threat but an opportunity for enormous growth. . . . Many of those who are anti-FTAA do not see the whole picture. For example, protesters . . . blamed NAFTA for the Mexican [peso] crisis in 1994 when . . . NAFTA actually helped reduce the negative effects significantly by lending a helping hand. You cannot blame an agreement like NAFTA or the FTAA for economic troubles. It will not make a country prosperous overnight. It needs time to reach its potential. But you can blame NAFTA for the speedy recovery Mexico had after the Mexican Peso Crisis. Although, it was not as speedy as most would have liked, it would have taken over 3 times longer if it wasn't for the help of Mexico's NAFTA partners. . . . It is important that the negotiators of the agreement educate the population of all the potential and good that it has to offer, especially since the FTAA is getting so much bad publicity.

The Time is Now

The FTAA process is a complex venture that undoubtedly bears costs. However, [the] FTAA could establish an important new framework of opportunities for regional integration, hemispheric cooperation and growth. Among other things, [the FTAA] could offer the possibilities of

- More secure hemispheric market access
  - A challenging incentive for productive transformation and preparation for globalization
  - A potential magnet for new FDI
  - A rationalization of existing strategies of regional integration
  - Synergies that contribute to a stronger multilateral system
  - Externalities that help to [lock in] policy reform

However, . . . [the] FTAA has much work left to do, but as President Bush . . . stated at the Summit of Americas, "Now is the time to extend these benefits of free trade throughout the entire hemisphere." Free trade could be beneficial for all. The real challenge is maximizing its potential.

Bibliography

Faux, Jeff. *"Failed Case for NAFTA—The most common claims."* The NAFTA and why they don't make sense.

"U.S Advances Bold Proposals in FTAA Negotiations to Create World's Largest Free Market in 2005." Office of the United States Trade Representative, 2003.

Background and Structure. 2005. http://www.doc.gov/ftaa2005/background.html.

Draft Text on General and Institutional Issues. FTAA.1 November 2003. http://www.doc.gov/ftaa2005.

Backgrounder: FTAA Offers Potential for Significant Increase in Trade Flows. US Department of State—International Informational Programs. http://usinfo.state.gov/regional/ar/trade/ftaa1.htm.

Crane, Philip M. *The FTAA: The Promise of Economic Prosperity and Strengthened Regional Partnerships.* http://usinfo.state.gov/journals/ites/1002/ijee/ftaa-crane.htm.

Levin, Sander M. *The FTAA: A Chance to Shape the Rules of International Trade.* http://usinfo.state.gov/journals/ites/1002/ijee/ftaa-levin.htm.

Otteman, Scott. *Why the FTAA Makes Sense for Business in the Americas.* http://usinfo.state.gov/journals/ites/1002/ijee/ftaa-otteman.htm.

Adolfo, Franco. *Building Trade Capacity in the Americas.* http://usinfo.state.gov/journals/ites/1002/ijee/ftaa-franco.htm.

Summary Table of US Government Actions in Compliance with the Mandates of the 1998 Summit of the Americas. December 2000. US Department of State—International Informational Programs. http://usinfo.state.gov/regional/ar/summit/fact7.htm.

Notes

i. US Trade Office Press Release 02/03.

ii. Detailed discussion on the merits of the FTTA cab be found in online Trade Publications of Coiel Webpage.

iii. Bilateral Trade Reports—Section XXII, Vol II, Released by the Trade Organizations of America.

1. Global Exchange Campaign—Article published in *Times* 'vol IXII' January 2003, pg. 32–34.

2. Summary Table of U.S Government Actions in Compliance with the Mandates of the 1998 Summit of the Americas. December 2000.

3. Roberto Bouzas and Gustavo Svarzman, *"The FTAA Process: What Has It Achieved and Where Does It Stand?"* The Leadership Council for Inter-American Summitry, Working Paper Series published by the Dante B. Fascell North-South Center, University of Miami, forthcoming.

Let's Harness Trade for Development: Why Oxfam Opposes the FTAA

Executive Summary

Oxfam . . . [is] opposed to the current proposal for a Free Trade Area of the Americas. We believe that substantial and wide-ranging changes are essential if the international trade and investment regime is to promote poverty eradication, respect for human rights and environmental sustainability. These changes will involve radical reform of trade policies, agreements and institutions at national, regional and international levels, moving in a very different direction than what is currently being envisioned for Hemispheric integration.

Like NAFTA . . . the FTAA . . . has been driven by the narrow commercial self-interest of business elites. The proposed FTAA, based on the extension of NAFTA to the Hemisphere, seeks to free corporations from government regulation, secure expanded markets for exporters and offer new guarantees to foreign investors—goals that more often than not conflict with the interests of the Hemisphere's farmers and workers and their families, and threaten the long-term prospects for poverty eradication and sustainable development.

We need to radically rethink our approach if trade and investment are to be part of the solution instead of part of the problem. Oxfam believes trade and investment agreements should be devised and judged on the basis of their contribution to poverty eradication, respect for human rights and environmental sustainability. We believe that trade and investment agreements should conform to global and inter-American rights and environmental covenants, and promote the achievement of agreed international human development targets.

Trade agreements signed in recent years go far beyond the exchange of goods to include rules on investment, services and intellectual property. They have removed conflicts between private and public interests from the political arena, placing them in the hands of unaccountable dispute-resolution panels. As such, they have had an enormous impact on the livelihoods of citizens and on their capacity to exercise their rights. What's more, these agreements have proscribed national policies that might mitigate their negative effects, restricting the ability of government at all levels to pursue sustainable development policies.

Virtually all the governments of the Americas are seeking trade and investment as ends in themselves, without a sufficiently careful reading of how they might support national development goals. The community organizations who are our overseas partners are particularly critical of their governments' apparent willingness to undercut human rights in order to attract foreign investment, and to forfeit alternative development options in return for possible access to the U.S. market. The United States seems intent on using the FTAA to weaken trade links between the European Union and Latin America, thereby strengthening its hand in any future global trade talks . . . None of this will bring the Americas closer to the fulfillment of the human development targets the international community has committed itself to achieving by 2015.

Oxfam is not against closer trading relations: Trade can contribute to equitable development and can be undertaken so as to enhance respect for human rights and environmental sustainability. We also believe that a rules-based system is the best way to achieve this. Latin America's longstanding dream of integration is worth cultivating. However, an agreement based on blanket liberalization of trade and investment rules, particularly one between countries of vastly different size and clout, will undermine the policy tools governments must have at their disposal for sustainable development.

This paper outlines key aspects of concern regarding the proposed Free Trade Area of the Americas, and suggests elements that an alternative fair trade agreement might contain. Of the many issues said to be on the negotiating table, five are of particular concern: agriculture, intellectual property, investment, market access, and the processes by which the agreement is being negotiated and would be administered.

An agreement based on the extension of NAFTA to the rest of the Hemisphere would constitute a setback to efforts to eradicate poverty and to promote equitable and sustainable development. The demands of a globalized world require a process and an agreement more in line with the democratic aspirations of the citizens of the Americas.

Key Issues

- Agriculture and Food Security: Trade and investment rules have made it harder for countries to implement national agricultural policies to promote food security and sustainable livelihoods, and to eradicate poverty. Minimum access obligations, for example, created to provide agribusiness with an entry into foreign markets, have facilitated dumping, undermined the livelihoods of small farmers, accelerated urbanization and stymied efforts at rural development.
- Intellectual Property: Over-zealous protection of corporate patent rights has unduly raised the cost of seeds, medicines and other technology-rich products essential to economic development. In the case of knowledge developed by community efforts (such as traditional strains of plants and breeds of animals), unbalanced intellectual property rules have also facilitated the removal of knowledge from the public domain to the detriment of small farmers.
- Investment: Measures to protect and promote investment have infringed on the capacity of government to protect the environment and promote public health and safety. NAFTA's Chapter 11, for example, by

granting corporations the power to sue for lost future profits due to public regulation, provides a powerful disincentive to public regulation of investor behaviour. NAFTA also bans performance requirements, a key policy tool to support social and economic development goals.

- Capital Controls: Lax rules on the movement of capital have contributed to devastating financial crises when speculators move vast amounts from country to country. Rather than remove controls, investment rules ought to encourage the channeling of long-term investment toward national development priorities.
- Market Access: Inequitable access to markets in the current trading system has perpetuated poverty. Thanks to IMF and World Bank conditionalities and WTO rules, the poorer countries of Latin America and the Caribbean have been obliged to open their economies to imports, while Canada and the United States have maintained barriers to the exports of their southern neighbours. This imbalance must be redressed.
- Special and Differential Treatment: Because of the vast differences in economic clout wielded by the countries of the Americas, a free trade area only makes sense if it includes significant resources transfers to its poorer members, as in the European Union. In a fair trade agreement, such special and differential treatment would go beyond longer transition periods to ensure poorer countries and regions have the policy tools and assistance to achieve equitable development.
- Transparency and Public Accountability: Because trade agreements have overruled national, provincial and local laws, public debate and parliamentary scrutiny should be an integral part of the negotiation process. The current process offers overwhelming access to business, and minimal access to civil society. Such a lack of transparency tends to favour corporate rights over citizens' rights. Conflicts between private and public interests should be resolved in the political arena, not by unaccountable dispute-resolution panels.

Agriculture

A large proportion of Latin America and the Caribbean people living in poverty (at least 60%) are rural and derive their livelihood from agriculture. This is especially true in the region's poorest countries. Agriculture not only provides the primary means for survival for the poor, it is the basis for local and regional development in much of the Hemisphere.

The economic dictums of the International Monetary Fund and the rules of the World Trade Organization have forced developing countries to eliminate supports for small farmers (such as public credit, price supports and marketing boards) while reducing tariff barriers on agricultural imports. Simultaneously, WTO's Agreement on Agriculture has allowed industrialized countries to continue their existing systems of agricultural supports.

Small farmers in Latin America and the Caribbean are thus locked into competition with subsidized imports, particularly from the United States, which drive down local prices. This has been the experience of corn farmers in Mexico following liberalization under NAFTA. Dumping of agricultural goods by the United States in the Caribbean, through loopholes in the WTO's anti-dumping provisions, has been devastating to the region's producers. Small farmers can find it equally difficult to compete with imports of unsubsidized staples from internationally competitive agricultural exporters such as Canada, Argentina, Brazil and Uruguay.

Agriculture is too important for poverty reduction and environmental sustainability to leave its development to market forces. A fair trade agreement would not undermine the right of developing country governments to devise and implement agricultural policies to improve the lot of small producers—including measures which constitute barriers to international trade—in order to promote food security, rural development, a more equitable distribution of assets and the sustainable use of natural resources. Similarly, government support to farmers in industrialized countries should be carefully targeted to meet social and environmental goals, and not be used as a means to capture overseas markets.

As well as fairer regulation of governmental subsidies, action is needed to regulate the activities of the huge corporations that dominate world trade in agricultural commodities—70 per cent of which is controlled by six or fewer companies. These corporations capture an increasing share of value in international supply chains, keeping poor men and women producing crops for export from escaping from poverty. Measures that effectively defend small farmers, such as farmer-controlled marketing boards, should be explicitly encouraged by trade agreements, rather than proscribed as the United States has proposed.

The downward trend and increasing volatility in international commodity prices negatively affects the income of small farmers supplying export markets and government revenue in commodity-dependent developing countries, such as the island nations of the Caribbean, thus reducing resources available for essential public investment in health, education and infrastructure. Tariff-escalation policies in Canada and the United States, by which tariffs are higher on processed agricultural products than on raw ones, stifle economic development in Latin America and the Caribbean.

Policy Proposals—Agriculture

- Trade rules must not undermine the right of developing countries to implement national agricultural policies that promote food security and sustainable livelihoods. In a fair trade agreement, this could be achieved by incorporating a food security clause, which would codify the types of interventions that developing countries could make exempt from trade liberalization commitments.
- All forms of public support for agricultural exports, including direct export subsidies and export credits provided by industrialized countries should be eliminated.
- A fair trade agreement would oblige the United States to re-design its domestic support policies so that they effectively promote social and environmental objectives, and no longer have negative impacts on small producers in Latin America and the Caribbean.
- The United States and Canada should improve market access for agricultural exports from Latin America and the Caribbean by substantially

reducing general tariffs, eliminating tariff escalation and reducing non-tariff barriers such as seasonal import restrictions. . . .

- A fair trade agreement should provide a framework for regulating the role of multinational corporations in international agricultural trade to allow for greater competition in international agricultural markets.
- Fair trade rules should encourage agricultural diversification and the public management of commodity supply and production, with the objective of stabilizing prices.

Intellectual Property

Rules on intellectual property must strike a balance between rewarding private innovation and promoting broader social objectives. Such rules must also balance the rights of patent holders with their obligations to society. Oxfam is particularly concerned about the potential negative impact of intellectual property rules on technology transfer to developing countries, on public health, and on poor people's ability to buy seeds, medicines, and other technology-rich products.

Economic development requires the sharing of technology. Current intellectual property rules guarantee monopoly benefits for the corporate owners of technology for periods as long as twenty years. The monopoly rents they collect allow them to control not only the use of technologies, but also the funds available for further research and development. While recognizing that inventors should receive fair compensation, the public interest would be better served by the sharing of technology, and by public control over research and development.

Access to essential medicines is perhaps the most evident problem in this regard. Key policy measures required by the huge and growing burden of disease among the poorest people of the Americas, such as the manufacture of generic versions of patented medicines or the sourcing of licensed versions on the world market, is severely restricted by current intellectual property rules. Applying NAFTA's patent rules to the Hemisphere, as the United States has suggested, would restrict those options even further. A fair agreement on intellectual property must allow governments the flexibility they need to protect and promote public health.

To offset the effect of such measures on private corporations' willingness to fund research and development, a fair trade agreement could create new public incentives for research and development on priority medicines and vaccines for diseases affecting the poor, including the creation of a Hemispheric fund financed by donors.

Proposed intellectual property rules seek to enforce corporate control over plant genetic resources, enabling companies to impose high prices for seeds and related agricultural products. Giving private companies monopoly rights over the production and marketing of important food crops threatens the livelihoods and food security of small farmers.

What's more, recent trade agreements have applied intellectual property rights originally intended for invented products to those derived from biodiversity and traditionally treated as the common property of local communities. Trade rules should do the opposite: reward community-based and traditional knowledge, and protect the rights and privileges of small farmers who have developed and maintained the plant varieties now being exploited for profit in northern laboratories.

Because patent rules can guarantee corporate control and monopoly rents, they are driving many of the developments in the field of agricultural biotechnology. Canada and the United States are seeking FTAA rules that will help promote their biotechnology exports. In the face of inadequate scientific evidence on the health and environmental risks, intellectual property rules should extend the precautionary principle and secure the rights of governments to restrict and/or require the mandatory labeling of genetically modified food and seed imports.

Safety and health issues aside, supplanting traditional crops with genetically modified ones that require the annual purchase of seeds and a brand-line of inputs limits poor farmers' access to the means of their survival, and undermines efforts to achieve national food security.

Policy Proposals—Intellectual Property

- Fair intellectual property rules should ensure a better balance between the interests of inventors and the public good than currently exists within NAFTA or the WTO. Member governments should be able to reduce the length and scope of patent protection required by the agreement in order to achieve broader social and developmental objectives. . . .
- Fair intellectual property rules should allow developing countries to make or import the cheaper generic medicines they vitally need. This means allowing countries more choice about their patent regime and including strong public health safeguards.
- To offset the effect of such measures on private pharmaceutical corporations' willingness to fund research and development, a fair trade agreement should create new public incentives for research and development on priority medicines and vaccines for diseases affecting the poor, including the creation of a Hemispheric fund financed by donors.
- Trade agreements must not undermine the right of developing country governments to determine 'sui generis' (of its own kind) regimes of intellectual property protection for plant varieties, including the option not to allow patents on living organisms and to outlaw contracts that prohibit the saving of seeds.
- Trade agreements must be consistent with the Convention on Biological Diversity so that patent approval is made conditional on prior informed consent, benefit sharing and the disclosure of the source of genetic material in order to combat biopiracy.

Investment

Foreign investment is one essential element of national development strategy, but a fair balance must be struck between the guarantees offered to investors and the public's need to orient investment toward national development goals, environmental sustainability and respect for human rights.

Privatization of public services is driving much of foreign investment activities in Latin America, with decidedly mixed results in terms of [poor people's] access [to essential services]. Rules governing investment must not undermine the regulatory capacity of government to restrict monopolistic behaviour by private corporations and ensure equitable and universal provision of essential services.

Interpretations by NAFTA's dispute-resolution panels of that agreement's investor/state provisions have significantly reduced the authority of governments to promote public health, protect the environment and derive benefits from foreign investment. NAFTA's Chapter 11 takes dispute resolution beyond government-to-government disagreements by granting corporations (and not citizens) the power to sue national governments for lost future profits for any measure "tantamount to expropriation." An appointed dispute-resolution panel adjudicates such cases on the basis of trade rules alone, making a mockery of international human rights law and providing a powerful disincentive to public regulation of investor behaviour.

NAFTA also bans performance requirements for foreign corporations, which governments have used to support social and economic development goals. Similarly, lax rules on the movement of capital under NAFTA contributed to Mexico's devastating financial crisis in 1996 when speculators removed vast amounts of money from the country. Rather than remove controls, investment rules ought to encourage the channeling of long-term investment toward national development priorities and away from volatile speculative ventures. . . .

Too often increased foreign investment has led to "social dumping"—the spread of dirty industries and the lowering of labour standards. A fair trade agreement must uphold agreed international labour and environmental standards, particularly the right of citizens to organize and advocate for their interests.

Policy Proposals—Investment

- A fair trade agreement should allow for strict controls on speculative or short-term portfolio investments that make no contribution to national development goals and increase the risk of economic instability.
- A fair agreement would establish fair rules on regulation of corporate assets to serve the public good. Such rules must redress the gross imbalance between the public interest and investor profit in NAFTA's Chapter 11.
- A fair agreement should include safeguards to enhance governments' ability to ensure fair competition and to assist populations disadvantaged by the effects of foreign investment.
- A fair agreement must uphold internationally recognized human, labour and environmental rights, and ensure that [they] are not undermined by the property rights of private investors.

Market Access

Trade liberalization has been an unequal bargain, with the greatest gains accruing to wealthy producers and industrialized countries. Most Latin American and Caribbean countries have suffered radical economic restructuring under IMF orders, in exchange for temporary debt relief, resulting in the de-industrialization of the region and a renewed reliance on primary exports. Latin American and Caribbean countries have opened up their economies far more rapidly than their northern neighbours. The results have undermined both livelihoods in poorer regions and the potential for developing new industries.

The costs of North American protectionism for Latin America and the Caribbean are huge. The sectors of greatest interest to small producers, agriculture and textiles, are subject to the highest trade barriers. Particular problems include escalating tariffs, which rise according to the level of processing, and obstruct developing country efforts to diversify into higher value production as a means of promoting industrialization and employment.

In the United States and Canada, tariffs on imports of fully processed food products are much higher than those on products in the first stage of processing. In addition, as average tariffs have fallen in most sectors, those countries have erected new, non-tariff, barriers which act to restrict entry to their markets, . . . for example, through the excessive use of anti-dumping measures.

The economic benefits obtained by developing country producers from improved access to industrialized country markets may have negative impacts on some low-income people employed in competing sectors in industrialized countries. Industrialized country governments should assist low-income groups to adjust to increased competition from imports through re-training, regional development programs and other targeted policies.

Policy Proposals—Market Access

- A fair trade agreement should encourage national governments in Latin America and the Caribbean to determine market access for foreign products and investment according to national development plans.
- A fair agreement should oblige Canada and the United States to make substantial reductions in tariffs applied to exports from developing countries, particularly peak and escalating tariffs.
- A fair agreement should [restrict] non-tariff barriers applied by Canada and the United States to exports from Latin America and the Caribbean, including the excessive use of anti-dumping and countervailing duty measures. . . .
- Canada and the United States should assist low-income groups in their own countries that are negatively affected by increased competition resulting from increased market access for Latin America and the Caribbean.

Rules and Mechanisms

Strong trade rules are essential if markets are to contribute to poverty eradication and sustainable development. But these rules must be fair and balanced, not tilted in favour of the interests of the rich and powerful at the expense of the poor and vulnerable. Balanced rules require a balanced process, one in which encourages transparency and public accountability in policy-making. The FTAA has been negotiated in secret, behind the backs of the societies most concerned with them. Large corporations have enjoyed privileged access to the negotiations through the Business Council of the Americas. Parliaments and civil society organizations have been kept in the dark. Proposals and drafts of a fair trade agreement should be submitted to public scrutiny through debate in the media, national consultations and hearings in national parliaments.

A fair trade agreement would not favour corporate rights over citizens' rights. To ensure this, an explicit reference would be included in the agreement's operating clauses to the pre-eminence of international human rights and environmental covenants. In addition, a fair agreement should include a complaints procedure by which citizens' organizations can challenge any perceived violations.

A key factor resulting in unfair outcomes is the unequal bargaining power among FTAA countries. Smaller countries have little or no representation in the process, putting them at a major disadvantage in relation to the well-resourced missions of wealthier countries. A fair agreement would minimize such capacity constraints and imbalances in political and economic power.

For this reason, special and differential treatment (SDT) for developing countries, already institutionalized in the WTO, should be a fundamental principle of a fair agreement. However, SDT must offer more than longer transitional periods for implementing the same rules as wealthier countries. Rather, there should be positive discrimination in the rules in favour of small producers and developing countries to ensure that poorer countries and regions have the policy tools and assistance to achieve equitable development.

A second key factor is the lack of civil society participation in trade policy-making. The current set-up, which offers limited space to a handful of NGOs, is clearly insufficient. Because much of Latin America is engaged in a fragile democratization process, and in all countries private corporations wield considerable clout, the capacity of the Hemisphere's governments to fairly represent the public interest in trade negotiations is questionable. For this reason, citizens' organizations that represent community interests should be at the negotiating table and their proposals should be considered on a par with those of the business community.

Policy Proposals—Rules and Mechanisms

- Mechanisms to operationalize special and differential treatment for poorer members should be incorporated into a fair trade agreement. SDT provisions should be reviewed on the basis of their contribution to developmental objectives and in support of the right of governments to devise and implement national strategies for poverty eradication, the promotion of human rights and environmental sustainability. Transition periods for implementing trade agreements should be based on development milestones not arbitrary dates.
- Fair trade negotiation processes should be designed to increase the capacity of the smaller members and civil society to participate effectively.

- All trade documents should be made automatically public. There should be greater public scrutiny of trade policy-making through more active involvement of national parliaments and increased opportunities for civil society involvement through regular national consultations.
- Civil society should be at the negotiating table, and their proposals should be considered on a par with those from the business community.
- Any dispute settlement system should be made fair and workable for smaller countries, should be based on human rights and environmental considerations, and should be transparent and accountable to the general public.
- Explicit reference to the pre-eminence of international human rights law and environmental covenants should be incorporated into the operational clauses of a fair trade agreement to ensure that trade rules cannot trump the rights of citizens.

Conclusion

Oxfam [has] supported community development for over thirty years in Latin America and the Caribbean. We have seen the potential of international trade and investment to help overcome scarcity and create employment opportunities. But we have also seen shortsighted trade and investment policies stymie our efforts and those of our [local] partners. The proposed Free Trade Area of the Americas poses a deadly threat to the livelihoods of the poorest of our neighbours, as well as to the long-term prospects for poverty eradication and sustainable development.

This paper identifies a number of elements that Oxfam believes could form the basis for a different approach, a Fair Trade Agreement. Other civil society organizations have also made cogent arguments for a fundamentally new approach. Trade and investment should be seen not as ends in themselves, but rather as means for achieving equitable and sustainable development.

The secrecy that characterizes the negotiations thus far is indicative that the public interest does not lie at the heart of the FTAA process. The debate must be brought into the open, and civil society's proposals considered on a par with those of the business community.

Oxfam believes that strong international rules are needed to manage trade in the interests of poverty eradication and sustainable development. But the FTAA as currently proposed favours only the narrow commercial interests of the most powerful nations and their large corporations. The demands of a globalized world require a process more in line with the democratic aspirations of the citizens of the Americas.

POSTSCRIPT

Is the Free Trade Area of the Americas (FTAA) Good for Latin America?

With the recent "move to the left" of several Latin American countries—particularly Venezuela and Bolivia—and their rejection of U.S.-led neoliberal trade policies such as those embodied in free trade agreements like NAFTA and the FTAA, a free trade agreement that would include all countries of the Western hemisphere at this time remains unlikely. Of particular significance to the FTAA's future was the Mar del Plata Summit held in Argentina in 2005. Amid massive protests and objection, proponents of the FTAA were unable to forge an agreement between the 34 potential participants, leading to claims that the FTAA was "dead," particularly by Hugo Chavez. However, 29 nations have agreed to reconvene negotiations in 2006.

With the emergence of the Bolivarian Alternative for the Americas as well as other opponents of neoliberal trade policies such as the Continental Social Alliance, the "anti-globalization" movements have gained in popularity. For example, at the most recent World Social Forum held in Caracas, Venezuela, in January 2006, participants established a number of objectives including ". . . maintaining a continental alert against any possible attempt to revive FTAA negotiations in any of its forms, and to forward the struggle against bilateral or regional free trade agreements in Central America, the Andean region, the Caribbean, and the new generation of agreements promoted by the United States, as expressed in the North American Security and Prosperity agreement, which furthers subordinate integration to the United States, including the area of 'security.'"

However, intergovernmental support for greater free trade has continued. Of particular interest to the continued promotion of the FTAA is the successful ratification of DR-CAFTA (Dominican Republic-Central American Free Trade Agreement). As of May 18, 2006, despite protests from a large percentage of citizens from many member nations, DR-CAFTA was approved and in effect for most of its participating nations, including the United States. Through the combination of NAFTA, DR-CAFTA, CARICOM—an agreement between a majority of Caribbean nations, and MERCOSUR—a common market trade agreement that generally includes the countries of southern South America, most countries in the Western hemisphere are participants in at least one trade agreement. It is speculated that these agreements may eventually form into one comprehensive agreement, thereby establishing a solid foundation toward the creation of the FTAA.

Although it is far too early to offer any conclusions as to what the positive and negative impacts of DR-CAFTA will be, the objections against DR-CAFTA are largely an echo of the critiques of NAFTA. Opinions on the merits

DR-CAFTA are primarily centered on large corporate agribusiness interests versus those of the small farmer, as well as the potential conflict of business objectives and environmental degradation, much like the concerns raised over NAFTA.

Many economists view the existence of trade agreements as a virtual inevitability and logical partnership for countries that share a particular geography. The European Union, ASEAN, NAFTA, CARICOM, MERCOSUR, and now DR-CAFTA are all examples and indications of a new compartmentalized economic system that continues to grow. And, with the political and philosophical divergence between North America and South America, the chances for one free trade agreement to include the entire Western hemisphere may not be initially plausible. However, perhaps it is not inconceivable that two free trade agreements—one in the North and one in the South—may eventually govern the economics of the Western hemisphere.

For an in-depth look at the benefits of the FTAA, read *Integrating the Americas: FTAA and Beyond* by Antoni Estevadeordal, Dani Rodrik, Alan M. Taylor, and Andrés Velasco. For an opposing view of the free trade agreements and neoliberal trade policies, see Maude Barlow, *Global Showdown: How the New Activists Are Fighting Global Corporate Rule*. In addition, for more perspectives on FTAA, visit http://www.ftaa-alca.org, http://www.stoptheftaa.org, and http:// www.latinbusinesschronicle.com/reports/columns/1205/farnsworth.htm.

ISSUE 18

Is International Aid Successfully Promoting Development and Stability in Latin America?

YES: Adolfo A. Franco, from "Poor Governance a Threat to Democracy in Latin America, U.S. Says," *Bureau for Latin America and the Caribbean, United States Agency for International Development* (May 25, 2005)

NO: J. Michael Waller, from "The Case for a Social Investment Fund for the Americas," Testimony Before the Committee on International Relations, U.S. House of Representatives, Subcommittee on the Western Hemisphere (November 5, 2003)

ISSUE SUMMARY

YES: Adolfo A. Franco, assistant administrator of the Bureau for Latin America and the Caribbean under the auspices of the U.S. Agency for International Development (USAID), testifies before the Subcommittee on the Western Hemisphere that international aid in Latin America is helping to foment democracy and support development.

NO: J. Michael Waller, Annenberg Professor of International Communication at the Institute of World Politics, argues before the same committee that international aid to Latin America has not been beneficial due to corruption, inabilities in effectively managing development efforts, and lack of law enforcement, among other issues.

Although international aid, or foreign aid, may appear altruistic in nature and largely removed from apparent controversy, the debate over its intentions and effectiveness has raged since the modern concept of foreign aid began after World War II. The first recipients of foreign aid were the war-ravaged countries of Western Europe. Europe needed to be rebuilt and, as part of the Marshall Plan, the United States was its key financier. The United States, of course, also spearheaded the reconstruction of Japan.

However, once Europe and Japan had financially recovered, international aid—oftentimes in the form of military aid—was used as a tool against the spread of communism. Riding the wave of success in Europe and Japan, U.S. President Truman enticed developing nations with the promise of advancing their own countries and providing hopeful solutions to famine, disease, and technological deficiencies. And, by garnering the support and alliance of these nations, the United States could inhibit communism from spreading elsewhere, particularly in Latin America.

Given this context, the deployment of aid to Latin America has come under much scrutiny. From a U.S.-led coup of a democratically elected president in Guatemala in 1954 to the U.S. support of the Contras in Nicaragua and contemporary issues related to debt, the goals and therefore viability of international aid have come into question.

International aid presents itself in two basic formats: humanitarian and developmental. Humanitarian aid generally focuses on issues that require immediate life-or-death attention such as providing food, medicines, and shelter as a result of natural disasters, droughts, civil wars, or other extreme conditions. Developmental aid is based on the premise of providing long-term solutions to remedy persistent or chronic issues such as insufficient infrastructure, failing educational systems, or poor health facilities.

Critics of international aid for development often cite inappropriate "top-down" methodologies used by international development agencies such as the United States Agency for International Development (USAID). These critics claim that development plans are shortsighted with little consideration given to future needs, environmental issues, and cultural practices, and that they undermine development efforts, resulting in little or no success. In addition, World Bank development loans in the 1970s and 1980s led to what is referred to as the Latin American Debt Crisis, leaving countries such as Mexico, Argentina, and Brazil saturated in foreign debt of nearly $100 billion apiece, creating a welfare-like dependency on food aid from the United States. Currently, Latin America has a $3 trillion debt, largely due to this legacy of developmental loans.

However, many feel that international aid has created subtantial benefits and opportunities for Latin Americans. Through health and educational programs, polio has been virtually eliminated from the continent. Illiteracy rates have been reduced by almost 50 percent, enrollment in secondary education has increased exponentially, and the number of telephones in countries such as Peru, Mexico, and the Dominican Republic has risen by over 1000 percent since 1970. In addition, many believe Latin America, in general, has never reflected more elements of peace, democracy, and stability than what is currently being experienced.

Adolfo A. Franco claims international aid has led to a surge of democracy throughout Latin America, the decline in corrupt governments, and increases in criminal justice, among other benefits. However, J. Michael Waller contends that levels of corruption and cronyism remain unchanged, debt problems still have not been resolved and, as suggested by recent elections in Latin America, many Latin Americans are unsatisfied with the results of U.S.-inspired policies and are looking toward domestically led solutions.

YES

Adolfo A. Franco

Poor Governance a Threat to Democracy in Latin America, U.S. Says

Latin America has made real progress toward democratic consolidation in recent decades, but violence, corruption and weak institutions in the region could undermine these democratic gains, according to Adolfo Franco, assistant administrator for Latin America and the Caribbean at the U.S. Agency for International Development (USAID).

In May 25 testimony before the House International Relations Committee's Subcommittee on the Western Hemisphere, Franco said that although democracy has taken hold in most of Latin America, democracy and good governance are not one and the same. . . .

To help Latin governments confront governance challenges, Franco said, USAID has allocated approximately $271 million in financial year 2005 for efforts to support democracy and encourage good governance.

He told lawmakers that the focus of USAID governance programs in the region is justice-sector modernization. The U.S. official noted that the region has made progress on a number of fronts toward more modern justice systems with USAID support—particularly the transition to oral, adversarial trials.

Franco noted that 12 Latin nations have adopted more modern accusatory, oral criminal procedures since 1992. He said that USAID has trained thousands of judges, prosecutors, litigators, law professors and community activists to smooth the transition to these more modern judicial systems.

In addition to USAID support for efforts to overhaul criminal procedures codes in the region, Franco said, USAID also supported the creation or strengthening of justice-sector institutions—including independent prosecutors, constitutional courts, judicial councils, and human-rights ombudsmen. He noted that USAID also continues to work with national and regional civil-society groups to improve the ability of citizens to monitor government functions and to ensure that governments are serving their interests. . . .

Following is the text of Franco's prepared testimony:

Testimony of Adolfo A. Franco,
Assistant Administrator,

Committee on International Relations United States House of Representatives Hearing, May 25, 2005.

Bureau for Latin America and the Caribbean,
United States Agency for International Development

before the

Committee on International Relations,
Subcommittee on the Western Hemisphere,
U.S. House of Representatives

Wednesday, May 25, 2005

Transparency and Rule of Law in Latin America

Mr. Chairman, thank you for the opportunity to appear before the Subcommittee on the Western Hemisphere of the House International Relations Committee. I have had the privilege to appear before you on a number of occasions over the past weeks, where I have discussed with you such issues as the state of democracy in the Western Hemisphere, rising crime and gang violence in Latin America and, most recently, key accomplishments related to Plan Colombia. Today, I will be discussing the related and equally important issues of transparency, rule of law, and governance in Latin America.

Last week, the elected presidents of Central America and the Dominican Republic met with President Bush to discuss the state of play of the Central America-Dominican Republic Free Trade Agreement. They said that the overriding benefit of CAFTA, even beyond its value in promoting economic growth and generating employment, is that it will strengthen democracy. They are right. The link between economic prosperity and democracy is becoming increasingly irrefutable. CAFTA-DR is teaching us that trade, democracy, and development are all means to the same end—freedom, security, and prosperity. We at USAID recognize this in all of our efforts to promote democratic consolidation and economic growth throughout Latin America and the Caribbean.

In 2001, when USAID Administrator Natsios took office, he commissioned a report entitled "Foreign Aid in the National Interest." The key message of that report was the importance of mainstreaming development into the national foreign policy process. The report's findings supported the vision laid out in the National Security Strategy of the United States, published in September 2002, which served as President Bush's vehicle for announcing his determination to help build strong democracies throughout the world. This has been a core task of USAID since its inception at the time of the Marshall Plan. Indeed, much of USAID's experience in implementing large scale democracy strengthening programs commenced in Latin America in the early 1980s and focused on addressing large-scale human rights abuses perpetrated under the notorious Central American dictatorships.

From Despotism to Democracy—Latin America Has Come a Long Way

In the early 1990s, Latin America emerged from two decades of authoritarian rule, violent civil strife, and widespread human rights violations. The Latin America we know today is largely democratic, as civilian governments have replaced military rule in nearly every country in the hemisphere. Indeed, many countries have now witnessed several generations of free and fair elections. As democracy has taken root, human rights violations have been drastically reduced and governments have taken actions to promote peace and reconciliation. Latin America has also witnessed an expansion of decentralization with central governments beginning to share power and responsibility with local governments. This has created new spaces of political participation for historically excluded populations and improved local governments' capacity to deliver on the promises of democracy.

The attitudes of governments in the region have also significantly evolved over the last fifteen years and political will to address these vital, but sensitive, subjects is on the rise. Rule of law and corruption have become central in political party platforms across the region, and governments are increasingly promoting initiatives to increase transparency, such as freedom of information legislation and the creation of ombudsman offices to monitor corruption allegations. "Corruption" is no longer an unmentionable word in the hallways of Latin American government, as it was just fifteen years ago, and governments are finally showing the will to aggressively prosecute official wrongdoing. . . .

Poor Governance Strains all Development Efforts

When governance and rule of law are weak, all efforts to promote democratic development suffer. The rule of law is an essential underpinning of democracy and a market economy. It establishes and protects legitimate democratic authority, safeguards human rights and civil liberties, provides a venue for dispute resolution, and is a necessary check against the abuses of executive power. Good governance and rule of law are critical to every sector in which USAID works, including economic growth, health, education, and the environment.

For example, efforts to reduce poverty and promote free trade and economic growth cannot compete with the offspring of bad governance, which include poorly defined property rights, high transaction costs and economic risks, corruption, and greatly reduced domestic and foreign investment. A prerequisite for trade integration is a rule-based system where contracts are honored, where governments provide the legal infrastructure needed for transparent enforcement, and where information can be exchanged openly and freely. . . .

In the health sector, we see the same trends affecting governments' ability to deliver much needed health services. A World Bank study last year concluded that even a very modest improvement in corruption levels results in a 29 percent decrease in infant mortality rates and a 52 percent increase in satisfaction among recipients of public health care. The same holds true for the education and environment sectors. In the education sector, expenditure leakages and bribes for services have been shown to eat up upwards of 50 percent of national education budgets. In the environmental arena, corruption in the extractive industries, such as forestry, mining, natural gas, and oil, is particularly destructive, not only due to the large sums of money typically involved, but also because of the long-term devastation that such activities can pose to a country's natural resource reserve if proper safeguards are not institutionalized.

USAID Programs

The United States continues to be Latin America's largest donor. President Bush has been firm in his commitment to the strengthening of democracy in our region, as evidenced by the steady increase in funding for democracy assistance since he came into office. In FY 2001, USAID's budget for building democracy, strengthening governance, promoting human rights, and addressing conflict in the Latin America and Caribbean region was approximately $106 million. This year, FY 2005, the USAID budget for the same activities is approximately $271 million. These numbers demonstrate President Bush's and Administrator Natsios' understanding that democracy-building is a long-term process that does not end with elections. As the President stated in a speech at the International Republican Institute last week, "When people risk everything to vote, it can raise expectations that their lives will improve immediately—but history teaches that the path to a free society is long and not always smooth."

USAID continues to be engaged in a number of efforts to strengthen the rule of law, promote justice-sector and legal reform, and increase transparency and accountability in Latin America. In fact, justice-sector modernization remains the largest focus of USAID governance programs in the region. Rule of law and justice reform initiatives are undertaken as part of democracy promotion programs, with the goal of establishing democratic authority, protecting rights, exerting a check on other branches of government, and complementing efforts to build security in post-conflict situations. In addition, legal reform activities such as commercial code reform, development of tax law systems, intellectual property rights protection, and commercial dispute resolution, are undertaken to promote economic growth.

With USAID support, the region has progressed on a number of fronts towards increasingly modernized justice systems—specifically, the transition to oral, adversarial trials and a consolidation of the independence of the judiciary. In 1992, Guatemala became the first country in Latin America to comprehensively reform its Criminal Procedures Code. Eleven countries followed in Guatemala's footsteps, resulting in twelve countries that have adopted some form of modern accusatory, oral criminal proceedings. This set the stage for the long-awaited elimination of the much-abused all-paper systems. As a result of these reforms, between 1982 and 2002, the incidence of pre-trial detention dramatically declined in many countries. In Mexico, for example, the level of pre-trial detention declined from 74 to 41 percent and, in Bolivia, from 90 to 36 percent. Oral criminal trials have also significantly reduced the length and cost of trials. In Bolivia, the length of trials dropped from an average of four years to four months, while the cost of trials decreased from an average of $2,400 to $400.

Since the 1980s, USAID has supported the creation of and strengthening of other justice-sector institutions, including independent prosecutors, constitutional courts, judicial councils, and human rights ombudsmen. USAID has trained thousands of judges, prosecutors, litigators, law professors, and community activists to ensure a smooth transition to modern judicial systems. In Honduras and Bolivia, every criminal judge in both countries was trained on their newly adopted criminal procedures. USAID also works with national and regional civil society networks to improve citizens' roles in monitoring government functions to guarantee that government is serving the interests of its constituents, and to ensure that citizens have access to information that will help them understand and evaluate government decisions.

The National Security Strategy clearly identifies development as the third key tool, along with defense and diplomacy, for achieving national security. We have come to recognize that security is the foundation upon which all progress in development rests. USAID is increasingly working with police and the range of other actors in the security sector chain—including the judicial and legal systems, the military, and communities—to address pressing security challenges in the region. To do so, countries must overcome the legacy of police in many Latin American countries as law-breakers rather than law enforcers. Community policing efforts in El Salvador, Jamaica, and Colombia are demonstrating that transforming the historically negative relationship between the police and the communities they serve into a collaborative relationship based on mutual trust, is not an unrealistic goal.

Here in the U.S., a common quip is that there are too many lawyers, too much law. However, in many other parts of the world, Latin America included, the opposite is often true. The issue is not too much law or too many rich lawyers, but too little access to law and often, not enough of it. Binding contracts and the courts that should justly and judiciously enforce them are often reserved for a small elite, while the majority of the country is left to deal with arbitrary action and decision. The challenge then is to increase the access and quality of justice for all citizens. In Guatemala, Colombia, and El Salvador, justice centers, justice houses, and alternative dispute resolution mediation centers are providing a variety of services to the poor, ranging from arbitration and witness protection to neighborhood dispute resolution and family violence response services. These justice centers and houses are not only increasing access to legal services, but also to other social services, and are making justice for the poor more swift and more effective.

USAID also supports the development of modern, computerized case-tracking systems to improve the administration of justice and reduce opportunities for corruption. In Guatemala, the number of lost files dropped from 1,000 in 1997 to 1 in 1999. Improvements in legal education and new merit-based selection systems are ensuring that more and more judges and prosecutors are selected based on their merit, rather than personal connections.

The legitimacy of governments is derived from the governed. Only if governments are accountable to democratic oversight and bound by and respectful of the rule of law can governments claim to act on behalf of the people. It is this legitimacy which gives governments the capacity to implement successful anti-corruption reforms and generates support from society for these reforms. In January of this year, the Administrator highlighted the need to address corruption when he approved USAID's new Anti-Corruption Strategy. Using the strategy as our guide, we will do more to spotlight the dynamics of grand corruption—corruption that involves the most vested, economic and political elite in a country and generally the largest sums of money. This will involve tackling the very incentives structures that allow those to benefit from the status quo. We understand that this is no small task. We will work closely with our colleagues at the State Department and other agencies, and reformers in the countries where we work, to study the problem and develop new programs to deal with grand corruption that complement our ongoing efforts to address lower-level administrative corruption. We will also improve our understanding of how corruption affects the various sectors in which we work and design multi- and cross-sectoral programs to address it. Finally, we will support reformers with rapid response assistance, and stand behind diplomatic initiatives that raise anti-corruption issues to the highest level. All of these efforts will help support United States leadership in combating corruption and building good governance across Latin America and the world.

Conclusion

The "Foreign Aid in the National Interest" report that I mentioned early on in my testimony rightly states that "no amount of resources transferred or infrastructure built can compensate for—or survive—bad governance. Predatory, corrupt, wasteful, abusive, tyrannical incompetent governance is the bane of development." The president's Millennium Challenge Account, or MCA, recognizes the fundamental correlation between governance and the effectiveness of development aid. Eligibility for MCA funds is contingent on, among other things, a government's commitment to "ruling justly." As President Bush stated, since "good government is an essential condition of development [the MCA] will reward nations that root out corruption, respect human rights, and adhere to the rule of law." That is, a government must first demonstrate the political will and clear commitment to addressing corruption and improving governance in their country before they will be considered for MCA assistance. USAID will continue to work closely with the Millennium Challenge Corporation on the MCA "Threshold Program"—an MCA program currently administered by USAID that supports countries the MCC has determined to be on the threshold of MCA eligibility. Three countries in Latin America were among the first to achieve eligibility for MCA assistance—Bolivia, Honduras, and Nicaragua—and two have attained MCA threshold status—Guyana and Paraguay. I look forward to continue working with my fellow panelists and colleagues in the Department of State, Millennium Challenge Corporation, and other agencies to promote economic growth and democratic consolidation in the Americas.

Our partnership with Latin American governments to strengthen the rule of law and increase transparency and accountability is one of mutual benefit. It is clearly in the U.S. government's interest to utilize our toolkit of diplomacy, defense, and development to counter the destabilizing effects that poor governance, corruption, and weak rule of law have on political and economic systems throughout Latin America, and the threats they pose to vital American interests. President Bush, during his meeting with the presidents of Central America and the Dominican Republic, emphasized the benefits of continued cooperation with our neighbors in Latin America. He stated, "The United States was built on freedom, and the more we have of it in our backyard, the freer and safer and more prosperous all of the Americas will be."

Working in partnership with Latin American governments, we can be true to the principles that President Bush and Secretary Rice have called essential to the health of all democracies—security, prosperity, and dignity. Working in partnership, we can honor the hundreds of thousands of Latin Americans that gave their lives in their struggle to leave a better, more democratic and just world behind for their children.

Mr. Chairman, this concludes my statement. I welcome any questions that you and other members of the Subcommittee might have.

J. Michael Waller

 **NO**

The Case for a Social Investment Fund for the Americas

T hank you, Mr. Chairman, for inviting me to testify today on the subject of U.S. bilateral development assistance in the Americas. This written statement discusses the following areas:

- In the post-9/11 world, U.S. international development assistance is officially on par with diplomacy and national defense, increasing its importance and its value to the public;
- Sustained public support for increased international development aid will depend in great part on ensuring the integrity of the aid programs against political or social manipulation;
- Political, economic and social trends in Latin America and the Caribbean in general are moving in a direction unfavorable to U.S. interests;
- Congress is handicapped in its ability to ensure effective expenditures of aid dollars because the chief agency in question has no means of measuring success or failure;
- Some strong supporters of bilateral development aid are uneasy, at best, about certain social-oriented development agendas and this could risk strong bipartisan support for a substantial development aid strategy;
- U.S. aid strategy requires focus and transformation;
- Successful long-term implementation of bilateral development programs requires a parallel public diplomacy and political warfare strategy;
- In keeping with the first main point, U.S. international development programming must be integrated with the larger global war on terrorism.

. . . Most recently I spent two years in El Salvador, which despite all its difficulties should be viewed as a real success story for U.S. assistance programs. El Salvador is as close as one can get to a worst-case scenario situation that was turned around completely thanks to a focused and long-term American commitment.

Bilateral development assistance to Latin America and the Caribbean, in addition to its morally correct humanitarian dimension, is an important U.S. foreign policy tool. Crafted skillfully and executed properly, it can serve the public at a time when U.S. interests around the world are being challenged at an intensity not seen since the height of the Cold War. . . .

The administration's *National Security Strategy*, an annual report required by Congress, is remarkable in that it elevates international development assistance

http://wwwc.house.gov/international_relations/108/90364.pdf

on par with diplomacy and national defense as a tool against the terrorists. This is a historic first.

The second chapter of the *National Security Strategy* states in its title that the U.S. will "Champion Aspirations for Human Dignity." This, too, is a landmark in the nation's national security doctrine, and one in which bilateral development aid can be a major player.

Unfortunately, while the administration called for "transformation" of the military and intelligence establishments, it did not call for "transformation" of the Department of State and USAID. However, in its 2002 report titled *Foreign Aid in the National Interest,* USAID described how it was integrating itself into the national security triad.

In short, the old-think of a scattergun approach to bilateral development aid, in which the U.S. had the brief luxury of experimentation with social engineering, with few if any considerations for national security priorities, is gone.

The administration has attempted a new approach with a Millennium Challenge Account (MCA), linking aid with private capital. [This] linkage is intended to reduce waste and create incentives for difficult reforms. Under the MCA, "The U.S. will channel these funds only to developing countries that *demonstrate, not promise*, a strong commitment to:

- "ruling justly (e.g., upholding the rule of law, rooting out corruption, protecting human rights and political freedoms)
- investing in their people (e.g., investment in education and health care)
- encouraging economic freedom (e.g., open markets, sound fiscal and monetary policies, appropriate regulatory environments, and strong support for private enterprise)."

The MCA is designed as a lever to encourage governments to pursue sound economic policies that allow people to be entrepreneurial: "we will reward nations that have more open markets and sustainable budget policies, nations where people can start and operate a small business without running the gauntlets of bureaucracy and bribery.". . .

Unfavorable General Trends

Is Latin America better off today than it was a decade ago? Let's look at the general trends:

- Levels of public corruption are generally at the same levels as before.
- Heavily centralized and bureaucratized national governments flourish with relatively few meaningful checks and balances.
- Crony capitalism remains buttressed by international loans, while keeping much of the populations out of the economy.
- Business and investment climate is generally less appealing to those with the capital to provide jobs and build infrastructure.
- Economies are depressed and even collapsing.
- Some populations show growing disillusionment with democracy and free markets.

- Weak law enforcement provides havens for smugglers and terrorists.
- Anti-U.S. populism becomes increasingly militant and self-confident.
- Mob action increasingly threatens rule of law and democratic governance.
- Political extremists and terrorist groups meet annually in an axis against the United States.
- Islamist terrorist support operations show increasing penetration and activity.
- New actors are emerging as hemispheric troublemakers.
- The successful inter-American security relationship is disintegrating.
- Illicit narcotics production is making a comeback in areas where it had been almost eradicated.
- Certain Latin American governments view the United States [as] an escape valve for their demographic and economic pressures, and as a permanent source of expatriate cash.
- An increase1 in economic dependency on Washington.

Within these general trends are pockets of real accomplishment that are testimony to the skill and dedication of U.S. aid workers as well as to people and officials in recipient countries. However, USAID lacks a means of measuring progress, making it impossible for Congress to determine the adequacy of programming and funding levels.

Are USAID Programs Really Monitored for Success or Failure?

. . . From my own personal experience on contract with USAID programs a decade ago, the aid organization tended to measure its success more in terms of the dollars it spent and the number of programs it sponsored, rather than the results it achieved. USAID contractors were told to write progress reports stressing the number of dollars spent and the quantity of certain programming, rather than measuring the quality and usefulness of the results.

Investigative data published in 2003 confirms my impressions of 1993. According to a January General Accounting Office (GAO) report, USAID remains structurally and procedurally incapable of providing Congress with adequate assessments of its programming. The GAO report stated:

> USAID faces difficulties in identifying and collecting data that would enable it to develop reliable performance measures and accurately report the results of its programs. USAID has taken several steps to try to overcome these difficulties, such as holding training seminars in field missions. However, although USAID has made a serious effort to develop improved performance measures, it continues to report numerical outputs that do not measure the impact of its programs.

. . . **It is urgent to establish an effective and credible metric.** Without one, it will be impossible to determine what is working, what is failing, where to cut back, and where to channel more funds.

What is "Social Development" and Who Carries It Out?

Metric or no metric, one should be leery when government planners create "investment" funds, or when well-meaning proponents call the unmonitored expenditure of tax dollars an "investment." One should also be cautious when political leaders, cause-driven non-governmental organizations (NGOs), and bureaucrats speak of using such "investments" to promote "social development" abroad.

Such jargon reminds one of the great failed social engineering experiments of the past. . . .

Will a "Social Investment Fund for the Americas" promote the self-sufficiency and productivity that so many people in the hemisphere desperately need? Or will it make those people even more dependent on constant handouts from inefficient bureaucracies and corrupt political machines? Is it designed to force those inefficient bureaucracies and corrupt political machines to open up, reform themselves, and break the cycle of political dependency at home? If so, what political and diplomatic tools are included in the package? If not, will it bolster those same bureaucracies and political machines and even make them become wards of USAID?

Will a "Social Investment Fund for the Americas" become another program that subsumes the U.S. national interest to the political or social agendas of well-meaning aid workers and special-interest groups? Will it become another foreign extension of domestic political and social battles? Will it promote practices that are morally or socially offensive to significant portions of the population in the recipient countries . . . ?

Toward Focus

The United States' well-intentioned bilateral aid programs for the hemisphere continue to be a mismash of soundly-devised initiatives combined with the illogically truncated remains of old programming combined with pet projects and feel-good headline grabbers. Taken together, they have not been conceived and constructed in ways that would maximize the impact of each assistance dollar. Many are driven by inertia from the past instead of forward-looking leadership. Others are driven by squeaky wheels at home.

Before Congress appropriates more aid dollars for Latin America, it should study the effectiveness of monies already spent, and ensure that any future resources are expended wisely. Some points to consider:

- Measure progress. Congress should demand that USAID provide a credible means of evaluating and accounting for its programs.
- Avoid dependency. Aid must be used sparingly so as to avoid a dependency relationship.
- Avoid crony contracting at home. With foreign aid such a huge business, there has been a tendency toward cronyism in the contracting process—not in Latin America, but here in Washington. Large

companies, built solely to subsist on USAID and related contracts, have mastered the Byzantine process of working with the federal government where smaller companies have not. It appears to the outsider that requests for proposals (RFPs) are rigged in advance to the advantage of the large firms, some of which act as aid mills that carry out the letter of the contract, but not congressional intent.

- Be more aggressive against waste, fraud and abuse. USAID programs are riddled with the equivalent of the Pentagon's fabled $600 toilet seats. All programming and practices must be cleaned out if the public is to support sustained development assistance.
- Dollars don't tell the story. Spreadsheets and dollar amounts seldom determine success. Some infusions of money can create impressive temporary results, but mean little for the long-term. Economic aid, healthcare projects, and environmental programs at the humanitarian level do little to help a society become self-sustaining.
- Structural reforms require sustained support. Some structural reform projects with promise have died on the vine for want of long-term funds or commitment.
- Assistance must be directed to where it does good. That means careful support for governments that have proven a commitment to reform, and non-support to the others. It also means well-targeted assistance to help empower non-governmental organizations, especially in countries where they would run afoul of the local government.
- Ensure that foreign aid works in the national interest. Our foreign aid program was developed as a policy tool to stave off and ultimately defeat Soviet expansion around the world. No less so today must it be utilized as a tool in the global war on terrorism.
- Integrate bilateral development aid with other tools of statecraft. Those tools include traditional diplomacy, public diplomacy, and in tougher cases, economic and political warfare.

Strong Public Diplomacy and Political Warfare Component Required

Political and social trends in much of Latin America and the Caribbean appear to be headed against the long-term interests of the United States. This challenge may be ameliorated by a combination of development assistance, public diplomacy, and tools that would allow policymakers to exert greater political leverage.

Organizations and governments hostile to the United States are operating throughout Latin America and the Caribbean to radicalize and organize groups and populations against pro-U.S. governments.

As the [U.S.'s] *National Security Strategy* suggests, one cannot expect bilateral development assistance and related programs to succeed without strong public diplomacy and political warfare components. In the Americas, as elsewhere around the world, the United States has allowed its once-effective public diplomacy machinery to disintegrate. Some of the disintegration has been willful, with unimaginative foreign policy leaders making conscious decisions to terminate important public diplomacy initiatives.

Consequently, in Latin America and the Caribbean, as elsewhere around the world, the U.S. has lost much of the leverage and human networks it had built for decades through its successful public diplomacy programs. The U.S. did away with crucial broadcasting, citizen exchanges, media services, cultural diplomacy, labor and entrepreneurial exchanges, and other education and training programs that had served the national interest so well in previous decades.

Two years after 9/11, the [Bush] administration has done a poor job of reviving public diplomacy—one would have to give it a failing grade—and has ceded the ground to the nation's adversaries and enemies. Examples in the Arab and Islamic worlds are well-known, but significant examples in the Western Hemisphere illustrate that the U.S. is losing the war of ideas because, to put it plainly, it has chosen not to engage.

The one-sidedness of the present war of ideas has allowed modestly funded extremist groups and movements to dominate public debate because the U.S. was not on the playing field. As Marcela Sanchez recently observed in the *Washington Post*,

> Throughout the hemisphere, new leaders are promulgating a kind of rhetoric about U.S. imperialistic ambitions eerily reminiscent of Cold War conspiracy theories of a generation ago. Such theories are not new. The problem this time around is that Washington is doing little to improve its image in the region and to counter such notions and the fears they engender. That leaves a vacuum too easily filled by the free flow of information— and disinformation—fueling anti-American sentiment in even the most distant corners of the continent.

Many U.S. policymakers don't take the threat seriously—and that is a danger to the national interest, Sanchez argues:

> Most in Washington dismiss such theories as hogwash that gives more credit than is due to a U.S. government absorbed in a new and formidable anti-terrorism war that has pushed Latin America backstage. But ridiculing this kind of theorizing as foolish or anachronistic ignores the fact that it is finding fertile ground among traditionally disenfranchised groups in the region whose destabilizing power is growing and whose leaders are gaining prominence.
>
> For groups as diverse as the *piqueteros* in Argentina, *cocaleros* in Bolivia, landless workers in Brazil, the Pachakutik indigenous movement in Ecuador and the Bolivarian Circles in Venezuela, there is one common thread: The belief that the U.S. role in the region is pernicious.

And the U.S. isn't attempting to counter them. Brazil, for example, has dispensed with its historically moderate foreign policy and now seeks a path of its own, leading other governments—as well as extremist and even terrorist organizations—in anti-U.S. coalitions. President da Silva's Forum of Sao Paulo is an annual networking meeting of most if not all the hemisphere's radical political parties, hung-over communist parties and former Soviet-backed guerrilla groups, and even terrorist organizations. Last year it met in Guatemala, with delegates and observers from the Irish Republican Army, the Popular Front for the Liberation of Palestine/General Command, the Saddam Hussein regime in Iraq, the Qaddafi regime in Libya, Castro regime in Cuba, and the Kim Jong-il regime in North Korea.

The failure to stem the new paranoid populism has allowed the movement to spread across the region and to begin toppling friendly, democratic governments. First was Argentina. Bolivia is the latest case in point. While working with the Bolivian government to eradicate coca production in the 1990s—a successful project that eradicated about 90 percent of the country's coca crops—the United States government shut down its public diplomacy programs in that country.

For more than two decades, the United States sent substantial assistance to the Chapare region of Bolivia. Recently, Bolivia has been the recipient of USAID programs worth $100 million a year to help farmers transition out of coca production and into legitimate commercial crops. Yet aid workers report that the Bolivian people knew almost nothing about the American assistance, or about U.S. intentions.

Meanwhile, a radical activist tied to the coca growers, Evo Morales, ran the only major radio station [in] the remote Chapare region, broadcasting inflammatory messages all day, every day. No other general broadcasting services operated in Chapare, so Morales dominated the airwaves—without any counter-programming. An American development professional wrote yesterday, "We have no effective public information campaign about U.S. objectives in the country."

Morales and the leader of the coca growers' union took advantage of economic dislocation and led the *cocalero* protests that forced President Gonzalo Sanchez de Losada from power on October 17. President Sanchez had been a key ally of the United States in the eradication of cocaine production. Yet he was ousted in a movement reportedly supported by European activists and Venezuelan President Hugo Chavez. The coca growers union leader then told Sanchez's vice president and successor, Carlos Mesa, [they had] 90 days to implement the *cocaleros'* agenda to resume large-scale production of the raw material for cocaine. The union leader threatened to continue a wave of violence against Bolivian society and the government if newly-installed President Mesa failed.

Integrate Bilateral Foreign Development Aid with The Global War on Terrorism

One might easily conclude that the United States has no effective security strategy for Latin America, and that it has willfully abandoned the tools it needs to influence the political climates in the region, while simultaneously not cultivating and supporting many of its friends and allies. It appears that the aid programs hemisphere-wide are uncoordinated and bound by little if any strategic vision. Policy priorities appear to be one-dimensional, in the case of counternarcotics and trade, and obsolete in such areas as military and police security, while development aid continues in isolation of pressing U.S. national interests.

The Americas is already a significant front in the global war on terrorism, and trends indicate that not only the narcoterrorists but Islamist terrorists from elsewhere in the world will increasingly use countries in the hemisphere with weak or corrupt institutions as bases of operation.

Bilateral development assistance must reward friends and punish enemies. It must never reward enemies or, through lack of full commitment or resources, end up punishing friends. Those approaches only strengthen our adversaries and weaken and alienate those who would be on our side. Aid also must be utilized as a means of reaching segments of society that may become valuable in penetrating, disrupting, uprooting, and destroying terrorist and terrorist-support networks.

We have far to go—far beyond social investment funds. As Stephen Johnson has observed, "Today, counternarcotics and counterterrorism are the main security concerns in the region, and the Department of State—with no apparent resources, training, doctrine, standardized procedures, or evaluation mechanisms characteristic of the U.S. military—is the lead agency."

POSTSCRIPT

Is International Aid Successfully Promoting Development and Stability in Latin America?

The debate over the effectiveness of international aid has raged since the conclusion of World War II. With inconclusive results, political motivations, and billions of dollars spent in the process, both supporters and opponents of international aid agree that measuring developmental successes and failures is inconsistent and oftentimes difficult to substantiate. In response to the need for a more precise method to manage, distribute, and evaluate aid recipients and developmental efforts, the United States—the single largest donor of international aid both around the world and to Latin America—has created a new international aid application and distribution system to more effectively meet developmental goals and reduce inefficiences.

The Millennium Challenge Account (MCA), established in 2004, reflects this new approach to development and is designed to support President Bush's plan to continually, and more effectively, increase the amount of funds dedicated to international aid in hopes of creating greater democracy and security throughout the world. The goal of the MCA is to provide a more systematic, open, and competitive vehicle by which countries who seek foreign aid may request funding. The application process consists of a set of 16 specific measures that each country must address, including elements focused on democracy, human rights, education of women, transparency of law, control of inflation, and the establishment of sound economic policies and practices, among others. Funding goes to those countries that score the highest in terms of approaching or meeting the established criteria. In 2006, Bolivia, El Salvador, Honduras, and Nicaragua were the Latin American representatives chosen to be eligible for international aid.

By using what is intended to be a more objective approach, the MCA hopes to eliminate many of the conflicts that have plagued international aid—corruption, political influence, conflicts of interest, distribution of aid to places that may not be adequately prepared that time to receive aid, and creation of systems that may not be appropriate for the specific needs of a particular country.

However, only a limited number of countries are chosen by the U.S. Congress to be considered eligible to apply for funding via the MCA. These countries are considered "threshold" countries, indicating they have not yet met a sufficient number of the goals of the MCA, but are judged to be making steady progress based on previous scores and other trends that may be reflective of progress. However, the process that determines which applicants are eligible to compete for MCA aid is argued by some to be more subjective, and therefore more susceptible to political influence, than that of the actual competition for aid. Therefore, the subjectivity of the application process may undermine the alleged transparency of the competition since a country may not participate if that country has not been previously approved to apply, such as Cuba. In 2006, 13 threshold countries were approved to compete for international aid, with Paraguay and Guyana being the only representatives of Latin America.

Although significant changes may increase the effectiveness of the application process, perhaps the biggest question mark related to international aid is rating its success. Clearly many positive changes have occurred since international aid became a development tool. However, questions have been raised as to the causes of these changes. What empirical evidence exists to show us that international aid is the cause of these changes—for better or for worse?

New information management systems such as AMP (Aid Management Platform) have recently shown promise in tracking funding, financial disbursements, and program coordination. And although programs like the MCA and AMP offer benefits to the distribution of international aid, the question of being able to identify direct benefits gained from international aid persists. Following significant systematic innovations like the MCA and AMP, an electronic reporting tool that would supply accurate developmental measures may one day be created to identify the performance and results of international aid.

For a more visual account of Latin America's Debt Crisis, view the 2001 documentary film, *Life and Debt*, directed by Stephanie Black, which explores the complications related to international aid and its connections to Jamaica's debt riots in the 1990s. For a more general comprehensive portrayal of the questions and issues surrounding developmental aid in Latin America, see Patrice M. Franko, *The Puzzle of Latin American Economic Development*. To better understand the mission, roles, and mechanisms of the United States Agency for International Development, visit http://www.usaid.gov. For additional information on the Millennium Challenge Account, visit http://www.mcc.gov.

Contributors to This Volume

EDITORS

ANALISA DeGRAVE is an assistant professor of Spanish in the foreign languages department at University of Wisconsin–Eau Claire where she is also a member of the Latin American Studies program. She received her Ph.D. and M.A. in Spanish at the University of Wisconsin–Madison and her B.A. in history and Spanish at Gustavus Adolphus College. She has published articles in scholarly journals on the concepts of utopia and dystopia in Latin American poetry. She previously worked with the Latino migrant community in Minnesota at Migrant Head Start and Migrant Health Services and was a volunteer with Project Minnesota–León in León, Nicaragua.

EVA L. SANTOS-PHILLIPS was born in Puerto Rico and received her undergraduate education at the main campus of the University of Puerto Rico. She received an M.Ed. at the University of Illinois–Urbana; an M.A. at California State University, Sacramento; and a Ph.D. at the University of California, Davis. She is professor of Spanish and coordinator of the University of Wisconsin–Eau Claire Latin American Studies program. She has traveled extensively in Latin America, and several of her articles on art and literature and film and literature have been accepted by refereed journals. She is currently researching a project on female Latin American documentary filmmakers.

STAFF

Larry Loeppke	Managing Editor
Jill Peter	Senior Developmental Editor
Susan Brusch	Senior Developmental Editor
Beth Kundert	Production Manager
Jane Mohr	Project Manager
Tara McDermott	Design Coordinator
Nancy Meissner	Editorial Assistant
Julie Keck	Senior Marketing Manager
Mary Klein	Marketing Communications Specialist
Alice Link	Marketing Coordinator
Tracie Kammerude	Senior Marketing Assistant
Lori Church	Pemissions Coordinator

JEFF DeGRAVE is an associate lecturer in geography at the University of Wisconsin–Eau Claire. He earned a B.A. in geography at Ohio University in 1993 and an M.A. in international affairs at Florida State University in 1996. He held the position of program manager for the Office of International Programs at West Virginia University and served as a consultant for the World Council of Credit Unions in the Latin America division. His research and teaching interests are Latin American geography and economic development.

AUTHORS

ANÍBAL ACEVEDO-VILÁ is the current governor of the Commonwealth of Puerto Rico. Acevedo has served in a Puerto Rico as a member of the House of Representatives (1993–2001) and resident commissioner (2001–2005). In the 2004 elections, Acevedo won the office of governor, defeating former governor Pedro Rosselló.

NAOMI ADELSON is a freelance journalist whose publications focus on Latin American and Latino issues. She recently published an investigative report, "Statistics on Mexicans Who Die in U.S. Tell a Sad Tale" in *El Tecolote* (November 2003).

MICHELLE ALLSOPP is a researcher at the Greenpeace Research Laboratories in the department of biological sciences at the University of Exeter, England. She has co-authored a number of Greenpeace reports including "Unseen Poisons in Asia" (2000), and "POPs in the Baltic" (2001), and co-authored "Pharm Crops—a Super-Disaster in the Making" (2005).

ALEJANDRO BERMÚDEZ writes for the *Catholic Information Agency for Latin America* (ACI-Prensa) based in Peru and is the editor-in-chief of the leading Spanish-language news Web site http://www.aciprensa.com. The International Catholic Union of the Press has honored him with two media awards. He is the author of the book *Yo Sobreviví a un Aborto* (Editorial Planeta-Tesitmonio, 2000).

GREG CAMPBELL is a freelance journalist and editor of *Fort Collins Weekly*. He previously served as editor of the *Boulder Weekly*. Among his publications, he has written two critically acclaimed books, *Blood Diamonds* (Westview Press, 2004), a look at the illicit diamond industry and terrorism, civil war, and violence, and *The Road to Kosovo* (Westview Press, 2000), a firsthand account of the struggle for peace during the breakup of Yugoslavia.

CANAL INTEROCEÁNICO DE NICARAGUA (CINN) is a multinational corporation comprised of construction, engineering, transportation, and investment firms from a number of different countries and is currently the leading candidate to construct a canal across Nicaragua.

ROBERT B. CHARLES was unanimously confirmed in October 2003 as Assistant Secretary of State for International Narcotics and Law Enforcement Affairs for the U.S. government. Prior to this appointment, Charles served in several departments at the federal level and taught government and cyber-law at Harvard University.

MARCELA A. CHAVÁN DE MATVIUK is an instructor and the director of curriculum and communication for the Center for Latino Leadership at Regent University. She completed her Ph.D. in intercultural and international communication at the Universidad Nacional de Córdoba, Argentina. The Organization of American States and Inter-American Development Bank awarded her for the course "How to Teach Ethics, Social Capital and Development in the University Context."

EDWARD L. CLEARY is a professor of political science and the director of Latin American studies at Providence College and a member of the Dominican order. He has authored numerous books and articles on religion and society in Latin America. His latest books are *Resurgent Voices in Latin America: Indigenous Peoples, Political Mobilization, and Religious Change* (co-author, Timothy J. Steigenga; Rutgers, 2004) and *The Struggle for Human Rights in Latin America* (Praeger Books, 1997).

BENJAMIN DANGL is the editor of UpsideDownWorld.org, a Web site uncovering activism and politics in Latin America, and TowardFreedom.com, a progressive perspective on world events. He is the author of *The Price of Fire: Resource Wars and Social Movements in Bolivia* (forthcoming in March 2007 from AK Press). He recently won a Project Censored Award for his coverage of U.S. military operations in Paraguay.

MARISOL DE LA CADENA is an associate professor of anthropology at University of California, Davis, is interested in the articulation of power and knowledge, and has authored a number of articles on race and culture. She details her research on twentieth-century Peru and questions of race, racial categories, and racial relations in *Indigenous Mestizos: The Politics of Race and Culture in Peru* (Duke University Press, 2000).

GUSTAVO A. DE LA RIVA is a researcher for the Centre of Genetic Engineering and Biotechnology in Havana, Cuba. He has authored and co-authored numerous articles on biotechnology including a 1999 article in *Plant Cell, Tissue and Organ Culture* and another in the *Electronic Journal of Biotechnology* (1998).

CHRISTINA DOS REIS earned her B.S. in management information systems from the University of Massachusetts–Dartmouth in May 2000 and her MBA in September 2004.

PAUL DRIESSEN is a senior fellow with the Committee for a Constructive Tomorrow and senior policy advisor for the Center for the Defense of Free Enterprise—nonprofit public policy institutes that study economic development, energy, international affairs, and the environment. He has lectured and written extensively on a variety of topics, including social responsibility, energy, and environmental policy.

BERNADETTE (BERNIE) DWYER is an Irish filmmaker and a journalist with Radio Havana in Cuba. With co-director Roberto Ruíz Rebo, she has created four documentaries, including "Mission Against Terror" (2004). Their award-winning documentaries have been shown at the Havana Film Festival and in Europe. Dwyer worked previously as a lecturer in women's studies at University College in Dublin.

DANIEL P. ERIKSON is senior associate for U.S. policy and director of Caribbean programs at the Inter-American Dialogue. His research and publications examine U.S. foreign policy challenges in the Americas. His articles have appeared in many publications, such as *Journal of Democracy* and *The Miami Herald*. He is coeditor of *Transforming Socialist Economies: Lessons for Cuba and Beyond* (Palgrave MacMillan, 2005).

BEA ERRY has worked as a Greenpeace researcher in the department of biological sciences at the University of Exeter, England. In 2001, she co-authored two reports for Greenpeace: "Toxic Chemicals in a Child's World: An Investigation into PVC Plastic Products" and "POPs in the Baltic."

TEHSIN FARUK earned her B.A. from Wilson College with a double major in business administration and economics and a minor in small business management. She received her MBA from the University of Massachusetts–Dartmouth in May 2004.

ADOLFO A. FRANCO was appointed by U.S. President George W. Bush in January 2002 as assistant administrator for the Bureau of Latin America and the Caribbean, for the U.S. Agency for International Development (USAID). Prior to this appointment, Franco held the role of counsel to the Majority on the House International Relations Committee and was president of the Inter-American Foundation.

MALA HTUN is an assistant professor of political science at the New School University. Her research areas are Latin American politics, gender and politics, and women and leadership. She is the author of *Sex and the State: Abortion, Divorce, and the Family under Latin American Dictatorships and Democracies* (Cambridge University Press, 2003). Htun holds a Ph.D. from Harvard University.

JUAN IZQUIERDO is a senior plant production officer for the United Nation's Food and Agriculture Organization at its regional office for Latin America and the Caribbean. He is the coordinator of technical activities related to crop production and biotechnology. He recently co-authored two articles on biotechnology and development that appeared in the *Electronic Journal of Biotechnology* (2005, 2001).

BRYAN KOFTON earned his B.S. in marketing (cum laude) from the University of Massachusetts–Dartmouth in June 1999 and his MBA degree in January 2004.

LULAWATCH is an electronic bi-weekly publication of the American Society for the Defense of Tradition, Family and Property whose corporate name is the Foundation for a Christian Civilization, Inc.

HEATHER MAC DONALD is a contributing editor to *City Journal*. Her publications have been printed in *The Wall Street Journal*, *Washington Post*, and *New York Times*, among others. She has written several books, including *Are Cops Racist?* (Ivan R. Dee, 2003) that explores the practices of law enforcement and addresses the notion of racial profiling. She was also awarded the 2005 Bradley Prize for Outstanding Intellectual Achievement.

CARLOS MALAMUD is a professor of history of the Americas at the Universidad Nacional de Educación a Distancia in Spain. He has published an array of articles on Latin American history. Two of his recent books are *Partidos Políticos y Elecciones en la Argentina: La Liga del Sur (1908-1916)* (UNED, 1998) and *Latin America and the Multinational Drug Trade* (with Elizabeth Joyce, Palgrave Macmillan, 1997).

CARLOS ALBERTO MONTANER is a writer and journalist whose syndicated column is found in newspapers in Latin America, Spain, and the United States. He is a former university professor, and his recent books include *Journey to the Heart of Cuba* (Algora, 2001), *Guide to the Perfect Latin American Idiot* (with Plinio Apuleyo Mendoza and Álvaro Vargas Llosa, Madison Books 2001), and *Twisted Roots: Latin America's Living Past* (Algora, 2003).

DHRUV NAG earned his MBA degree from the University of Massachusetts–Dartmouth in January 2005.

NICARAGUA NETWORK'S ENVIRONMENTAL COMMITTEE is part of NicaNet, a grassroots organization that addresses social justice, human rights, U.S. foreign policy, and environmental issues in Nicaragua through collaboration with domestic and international non-governmental organizations.

CHARLES (CHARLIE) NORWOOD is currently in his sixth term as a congressperson in the U.S. House of Representatives and serves the people of Georgia's Ninth District. He is a Republican and is the chair of the Subcommittee on Workforce Protections of the Education and Workforce Committee, and vice chair of the Subcommittee on Health of the Energy and Commerce Committee.

OXFAM CANADA is a non-profit international development organization that assists in the creation of community programs involving democratic development, the improvement of health, food security, and nutrition, and advocating women's rights, among other issues.

LINDA PANETTA is a photojournalist who directs her efforts on environmental, cultural, and human rights issues, primarily focusing on areas of conflict including much of Latin America, Afghanistan, and Iraq. She garnered two honorable mentions in 2005 by the Catholic Press Association (published in the *National Catholic Reporter*) for Best Photo Story for "Iraq Diary" and Best General News Photo for "Iraq's Search for a Future."

KENT PATERSON is a freelance writer and chief editor of Frontera NorteSur, an on-line Web site dedicated to news and analysis concerning the U.S.-Mexico border. He has covered Latin America for over 20 years and regularly appears on radio stations worldwide. His publications include entries in *Ecoamericas,* the *New Mexico Business Weekly,* and *Crosswinds,* and he authored the award-winning book, *The Hot Empire of Chile* (Bilingual Review Press, 2001).

JAMES PETRAS is a Bartle Professor (Emeritus) of sociology at Binghampton University in New York and an advisor to the Brazilian landless workers' movement and the unemployed workers' movement in Argentina. He has authored numerous books and articles and provides international commentary for the magazine, *Canadian Dimension.* With Henry Veltmeyer, he has recently published *Social Movements and State Power: Argentina, Brazil, Bolivia, Ecuador* (Pluto Press, 2005) and *Globalization Unmasked: Imperialism in the 21st Century* (Fernwood Publishing, 2001).

SILVIA RIBEIRO works with the Action Group on Erosion, Technology and Concentration in Mexico as a researcher and program manager. As an advocate, researcher, and journalist, she has focused on social and environmental issues and has attended several negotiations of United Nations environmental treaties. She has authored articles on environmental topics and was the editor of the Latin American magazine *Biodiversidad, Sustento y Culturas* (1994–1999).

PEDRO ROSSELLÓ is a Puerto Rican senator who was the sixth governor of the Commonwealth of Puerto Rico from 1993 to 2001. He studied medicine at Yale and later specialized in general and pediatric surgery at Harvard University. He also holds a master's in public health and a degree in education.

LUIS SUÁREZ SALAZAR is a professor of history and political science at the Universidad de La Habana and the Instituto Superior de Relaciones Internacionales. One of his most recent books is *El Siglo XX1: Posiblidades y Desafios para la Revolución Cubana* (La Habana, 2000).

ROXANA VÁSQUEZ SOTELO is a Peruvian lawyer and a member of the Latin American and Caribbean Committee Defense for Women's Rights. She coordinates the regional campaign that supports the Inter-American Convention on Sexual and Reproductive Rights (CLADEM). One of her most recent books is *Derechos Sexuales, Derechos Reproductivos, Derechos Humanos* (Latin American and Caribbean Committee for the Defense of Women's Rights, 2002).

KARTIK SUBRAMANIAN earned his MBA degree from the University of Massachusetts–Dartmouth in May 2003.

HENRY VELTMEYER is a professor of sociology and international development studies in St. Mary's University in Halifax, Nova Scotia. His work focuses on issues related to the political economy and sociology of development, with an emphasis on Latin American development, globalization processes, government policies, and social movements. With James Petras, he co-authored *Social Movements and State Power: Argentina, Brazil, Bolivia, Ecuador* (Pluto Press, 2005) and *Globalization Unmasked: Imperialism in the 21st Century* (Fernwood Publishing, 2001).

J. MICHAEL WALLER holds the Walter and Leonore Annenberg Chair in International Communication at the Institute of World Politics and is the executive editor of *Demokratizatisiya,* a journal dedicated to post-Soviet democracy. He has written for *USA Today,* the *Washington Times,* and the *Wall Street Journal*, among others, is the author of several books, including the award-winning *Secret Empire: The KGB in Russia Today* (Westview Press, 1994), and has recently published *Dismantling Tyranny: Transitioning Beyond Totalitarian Regimes* (ed. with Ilan Berman, Rowman & Littlefield, 2005). He also served in the U.S. House of Representatives and Senate, on the White House Task Force on Central America, the U.S. Agency for International Development, and the Office of the Secretary of Defense.

RAÚL ZIBECHI is a professor, journalist, and researcher at the Universidad Fransicana de América Latina. He is on the editorial board of the weekly *Brecha de Montevideo* (Uruguay), a monthly contributor to the International Relations Program's Americas Program. In 2003, Zibechi received the José Martí award from Prensa Latina. He recently published *Genealogía de la Revuelta: Argentina, Sociedad en Movimiento* (Nordan-Letra Libre, 2003).

Index